MW01094849

THE LINCOLN FUNERAL TRAIN

The Final Journey and National Funeral for Abraham Lincoln

Scott D. Trostel

CAM-TECH PUBLISHING
P.O. Box 341
Fletcher, Ohio 45326-0341

Printed in the United States of America

First printing
10 9 8 7 6 5 4 3 2

Library of Congress Cataloging-in-Publication Data

Trostel, Scott D.
The Lincoln funeral train : the final journey and national funeral for Abraham Lincoln / Scott D. Trostel.
p. cm.
Includes bibliographical references and index.
ISBN 0-925436-21-6 (hardcover)
1. Lincoln, Abraham, 1809-1865—Funeral journey to Springfield. 2. Lincoln, Abraham, 1809-1865—Death and burial. 3. Presidents—United States—Death. I. Title.
E457.52 .T78 2002
973.7'092—dc21

2002004465

ISBN 0-925436-21-6

Abraham Lincoln

"The account of the funeral journey will form one of the most intensely impressive chapters of the history which some future Masauley will write of the momentous events through which our nation is now passing. It is the manifestation of public grief and popular appreciation, which will stand among ordinary observances of the death of a Statesman, as would Bunker Hill Monument among the unpretending monuments of a country churchyard." - *Ohio State Journal, Columbus, Ohio, May 1, 1865*

PREFACE

The basis for this book comes from an article in the *Piqua Daily Call*, my hometown newspaper, dated April 29, 1865. A local historian, Leonard Hill, whom I later knew as a collegue, wrote an account of the train's passage through Piqua, Ohio, upon the 100th anniversary of its passage. I was 13 years old when I read accounts of this great man and the funeral train. I still have a copy of that article. That article became the basis of a collection of loose notes, compiled over years of travel and research for other books. The rest is history ... as they say. This story is one of the national funeral of the Chief Magistrate, Abraham Lincoln, and of the first national funeral in the United States in 1865. The funeral was conducted using trains which carried his coffin, and that of his son Willie, over 1,600 miles.

In the era immediately following the assassination of Lincoln, several books depicting some portion of the events of the funeral train were written as memorial tributes. Opposed to the multimedia sources today, back then media were the printed words of newspapers and books. At the time most were written, their focus appears to have been to portray the sorrow of the Country. This book takes a close-up look at the larger human side along the route as well as the route, the cars, locomotives, trains and the tremendous logistics required to make the journey. In 1865 trains were crude, undependable, without constant communications and lacked safety devices. The locomotives were of steam propulsion, used wood for fuel and made frequent water stops. The rails were of iron and subject to rapid wear.

Some of the better logistical minds used in the United States Military Railroad operations were employed to handle the many trains, cars and locomotives required for what many consider as just a single train. It was many trains making up the funeral cortege. At times two three and even four trains moving in unison on separate legs of the long journey. Telegraph was the most technological advanced form of communication known. The trains did not have air brakes at the control of the engineer. He was reliant on brakemen stationed on each car to hand crank the brakes as directed by his whistle signals. There were no automatic knuckle couplers, but the dangerous link-and-pin couplers. Car wheels and locomotive boilers were made of sometimes unreliable cast iron. Steel was just being introduced to the railroads at this time. The locomotives were steam boilers, using wood as fuel to boil water for the production of steam. Fuel stops were required about every 80 miles to replenish the water in the tender tank, and wood for fuel. The rail cars were of wood construction. The speed of trains were an head-spinning 20 miles-per-hour average.

The trains were an intricate part of the grand plan for a national memorial to honor Lincoln. As plans unfolded, major cities were selected for stops and memorials. At many of these cities, the most convenient place to off-load the coffin would not have allowed a proper memorial parade or other public expressions. Places like Baltimore, Philadelphia, New York City and Cleveland had the train spotted great distances from the site of the planned memorial just to accommodate the public displays of sorrow and massive processionals. These events were not well documented, and no books have ever attempted to document the rail and parade routes, nor the many minor stops enroute for local memorials. The train passed under many memorial arches enroute, including those made of evergreens, flags and crepe.

Portions of this book reads different than some previously published Lincoln funeral train texts. This text explores extensive local coverage of the individual events along the route and relied less on the national accounts largely used in previous text. There is a difference in the accounts as written from the perspective of the reporter on the train and those at trackside who witnessed the planning and local efforts.

The national funeral was planned, and executed by hundreds of people along the route. Women decorated the locomotives at many places, but were largely excluded from riding on the train. Not many photos of the train have survived.

Photography was still a new and bulky innovations requiring wet film plates, big cameras and portable dark rooms. Night photography was unheard of at this time. From Albany, New York to Springfield, Illinois, there are no pictures of the train in motion.

Many of the Generals of Civil War fame were on the train, as were many state and territorial governors. A full list of all those who came and went at various times has never been discovered. Those charged with establishing a record did not do a good job recording the details. Before the train reached Springfield, Illinois, the presidential private car *United States* was put up for sale.

The legends generated about the train over following years are examined, and some dispelled.

ACKNOWLEDGMENTS

I am indebted to many people. The late Richard L. Hoover, provided era timetables to compare against other sources. Rosemary Rath-Quinn, for her intensive research into the events during the train's stay in New Jersey. Craig Harmon, Director of the Lincoln Highway Museum for the loan of his papers. National Archives, Library of Congress, Ohio Historical Society, Illinois State Library, New York State Library, Philadelphia Free Library, Lancaster Public Library, State Railroad Museum of Pennsylvania, Allen County (Ohio) Historical Society, Charles Bates and John H. Keller Sr., for their efforts.

Wayne Wesolowski's knowledge of the funeral car *United States* and locomotives is second to none. His traveling model of the Funeral Train is a masterful work to be held in the annals of Lincoln history. I am especially greatful for the time and information he passed along. The Benedictine University Library at Lisle. Illinois, for access to their extensive collection of Lincoln funeral papers. This library is a highly qualified resource for the serious Lincoln scholar.

Rachel Cron, Local History Director of the Flesh Public Library, at Piqua, Ohio, for her time and efforts in gathering microfilms from far and wide. The films were always delivered with a smile. To Diedre Douglas for her everpresent help in finding some of the rather obscure subjects in the focus of the writing. Jerry W. Fisher, who always provides a great deal of help in getting my topics focused. Dick Virts, of the Champaign County (Ohio) Historical Society for his efforts in helping with the mysteries of the train"s passage between Columbus and Indianapolis. Charles Huppert of Indianapolis, a thorough historian steeped in the Lincoln ways of Indiana. Nancy Baxter of Guild Press of Indiana for her efforts in opening up the mysteries of the trains passage north of Indianapolis. My daughter Elizabeth, for taking time from a busy college schedule to dig out the Harrisburg, Pennsylvania, newspapers microfilms and copy them. Valarie for reading the manuscript while attending college to become a history teacher.

Bob Wayner for his in-depth knowledge of the early days of the Field & Pullman sleeping car enterprise and for his time at the New York City Library. His efforts cleared up many mis-statements that evolved over time about Lincoln's passage from Chicago to Springfield.

Christopher T. Baer, Assistant Curator, Manuscripts and Archives, Hagley Museum and Library, Greenville, Delaware, for his efforts to define the routing of tracks and railroad around Philadelphia in 1865, and for his knowledge of the Camden and Amboy Railroad at the time of the Civil War.

Rebekah Ambrose of the Onondaga Historical Association of Syracuse, NewYrok for her efforts in gathering many articles on the pasaage of the train in and around Syracuse.

Roberta Chandler and the Lovell Historical Society for their notes on William Durgin, the last surviving member of the Veteran Reserve Guard of Escort, and one of the eight pallbearers for the journey.

Juda Moyer, Troy (Ohio) Historical Society Archivist, for her help in finding the accounts of the train at Piqua, Ohio, as seen through the eyes of a Tory, Ohio, reporter. Sharon O'Brien, Reference Librarian, Troy (New York) Public Library for her help in uncovering some of the details of the Albany, New York stop.

Anne Calhoun, Reference Librarian at the B & O Museum in Baltimore, Maryland, for her help in putting the pieces together for the first leg of the trip from Washington to Baltimore.

To the several libraries and archives who answered inquiries without any acknowledgement Your contribution is most appreciated.

DEDICATION

To

John H. Keller Sr.
(1909 - 2002)

A very kind and extremely dedicated man, who met everyone with humility, dignity and respect. He was a passionate advocate for the plight of the working people. He quietly lived his life by example of service, never seeking recognition. His service to God was his humanitarian service to his fellow man. Each day he set out to accomplish something or to be actively involved in making his hometown a better place. He taught us how important every person in all walks of life really are. He touched us one and all. We are all better for his time with us.

CONTENTS

PRESIDENT'S FUNERAL.

At a meeting of the Citizens, held at Border Hall, on Saturday Evening, April 15, 1865, the following Programme was arranged and adopted for the funeral ceremonies, to take place on

Wednesday, April 19th, 1865.

The Procession will form on the Public Square at 10 o'clock a. m., and march in the following order, under the direction of the Chief Marshals, Cols. W. N. Foster and Stephen Johnston :

MUSIC.
THE MAYOR OF THE CITY.
CITY COUNCIL.
CITY OFFICIALS.
ORATOR OF THE DAY.
CLERGYMEN.
RETURNED SOLDIERS.
NATIONAL GUARDS.
CITIZENS.
FREE AND ACCEPTED MASONS.
INDEPENDENT ORDER OF ODD FELLOWS.
ANCIENT ORDER OF DRUIDS.
TUREN VEREIN.
FIREMEN.

Oration by Hon. G. V. Dorsey.

Order of procession and other arrangements in detail, will be made by the Marshals on the day of exercises.

It is requested that all business will be suspended and the houses appropriately decorated, as far as practicable.

All the above named individuals, and societies, &c., are expected to join in the procession without further notice.

The bells of the different churches and the City Hall, will be tolled from 11 till 12 o'clock.

Handbill announcement for local memorial services at Piqua, Ohio, on April 19, 1865. These services coincided with the national funeral for Abraham Lincoln. A few days later the village of Piqua learned it would receive the funeral train of Abraham Lincoln on April 30, 1865, while the railroad serviced the train en route. -- *Flesh Public Library collection*

THE EVENTS OF APRIL 14 AND 15, 1865

When it became known that the rebels would surrender, ending the Civil War, many of the northern states scheduled a day of thanksgiving to celebrate the end of hostilities. Ohio Governor John Brough, issued such a proclamation to his state April 8, 1865: "It is therefore recommended that Friday next, the 14th day of April - being the anniversary of the fall of Fort Sumter - be generally observed by the people of the State, as a day of Thanksgiving to God, and general rejoicing; that religious assemblages and observances mark the day, and the evening be given to bonfires, illuminations and the thundering of artillery, public assemblages and speeches, and such other manifestations as may be suggested to appropriately mark the heroic deeds of our armies, and the general joy of our people at the early restoration of the Constitution and good government."

The celebrating at Cleveland on Good Friday, April 14th, marked an end to the long harsh winter of war. People demonstrated with wild delight and joy, all forms of jubilant expression. All businesses were closed. There was cheering, salutes of cannons and martial music. As soon as the cannons stopped, church bells took up. People filled the churches to capacity, at the news the war was over. On the northeast corner of the Public Square the convention of working men of Cleveland gathered to express their relief and joy. Flags floated gaily. An effigy of Jefferson Davis was hung from Hawk's News Room.

That evening, bonfires were kindled along Superior Street and sky rockets were fired. The streets were packed with people celebrating until a late hour. Events of an entirely different nature that would soon involve Cleveland were unfolding in Washington, D.C.

The President and Mrs. Lincoln did not leave for Ford's Theater until 8:15 p.m., playing there was "Our American Cousin." President Lincoln, talking with Speaker of the House Skyler Colfax, is reported to have said that Mrs. Lincoln had not been well, because the papers announced that General Grant was to be present. Instead, Grant had gone north, to New Jersey, and Lincoln did not wish to disappoint the audience. He is reported to have urged Mr. Colfax to go along with him.

The dastardly deed was done during the third act, at about the ten o'clock hour. Lincoln was carried across the street to Petersen's Home and tended for his injuries.

The first dispatch with the shocking news was issued out of Washington at about 12:30 a.m., on April 15th. When it reached Cleveland, it was immediately posted on the newspaper bulletin boards. The joy of peoples hearts ceased, their celebrating had turned into shock, and in a few hours into mourning.

The first dispatch indicated the wound was perhaps mortal. A second dispatch indicated the President was not expected to live through the night. The third gave details of the attack.

Newsboys were on the street by 5:00 a.m. with papers announcing the President had been shot. Lincoln expired at 7:22 a.m., and the news went out rapidly.

By 9:00 a.m. the dreaded news reached Cleveland and the Mayor G. B. Senter issued a proclamation requesting all businesses to stay closed and for a public expression on the Public Square at 3:00 p.m. Speeches were delivered by ex-Governor David Todd and current Governor John Brough. The sadness hit Brough especially hard. He had been both

ASSASSINATION OF PRESIDENT LINCOLN !!!
He is Shot Through the Head, While in the Theater
Wound Pronounced Mortal !

Headlines of *Cleveland Morning Leader*, newspaper for April 15, 1865

a client of the Lincoln law firm in railroad matters, and a personal friend for over 15 years. Little did he know that in coming hours he would be summoned to Washington and requested to co-Chair the arrangements committee for the funeral train.

The United States reeled under the news on the day before Easter. The war was over, but hope had turned into grief. The preliminary arrangements for Lincoln's funeral were immediately undertaken.

At Springfield, Illinois, the Mayor, J. S. Vredenberg, called an emergency meeting of the City Council for 10:00 a.m. Upon adjournment, a meeting of the citizens was called for noon on the State House lawn, where speakers were heard and several resolutions expressing sorrow and support for the new president were passed. One other citizens' resolution was passed. "*Resolved*, That inasmuch as this city has, for a long time, been the home of the President, in which he has graced with the kindness of heart and honesty of purpose, all the relations of life, it is appropriate that its 'City of the Dead' should be the final resting place of all of him that is mortal, and to this end we respectfully request the appointment of a committee on the part of the City Council, to set in conjunction with the Governor of the State, with a view of bringing hither his remains for interment."

Appropriate telegraphic messages were dispatched to Governor Richard Oglesby, in Washington, and himself, putting certain actions into motion with respect to an Illinois burial for the dead President.

Back in Chicago, a public meeting had been called for Saturday evening at Bryan Hall to hear speakers and adopt resolutions further supporting the actions of Governor Oglesby, in Washington and requesting the Lincoln family to consider Illinois as the site for burial of President Lincoln. "*Resolved*, That the people of the State of Illinois claim the honored remains of her great son and glorious martyr, Abraham Lincoln, and after the public funeral obsequies shall have transpired at the capitol of the nation, that we request the relatives of the distinguished deceased to allow his remains to be brought home to repose in the genial free soil of his adopted State, and at his chosen home."

"*Resolved*, That Governor Oglesby, Lieutenant Governor Bross, our Senators and members of the House of Representatives in Congress from this State, be requested to act as a committee to carry out the wishes of the people of the State of Illinois."

At 2:00 p.m. on April 15th, Governor Oglesby, convened a meeting of Illinois citizens to take preliminary action in connection with the duties of the State. They consisted of: *Gentlemen of Committee Expressive of Purpose* - General J. W. Haynie, G. R. Edwards, Hon. W. P. Kellogg, C. H. Fox and E. F. Bridges. *Committee to Confer with Lincoln Family* - Gov. Richard J. Oglesby, General Joseph W. Singleton, General J. Farnsworth, Senator (and Ex-Governor) Richard Yates, Major General David Hunter, Lieutenant General U. S. Grant, Colonel James J. Loomis and Hon. W. P. Dole. *Committee of Arrangements* - Hon. John Wilson, General John A. Rawlings, Hon. Ward H. Lamon, John A. Jones, Hon. D. L. Phillips, W. W. Danhower and James Fishback. It appears the Committee to Confer with the Lincoln Family met with them later that day, then reported to Governor Oglesby at 7:00 p.m. that evening.

In the forenoon of Easter morning, April 16th, the Illinois Committee met with Mrs. Lincoln, in accordance with the Chicago Reso-

Abraham Lincoln

lution of April 15. According to the *Chicago Evening Journal*, they, "... asked that after the funeral, the President's remains be escorted to Springfield, Ill. instead of being removed to the Congressional Cemetery, as now proposed."

Monday, April 17, saw the people of influence assemble in Springfield to seek a formalized purpose. Before noon a group led by Lt. Governor Bross visited Oak Ridge Cemetery and the Mather Place, seeking a proper burial site. The decision was made in favor of the Mather Place because, "... it is in the heart of the city and accessible to all classes of people rich and poor." They expressed the problem with the Oak Ridge Cemetery as being, "... distant from town, and many times during the year hard to reach."

The citizens met at the Secretary of State's office at 8:00 p.m. that night. Without the desires of the Lincoln family this committee planned on a Springfield burial. The newspapers stated; "... the occasion will bring a vast concourse to this city as was never before witnessed to this or any other state." After the meetings of the Springfield, Illinois, Committee, a number of Illinois residents were appointed to proceed to Washington with the expressed purpose to respectfully remove the remains back to Illinois for burial. The group was lead by the Honorable Jesse K. DuBois, Honorable Lyman Trumbull, former Governor Richard Yates, Honorable John T. Stewart, Honorable Shelby M. Cullom, General I. N. Haynie, General John A. McClernand, The soon-to-be ex-Mayor of Springfield, J.S. Vredenberg and Mayor-elect of Springfield, Thomas J. Dennis. Some of the gentlemen were already in Washington, and others departed immediately for Washington.

In a dispatch to the Citizens of Illinois, dated April 17, Governor Oglesby reported; "Although final arrangements had not been determined upon ... it was arranged that the body of the President was to be taken to Illinois for interment." The outcome of several additional meetings is not reported. Events and announcements pertaining to the train and its proposed route through late on the 19th indicate things were unsettled with respect to the whole proposition of the burial in Springfield, or Chicago, Illinois.*

On Monday, April 17, Illinois Governor, Richard J. Oglesby, announced to the People of the State of Illinois, the national funeral ceremonies for the lamented Chief Magistrate would take place in Washington, D.C. on April 19 at noon. He urged all of Illinois to meet in their respective churches and places of worship that day to observe in such a manner as the occasion of that solemn hour would suggest. Meanwhile, Ohio Governor John Brough, had been summoned from his Cleveland home to Washington by Secretary of War Edwin Stanton. On April 18th Indiana Governor Oliver Morton, departed for Washington to attend the funeral services of his friend and President.

---

* Records indicate Mary Lincoln's initial first choice was for burial in Chicago, followed by Washington D.C. She did not want any part of the Springfield site selection (Mather Place) in the downtown area. It would thus appear all other plans including the route of the train and its schedule were tenative at best, and this would account for the several changes in both route and departure dates announced between April 17 and late on the 19th. Her final selection was the Oak Ridge Cemetery to the north of Springfield. To that end the City of Springfield offered 28 acres of ground for the erection of a suitable memorial. On May 5, 1865, Robert Lincoln settled on an approximate three acre site.

PLANNING THE FUNERAL TRAIN AND THE UNITED STATES MILITARY RAILROADS

Secretary of War, Edwin M. Stanton, was the person most directly charged with the details of arrangement for the burial of President Abraham Lincoln. It appears he was ill-prepared to end isolated hostilities in the south and plan a national funeral. He summoned help from several quarters to get the painful tasks ahead into motion.

Among the early obligations was to get a determination of Lincoln family wishes. The task was not easy. If it had been solely the decision of Mary Lincoln, she would have taken her husband's remains and headed straight to Chicago, Illinois, for burial. Mrs. Lincoln, was described as very reluctant to yield to any extended public ceremony. She held a dim view of anything other than her husbands expressed wishes. It took the combined pleadings of personal friends and relatives who were arriving to attend the Washington, D.C., memorial services to convince her an extended itinerary with the funeral train was in the public interest. Mrs. Lincoln, finally granted Secretary Stanton, permission for extended services on the way to an Illinois burial, though she deplored the thought of public exhibition of her deceased husband's person.

While the Lincoln wishes were being heard, Stanton, appointed a committee headed by Ohio Governor John Brough, who was in Cleveland, Ohio, the day of the terrible news. He left for Washington, as soon as the telegraph from Stanton was received. Baltimore & Ohio Railroad president John Garrett, who was in nearby Baltimore, was also requested to co-chair a committee to oversee planning for the route and operation of the funeral train.

Brough had been president of the Indianapolis & Madison Railroad in Indiana. While holding Ohio's office of Governor, he was at this point also President of the Bellefontaine and Indianapolis Railroad, an important line at this day running between Cleveland, Ohio and Indianapolis, Indiana. He had been a long time friend and also a railroad client of Lincoln's since 1850. Garrett was a key transportation advisor to Lincoln during his term as President, and also a personal friend of Edwin Stanton.

On April 18th, three days before the trains' departure, the route was still tentative. Mrs. Lincoln, was not easily yielding to the request for an extended funeral train, extended public memorials and a Springfield burial. She was apparently holding steadfast into the late evening hours of April 19, insisting the train go directly to Springfield apparently via the Pennsylvania Railroad and connecting lines of the Toledo, Wabash and Great Western Railroad. Her wishes were that President Lincoln could lay in state at the state capitols en route.

During the 18th, first plans indicated the train would depart Washington on April 20th, and go via Baltimore, Philadelphia, New York, Albany, Buffalo, Cleveland, Toledo and Chicago, Illinois. Preliminaries indicated it would stop in Cleveland on the 22nd, and stay over the 23rd before continuing on. At 3:20 a.m. on the morning of April 18, Stanton sent Cleveland Mayor, G. B. Senter a telegram stating the remains would pass through Cleveland, but details were not determined.

In Washington, Brough and Garrett had brought the Illinois Committee together to develop a detailed plan for the route. There is no clear origin of the decision for retracing the route of his 1861, inaugural train. It may be the Committee determined their suggested route was the most direct to the state capitals, in keeping with Mrs. Lincoln's wishes. The fact remains hidden from history.

The desired route of the train had been

furnished to Brough and Garrett by the Illinois Citizens Committee. The route was modified at least twice, during the hours that followed. That committee, was headed by Governor Richard J. Oglesby, and Senator Richard Yates.

Legend has stated the Illinois Committee wanted to retrace the 1861 route to Washington, D.C. There was considerable difference in more than 800 miles of trackage west of Cleveland, Ohio. History reveals it was likely a visitation of principal cities along the route, and state capitals en route, and not a retracing of the 1861 trackage. In that distance west of Cleveland only 64 miles in Indiana would be over 1861 trackage. The initial route plan excluded the capitol cities of Columbus, Ohio, and Indianapolis, Indiana.

After the Ohio and Indiana segments were finalized, the route from Columbus to Indianapolis via Cincinnati was not considered. A more direct route was planned. It had to be verified, which of two parallel routes between Columbus and New Paris, Ohio, on the Ohio - Indiana border was most viable, the southern route via Dayton, Ohio, or a northern route via Urbana, Piqua, and Greenville. The northern line had been opened for trains less than two weeks at the time of Lincoln's death.

When Lincoln left Springfield for Washington, in 1861, he went directly from Springfield to Indianapolis. With the additional Chicago stop added to the funeral train's route, that new segment would have to be included between Indianapolis and Springfield.

The other major city on the 1861 route,

Cincinnati, Hamilton & Dayton

AND

DAYTON & MICHIGAN RAILROADS.

TO ALL OFFICERS AND EMPLOYEES.

The Funeral Ceremonies of the late President of the United States, will take place in the City of Washington, on Wednesday, the 19th inst., at 12 o'clock, noon.

As there will be services held throughout the Country in the different churches on the day and at the time above mentioned, I invite the attendance to said service, at such church as they may select, of all the employees of these Roads, whose duties will permit. The Company hereby allows the proper time for such attendance.

This circular is not to be understood so as to interfere with the running of the several trains.

GEN'L SUPERINTENDENT'S OFFICE,
Cincinnati, O., April 18th, 1865.

D. McLAREN,
Gen'l Supt.

A copy of the circular for the Cincinnati, Hamilton & Dayton and Dayton & Michigan Railroads (Baltimore & Ohio Railroad between Cincinnati and Toledo, Ohio,) dated April 18, 1865, inviting employees to attend services of any church they select in respect to the national funeral for Abraham Lincoln on April 19, 1865. -- *Benedictine University collection*

The Two Gentlemen Most Responsible for the Burial Arrangements and the Funeral Train

Edwin M. Stanton
Secretary of War

General Daniel C. McCallum
General Manager,
United States Military Railroads

Boh photos courtesy Library of Congress, Prints & Photographic Div. Digital I.D. # cwp 4a40408 and cwp 4a40353

Pittsburgh, Pennsylvania, was not included in the funeral train's final itinerary. It would have added another day to the train's schedule. A Pittsburgh delegation was invited to attend the services at Philadelphia.

On April 18th, the Committee made details of arrangements and the train's timetable public, even though it was unsettled. This timetable suggested a route via New Jersey, and New York, but Mrs. Lincoln remained steadfast in her desires to go directly to Chicago or Springfield from Washington, which put Stanton and the Illinois Committee in a difficult situation. On April 19, the Committees announced the New York route was still tentative. The only thing that was clear was that there would be a funeral train, but over what route? Compounding the problem were the petitions and requests from cities at many places to host the remains of the President for a ceremony. The telegraph from St. Louis, Missouri, on April 19, 1865, is typical.

"Mrs. President Lincoln: The authorities of Saint Louis have made the most elaborate arrangements befitting the solemn occasion to receive with the honors due to the departed chief his mortal remains. Please grant to us and the people west of the Mississippi, who loved him so well, the respectful request to direct his body to pass by way of Cincinnati to Saint Louis, thence to Springfield."

"JAS. H. THOMAS, Mayor of Saint Louis. WM. TAUSSIG, President St Louis County Committee." It was received in Washington on April 19, at 9:10 p.m.

Cincinnati, Ohio, appointed a committee of six to have the funeral train pass through

WAR DEPARTMENT ORDERS FOR THE TRAIN AND ITS OPERATION

War Department
Washington City, April 18, 1865.

His Excellency Governor Brough, and John W. Garrett, Esq., are requested to act as a Committee of Arrangements of transportation of the remains of the late President, Abraham Lincoln, from Washington to their final resting place. They are authorized to arrange the timetables with the respective railroad companies, and do and regulate all things for safe and appropriate transportation. They will cause notice of this appointment, and their acceptance, to be published for public information.

EDWIN M. STANTON,
Secretary of War

Messrs. Brough and Garrett promptly accepted their appointments, and entered upon discharge of their duties. Upon preparation of their report, the following order was issued

their town, both towns acting jointly on attracting the train.

Requests were made to have the remains travel to the eastern states. "Cannot the funeral train pass through a portion of New England? Do me the favor of tendering to the War Department for that purpose a train from New York to Albany via New Haven, Hartford, and Springfield. In no portion of our common country do the people mourn in deeper grief than in New England. This slight divergence will take in the route the capital of Connecticut and also important points in Massachusetts. C. W. CHAPIN, President. Western Railroad Corporation."

On Stanton's signature, the War Department sent a telegraph on the morning of April 19, stating the train would pass through central New York State. During the afternoon another telegraph was sent, stating the train would be routed over the Pennsylvania [Central] Railroad, the Pittsburgh, Fort Wayne & Chicago Railroad, and the Toledo, Wabash and Great Western Railway. Another telegram is dated 1:00 a.m. April 19, to General Dix stating, "Arrangements for conveying the President's remains to Springfield have been changed this morning. They will go directly from Washington to Philadelphia, Harrisburg, Pittsburgh, Fort Wayne, and then to Springfield." Had that plan prevailed, the train would have avoided New York State completely.

At 11:00 p.m., that night yet another and final telegraph was sent by Edwin Stanton, to Major General John Dix, confirming the final route: "It has been finally concluded to conform to the arrangements made yesterday for the conveyance of the remains of the late President Abraham Lincoln, from Washington to Springfield, viz: by way of Baltimore, Philadelphia, Harrisburg, New York, Albany, Buffalo, Cleveland, Columbus, Indianapolis, and Chicago to Springfield." Mrs. Lincoln had yielded again and the route was set. She did not attend the train at any point. The train did not pass through Pittsburgh, Cincinnati or St. Louis. While the final schedule included Columbus, Ohio, and Indianapolis, Indiana, neither was included on the tentative list, the train having been planned to travel along Lake Erie from Cleveland to Toledo and Chicago. That plan was changed sometime on the 17th.

Meanwhile, the Springfield Committee had arrived at Washington to escort the remains back to Illinois.

PUTTING THE PLANS TOGETHER

As soon as the news of Lincoln's death became known nationally, the major eastern railroads quickly responded, offering special trains intended to move the lamented Presi-

War Department
Washington City, April 18, 1865

Ordered:
First: That the following report, the arrangements therein specified, be approved and confirmed, and that the transportation of the remains of the late President, Abraham Lincoln, from Washington to his former home, at Springfield, the capital of Illinois, be conducted in accordance with the said report and the arrangements therein specified.
Second, That for the purpose of said transportation the railroads over which said transportation is made be declared military railroads, subject to the orders of the War Department, and that the railroad and locomotives, cars and engines engaged in said transportation be subject to military control of Brig. Gen. McCullum, superintendent of military railroad transportation; and all persons are required to conform to the rules, regulations, orders and directions he may give or prescribe for the transportation aforesaid; and disobeying said orders shall be deemed to have violated the military orders of the War Department, and shall be dealt with accordingly.
Third, That no person shall be allowed to be transferred upon the car constituting the funeral train save those who are specifically authorized by the order of the War Department. The funeral train will not exceed nine cars, including baggage car, and the hearse car, which will proceed over the whole route from Washington to Springfield, Illinois.
Fourth, At the various points along the route, where the remains are to be taken from the hearse car by State or municipal authorities, to receive public honors, according to aforesaid programme, the said authorities will make such arrangements as may be fitting and appropriate to the occasion, under direction of the military commander of the division, department or district, but the remains will continue always under the special charge of the officers and escort assigned by this Department.
By order of the Secretary of War.

E. D. TOWNSEND
Assistant Adjutant General

dent back to Springfield, Illinois. The Pennsylvania, and Baltimore & Ohio Railroads quickly offered any service they could render.

Edwin Stanton assigned the details for assembling the funeral train to General Daniel C. McCallum, who had charge of the United States Military Railroads. To that end, McCallum had an established and proven reputation for getting railroads under his command into top operating condition. He had been appointed General Manager of United States Military Railroads, February 11, 1862, having come from the Erie Railroad. In several decisive battles, he was able to muster troops and equipment to get supplies to the front rapidly. Now he would turn to friend and Baltimore & Ohio Railroad president John W. Garrett, who had worked closely with McCullum, in the movement of troops and supplies during the past three years. Garrett was used to the urgency. His railroad had been a key player in the shifting battles of the Civil War. Though still pressed by war demands, damage and recent floods, the B & O supplied two new locomotives, six passenger cars and a baggage car for use in the train on April 21.

Orders quickly went to Benjamin Lamason, at the United States Military Railroads mechanical department to have the presidential railroad car, *United States* modified for funeral duty. Immediate car modification was begun in the Alexandria, Virginia Shops. The platform railings on the end where Lincoln's coffin would be loaded had to be removed, and rollers installed for the easy movement of the coffin. Two catafalques had to be fabricated and installed. Under the superintendence of John Alexander, upholsterer for the Executive Mansion, appropriate emblems of mourning, black drapery, white and black rosettes, and silver fringes and tassels had to be gathered and applied to the exterior of the car. He richly draped the

REPORT OF MESSRS. BROUGH AND GARRETT

Washington City, D. C. April 18, 1865

Hon. E. M. Stanton, Secretary of War:
Sir--
Under your commission of this date, we have the honor to report--
1. A committee of the citizens of the State of Illinois, appointed for the purpose of attending to the removal of the remains of the late President to their State, has furnished us with the following route for the remains and escort, being with the exception of two points, the route traversed by Mr. Lincoln from Springfield to Washington:
Washington to Baltimore, thence to Harrisburg, Philadelphia, New York, Albany, Buffalo, Cleveland, Columbus, Indianapolis, Chicago to Springfield.
2. Over this route, under the counsels of the committee, we have prepared the following time card, in all cases by special train:

interior of the car with black curtains, and the entire furniture shrouded in black. A plain stand covered with black cloth, was placed in the car, at one end and on this rested the remains of the President. On a similar stand, at the other end of the car, was the coffin holding the remains of Willie Lincoln.

By military order the funeral train consisted of not less than nine cars, all but two of them furnished in succession by the chief railways over which the remains were transported. The two through cars consisted of the *United States*, containing the body, was originally built for the convenience of the President and other government officers in traveling over the United States Military Railroads. This car contained a parlor, sitting room, and sleeping apartment. It had been richly draped in mourning within and without, the heavy black drapery being relieved with white and black rosettes, silver fringes and tassels. The second through car was the Officers Car.

The other cars of the train were new and elegant, and tastefully draped in mourning. The locomotive was also heavily draped. The funeral car was in the charge of Mr. John McNaughton, United States Military Railroads. His interest was in making sure the car was mechanically sound over this long journey, and to see to its daily inspection and any maintenance requirements.

Brigadier-General Daniel C. McCallum had charge of the general arrangements for the running of the train. It was a military train under military command, and operated over all railroads directly on the authority of the United States Government.

A pilot engine, furnished by the several railway companies on the route, preceded the train over each line of the roads traversed. It usually pulled one car with a local delegation on board for each leg of the journey.

A variety of locomotives pulled the funeral special. Locomotive design was still in its infancy. There were few motive power standards and most engines stayed close to their home shops. At least 42 locomotives were used on the journey to Springfield.

Locomotives at this date were relatively light, weighing on average from 15 to 25 tons. Steam power was the technology of the day, which required a constant supply of wood for fuel to heat the water, and water to supply the boiler. Hence the need for frequent fuel and water stops, and many locomotive changes. All firing of the locomotives was by hand. Air brakes had not been invented, requiring railroad brakemen to stand on each car and listen for a series of whistle signals to know when to apply the hand brake and when to release the hand brake on each car.

Some 80 passenger cars were used over the course of the journey. The cars were coupled together by a link-and-pin coupler, a rather dangerous and untrustworthy device of the day, The links were not always reliable and might suddenly break, releasing cars from anywhere behind the locomotive. A runaway might result if they were climbing a

TIME CARD

Leave Washington, Friday morning, April 21, at 8 o'clock, and arrive at Baltimore at 10 o'clock a.m.
Leave Baltimore, at 3 o'clock p.m., and reach Harrisburg at 8:20 p.m., same day.
Leave Harrisburg 12 o'clock noon, Saturday, 22, and arrive in Philadelphia at 5:30 p.m.
Leave Philadelphia 4 a.m., Monday 24, and arrive New York at 10 o'clock a.m. same day.
Leave New York City 4 p.m. Tuesday, 25, and arrive in Albany at 11 p.m. same day.
Leave Albany at 4 p.m., Wednesday, 26, and arrive at Buffalo at 7 a.m. Thursday, 27.
Leave Buffalo, at 10:10 p.m. the same day, and arrive in Cleveland at 7 a.m. on Friday, 28.
Leave Cleveland at midnight, same day, and arrive in Columbus at 7:30 a.m. Saturday 29.
Leave Columbus at 8 o'clock p.m. Saturday, 29, and arrive in Indianapolis at 7 a.m. Sunday, 30.
Leave Indianapolis at 12 midnight, Sunday, and arrive in Chicago at 11 a.m. Monday, May 1.
Leave Chicago at 9:30 p.m. Tuesday, May 2, and arrive in Springfield at 8 o'clock a.m. Wednesday, May 3.
The route from Columbus to Indianapolis is via the Columbus & Indianapolis Central Railway, and from Indianapolis to Chicago via Lafayette & Michigan City.

3. As to the running of these special trains, which, in order to guard, as far as practicable, against accidents and detentions, we have reduced to twenty miles per hour, we suggest the following regulations:

1. That the time of departure and arrival be observed as closely as possible.
2. That material detentions at way points be guarded against as much as practicable, so as not to increase the speed of trains.
3. That a pilot engine be kept 10 minutes in advance of the train.
4. That the special train, in all cases, have the right of road, and all other trains be kept out of its way.
5. That the several railroad companies provide a sufficient number of coaches for the comfortable accommodation of the escort, and a special car for the remains; and that all these, together with the engines, be appropriately draped in mourning.
6. That where running time of any train extends beyond or commences at midnight, not less than two sleeping cars be added, and a greater number if the road can accommodate them, sufficient for the accommodation of the escort.
7. That two officers of the United States Military Railway Service be detailed by you, and dispatched at once over the route to confer with the several railway officers, and make all necessary preparations for carrying out these arrangements promptly and satisfactorily.
8. That this programme and these regulations, if approved, be confirmed by an order of the War Department.

Respectfully submitted,
JOHN BROUGH
JOHN W. GARRETT *Committee*

grade, in which case the urgent services of the brakemen would be needed to stop the cars.

The cars themselves were of wood construction, with iron wheels, each being approximately 40 to 45 feet long. Heating was provided by a wood stove, and lighting was provided by oil lamps. Dining cars were a novelty, not in common use. To obtain refreshment required periodic stops by the train for the members to refresh themselves at trackside eating establishments. In at least two instances prepared food was placed on the train and consumed while in-transit. Three other formal meal stops were made en route, all other meals were served while the cortege was at a layover city for a memorial.

GENERAL RULES AND REGULATIONS FOR THE OPERATIONS OF THE TRAINS

The Pilot Engine and usually one coach operated over the tracks first, as a security buffer, followed by Funeral Train. The space between the trains was to average approximately 10 minutes.

The funeral train was not to pass stations at a speed greater than five miles per hour, the engine man tolling his bell as the train passed through the station and town.

TELEGRAPH MESSAGE APPOINTING GENERAL OFFICERS FOR THE TRAIN

War Dept., Adjt. General's Office
Washington, April 20, 1865

General Order)
)
No. 72.)

The following general officers and guard of honor will accompany the remains of the late President from Washington to Springfield, the capital of the State of Illinois, and continue with them until they are consigned to their final resting place:

Bvt. Brig. Gen. E. D. Townsend, Assistant Adjutant General, to represent the Secretary of War
Bvt. Brig. Gen. Charles Thomas, Assistant Quartermaster General
Brig. Gen. A. B. Eaton, Commissary General of Subsistence
Bvt. Maj. Gen. J. G. Barnard, Lieutenant Colonel of Nngineers
Brig. Gen. G. D. Ramsay, Ordnance Department
Brig. Gen. A. P. Howe, Chief of Artillery
Bvt. Brig. Gen. D.C. McCallum, Superintendent Military Railroads
Maj. Gen. D. Hunter, U.S. Volunteers
Brig. Gen. J. C. Caldwell, U.S. Volunteers
Twenty-five picked men, under a captain.

By order of the Secretary of War
E. W. TOWNSEND
Assistant Adjutannt-General

Telegraph offices upon the entire route were kept open during the passage of the funeral train, and as soon as the train had passed a station the operator at once gave notice to that effect to the next telegraph station.

Communications between the pilot engine and the funeral train was solely via telegraphic messages. This required the pilot engine to receive messages at each telegraph station advising of the funeral trains location. Most of these messages were "handed-up" to the slowly passing train crew, or by coming to a full stop for that information, if necessary.

Security was beefed up for the trains passage along the entire route. Guards were posted at bridges, curves, tunnels, switches and other places to satisfy the safe passage of the trains. A safety signal would be shown at each switch and bridge, and at entrance upon each curve, indicating that all is safe for the passage of pilot and train—each man in charge of a signal knowing personally such to be the case. The signal in daylight, to be a white flag, and at night a lantern.

The pilot engine was to carry two red* lights in the night, and an American flag, draped, during daylight, indicating that the funeral train was following. The pilot train carried red lights, flags and extra men, to immediately give notice to the funeral train, in case of meeting with another train or a difficulty on the route that might cause a delay.

The engine men in charge of the funeral train were fully instructed to keep a sharp lookout for the pilot engine and its signals.

*A red light hung from the front of a moving locomotive indicated another section of the train was following. At a later time the color was changed to green.

GENERAL ARRANGEMENT OF THE FUNERAL TRAIN

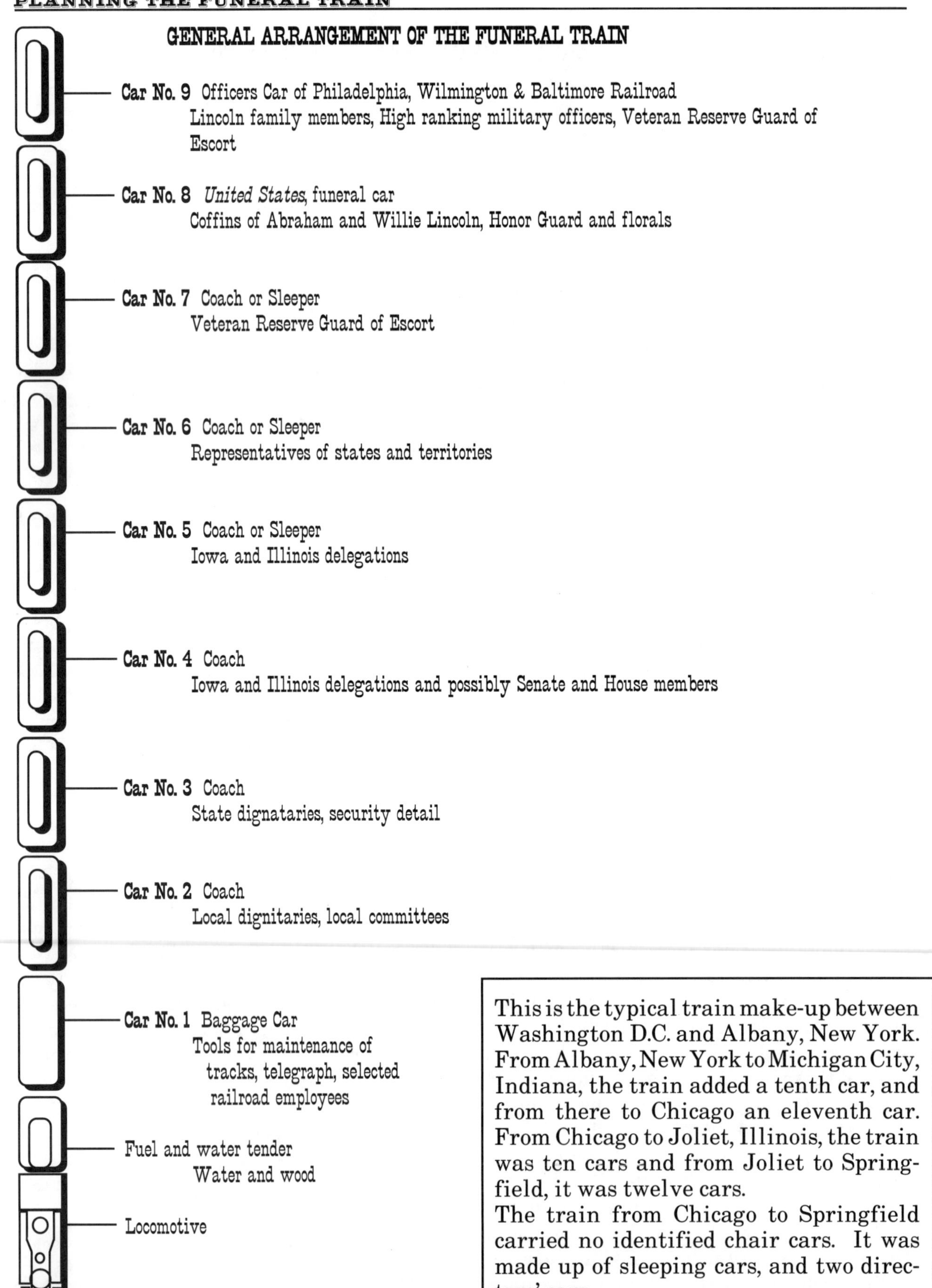

This is the typical train make-up between Washington D.C. and Albany, New York. From Albany, New York to Michigan City, Indiana, the train added a tenth car, and from there to Chicago an eleventh car. From Chicago to Joliet, Illinois, the train was ten cars and from Joliet to Springfield, it was twelve cars.
The train from Chicago to Springfield carried no identified chair cars. It was made up of sleeping cars, and two directors' cars.

TELEGRAPH MESSAGE APPOINTING VETERAN RESERVE GUARD OF ESCORT FOR THE TRAIN

Headquarters 1st Brigade V. R. C.
Washington, D, C„ April 19th 1865.

General Order)
)
No. 36)

Pursuant to orders from Headquarters Department of Washington, requiring that one Captain, Three subalterns and twenty five 1st Sergts. be detailed as a guard of honor to escort the remains of the late President to their final resting glace in Illinois, and that the detail consist or the best and most reliable men in the command. The following named officers and 1st Sergeants are detailed for this duty and the Commanding officer Captain James McCamly will report for instruction to Brig. Genl. E. D. Townsend, A.A.G. at the War Dept. at 10 o'clock A.M. tomorrow the 20th Inst.

Capt. Jas. M. McCamly,	9th	Regt.	Vet. Res. Corps.
1st. Lieut. J. R. Durkee,	7th	Regt.	Vet. Res. Corps.
2nd. Lieut. E. Murphy,	10th	Regt.	Vet. Res. Corps.
3rd. Lieut.E. Hoppy,	12th	Regt.	Vet. Res. Corps.
1st Sergt. Chester Swinehart,	Co. D,		7th Regt. Vet. Res. Corps.
1st Sergt. John R. Edwards,	Co. E,		" " " " "
1st Sergt. Samuel Carpenter,	Co. H,		" " " " "
1st Sergt. Adison C. Cornwell,	Co. I,		" " " " "
1st Sergt. Jacob F. Nelson,	Co. A,		9th Regt. Vet. Res. Corps.
1st Sergt. Luther E. Bulock,	Co. E		" " " " "
1st Sergt. Patrick Callaghan,	Co. H		" " " " "
1st Sergt. A. J. Marshall,	Co. K,		" " " " "
1st Sergt. Wm. P. Daly,	Co. A,		10th Regt. Vet. Res. Corps.
1st Sergt. James Collins,	Co. D,		" " " " "
1st Sergt. Wm. W. Durgin,	Co. F,		" " " " "
1st Sergt. Frank P. Smith,	Co. C,		" " " " "
1st Sergt. George E. Goodrich,	Co. A,		12th Regt. Vet. Res. Corps.
1st Sergt. Frank Carey,	Co. E,		" " " " "
1st Sergt. Augustus E. Car,	Co. D,		" " " " "
1st Sergt. Wm. H. Noble,	Co. G,		" " " " "
1st Sergt. John Karr,	Co. D.,		14th Regt. Vet. Res. Corps.
1st Sergt. John P. Smith,	Co. I,		" " " " "
1st Sergt. John Hanna,	Co. B,		" " " " "
1st Sergt. Floyd D. Forehand,	Co. I,		18th Regt. Vet. Res. Corps.
1st Sergt. I. M. Sedgwick,	Co. H.,		" " " " "
1st Sergt. Rufus W. Lewis,	Co. E,		" " " " "
1st Sergt. John P. Barry,	Co. A,		24th Regt. Vet. Res. Corps.
1st Sergt. Wm. H. Wiseman,	Co. E,		" " " " "
1st Sergt. James M. Pardun,	Co. K,		" " " " "

By Command of
Col. George W. Gile,
H. M. Brewster,
Capt. and A.A.A.G.

During the day it included looking for a smoke plume close by, which would be a clear warning to prepare to stop.

The pilot and funeral train were granted the entire right to the line during its passage, and all trains of every description were ordered into sidings and to be kept out of the way of the two trains.

Because of the lack of standard time zones each railroad forming the route was authorized to use its own standard time, to establish a local schedule, and there were many time zones.

THE VETERAN RESERVE GUARD OF ESCORT

The twenty-nine men who composed the Veteran Reserve Guard of Escort (pallbearers and immediate escort), to accompany President Lincoln's body from Washington, D.C., to Springfield, Illinois, were battle seasoned veterans who had exhibited meritorious service, but who were unfit for regular duty, due to an injury or other war related infirmity. After sufficiently recovering, the men were reassigned to the Invalid Corps and given light duty service while retained in active duty status. Late in the war the Invalid Corps was renamed the Veterans Reserve Corps.

The select unit comprised men who, according to records, "... were selected with reference to their age, length of service and good soldierly conduct ...." The men came from 12 states, with seven from New York and four from Pennsylvania. Three were from Ohio, three from Wisconsin and three from Massachusetts. The states of Missouri, Indiana, Maine, Michigan, Illinois, New Hampshire and Connecticut were represented by one man. The average age of the men was twenty-six. At least one was an immigrant. All had worked common labors.

No other special criteria was used in consideration of their selection, William W. Durgin recalled, in 1927, how he was selected. In his words, "My assignment to the Lincoln Escort was of a considerable surprise. I fell in with my Company on the morning of the funeral [April 19th at Washington, D.C.] and with them, and other troops marched down Pennsylvania Avenue and halted in front of the White House. P. D. Dewit was Colonel of the Regiment. While my Regiment waited in line, I heard a General asking for a detail of men for the funeral. I heard the Colonel say, 'I guess this is the man for whom you are looking.' referring to me. General Townsend detailed me to go into the White House with several of the men who had been selected.

"Once inside the White House I got the surprise of my life. General Townsend said, 'I want you for one of the bearers'. There were eight bearers in all, and five of us, Smith,

Headquarters 1st Brigade V. R. C.
Camp Fry, Washington, D, C„
April 20, 1865.

Special Order)
No. 88)

Pursuant to orders from Headquarters 1sr Brigade V. R. C. requiring that 4 (four) First Sergeants should be selected with reference to their Age, length of service, and good soldierly conduct for escort duty to the remains of President Lincoln to Springfield, Illinois, 1st Sergeant William W. Durgin of Comp. F. 10th Regiment V. R. C. is hereby detailed for that duty and will report to Capt. McCamly 9th Regiment Vet. Res. Corps at Camp Fry at 9 o'clock a.m. this day (20 instant).

By Command of
Major George Bravers
Commanding Regiment
F. E. O'Connors
1st Lieut Co. D. 10th Rgt. V. R. C. and Adjutants

Notification of selection to Veteran Reserve Guard of Escort on April 20, 1865.

[1] Durgin states Leach was a bearer. He was included as part of the Washington funeral, but was not on the Funeral Train.

WAR DEPARTMENT,
Washington City, April 20, 1865.

Bvt. Brig. Gen. E. D. TOWNSEND,
Assistant Adjutant-General, U.S. Army:

SIR:

You will observe the following instructions in relation to conveying the remains of the late President Lincoln to Springfield, Ill.

Official duties prevent the Secretary of War from gratifying his desire to accompany the remains of the late beloved and distinguished President Abraham Lincoln from Washington to their final resting place at his former home in Springfield, Ill., and therefore Assistant Adjutant-General Townsend is specially assigned to represent the Secretary of War, and to give all necessary orders in the name of the Secretary as if he were present, and such orders will be obeyed and respected accordingly. The number of general officers designated is nine, in order that at least one general officer may be continually in view of the remains from the time of departure from Washington until their interment.

The following details, in addition to the General Orders, No. 72, will be observed:

1. The State executive will have the general direction of the public honors in each State and furnish additional escort and guards of honor at places where the remains are taken from the hearse car, but subject to the general command of the departmental, division, or district commander.
2. The Adjutant-General will have a discretionary power to change or modify details not conflicting with the general arrangement.
3. The directions of General McCallum in regard to the transportation and whatever may be necessary for safe and appropriate conveyance will be rigorously enforced.
4. The Adjutant-General and the officers in charge are specially enjoined to strict vigilance to see that everything appropriate is done and that the remains of the late illustrious President receive no neglect or indignity.
5. The regulations in respect to the persons to be transported on the funeral train will be rigorously enforced.
6. The Adjutant-General will report by telegraph the arrival and departure at each of the designated cities on the route.
7. The remains, properly escorted, will be removed from the Capitol to the hearse car on the morning of Friday, the 21st, at 6 a.m., so that the train may be ready to start at the designated hour of 8 o'clock, and at each point designated for public honors care will be taken to have them restored to the hearse car in season for starting the train at the designated hour.
8. A disbursing officer of the proper bureau will accompany the cortege to defray the necessary expenses, keeping an exact and detailed account thereof, and also distinguishing the expenses incurred on account of the Congressional committees, so that they may be reimbursed from the proper appropriations.

EDWIN M. STANTON,
Secretary of War.

The orders to General E. D. Townsend for his representation of Secretary of War Edwin Stanton, on the funeral train, conduct en route and expenses.

Leach, Daly, Collins and myself were from my outfit."[1]

It would appear General Edward Townsend had some influence over the selection of part of the escort, and the selection was carried out on April 19th and 20th.

The bearer duties included carrying the coffin on their shoulders from the hearse into and out of the Capitol, from the hearse to the train at every stop where a state ceremony was conducted, guarding the coffins of President Abraham Lincoln and that of his son Willie, on the train, and escorting the remains from the train to that designated site for each state ceremony. In addition, seventeen other men with the rank of First Sergeant comprised the immediate escort of honor. They walked beside the bearers with swords drawn, and acted in an official capacity of protection to the remains. Additionally, they were assigned to guard the presidential funeral car *United States,* while in station. At every town where the train was held, at least three members of the Guard secured the car and kept watch over the coffin of Willie.

For their honored service, each select member of the twenty-nine Veteran Reserve Guard of Escort was awarded the Medal of Honor.[2] Each medal was personally inscribed: "The Congress To *1st Sergeant Wm. H. Wiseman Co. E. 24th* Vet Res Corps of Escort to remains of President Abraham Lincoln April 1865."

THE PRESIDENTIAL RAILROAD CAR *"United States"*

From the beginning the train would be something never before equaled. No ordinary car would be used, but the special presidential car just completed, but never before used by the President. Mr. Lincoln actually made fewer than four official trips[3] by rail during his presidency. The most noteworthy was a spectacular trip to West Point, New York, in June, 1862, to consult with ailing General Winfield Scott. The *New York Herald* reported, "Thus, in only eleven hours the Chief Magistrate had traveled from Washington to West Point—a distance of nearly three hundred miles."

Sometime in 1863, the construction of a special presidential car was authorized, probably by Brevet Brig. General Daniel McCallum, Director of the United States Military Railroads. Its construction was undertaken at Alexandria, Virginia, in the stockade protected Car Shops of the United States Military Railroads. Benjamin Patten Lamason was the Superintendent of Car Repair and designer of the car. William Henry Harrison Price was the shop foreman with direct responsibility for its construction. Perhaps following the custom of design for European royalty, it was one of the most opulent cars of its time. With sixteen wheels for a smoother ride, rounded monitor ends, fine woodwork, upholstered walls, etched glass windows, the *United States* represented the finest in car construction.

Mr. Price writes in *Locomotive Engineering*, September 1893, that no armor plating was used in the walls as was later rumored. The car contained three rooms for work and sitting, but without cooking facilities. The large scoop-like devices on the roof are for air movement over simple stoves at the ends of the car. Designed as a "compromise" car it had extra wide wheel treads for use on standard gauge up to, and including, five foot gauge that was common in both the north and south. A large United States crest was painted for the sides of the car since no official presidential seal existed at the time.

General Herman Haupt of the United States Military Railroads stated, "The President himself never affected style or required anything more than ordinary accommoda-

[2] In June of 1916 a panel of five retired Generals reviewed the criteria under which Medal of Honor Recipients were bestowed their accolades. They decided the men comprising the Guard of Honor did not meet the minimum requirements for courage, "Above and Beyond the call of duty". The medals were rescinded and made illegal to wear by the Guard when Congress, in 1917, limited the medal for only extreme valor in combat.

[3] Lincoln also traveled by rail to Gettysburg, Pennsylvania in November, 1863 and to Philadelphia in June, 1864.

tions."

No drawings for the car have been discovered, and accounts of its interior are left to the several local accounts of the car appearing in newspapers along the route. The *Poughkeepsie Eagle*, in its April 26, 1865, edition, makes a rather interesting description of the car as it had been redecorated for funeral hearse service. "The front of this car outside was heavily draped with emblems of mourning, the upholstering being of red and green. Here rested the coffin in which Willie Lincoln's remains were deposited. The top of the coffin was covered with fresh flowers, sculpted in the shape of a shield, also a wreath was attached and has the following inscription on it: "From the ladies at York, Pa*." In this part of the car were heavily upholstered arm chairs of a handsome pattern. From the center of the ceiling hung a magnificent chandelier. In the center [of the car] was a state room splendidly fitted up with everything necessary. All the upholstered work was heavily draped in black. The rear part of the car was set apart for the remains of our late illustrious President. Here as well as in the forward part, the sides, ceiling and upholstered work was heavily draped, the head of the coffin, in which reposed all that remained of Abraham Lincoln, being towards the doors. The fittings inside the car were magnificent in every respect. Marble top wash stands, mirrors, tapestry velvet carpet, in fact everything that was necessary predominated. The outside of the car was also heavily draped, the mournful cloth being looped up with clusters of silver stars and bordered with silver fringe. In the center panels [between the center windows of the car] on either side are the words, "United States," just below the words is a cluster of flags and shields, the whole arrangement set off by an eagle."

W. H. H. Price, Master Car Builder and foreman for construction of the *United States* wrote his recollections in the September 1893 issue of *Locomotive Engineering*.

"From time to time since 1866, the writer has noticed in the press and railway journals different articles in regard to the car which was built during the war for the private use of President Lincoln, and, as this important relic (now the property of the Union Pacific Railway) is likely to attract considerable interest among the exhibits at Chicago, he undertakes to state for the benefit of the reading public what he knows of its history. It may be added without impropriety that there is probably no one now living more conversant with this matter than the writer, as will be shown before he is through."

"Soon after the beginning of the war, the old railroad shops at Alexandria, Virginia, were enlarged by the government for the purpose of building and repairing cars. The work was under the immediate supervision of Mr. B. P. Lamason, Superintendent in charge of all car work in Virginia, and the writer was one of his foremen."

"Some time during the year 1863 superintendent Lamason either conceived the idea or had received instructions to build a private car for the use of the President. The work was begun in November of that year, and was completed in February 1865. The car was designed for the general use of the President, and not exclusively for the purpose of conveying him to and from the front, as is generally supposed; neither was the car cased inside with iron as stated by some writers."

"As the car was completed but a short time before the assassination of the President, the first trip it ever made was to bear his lifeless remains with those of his son, which had been disinterred from Washington to Springfield, Ill."

"After the car was finished, it was photographed by the Government Photographer, from a copy of which, now in the possession of the writer ..."

"In design the car was similar to those in use on the Pennsylvania Railroad; it was 42 feet long inside and had a raised roof with

* It is believed, when this article was written, on April 26, 1865. the floral wreath from the ladies of York, Pennsylvania, had been moved from Abraham Lincoln's coffin to that of his son Willie. The ladies at York, Pennsylvania, had placed a wreath on the coffin of Abraham Lincoln, on April 21, 1865, and since that time the President's coffin had been removed from the car three times, and many florals added.

circular ends. The inside of the car was upholstered on sides and ends from the seat rail to head lining, and was divided into three compartments, viz., drawing-room, parlor and state room, the latter being the center of the car. The drawing room and parlor were connected by an aisle extending along the wall inside the car, and in the drawing-room end a salon was placed. The upper deck was painted a zinc white, with coats of arms of the different states in the panels.

"The car was originally planned to run on two trucks, but after being raised, braced and bolted, Mr. Lamason changed his mind and decided to mount it on four trucks, which necessitated changing the bolsters and considerable other work. The body bolsters were Ambrose Ward's patent, and the sides of the car were covered by brass-capped nuts."

"Each two pair of trucks was connected by means of a truss, with main center plate in center, and four guide center plates with curved slots, one on each truck. There were eight side bearings made of spring steel and rubber."

"The spread of the trucks was 4 feet, 10 inches; wheels 33 inches, cast iron with broad tread. The springs in truck bolsters were hung on old style long hangers, no sand board, but bottom of hangers tied with "U" shaped under rods."

"No equalizing bar was used, the elliptic springs being placed on top of the oil boxes. The pedestals were cast iron of a pattern so elaborate as to be difficult to describe, Mr. Lamason having spent weeks in designing them."

"The outside of the car was painted a rich chocolate brown, and polished with oil and rotten stone with the bare hand. It was trimmed with faint lines in red, and all its salient points of knobs, angles and bolt heads tastefully gilded. In the oval center, on [the] side of [the] car, was painted the United States Coat of Arms, represented by an American eagle, with outstretched wings resting upon a shield, above which appeared a halo of stars upon a groundwork of clouds. Above it,

Photo of the *United States*, decorated in emblems of mourning, including silver fringe, tassels, and crape festoons. The end of the car nearest the photographer would hold the coffin of Willie Lincoln. The far end of the car would hold the remains of President Abraham Lincoln. The man on the far end of the car is claimed to be Myron H. Lamson, a mechanic who helped remodel the car for funeral duty. Photo is probably taken on April 20, 1865. The car is sitting outside the shop door at the U. S. Military Railroads at Alexandria, Virginia. In 1908 the Grand Army of the Republic meeting issued a postcard of this car useing this scene. -- *Library of Congress*

in the center of the panel above the coat of arms, in small gold letters placed in a circle, were the words 'United States.' The car was ornamented in gold, but neither number nor name except as described."

After the journey to Springfield was completed, Addison Cornwell, one of the Honor Guards on the train, is said to have told a neighbor in his home at Syracuse, New York, "... that upon arriving at their destination, the soldier guards had divided the pall and fringe."

Sidney D. King, Assistant Master Car Builder at the Alexandria Shops, in a 1903 letter makes additional observations about the legend the car was armor plated. "I ... was in the shops constantly while the car was being built, and am certain that no armor was used in its construction." He goes on to make additional observations. "Just when the fact of its being built came to his [Lincoln's] knowledge I do not know, but as I recollect it, some of the New York newspapers opposed to his administration took up the matter and presented it in a very unfavorable light. It stood in the shop for some months at least after making one trial trip. It was really magnificent for those days, and every available convenience was used ...."

Discussing its use and return to Virginia, Mr. King writes, "When the car made its first real journey, that from Washington to Springfield, Illinois, bearing the dead body of the President to its final resting place, it was elaborately draped in black cloth, with silver bullion fringe, silver spangled stars and large silver tassels about nine inches long and three inches in diameter. There were also many black tassels used about the biers on which rested the two coffins -- that of the President and his son.

"These 'funeral trappings' were removed on return of the car to Alexandria and divided up as relics."

There is another account by W. H. H. Price, suggesting that when the car was returned to Alexandria, Virginia, it was still draped in black crape, which was removed, carefully boxed and sent to the Treasury Department. Orders were apparently issued that no souvenir samples of the fabric were to be taken. Some of the relics have survived in private collections.

OFFICERS CAR

The Directors' Car of the Philadelphia, Wilmington and Baltimore Railroad

Presdential private car *United States*, built in 1864. It was constructed at Alexandria, Virginia in the Car Shops of the Military Railroads. Benjamin Fatten Lamason, the Superintendent of Car Repair was designer of the car. William Henry Harrison Price, the shop foreman had direct responsibility for its construction. -- *Library of Congress*

Major General Edward D. Townsend, the senior officer on the funeral train. He represented Secretary of War Edwin Stanton, on the train, made formal reception speeches enroute, and extended the courtesy of the United States. Edwin Stanton was still involved in quelling the unrest in the southern states and could not attend the train. -- *Collection National Archives*

The last car on the train was the Directors' Car of the Philadelphia, Wilmington and Baltimore Railroad. It was offered by the officers' of the P W & B for the personal use of family and significant members of the committee.

The *Harrisburg Patriot and Union* offered a description of the car while it was at Harrisburg on April 22. " ... a highly ornamented and finished car, the ground color of which was bright vermillion, striped with yellow and other colors, creating a rich and regal effect, subdued, however, by heavy drapery of black alpaca. It was the officers car for the Philadelphia, Wilmington and Baltimore Railroad. It was divided into compartments for sitting, dining and sleeping." This car plus the *United States* were the only two cars to make the entire journey to Springfield, Illinois.

A second Directors' Car was added by the Michigan Central Railroad for the leg of the trip from Indianapolis to Chicago on May 1st, and to Springfield on May 2, 1865.

APRIL 19, 1865

Silence interrupted by the gentle searing sounds of rain abounded as the daylight broke across the eastern sky on that rainy Wednesday morning. Members of the Baltimore City Council, Mayor and corporate authorities marched in procession to Camden Station of the Baltimore & Ohio Railroad, where a special two car train awaited to carry them to the National Funeral at Washington, D.C. They were among crowds arriving in the Capitol city to pay their last respects to the slain president.

The Baltimore delegation observed the tracks between Baltimore and Washington were receiving attention to make sure they were in the best of condition for the passage of the train.

Upon arrival in the B & O station near the Capitol, they were met by the Washington Committee, escorted to City Hall and from there to the presidential mansion. They were admitted to the East Room and permitted to attend funeral services in the East Room before moving the body to the rotunda.

With the responsibility for the movement of the funeral train squarely in the hands of General Daniel McCullum, on this date he dispatched two aids, Colonel H. L. Robinson and Captain J. C. Wyman to refine details of the journey with each railroad, and set ceremonial schedules with the local authorities. With their job came the development of detailed station schedules, stops for brief ceremonies, water and fuel stops, changing of the locomotives and a myriad of other details. The logistics of a ferryboat move at Jersey City, and of not just the coffin, but also two railroad cars, had to be precisely understood. A second ferry move was required at Albany, but the train could be moved north a few miles where the bridge crossed the Hudson River. Colonel Robinson is reported meeting the train at several locations, and it appears he took care of details up to the time of arrival. Captain Wyman appears to have been the forward man to make preliminary arrangements. By the time Wyman reached Ohio, he was nearly a week ahead of the train.

It is quite evident they were in contact with the other working officers to recommend and arrange the meal stops and lodging for the funeral escort en route. Captain Charles

Penrose, Quartermaster and Commissary of Subsistence, who was on the train, took care of lodging and meal arrangements en route, sending telegraph messages in advance of the train to schedule requirements for the rest and nourishment of the funeral escort.

The Governors of states through which the train would pass were afforded the opportunity to receive the remains coming into their respective state and to arrange the ceremonies at each place where the coffin would be removed from the train for the ceremony. With the train just over 24 hours from leaving Washington, there was little time for elaborate reception ceremonies in Baltimore, Maryland, and Harrisburg, Pennsylvania. Detailed instructions were dispatched to each governor. Governor Andrew Curtin, of Pennsylvania released the telegraph messages to the newspapers, and they were printed in many of the daily papers:

"The remains of the late President, Abraham Lincoln, will leave Washington on Friday morning at 8 o'clock to go by way of Baltimore to Harrisburg and thence to Philadelphia and New York by the timetable as arranged. The remains will reach Harrisburg at 8 P.M. on Friday and leave at 12 noon on Saturday for Philadelphia, where they will remain until 4 o'clock Monday morning and then be conveyed to New York. A copy of the timetable and program will be forwarded to you tomorrow."

"You are respectfully invited to meet the remains with your staff at such point as you may designate to this Department and accompany them so far as you are pleased to go. You will please signify to this Department by telegraph where you will join the remains; whether you will take charge of them at Harrisburg; where you will have them placed while they remain at the capital of your State; and what honors you desire to pay while there."

Governor Curtin's reply, also printed in the papers, "I propose to take charge of the remains at the line of the State and to accompany them until they leave the State. They will be placed in the Capitol at Harrisburg. All the military honors that can be arranged will be shown. Measures are being taken for that purpose."

Simultaneously he issued his proclamation to the public: "The remains of the murdered patriot, Abraham Lincoln, President of the United States, will arrive in the State on Friday evening next on their way to the place of interment in Illinois.... I recommend that all business be suspended during their passage through the State. Local authorities and people everywhere to join the State authorities in paying honor to the memory of the martyred statesman who has fallen a victim to the savage treason of assassins.

New York State is the only state along the route where the governor did not personally receive the remains at the river crossing from New Jersey, nor were they escorted by the governor west of Albany.

A national day of mourning was set on April 19th, and the Governors of each state set their own day of state mourning. Ohio selected the date of May 4, as the date, to coincide with the burial.

THE EARLY HOURS OF APRIL 21

As the hours of early morning darkness quietly slipped by, the Washington area railroads were well under way with final preparations for the beginning of the funeral trains.

At the United States Military Railroads shop in Alexandria, Virginia, the *United States* was given its final inspection in its new role as a funeral car. Benjamin Lamason and others were busy making sure the untested car was ready for a flawless trip over 1,600 miles.

In the predawn hours the train was being assembled. The *United States*, now modified to a funeral car and appropriately decorated in emblems of mourning for its initial trip, had to meet the rest of the funeral train across the river in Washington, D.C.

The shop doors were opened and upon authority, a waiting locomotive moved down and coupled to the car. Military guards were on the car. The movement of the car was across the Washington, Alexandria and Gerogetown Railroad. A railroad about seven miles long, built in 1862, under War Department orders to connect the Baltimore & Ohio Railroad, the only railroad then serving Washington, D.C., with the Orange & Alexandria Railroad, across the Potomac River. This line was a vital link in the Union war efforts, including a bridge nearly a mile long across the Potomac. It was the first piece of railroad operated by the United States Military Railroads.

From Alexandria, the single car and locomotive crossed the Potomac River on Long Bridge, entering the District of Columbia at Maryland Avenue. It commenced up the tracks to the Capitol, where tracks turned north, heading across Pennsylvania Avenue, entering First Street, and exiting eastward near Indiana Avenue, going east on C Street the short block to the B & O yard and station.

The Officers Car of the Philadelphia, Wilmington and Baltimore Railroad was fitted with emblems of mourning at Philadelphia, Pennsylvania, and hauled to Baltimore, Maryland, where it was switched over to the Baltimore & Ohio Railroad for final movement to Washington. The B & O fitted its train in appropriate emblems of mourning at Baltimore, though details are sketchy at best. The eight cars were moved to Washington, during darkness.

The *United States* had to be switched in between the waiting Officers Car, and six coaches and a baggage car, for completion of the nine car funeral train.

The details of this move are not well recorded. It is clear that military guards were posted along the first miles of the railroad to assure safe uninterrupted movement of the funeral cars toward the north side of the Capitol.

This is Long Bridge, which connected Washington D. C. to Alexandria, Virginia, over the Potomac River during the Civil War. This view looks toward Alexandria. The Presdential funeral car *United States*, crossed here on April 21, 1865. The seven mile trip from Alexandria, with the single car and locomotive entered the District of Columbia at Maryland Avenue. It commenced up the tracks to the Capitol, where tracks turned north, heading north across Pennsylvania Avenue, entering First Street, and exiting eastward near Indiana Avenue, going east on C Street the short block to the B & O yard and station. -- *Phots courtesy Library of Congress, Prints & Photographic Div. Digital I.D. # cwp 4a40229*

DECORATIONS OF MOURNING TO THE TRAIN

Funeral car *United States*

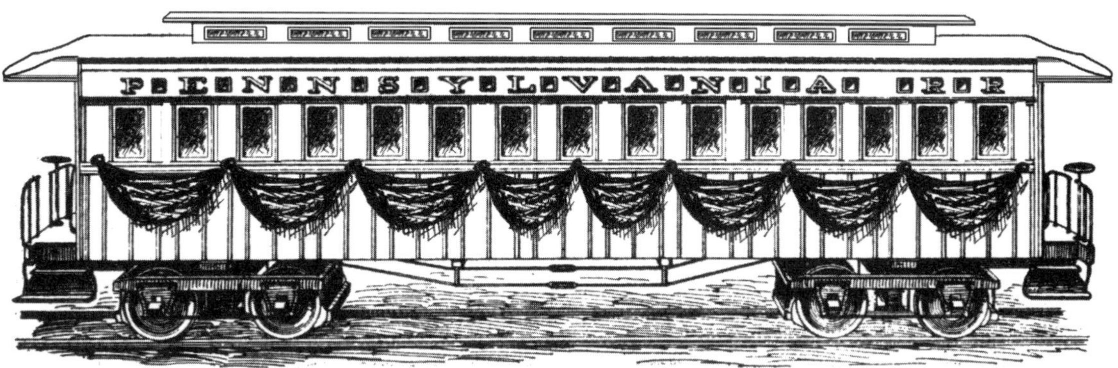

Typical coach with emblems of mourning. This example is from the Pennsylvania Railroad

Typical coach with emblems of mourning. This example is from the Michigan Central Railroad

Typical style of decoration used on locomotives assigned to pull the Lincoln Funeral Train.
Based on a locomotive of the Columbus & Indianapolis Central Railway

Typical locomotive tender decorating style

Front View
Typical locomotive decoration

RECURRING THEMES AND EXPRESSIONS OF MOURNING

As the train moved north out of New York, recurring themes of mourning were reported. The two most common uses were that of thirty-six ladies dressed in white and wearing a black sash. The depiction of the Weeping Goddess of Liberty and arches draped over railroad tracks were also very popular.

ARCHES OVER THE RAILROAD

Washington D.C.	Evergreen
Yonkers, New York	Evergreen
Hastings, New York	Evergreen
Tarrytown, New York	Fabricated
Sing-Sing, New York	Fabricated
Croton, New York	Floral
Cold Springs, New York	Evergreen
Amsterdam, New York	Fabricated
Fonda, New York	Fabricated
Oneida, New York	Fabricated
Cleveland, Ohio	Fabricated
Urbana, Ohio	Evergreen (too narrow, taken down before train arrived)
Piqua, Ohio	Flaming gas
New Paris, Ohio	Evergreen
Richmond, Indiana	Evergreen
Cambridge City, Indiana	Evergreen
Dublin, Indiana	Evergreen
Knightstown, Indiana	Evergreen
Lebanon, Indiana	Evergreen
Westville, Indiana	Fabricated
Michigan City, Indiana	Fabricated
Chicago, Illinois	Fabricated
Joliet, Illinois	Evergreen and Fabricated
Bloomington, Illinois	Evergreen
Lincoln, Illinois	Fabricated
Elkhart, Illinois	Fabricated
Williamsville, Illinois	Fabricated

EXPRESSIONS OF SORROW DEMONSTRATING ALL THIRTY SIX STATES ARE IN THE UNION

LADIES DRESSED IN WHITE

At many stations along the route reference is made to having thirty six ladies dressed in white. Some sang, some waived flags, others stood with arms interlocked, or holding a single flower Such scenes are mentioned at the following locations:

Herkimer, New York
Dunkirk, New York
Columbus, Ohio
Piqua, Ohio
Greenville, Ohio
Michigan City, Indiana
Chicago, Illinois
Atlanta, Illinois

THIRTY-SIX GUN SALUTE

April 19 at all military forts, arsenals, stations and West Point.
April 28, Cleveland, Ohio, upon arrival of the train at Euclid Street Station.
May 1, Illinois Orders at sunset.
May 3, Illinois Orders at sunset.
May 4, Springfield, Illinois, at sunset.

THIRTY-SIX STARS

On dias at Baltimore, Maryland
On pagota at Cleveland, Ohio.
On dias at Columbus, Ohio.
On roof of catafalque at Chicago, Illinois.
On roof of catafalque at Springfield, Illinois.

ROUTE MAP
of
The Abraham Lincoln Funeral Train
April 21 - May 3, 1865

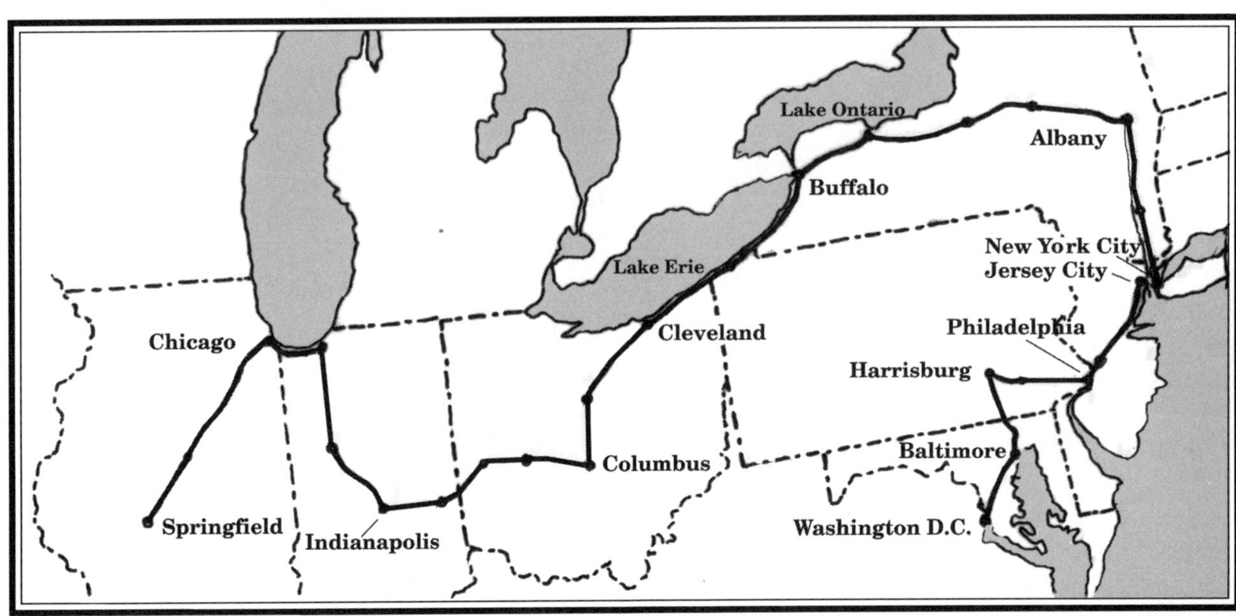

History has wrongly suggested, many miles of the Lincoln funeral train route retraced his 1861 inauguration mileage. Almost 50% of the miles, 827 miles, of the funeral train route was over trackage not traversed by the 1861 inauguration train. The principal towns visited by the funeral train were the same with three exceptions. Pittsburgh, Pennsylvania and Cincinnati, Ohio, were not included on the funeral train schedule. Chicago, Illinois, was the addition to the schedule.

The only place west of Cleveland, Ohio, where Lincoln's funeral train retraced original trackage of the 1861 route was the 64 miles between Indianapolis and Lafayette on the Lafayette and Indianapolis Railroad.

PRINCIPAL TOWNS VISITED BY LINCOLN IN 1861 AND 1865

1861 INAUGUARATION	1865 FUNERAL
Springfield, Illinois	Springfield, Illinois
----	Chicago, Illinois
Lafayette, Indiana	Lafayette, Indiana
Indianapolis, Indiana	Indianapolis, Indiana
Cincinnati, Ohio	----
Columbus, Ohio	Columbus, Ohio
Pittsburgh, Pennsylvania	----
Cleveland, Ohio	Cleveland, Ohio
Buffalo, New York	Buffalo, New York
Albany, New York	Albany, New York
New York, New York	New York, New York
Trenton, New Jersey	Trenton, New Jersey
Philadelphia, PA	Philadelphia, PA
Harrisburg, PA	Harrisburg, PA
Baltimore, Maryland	Baltimore, Maryland
Washington, DC	Washington, DC

SCHEDULE OF THE FUNERAL TRAIN ROUTE

April 21, 1865 96 miles Washington, D. C. to Harrisburg, Pennsylvania
Via Baltimore & Ohio Railroad Washington, D.C. to Baltimore, Maryland, Camden Station
Via Northern Central Railway N.C Ry Sation, Baltimore, Maryland to Harrisburg, Pennsylvania
DEPART Washington DC 8:00 AM ARRIVE BALTIMORE 10 AM Camden Station
DEPART BALTIMORE 3:10 PM NC Ry. Station ARRIVE Harrisburg 8:35 PM
On track time for the train 6 Hours

April 22, 1865 106 miles Harrisburg to Philadelphia, Pennsylvania
Via Pennsylvania Railroad DEPART Harrisburg 11:15 AM, ARRIVE Philadelphia 4:50 PM
On track time for the train 5 Hours 35 Minutes

April 24, 1865 86 miles Philadelphia, Pennsylvania to New York, New York
Via Philadelphia and Trenton Railroad DEPART Philadelphia 4:00 AM Kensington Station,
Camden & Amboy Railroad
New Jersey Railroad and Transportation Company
ARRIVE Jersey City, New Jersey 10:00 AM via ferry boat New Jersey to New York City, N.Y. ARRIVE 11:00 AM
On track time for the train 6 Hours

April 25, 1865 141 miles New York, New York to Albany, New York
Via Hudson River Railroad DEPART New York City 4:15 PM from Hudson River RR depot, ARRIVE Albany 10:55 PM
On track time for the train 6 Hours 40 Minutes

April 26 - 27, 1865 298 miles Albany, New York to Buffalo, New York
Via New York Central Railroad DEPART Albany 4:00 PM, ARRIVE Buffalo 7:00 AM
On track time for the train 15 Hours

April 27 - 28, 1865 183 miles Buffalo, New York to Cleveland, Ohio
Via Buffalo and State Line Railroad, and the Cleveland and Erie Railroad DEPART Buffalo, New York 10:00 PM, ARRIVE Cleveland 7:00 AM at Cleveland Union Depot. Move in reverse move over *Cleveland & Pittsburgh Railroad* to Euclid Street Station.
On track time for the train 9 Hours

April 29, 1865 135 miles Cleveland, Ohio to Columbus, Ohio
Via Cleveland, Columbus and Cincinnati Railway DEPART Cleveland midnight from Euclid Street Station ARRIVE Columbus 7:00 AM Union Depot
On track time for the train 7 Hours 30 Minutes

April 29 - 30, 1865 188 miles Columbus, Ohio to Indianapolis, Indiana
Via Columbus & Indianapolis Central Railroad DEPART Columbus 8:00 PM C & IC Depot, ARRIVE Indianapolis 7:00 AM
On track time for the train 11 Hours

May 1, 1865 210 miles Indianapolis, Indiana to Chicago, Illinois
Via Indianapolis & LaFayette Railroad; Louisville, New Albany & Chicago, Railroad; Michigan Central Railroad DEPART Indianapolis midnight, ARRIVE Chicago 11:00 AM
On track time for the train 11 Hours

May 2 - 3, 1865 184 miles Chicago, Illinois to Springfield, Illinois
Via Chicago & Alton Railroad DEPART Chicago 9:30 PM ARRIVE Springfield 9:00 AM
On track time for the train 11 Hours 30 Minutes

The Funeral Escort out of Washington, D.C.

The following is a list of the gentlemen prominent in civil and military life, officially appointed to accompany the Funeral Train:

RELATIVES AND FAMILY FRIENDS.

Judge David Davis, United States Supreme Court.
C. M. Smith and N. M. Edwards, brothers-in-law of Mrs. Lincoln.
General John B. S. Todd, cousin to Mrs. Lincoln.
Charles Alexander Smith, brother of C. M. Smith.

GUARD OF HONOR.

Major General David Hunter.
Brigadier General E. D. Townsend.
Brigadier General Charles Thomas.
Brigadier General A. D. Eaton.
Brevet Major General J. G. Barnard.
Brigadier General G. D. Ramsey.
Brigadier General A. P. Howe.
Brigadier General D. C. McCallum.
Brigadier General J. C. Caldwell.
Rear Admiral C. H. Davis, United States Navy
Captain Wm. R. Taylor, United States Navy.
Major T. H. Field, United States Marine Corps.

GENTLEMEN ON DUTY.

Captain Charles Penrose, Quartermaster and Commissary of Subsistence of the entire party.
Ward H. Lamon, Marshal of the District of Columbia.
Dr. Charles B. Brown, Embalmer.
Frank T. Sands, Undertaker.
B. P. Lamason, U.S. Military Railraods, car designer
John McNaugtn, Mechanical Department, U.S. Military Railroads.

MEMBERS OF CONGRESS ACCOMPANYING THE REMAINS.

The following members of the Senate and House of Representatives had been specially invited to accompany the remains to Springfield:

Mr. Pike, Maine.
Mr. Rollins, N. Hampshire.
Mr. Baxter, Vermont.
Mr. Hooper, Massachusetts.
Mr. Dexter, Connecticut.
Mr. Anthony, R. Island.
Mr. Harris, New York.
Mr. Cowan, Pennsylvania.
Mr. Schenck, Ohio.
Mr. Smith, Kentucky.
Mr. Julian, Indiana.
Mr. Ramsay, Minnesota.
Mr. T. W. Terry, Michigan.
Mr. Harlan, Iowa.
Mr. Yates, Illinois.
Mr. Washburne, Illinois.
Mr. Farnsworth, Illinois.
Mr. Arnold, Illinois.
Mr. Shannon,California.
Mr. Williams, Oregon.
Mr. Clarke, Kansas.
Mr. Phelps, Maryland.
Mr. Whaley, West Virginia.
Geo. T. Brown, Sergeant-at-Arms of the Senate
Mr. Nye, Nevada
Mr. Hitchcock, Nebraska.
N. G. Ordway, Sergeant-at-Arms of the House of Representatives
Mr. Bradford, Colorado.
Mr. Wallace, Idaho.
Mr. Newell, New Jersey.

THE DELEGATES FROM ILLINOIS.

The following are the names of the delegates from Illinois appointed to accompany the remains to their last resting place:
Gov. Richard J. Oglesby
Hon. Thomas A. Haine.
Gen. Isham N. Haguie,
Hon. John Wentworth.
Adjutant General Illinois. Hon. S. S.Hayes.
Col. Jas. H. Bowen, A.D.C. Col. R. M. Hough.
Col. M. H. Hanna, A. D.C. Hon. S. W. Fuller.
Col. D. B. James, A.D.C. Capt. J. B. Turner.
Maj. S. Waite, A.D. C. Hon. J. Lawson.
Col. D. L. Phillips, U. States Hon. C. L. Woodman.

Marshal of the District of Hon. G. W. Gage.

Illinois, A.D.C.
Hon. Jesse K. Dubois.
Hon. T. J. Stuart.
Col. John Williams.
Dr. S. H. Melvin.
Hon. S. M. Cullom.
Gen. John A. McClernand.
Eon. Lyman Trumbull.
G. H. Roberts, Esq.
J. Connisky, Esq.
Hon. L. Talcott.
Hon. J. S. Fredenburg.
Hon. Thomas J. Dennis.
Lieut. Gov. William Bross.
Hon. Francis E. Sherman,Mayor of Chicago.

GOVERNORS OF STATES

Gov. Richard J. Oglesby, of Illinois, (Listed in Illinois Delegation)
Governor Oliver P. Morton, of Indiana;
Governor John Brough, of Ohio;
Governor William Stone, of Iowa, together with their aides.

VETERAN RESERVE GUARD OF ESCORT

Captain James M. McCamly, Co. A, 9th VRC,
First Lieut. Joseph R. Durkee, Co. E, 7th VRC,
Second Lieut. Edward Murphy, Co. B, 10thVRC
Second Lieut.Edward Hoppy, Co. C, 12th VRC,
Sergt. Chester Swinehart, Co. D, 7th VRC,
Sergt. John R. Edwards, Co. E, 7th VRC
Sergt. Samuel Carpenter, Co. H, 7th VRC
Sergt. Adison C. Cornwell, Co. I, 7th VRC
Sergt. Jacob F. Nelson, Co. A, 9th VRC
Sergt. Luther E. Bulock, Co. E 9th VRC
Sergt. Patrick Callaghan, Co. H 9th VRC
Sergt. A. Judson Marshall, Co. K, 9th VRC
Sergt. William P. Daly, Co. A, 10th VRC
Sergt. James Collins, Co. D, 10th VRC
Sergt. William W. Durgin, Co. F, 10th VRC
Sergt. Frank P. Smith, Co. C, 10th VRC
Sergt. George E. Goodrich, Co. A, 12th VRC
Sergt. Frank Carey, Co. E, 12th VRC
Sergt. Augustus E. Car, Co. D, 12th VRC
Sergt. William H. Noble, Co. G, 12th VRC
Sergt. John Karr, Co. D., 14th VRC
Sergt. John P. Smith, Co. I, 14th VRC
Sergt. John Hanna, Co. B, 14th VRC
Sergt. Floyd D. Forehand, Co. I, 18th VRC
Sergt. Irvin M. Sedgwick, Co. H., 18th VRC
Sergt. Rufus W. Lewis, Co. E, 18th VRC
Sergt. John P. Barry, Co. A, 24th VRC
Sergt. William H. Wiseman, Co. E, 24th VRC
Sergt. James M. Pardun, Co. K, 24th VRC

REPORTERS FOR THE PRESS

L. A. Gobright - Associated Press
C. R. Morgan - Associated Press
U. H. Painter - Philadelphia Inquirer
E. L. Crounse - New York Times
G. B. Woods - Boston Daily Advertiser
Dr. Adonis - Chicago Tribune
C. A. Page - New York Tribune

Of the 1861 escort that accompanied Mr. Lincoln from Springfield to Washington, but three left Washington with the funeral train: Judge David Davis, of Illinois, Major-General David Hunter, and Ward H. Lamon, Marshal of the District of Columbia. Lamon was the only person to make both the 1861 and 1865 trips.

Several newspapers report 25 prominent black men also on the train, at Washington, D. C., going through to Springfield, even though their names do not show up on the invitation list. Among that group, Frederick Douglass, advisor to Lincoln, on anti-slavery issues is reportedly seen boarding the train.

No women were admitted to ride the train until it reached Michigan City, Indiana, on May 1st, where the Chicago Committee of One Hundred Citizens included women and at least one negro man. They remained with the train to Springfield.

A regional military escort, which changed at each city of viewing, also rode the train. It was typically composed of 50 hand-picked men from a state National Guard or Veteran Reserve Guard Unit. Little information remains of the units/regiments selected.

Local delegations for larger cities along each leg of the route usually rode some portion of that specific leg. The mayor and Common Council members for the towns where a planned stop would be made enroute rode.

This was certainly a national funeral by the people.

AN INTERIOR VIEW OF THE RAILROAD CAR CONVEYING THE REMAINS OF PRESIDENT LINCOLN

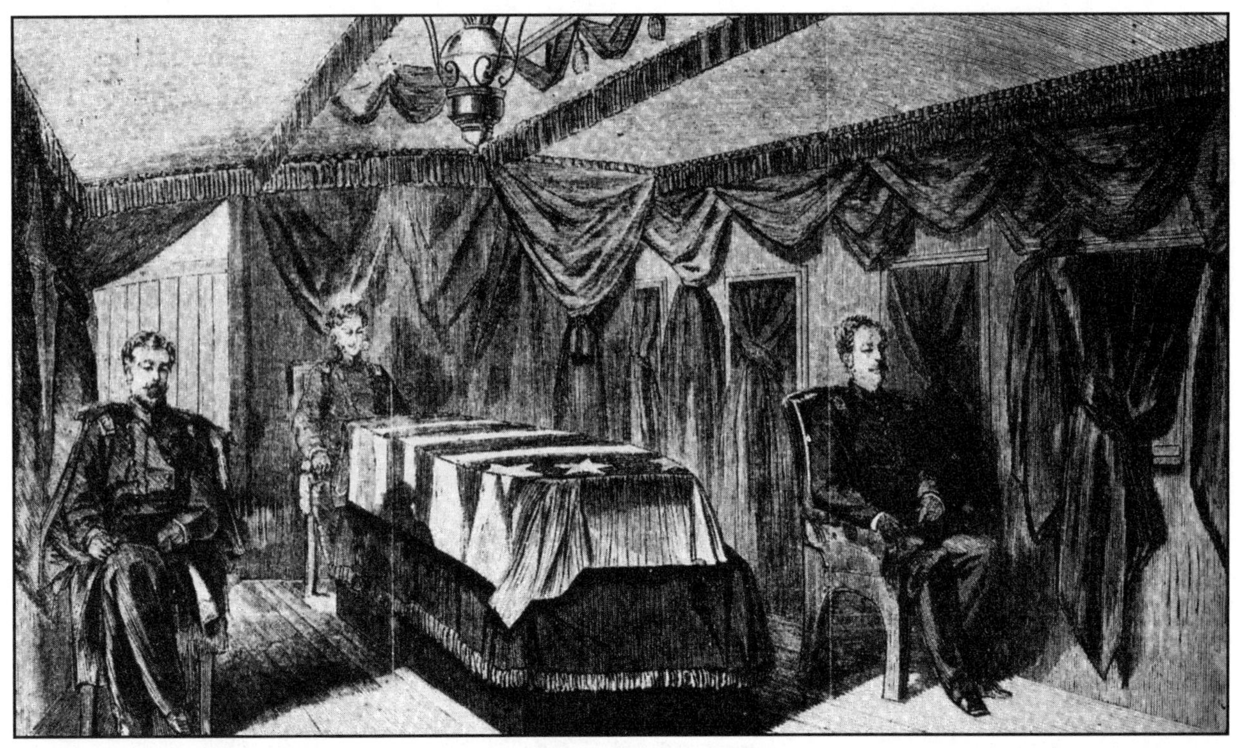

Illustration of the interior of the funeral car *United States* with the coffin of President Abraham Lincoln. The interior was of black walnut woodwork, curtins of light green silk; the ceiling was paneled with crimson silk gathered into a rosette in the center of each panel. In this view Lincoln's coffin is depicted in the sitting room of the car. This view depicts an honor guard from the military service. Each of these officers were from the select group appointed by E. M. Stanton, to accompany the remains to Springfield. -- *New York Public Library collection*

GENERAL ARRANGEMENT DRAWING OF THE FUNERAL CAR INTERIOR

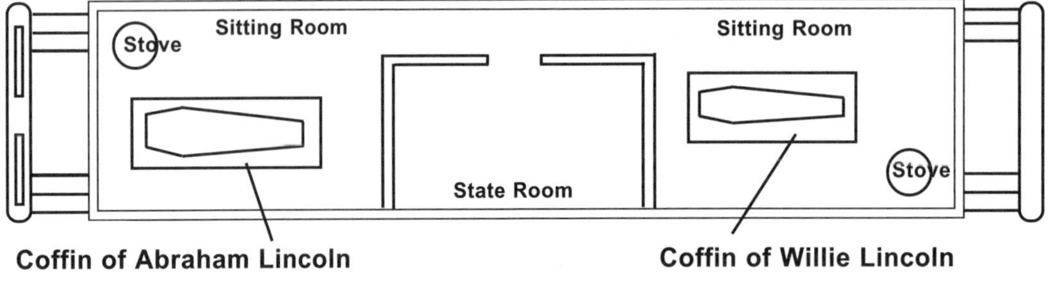

There are no discovered drawings for *United States*. This drawing is based solely on descriptions of those who built the car.

APRIL 21, 1865
WASHINGTON - BALTIMORE - HARRISBURG

Silence interrupted by the gentle searing sounds of rain abounded as daylight broke across the eastern sky on that rainy Friday morning. Notwithstanding the early hour, and inclement weather, large numbers of citizens had collected for the purpose of rendering a last mark of respect to the mortal remains of Lincoln.

At about 6:00 a.m. the members of the Cabinet, the Illinois Delegation, the pallbearers, and several officers of the army, with Senators and other distinguished visitors, assembled in the rotunda of the Capitol Building where Lincoln lay in state.

The unfolding events marked final honors in Washington and the start of a national funeral procession of immense proportions on the long journey home.

In the rotunda, and after taking a final look at the corpse, the Rev. Dr. Phineas Densmore Gurley offered a brief prayer, the only ceremony at the Capitol.

The coffin was closed and removed to a hearse by the same sergeants who carried the corpse on Wednesday, and under a guard of honor composed of the companies of Captains Cromee, Bush, Hildebrand and Dillon, of the Twelfth Veteran Reserve Corps. Under the command of Lieutenant Colonel Bell, the remains were taken to the depot, the Cabinet and others following.

Meanwhile, the remains of little Willie Lincoln, who died in February 1862, were removed to the depot, and placed in the same car with the remains of his lamented father. His metal coffin was placed in a handsome black walnut coffin, and silver mounted the prior day. A silver plate on the burial case was inscribed, "William Wallace Lincoln, born December 21st, 1850, died February 20th,

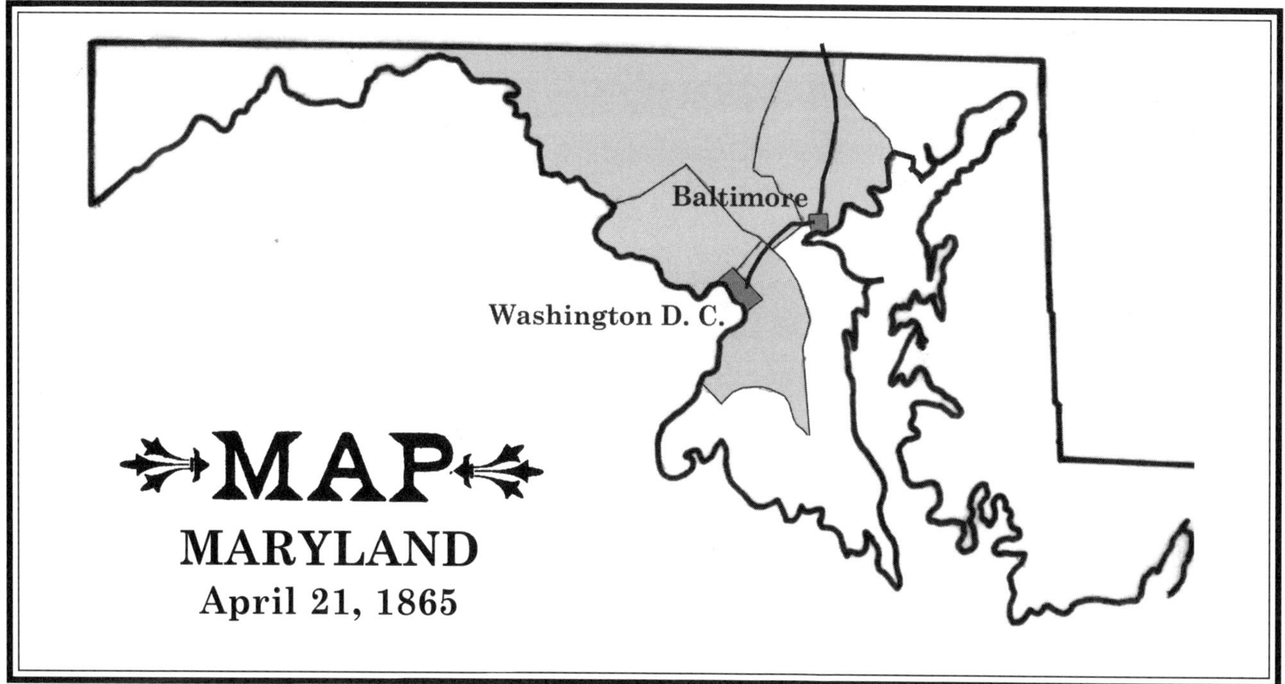

Railroads used: Washington D. C. to Baltimore, Maryland -- Baltimore & Ohio Railroad
Baltimore, Maryland to Harrisburg, Pennsylvania -- Northern Central Railroad

ROUTE MAP
Washington D.C. to Baltimore, Maryland
April 21, 1865
38 miles

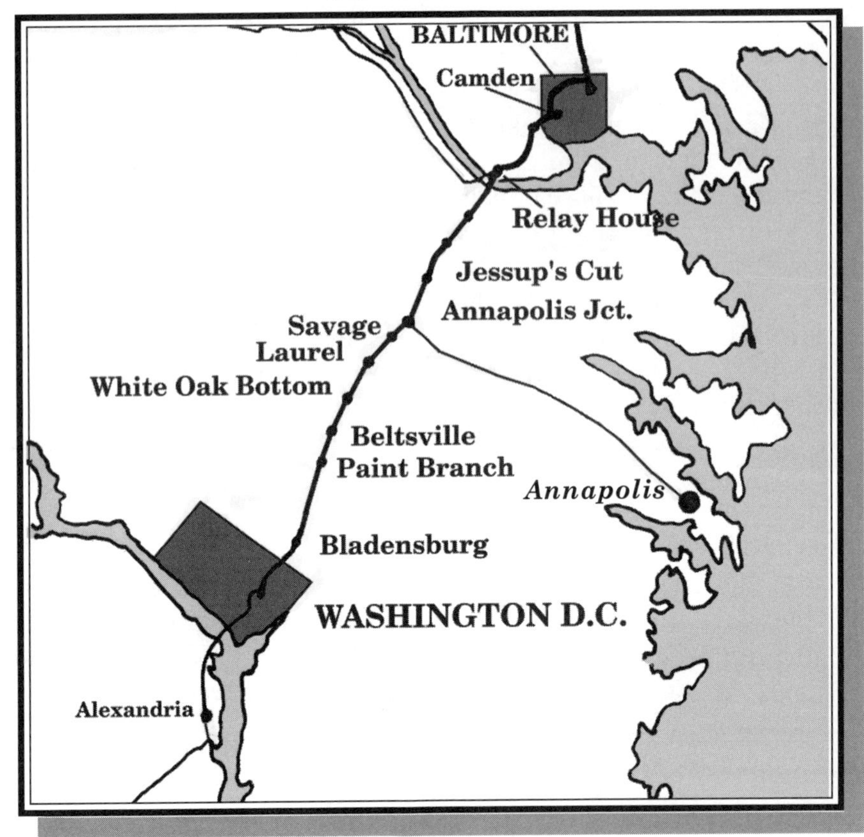

Railroads used: Washington, D.C. to Baltimore, Maryland -- Baltimore & Ohio Railroad

ITINERARY
Washington to Baltimore

Via Baltimore & Ohio Railroad
Washington, D.C. DEPART: 8:00 AM
Bladensburg
Paint Branch
Beltsville
White Oak Bottom
Laurel
Savage
Annapolis Jct.
Jessups Cut
Elkridge Landing
Relay House
St. Denis
Camden
BALTIMORE ARR: 10 AM Camden Station

Illustration of New Jersey Street Station, Baltimore & Ohio station at Washington D.C. where the Lincoln funeral train originated. Built in 1852, this station stood at the intersection of New Jersey Avenue and "C" Street. It was just two short blocks from the capitol building to this station for the Lincoln's funeral cortege. It stood until 1907. -- *B & O Museum collection*

1862." The remains of father and son were placed on the *United States.* A stand to support the coffin, covered with black cloth, was placed in the car on which the remains of the President were placed, and on a like stand, at the opposite end, the remains of little Willie rested.

During the prior day, the car was decorated with emblems of mourning, the windows being hung with black curtains, and the entire furniture robed in black. Along the top outside was a row of mourning gathered to black and white rosettes, and another similar row extended around the car, below the window. This car was in the charge of Mr. John McNaughton, of the United States Military Railroads.

The coffin having been moved from the Capitol a few short blocks to the station, the Veteran Reserve Guard of Escort removed it from the hearse and carried it through the depot to the awaiting train. Followed were the distinguished gentlemen, civil and military. The military, as soon as the remains had passed them, formed a line in front of the building. A strong guard was placed at all approaches, with no person being allowed but officers of the army and navy, the delegations going with the trains, and the passengers for the Baltimore-Philadelphia train leaving at 7:30 a.m.

Lincoln's coffin was passed through the

FREE TRANSPORTATION

War Department
Adjutant-General's Office
Washington, April 20, 1865

U. H. Painter, Esq., correspondent of the PHILADELPHIA INQUIRER, is invited to accompany the remains of the late President ABRAHAM LINCOLN, from the city of Washington to Springfield, Illinois.
By order of the Secretary of War

E. D. TOWNSEND
Assistant Adjutant General

Washington D.C.

April 21, 1865

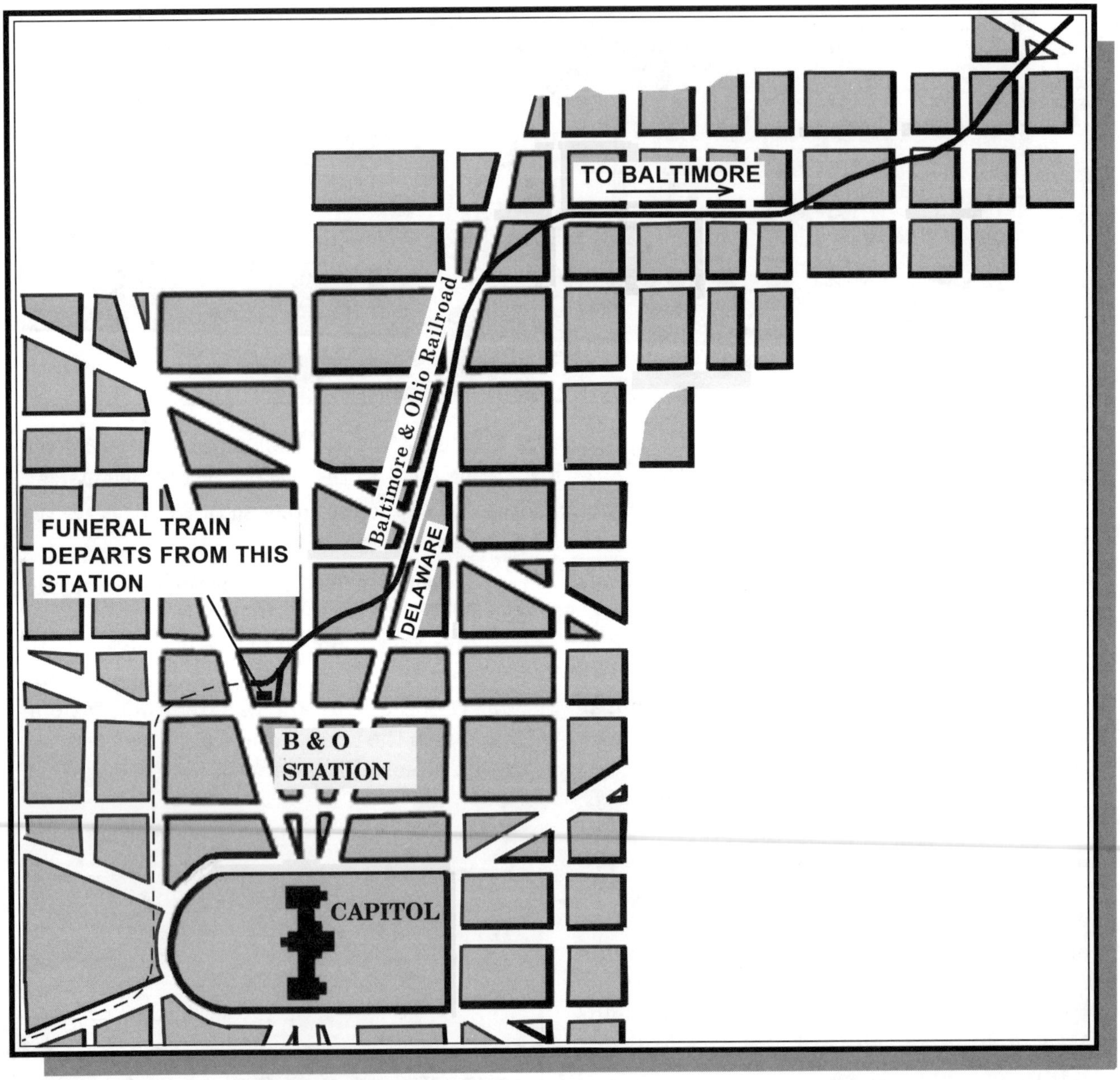

TO BALTIMORE

Baltimore & Ohio Railroad

FUNERAL TRAIN DEPARTS FROM THIS STATION

DELAWARE

B & O STATION

CAPITOL

After the train left the B & O depot in Washington, it followed the tracks two city blocks over to Delaware Street, running about four blocks down that street before swinging onto "I" Street for four blocks, then finally angling north and departing the city. The streets were crowded with the masses as they watched the funeral train of the second father of our country pass by. -- *Traced from a map at the Library of Congress*

narrow end door of the *United States* via the rollers. The Veteran Reserve Guard of Escort picked it up, placing it on the catafalque which had been prepared for its reception. At the door of the car the Rev. Dr. Gurley again briefly addressed the God of the living and the dead in a solemn and appropriate prayer as thousands wept.

Captain Robert Lincoln, and family friends escorted the remains to the depot, and witnessed their loading on the train. Then he returned to the White House to tend his grieving mother. He did not leave Washington for the Springfield burial until the afternoon of May 1, 1865.

At the back of the depot Captain Camp, of the Soldiers Rest, posted a guard, and kept the crowd back, a large number of persons having gathered. There were quite a number of officials present as the train was being made ready, among whom were Secretaries Stanton, Usher, Welles, McCulloch and Post Master General Dennison, Attorney-General Speed, Lieutenant-General Grant, Generals Hunter, Hardee, Barnard, Rucker, Townsend, Ekin, Eaton, Howe, Gen. McCullum, Captain Camp, of Soldiers' Rest, and others of the army. Admiral C. H. Davis, of the Bureau of Navigation, Captain W. R. Taylor and Major Feld of the Marine Corps were also present.

As the time for departure of the train drew near the parties, estimated at this time to be 150 men, who were holding tickets took their place in the coaches. No women were permitted to ride the train until it reached Michigan City, Indiana. The station, which since the death of the President, had worn mourning on the outside, was elaborately draped inside, the work having been done the day before, under the direction of Mr. George

The Lincoln Funeral Train ready to depart the Baltimore & Ohio Railroad's New Jersey Avenue Station in Washington, D. C., April 21, 1865. The *United States* is the second from the last car. In the background is the newly completed capitol dome, which was just a few city blocks away. -- *Illustration by Author based on accounts and photos.*

S. Koontz, the General Agent of the Baltimore & Ohio Railroad. Every window and door frame was draped, and heavy festoons falling from the cornice of the main saloon, and a large flag covered with crepe angling over the door leading to the platform. Over the gate to the platform a large arch was covered, running the entire length of the platform. The train was composed of nine cars, seven of them being coaches of the Baltimore and Ohio Railroad. One funeral car the *United States,* was from the United States Military Railroads. The last, the Officers Car intended for the family and the Congressional Committee, was sent by the Sam Felton, President of the Philadelphia, Wilmington and Baltimore Railroad. The Officers' car contained a parlor, chamber, dining-room and a small kitchen, and was elegantly furnished.

The train was put together by Mr. John Collins, dispatcher of trains. The locomotives selected for the initial leg of the trip were brand-new Baltimore and Ohio Railroad class G 4-4-0's, Numbered 238 and 239, manufactured by Thatcher Perkins, Master of Machinery, in Baltimore. Mr. Koontz, and Walker the Passenger Agents, saw that the passengers were properly seated. The train was under immediate charge of Baltimore & Ohio Railroad Conductor, Captain J. P. Dukehart, who went through with the remains to Springfield, as special aid to General McCullum. The engine to go before the train as the pilot was No. 239, of which William Galloway, was the Engineer, and James Brown, Fireman. It was heavily draped in mourning, all the brass being covered, while in front there were two large flags fringed with mourning, and four smaller ones on the engine. The tender was also heavily draped.

At precisely 7:50 a.m., after directions had been given by Major-General Meigs and General McCullum, the pilot locomotive and a single coach started north. In the coach was mostly railroad personnel and military staff to make sure the tracks were clear.

Shortly after the pilot train started, all who were to accompany the remains took their places in the cars. At precisely 8:00 a.m. the funeral train began one of the most sorrowful journeys ever undertaken on an American railroad. A single steam locomotive sounded its whistle and slowly the great driving wheels began to roll, with the nine car train following. The locomotive burned wood fuel. Cords of fuel were stacked neatly in the tender, undoubtedly selected from dried hardwood to provide maximum heat in the fire box.

To understand the complex nature of the task being undertaken with this lengthy journey, one must consider the trains lacked air brakes, automatic couplers or even radio's. A staff of brakemen were required to ride outside on the platform of some railcars and listen for whistle signals from the locomotive engineer to know when to begin to hand crank the hand brake wheels and bring the train to a stop, or to release them.

Eyewitness accounts indicate when the "proceed" signal was given, the bell on the locomotive was tolled. Then the bells on some of the other nearby engines tolled simultaneously, and slowly the train began moving from the station. The members of the Cabinet, and others who were on the platform, as well as the crowd gathered in the rear of the depot with heads uncovered until the train passed out of view. The military escort remained in line along the front of the depot platform until the train started. As it commenced to move, they presented arms as a last token of respect. As the train moved by the Soldiers' Rest, which was immediately in the rear of the depot, the Eighth Regiment United States Colored Artillery, who were there finishing their breakfast, jumped to formation, drew in line and presented arms. It is reported there was not a dry eye among the men. Everyone stood at attention until the train rolled out of sight.

The engineer in charge of No. 238, was Thomas Beckitt, whose fireman was C. A. Miller, and on the engine was Mr. John R. Smith, Supervisor of Engines of the Baltimore and Ohio Railroad, to personally oversee the locomotive operations.

The Baltimore & Ohio Railroad's Camden Station on Camden Street at Baltimore, Maryland, in 1865. This was the arrival station in Baltimore for Lincoln's funeral train. This view looks west across the front of the station. The train arrived to the rear of the building. Below and out of the picture the rails continued north to the Northerm Central Railroad where the funeral train departed for Harrisburg, Pennsylvania. -- *B & O Museum collection*

WASHINGTON, D.C. to BALTIMORE

The first mile of the next 38 was largely over the Streets of Washington. After the train left the depot, it followed the tracks two city blocks over to Delaware Street, running about four blocks down that Street before swinging onto "I" Street for four blocks, it finally angled north and departed the city. The streets were crowded with the masses as they watched the funeral train carrying the deceased remains of the second father of our country pass by. The next 37 miles of the funeral train's journey to Baltimore was over the Baltimore & Ohio Railroad.

Along the route guards came to present arms as the train passed them. The 116th New York Volunteers, riding on the B & O, were on their way south to Washington, D.C. for provost duty. About 12 miles north of Washington, their train was put in a siding and held until the Funeral Train had passed. "... our train slackened its speed, and the slow tolling of our engine bell announced the approach of the funeral cortege."

The 29th Maine was on another troop train north of Washington, which was held in a siding to allow President Lincoln's funeral train to pass. All the regiments' men removed their hats and stood in silence while the funeral train passed in the morning mist.

Few other people were visible along the tracks until the train was north of Annapolis Junction. Two stops were made, the first at Annapolis Junction, where Maryland Gov. A. W. Bradford, the Lieutenant Governor and Baltimore City Officials joined the mournful procession. The buildings were draped in black and two locomotives standing on a siding tolled their bells. The crowd estimated at 500 people stood silent. A second brief stop was made at Relay Station, nine miles from Baltimore, to permit a party of ladies to lay floral tributes on the coffin. This was the first of many local expressions of sorrow frequently repeated over the next 1,600 miles.

It was over this same stretch of track that Abraham Lincoln had traveled on February 23, 1861, under the cover of darkness, veiled in secrecy, being carried to his inaugu-

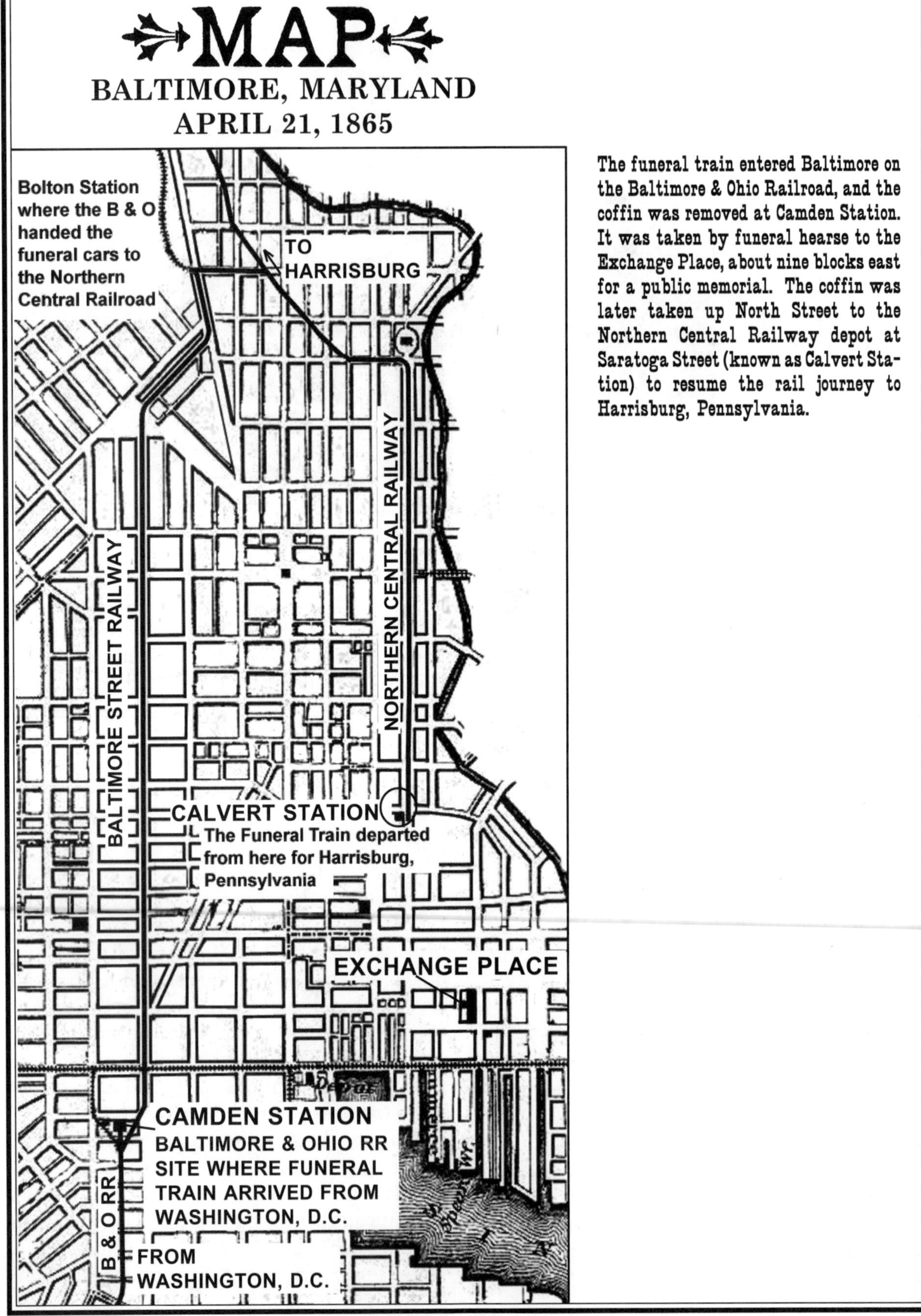

The funeral train entered Baltimore on the Baltimore & Ohio Railroad, and the coffin was removed at Camden Station. It was taken by funeral hearse to the Exchange Place, about nine blocks east for a public memorial. The coffin was later taken up North Street to the Northern Central Railway depot at Saratoga Street (known as Calvert Station) to resume the rail journey to Harrisburg, Pennsylvania.

ration as president in Washington, D.C. In the early days of the Civil War, word had it that conspirators would attempt to attack Lincoln's train.

There was a great anxiety for the safety of the remains of the President and the 150 on the train for most of the route. The concerns were highest until the train was north of Philadelphia.

The public outpouring of sorrow came as no surprise, although it was overwhelming to the emotional nature of the train's purpose. The train maintained its 20 miles-per-hour speed, passing by almost continuous lines of mourners who kneeled, stood with heads bowed and presented personal memorials to the memory of the slain president.

Baltimore was reached at 10:00 a.m. A heavy rain fell, yet with unanimity, in that city never equaled, the citizens testified their high regard for the honored dead in every expressive mode.

Long before daylight had broken over the city, the streets were thronged with citizens hastening to the different localities assigned for the assemblage of the different clubs and associations to join the procession. In spite of the inclement weather, people of all ages and races, gathered about the Camden Station of the Baltimore and Ohio Railroad. Camden Station was to the west of the main business area. By 8:00 a.m., it was reported the crowds were so great that it was almost impossible to move on any of the footwalks surrounding the depot buildings.

The depot buildings, and locomotives in the yards were tastefully draped. Every arrangement had been made in this department by the Master of Transportation, William Prescott Smith, to insure no delay or interruption in the proceedings. Lieutenant Governor Cox, with a portion of the Governor's staff, General Berry and staff, Honorable William B. Hill, Secretary of the State, and others accompanied the train.

From Camden Station it was about nine blocks to the Exchange Building where the body of Lincoln lay in state until about 2:30 p.m.

The train pulled into the station, the *United States* was the eighth car in the train, a goodly distance from the station or the platform. The back of the train was switched to a nearby parallel track for easy removal of the coffin. The buildings and yards were carefully guarded by the military.

CAMDEN STATION,
April 21, 1865.

Hon. EDWIN M. STANTON,
Secretary of War:
Just arrived all safe. Governor Bradford and suite and General E B. Tyler joined at Annapolis Junction.

E. D. TOWNSEND,
Assistant Adjutant-General.

BALTIMORE MEMORIALS

Baltimore having been reached , the citizens testified their high regard for the honored dead in every expressive way. Work was suspended; the hum of traffic was hushed; all turned aside from their usual vocations to unite in the observance of the day, and paid reverence to the great departed.

The streets were thronged with citizens,. In spite of the misty weather, people gathered about the Camden Station of the Baltimore and Ohio Railroad. It was reported by 8:00 a.m. that the crowd was so great that it was almost impossible to move on any of the foot walks surrounding the depot buildings.

When the car bearing the body reached the depot, the coffin was removed by the Veteran Reserve Guard of Escort, and, escorted through the depot buildings to the hearse awaiting its reception on Camden Street. The body of this hearse was almost entirely composed of plate glass, and drawn by four black horses. Owing to the presence of large detachments of the army in Baltimore, the military escort was exceedingly imposing. The various commands were thoroughly equipped. The entire column was under command of Brigadier General H. H. Lockwood, attended by his staff. It formed a line on

Eutaw Street, the right resting on Conway Street, and moved in reverse order a few minutes after 10:00 a.m. The rear of the escort was brought up by a large number of officers of various departments, including medical and other branches, all mounted.

The procession moved over Baltimore streets for nearly three hours, cutting precious time from those wanting to view the remains laying in state and pay their respects.

A few moments before 1:00 p.m., the head of the procession arrived at the southern front of the Exchange. As the head of the military escort reached Calvert Street the column was halted, and the hearse, with its guard of honor, passed between the lines, the troops presenting arms, and the bands of music wailing out the plaintive tune, *Peace, Troubled Soul.* The general officers dismounted and formed, with their staffs, on either side of the approach from the gate to the main entrance of the Exchange. The remains were then removed from the hearse and carried slowly and reverently into the building, being placed on a catafalque prepared for them.

After the coffin had been properly placed, the cover was removed. Officers present passed slowly forward, on either side of the body. The civic part of the procession followed, and the general public was then admitted for the next ninety minutes.

The catafalque was erected immediately beneath the dome. It consisted of a raised dais. From the four corners rose graceful columns, supporting a cornice extending beyond the line of the base. The canopy rose to a point fourteen feet from the ground, and terminated in clusters of black plumes. The whole structure was described as richly draped. The floor and sides of the dais were covered with black cloth, and the canopy was formed of black crape, with the rich folds drooping from the four corners and bordered with silver fringe. The cornice was adorned with silver stars, while the sides and ends were similarly ornamented. The interior of the canopy was of black cloth, gathered in fluted folds. In the central point was a large star of black velvet, studded with thirty-six stars, one for each State in the Union. The floor of the dais on which the body of the martyred patriot rested, was bordered with evergreens and a wreath of spiral azaleas, calla lilies, and other choice flowers.

Only a small portion of the throng in attendance were able to obtain a view of the remains. At about 2:30 p.m., to the regret of many thousands, the coffin was closed. The Veteran Reserve Guard of Escort removed the coffin to the hearse. The procession then reformed and took up its mournful march toward the depot of the Northern Central Railway.

A greatly disappointed public demanded to be allowed to pass through the hall and see the place where the remains had lain, and for days afterward a steady stream of people passed through.

While the procession and public viewing was being held, the Baltimore and Ohio Railroad had to take the cars north over street railway tracks in the middle of Howard Street, for interchange with the Northern Central Railway at Bolton Station. History indicates the movement of interchange cars was conducted between Camden Station and Bolton Station employing teams of horses to tow the cars. Once the two dedicated cars were delivered to the Northern Central, they had to be backed down to the Calvert Station, the site of departure north of the Exchange. Seven cars from the Northern Central Railway were added for the next leg of the journey to Harrisburg. At this date the Northern Central was

BALTIMORE,
April 21, 1865.

Hon. E. M. STANTON,
Secretary of War:
Ceremonies very imposing. Dense crowd lined the streets; chiefly laboring classes, white and black. Perfect order throughout. Many men and women in tears. Arrangements admirable. Start for Harrisburg at 3 p.m.

E. D. TOWNSEND,
Assistant Adjutant-General.

ROUTE MAP

Baltimore, Maryland to Harrisburg, Pennsylvania
April 21, 1865
58 miles

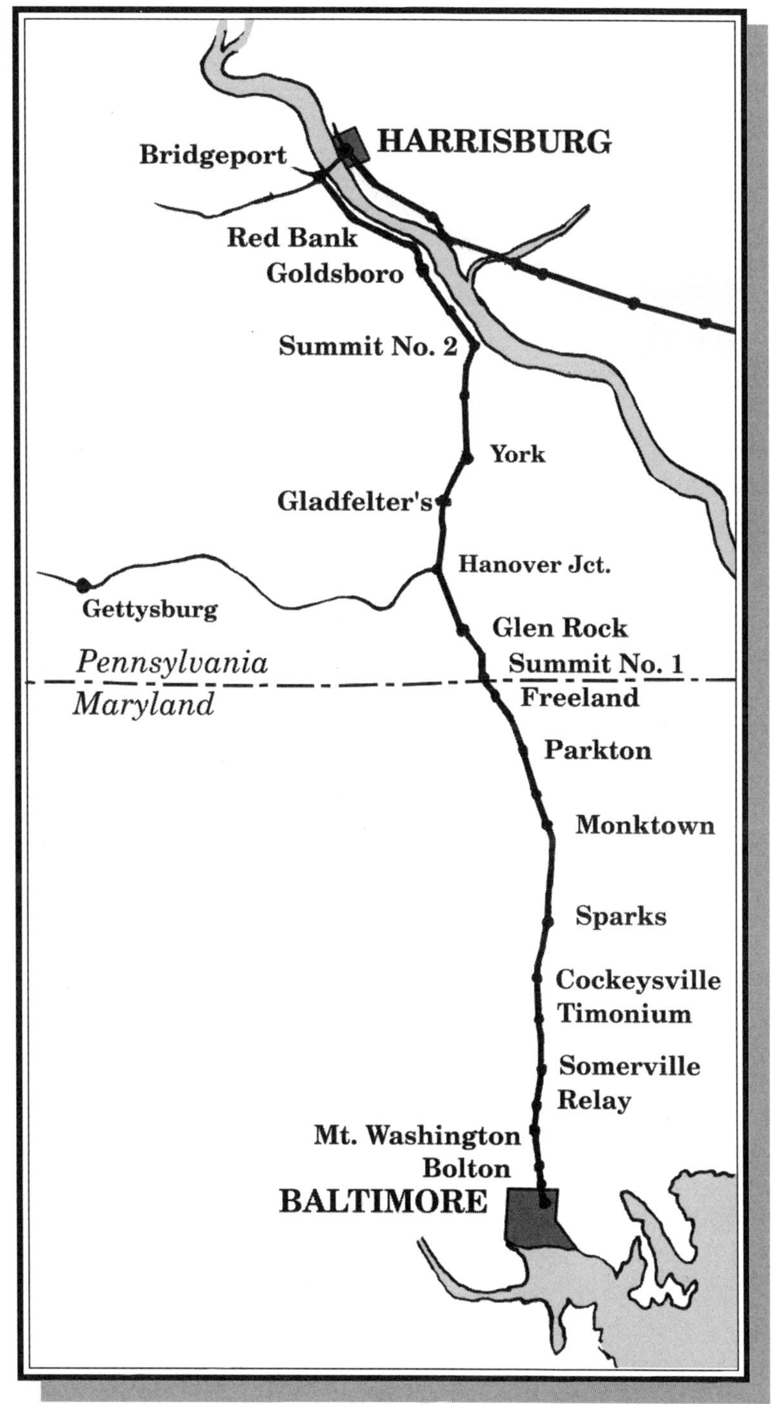

Railroads used: Baltimore, Maryland to Bridgeport, Pennsylvania -- Northern Central Railway
Bridgeport to Harrisburg -- Cumberland Valley Railroad

PROCLAMATION!!

The remains of our late lamented President will reach York at six o'-clock this evening, en route for Springfield, Ill. In order to render proper respect to the Funeral Cortege, the following order will be observed by the citizens:

1, All places of business will be closed from four o'clock, this evening, and under the Proclamation of the Governor of the State, will continue closed while the remains are within the limits of the State.

2. At five o'clock, P. M., the military and citizens will assemble in Centre Square, where a procession will be formed, and will march to the Railway Station. All citizens are expected to unite with the procession.

3. At the Rail-road a line will be formed, the right resting in front of the Station-house, and extending along the Rail-road in the direction of Baltimore. During the passing of the train the line will remain uncovered.

4. The citizens are requested to take their flags and drapery of mourning to Water Street, and suspend the same along the buildings on the line of the Rail-road.

5. The bells will be tolled while the remains are within the Borough limits.

6. Col. J. A. Stahle will act as Chief Marshal on the part of the citizens.

DAVID SMALL,

YORK, Pa., April 21. CHIEF BURGESS.

York, Pennsylvania, handbill proclaiming trackside services for the Lincoln Funeral Train, en route April 21, 1865. Handbills were common at this era because many smaller newspapers were only printed as a weekly. -- *Benedictine University collection* **BELOW: Conductor's Badge thought to have been worn on the Northern Central Railway.**

a very busy line hauling troops, goods and materials of the armies. The road had enhanced its fleet of locomotives, using the heavier 4-6-0 wheel arrangement locomotives. These are the likely locomotives used for the trip to Harrisburg.

The viewing at the Exchange ended and the procession left to march another six blocks to Calvert Station of the Northern Central Railway. There the refreshed train would resume its remaining 58 miles to Harrisburg, Pennsylvania.

BALTIMORE to HARRISBURG

The funeral train departed in the rain for Harrisburg via the Northern Central Railway, also known as the Sesquahanna Railway. From Baltimore to York, Pennsylvania, this line had been double tracked to handle the massive amounts of war traffic it was experiencing. The pilot locomotive departed with knowledge the funeral train would stop at the Maryland-Pennsylvania State Line to pick up the Pennsylvania Governor Andrew G. Curtin and suite.

Governor Curtin had been confined to

bed because of illness in the days before. He came from Harrisburg on a special 1:00 p.m. train with his staff to meet the funeral train and to escort it through the Keystone State as a proper host.

On this stretch of the Northern Central Railway, it had been ordered to have the bridges burned on April 20, 1861, in the very early days of the Civil War. They did not want to transport troops of either Union or Confederate armies, thus cutting the city off from further troop movements and isolating Washington D.C. by rail. The bridges were restored by late May 1861. The artery was an important transportation link in the war efforts and were heavily guarded.

In early July 1863, the Confederate raiders destroyed 19 additional bridges on the line between York and Harrisburg, Pennsylvania. Now the recently rebuilt line carried the train of the martyred president for a nation to mourn.

The train and all arrangements until leaving Harrisburg were under the immediate charge of the Superintendent of the Northern Central Railway, Mr. J. N. DuBarry and his assistant W. D. Hayes. At every point along the entire route significant tokens of sorrow and respect were manifested by large concourses of people. The individuals being able to show a last tribute of respect to the earthly remains of the Chief Magistrate, to express in common with their fellow citizens the sense of loss which the United States had sustained.

The first miles north of Baltimore presented scenes of gathered masses in wet clothes, standing about the crossings and along the margins of the railroad in the rain. The scene was most sad with many bared heads, weeping as they witnessed the passing train. Whole crowds were seen kneeling on the ground, or standing in reverent respect for the slain President. Clergymen were leading groups in prayers and hymns as the train slowly passed. The funeral escort knew this first national funeral would be overwhelming beyond anything they could have imagined.

As the Funeral Train passed Somerville, north of Baltimore, the ladies of the Female Seminary formed a line along the tracks, and displayed an American flag draped in mourning. The gentlemen who accompanied them stood with uncovered heads, silent and humble. A water stop was made at Parkton about 5:00 p.m. No mention of any local memorials is made.

At the Pennsylvania State Line, Summit No. 1 on the schedule, Governor Andrew Curtin met the train, accompanied by his staff. He was cordially greeted by Maryland Governor Bradford, who remained with the train to Harrisburg. The train resumed the slow pace. Both state parties rode in the first car behind the locomotive.

Just up the track a few miles, at Hanover Junction, Pennsylvania, on November 18, 1863, Lincoln had gone west to the village of Gettysburg, Pennsylvania, where he delivered a short speech, *The Gettysburg Address*, at the dedication of the National Cemetery established there after the Battle of Gettysburg.

COMING ONTO THE TRAIN

At the Pennsylvania State Line, Gov. A. G. Curtin met the train, accompanied by his staff, consisting of
Adjutant-General Russell,
Quartermaster-General Reynolds,
Inspector-General Lemuel Todd,
Surgeon-General James A. Phillips,
Colonels R. B. Roberts, S. B. Thomas, Frank Jordan and John A. Wright.
General Cadwalader, commanding the Department of Pennsylvania, accompanied Governor Curtin. The General's staff consisted of Major W. McMichael, A.D.C., Captain L. Howard.

DEPARTING FROM THE TRAIN

Governor Bradford, who was in the front car with his staff, consisting of:
Adjutant-General Berry,
General Edward Shriver and
Lieutenant Colonels Thomas J. Morris, Henry Tyson and A. J. Ridgeley.

NORTHERN CENTRAL RAILWAY

SPECIAL SCHEDULE

FOR

The President's Funeral Train,

For Friday, April 21, 1865, and to remain in force for that day only.

This Train has the right of Road against all Passenger, Freight and other Trains.

All Passenger, Freight and other Trains must keep entirely out of the way of this Schedule, as provided in special orders printed below.

Baltimore,	Leave	3.00 P. M.
Bolton,	"	3.06 "
(End of Double Track,)	"	3.11 "
Relay,	"	3.27 "
Timonium,	"	3.44 "
Cockeysville, (End of Double Track)	"	3.56 "
Sparks',	"	4.14 "
Monkton,	"	4.27 "
Parkton,	"	4.50 "
Freeland's,	"	5.10 "
Summit No. 1.	Arr.	5.20 "
	Leave	5.25 "
Glenrock,	"	5.42 "
(End of Double Track,)	"	5.45 "
Hanover Junction,	"	5.55 "
Glatfelter's,	"	6.03 "
York,	Arr.	6.30 "
	Leave	6.35 "
Summit No. 2,	"	6.53 "
Conewago,	"	7.05 "
Goldsboro',	"	7.21 "
Red Bank,	"	7.39 "
Bridgeport,	"	7.55 "
Harrisburg,	"	8.10 "

FAST FREIGHT SOUTH failing to make Cockeysville, (end of Double Track,) on time, will keep ONE HOUR off of time of Special Schedule, and remain on Siding until the Special Train passes.

MAIL TRAIN SOUTH arriving at Parkton on time, will remain there until Special Train passes. Failing to make Parkton on time, it will keep 40 minutes off of the time of Special Schedule and remain on Siding until Special Train passes.

LOCAL FREIGHT, NORTH AND SOUTH—York and Baltimore—are annulled for this day.

LOCAL FREIGHT SOUTH, AND COAL TRAINS SOUTH will not pass Cumberland Valley Rail Road Crossing at Bridgeport, until the Special Train arrives and passes on to the Cumberland Valley Bridge.

ALL GRAVEL AND CONSTRUCTION TRAINS will lay off and will not occupy Main Track between Bridgeport and Baltimore after 12 mid-day of Friday until Special Train passes.

PARKTON ACCOMMODATION, SOUTH, will not leave Parkton until Special Train passes.

A PILOT ENGINE will run on the time as printed on this Schedule, carrying Flags for Special Funeral Train, which will follow ten (10) minutes after the Pilot Engine.

J. N. DUBARRY, Gen'l Supt.

Office Northern Central Railway, Baltimore, April 21, 1865.

Benedictine University collection

It was dusk as the train neared York at 6:40 p.m. The town bells could be heard announcing the sorrowful arrival of the train.

According to the *York Cartridge Box*, for April 22, 1865, "Through neglect or disrespect for the memory of the illustrious dear - and it is believed to be the latter - the rebel sympathizers who have charge of the public building of York County, failed to clothe the Court House with the habiliments of mourning. This, however, was done, not by the County officials, not by the citizens of the borough, but by and at the expense of the officers, convalescents and patients of this hospital thus rebuking them for their disloyalty and want of proper respect. "

This important junction town on the railroad was the scene of special events. The locomotives required water in order to continue their journey to Harrisburg. While this activity was under way, a brief memorial service was conducted. A brass band from the United States Hospital played a mournful dirge during the trains stay. While the refueling activity was proceeding, a line opened in the crowd, and several ladies in black appeared. They were met by General Townsend and McCullum. In a moment, a large wreath was carried down to the train by a soldier. This is the second recorded site where ladies requested permission to enter the car and lay a wreath of flowers on the President's coffin.

After a brief discussion, General Edward Townsend, Secretary of War Edwin Stanton's representative, granted the request, with a modification that six ladies might perform the service. During the performance of a dirge by the band the flowers were carried in procession up and into the funeral car, while the bells tolled. All the men stood, heads uncovered. The ladies who made entry to the car were; Mrs. Samuel Smalley, Mrs. Henry E. Miles, Mrs. David E. Smalley, Miss Plover, Miss Louisa Ducks, Miss Susan Smalley and Miss Jane Lattimol, three on each side of the coffin; after being handed the wreath they placed it in the center of the coffin and then departed. York community leader, Aquilla Howard, a Negro man, on behalf of the city of York, placed a second wreath on Abraham Lincoln's coffin.

Those who witnessed the scene were reportedly bitterly weeping. The wreath was very large, about three feet in circumference. The outer circle was of roses, and alternate parallel lines were composed of white and red flowers of the choicest description. This expression became common after the train left New York City.

The bells of the town continued to toll and the band sounded appropriately mournful strains. The hand of affection could not have contributed a more choice and delicate tribute to the departed.

Departing York at 6:50 p.m., the train soon neared Mt. Wolf, Pennsylvania. The railroad ran parallel to and within close proximity of the Sesquahanna River. Threatening clouds grew as the train continued north.

Traversing the west bank of the river, it continued through to Bridgeport, a railroad junction on the west side of the Sesquahanna across from Harrisburg. As the train prepared to cross, a military corp fired a cannon on the Harrisburg side of the river to announce the train's approach.

The train accessed the bridge of the Cumberland Valley Railroad, at Bridgeport, slowly crossing the great Sesquahanna River, then exiting to Harrisburg on the east side and swinging onto the west leg of the wye track before entering the station. About the time the train started across the great bridge, a heavy rain storm set in, accompanied by vivid flashes of lightning and thunder. It was described in the *Harrisburg Patriot and Union* as, "... typical of the national gloom and of heaven's wrath upon the bloody crime that had been committed."

ARRIVAL AT HARRISBURG

Crowds and vast numbers of people had gathered all day to witness the train and the funeral procession. The train entered town after dark, quickly entering upon the tracks of the Pennsylvania Railroad, and stopping at the massive station at 8:35 p.m., some 15 minutes past the scheduled time. The rain had suddenly increased in intensity. The arrival was announced by a 21-gun national salute. The Courthouse bell tolled, calling the citizens to assemble. Order and sobriety was observed to a degree worthy of all praise on the Streets of Harrisburg.

The thick mist had turned into a rain so violent it was almost unendurable. Thousands of people who had gathered near the Market Street Station sought shelter indoors and under awnings, but the military guards bravely stood their posts in the pelting rain. It had become clear to those assigned to accompany the train, the expressions of sorrow were overwhelming beyond their wildest dreams.

Harrisburg was a vital city on the growing Pennsylvania Railroad, and its President, J. Edgar Thomson, had acted strongly in support of the Union during the Civil War. He was equally determined his railroad would be a proper host to serve the nation at this

The Pennsylvania State House at Harrisburg, Pennsylvania, where Lincoln lay in state during the first night of the funeral journey on April 21 and April 22, 1865. -- *History of Dauphin and Lebanon Counties, Pennsylvania, 1883*

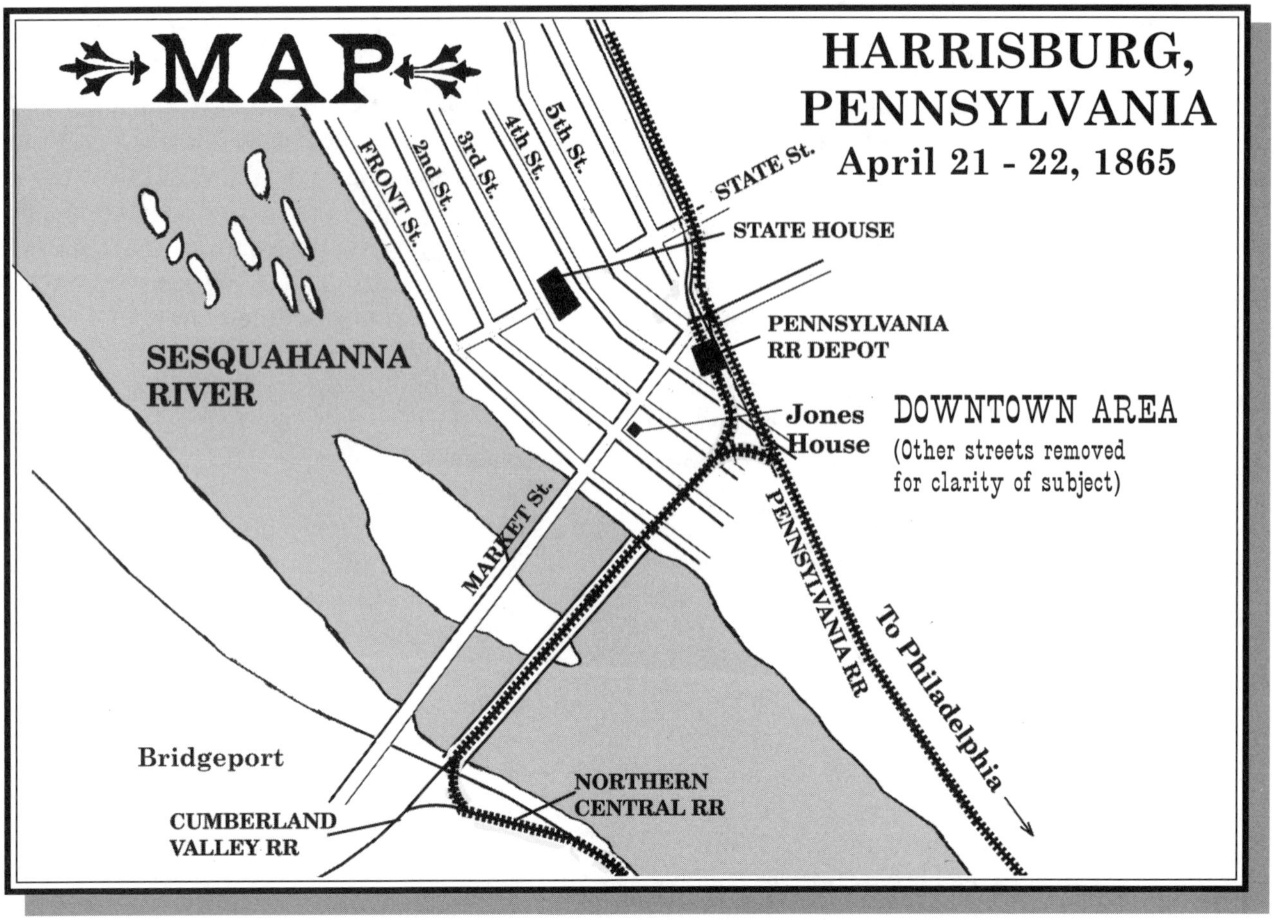

MAP

HARRISBURG, PENNSYLVANIA

April 21 - 22, 1865

FRONT St.
2nd St.
3rd St.
4th St.
5th St.
STATE St.
STATE HOUSE
PENNSYLVANIA RR DEPOT
Jones House
DOWNTOWN AREA
(Other streets removed for clarity of subject)
SESQUAHANNA RIVER
MARKET St.
PENNSYLVANIA RR
To Philadelphia
Bridgeport
NORTHERN CENTRAL RR
CUMBERLAND VALLEY RR

This view of the Funeral Train at the Harrisburg station is on the morning of April 22, 1865, at the Pennsylvania, Railroad. The car United States had to be stripped of its wet mourning emblems during the night and rehung with dry crape, lacking the silver fringe. This is the Harrisburg styling. It was replaced at Philadelphia, and the silver fringe was added. The view looks west, the end of the station in the picture is the east end. The train crossed into Harrisburg over the Cumberland Valley Railroad bridge to the east. Note one side of the station is draped in signs of mourning, while the other side is not.

The official schedule of procession to escort the remains to the train at Harrisburg, Pennsylvania:

PROCESSIONAL ESCORT TO THE DEPOT.
Full Band.
Military.
Detachment of Regiments stationed at Camp Curtin, carrying regimental and national flags, draped.
Martial music, with muffled drums.
Veteran Reserve Corps.
Martial Music.
1st New York Artillery, Battery A - guns draped in mourning.
201st Regiment Mounted Infantry.
Chief Marshalm Col. Henry McCormick.
Aids.
Cols. Alleman, Williams, Jennings, Major McCormick.
Clergy, flanked by Police of the City.
Hearse, containing Remains, Guard on sides, flanked by Pall Bearers.
General Cadwalader and Staff.
Governor Curtin, Attorney General Wm. M. Meredith and Secretary Eli Slifer, in carriage.
Carriages containing other distinguished persons.
Gen. Russell and Governor's Staff.
Assistant Marshals Alex. Koser and H. C. Shaffer.
Members of the Senate and House of Representatives.
Full Brass Band.
Judges of the Court.
Members of the Bar.
County officers.
Marshal, W. K. Verbeke.
Members of Council.
Committee of Arrangements.
Delegation of citizens of Pittsburg, under the Marshalship of Mayor Lowry.
Assistant Marshalls, Col. D. J. Unger and Maj. J. Brady.
Soldiers of war of 1812.
Honorably discharged soldiers.
Fire Companies.
Friendship No. 1
Marshal, W. A. Parkhill
Members dressed in red shirts, black pants and New York hats.
Hope No. 2
Marshal, W. H. Kepner.
Flag draped.
Members, dressed in gray shirts, black pants and New York hats.
Washington No. 4.
Marshal, Wm. Alricks.
Members Dress, citizens clothing; New York fire hats.
Mount Vernon Hook and Ladder No. 5;
Marshal, S. D. Ingram.
Members Dress, red shirts, black pants, New York hats.
Paxton Hose No. 6; Marshal, B. F. Shoops.
Members Dress, blue shirts, black pants, felt hats.
Masonic Lodge.
Knights Templar.
Dauphin Encampment, I. O. of O. F.
Carrying a beautiful black silk banner.
Salem Lodge - red silk banner.
Other civic organizations.
Young Men's Christian Association.
Quartermaster's employees.
Citizens and strangers.
Colored citizens.

moment, and a solemn privilege to move the martyred President on his final journey.

Due to the intense storms the civic portion of the procession was disbanded and the remaining military and government portion took the coffin from the train directly down Market Street to Second, up Second to State, and up State to the Capitol. The route was illuminated by burning red lights at short intervals along the route.

The passenger station, a large brick structure with covered train shed had been built in 1857, and featured twin towers, one at each end of the structure for the spotting of incoming trains.

While the train was in Harrisburg, it was kept in the great train shed. On this first night out a guard was posted around the *United States* and Officers Car. The guard included the Veteran Reserve Guard of Escort not assigned pallbearer duty, and local constables. This was a standard practice at every stop during the journey.

During the night wet decorations had to be refreshed on the *United States* and the Officers Car. The black crepe, silver fringe and tassels were removed, and hastily replaced to whatever degree time and materials permitted. The train left Harrisburg without the silver ornamentations, and it was not placed back on the cars until the train reached Philadelphia.

SCENE AT THE CAPITOL

The remains were taken directly to the Hall of the House of Representatives, where they lay in state. Thousands had gathered at Capitol Park for the opportunity to view the remains. A guard had been placed at the Capitol, but after the body had been placed in the building, the crush became so great the guards were pushed back and an immense crowd rushed to the doors of the rotunda. Citizens were permitted into the Hall about 9:30 p.m., passing the coffin, and exiting via windows. The silence of death pervaded the Hall even though it was disorderly outside. At midnight the Hall was closed to visitors and the guard set for the night. This city and Philadelphia were the two cities en route to close the remains from public visitation during the night hours.

The doors to the House of Representatives were reopened at 7:00 a.m. Viewing was closed at 9:00 a.m. For the next hour visitation was reserved for those who participated in the escort from the Capitol.

Because of the change of plans, many coming in to view the memorial procession in the morning had no knowledge it had been cancelled. The railroads were busy making preparations to handle the extra trains when the changes were announced. Still, the crowds came.

> HARRISBURG,
> April 21, 1865.
>
> Hon. E. M. STANTON,
> Secretary of War:
> Arrived here safely. Everything goes on well. At York a committee of ladies brought a superb wreath and laid it on the coffin in the car.
>
> E. D. TOWNSEND,
> Assistant Adjutant-General.

This is Pennsylvania Railroad locomotive Number 331, the locomotive that pulled the funeral train from Harrisburg to Philadelphia, Pennsylvania, on April 22, 1865. The engineer is J. A. Miller. The photo was likely taken at Harrisburg.

APRIL 22, 1865
HARRISBURG - LANCASTER - PHILADELPHIA

Security for the train and along the railroad had been successful during the first day's journey.

This days' journey, some five hours and thirty-five minutes, was the only made entirely during daylight hours. It would prove to be an overwhelming manifestation of public grief and popular appreciation. Crowds were well in excess of anything imagined by the organizers of the train.

As dawn broke on Saturday, April 22, it was still raining at Harrisburg. The Cumberland Valley Railroad brought an unheard of twenty car train filled with mourners into town near dawn to attend the viewing and witness the procession. The Pennsylvania Railroad was also bringing trains of mourners for the viewing. Public viewing, that was extended two additional hours, ended at 9:00 a.m. The original schedule had intended for an 8:00 a.m. processional parade over city streets, but the time was changed to 10:00 a.m. because of the unceasing rains. By the time of the appointed hour an estimated 40,000 people lined Harrisburg's streets to watch the hearse carry the coffin back to the Pennsylvania Railroad depot.

To prevent the streets from being overrun by the crowds, the military were again in line to maintain a clear path for the procession to pass. The Veteran Reserve Guard of Escort removed the coffin from the statehouse and, in the rain, carried it to the waiting hearse. At 10:20 a.m. the procession began, following the route of State Street to Front Street, and Front to Market, and back

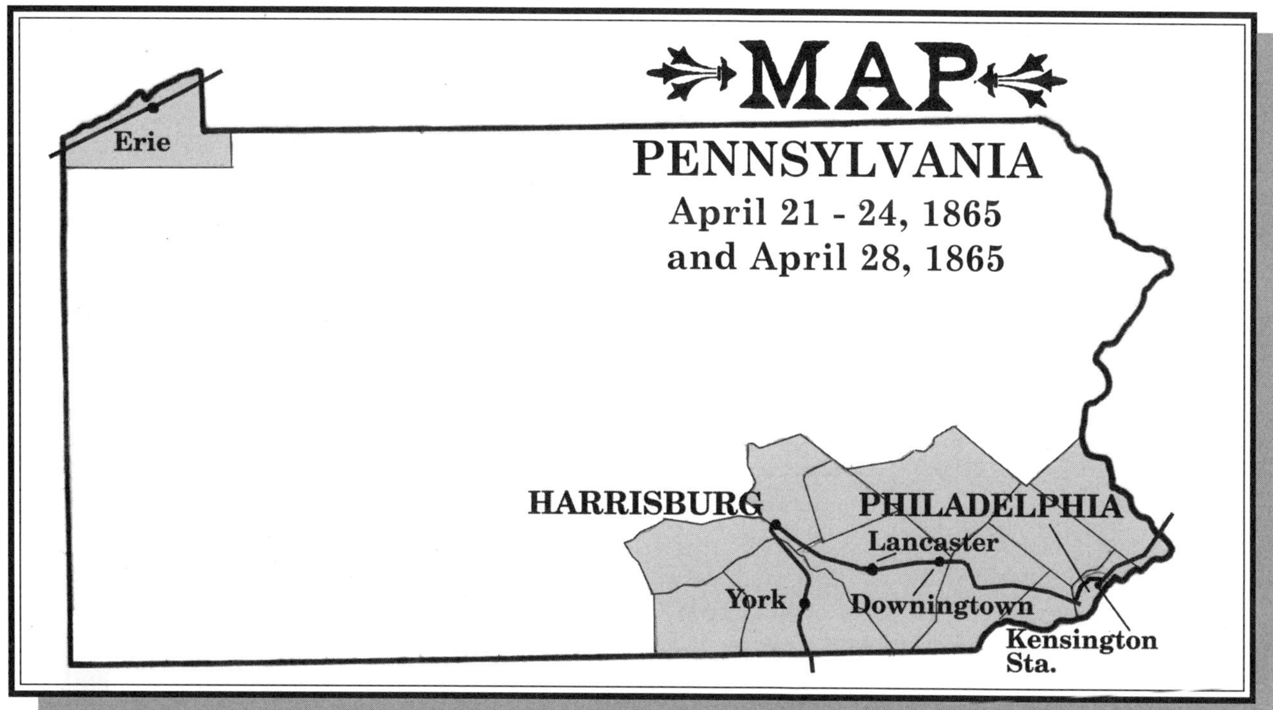

Pennsylvania is the only state on the funeral train route to have been visited twice. The first time was from April 21 through April 24, 1865. The second visit to the state came in the early morning hours of April 28, 1865, when the train passed through the short stretch near Erie, Pennsylvania.

The funeral train at the Harrisburg, Pennsylvania station on the morning of April 22, 1865, at the Pennsylvania, Railroad. The locomotive is Pennsylvania Railroad Number 331, of the 4-4-0 wheel arrangement. The train is facing west in this view. The whole train had to be turned in order to head east to Philadelphia.

to the Pennsylvania Railroad Depot, where the guarded train stood waiting.

The train was drawn up across Market Street, to receive the remains. The Veteran Reserve Guard of Escort removed the coffin from the hearse and placed it directly on the awaiting *United States*. Members of the funeral escort in the procession left their carriages and quickly entered the train. It had been suggested the escort delegates be on the train prior to the arrival of the coffin in preparation for the early departure.

At 11:05 a.m., almost an hour early, the pilot train lead by Pennsylvania Railroad locomotive Number 286, engineer, John McNeal, departed with a single coach. Just ten minutes later to the sound of the locomotive whistle, the nine car funeral train, lead by Pennsylvania Railroad locomotive Number 331, engineer, John E. Miller, slowly departed Harrisburg, for the 106-mile journey to Philadelphia. Both locomotives were of the lighter 4-4-0 wheel arrangement.

Departing, the funeral train was pulled backwards through a wye track so it could be turned. This occurred just east of the station. Properly positioned, the whole train was ready to begin the journey east to Philadelphia. The *Harrisburg Patriot and Union* indicated the order of the train at the station was a locomotive, baggage car, Officers Car, *United States* and six coaches. Photos taken at this time indicate it is exactly the opposite. A yard switcher was likely used to pull the train backwards for the purpose of changing its direction.

DEPARTING HARRISBURG

At this hour the rains stopped and the sun burst through the clouds and across the eastern Pennsylvania landscape. The margins along the tracks were lined with people who wanted to catch a glimpse of the coffin or to express their sorrow. A few miles beyond Harrisburg a large national flag with appendages was spread upon the grass and crowds of people with heads uncovered, stood on either

TIME TABLE

Pennsylvania Rail Road.-----Philadelphia Division.

SCHEDULE
FOR
SPECIAL TRAIN,
WITH THE REMAINS OF PRESIDENT LINCOLN,
TO BE RUN FROM
HARRISBURG TO PHILADELPHIA.
On Saturday, April 22d, 1865.

LEAVE EASTWARD.

Stations.	Distance	TIME.	Special Instructions.
HARRISBURG,		11 00	A. M.
Highspire,	6.2	11 19	
Middletown,	3.7	11 30	
Branch Intersection,	1.0	11 33	
Conewago Siding,	4.6	11 46	
Elizabethtown,	3.0	11 55	A.M.
Kuhnz's Siding,	3.2	12 04	P. M.
Mount Joy,	3.2	12 14	
Landisville,	4.4	12 27	
Kauffman's Siding,	3.3	12 37	
Dillerville,	3.3	12 47	
Lancaster,	1.2	12 55	
Bird-in-hand,	7.0	1 15	
Gordonville,	3.3	1 25	
Leaman Place,	1.1	1 28	
Kinzer's,	3.2	1 37	
Gap,	2.9	1 46	
Christiana,	2.5	1 53	
Penningtonville,	1.5	1 57	
Parkesburg,	3.1	2 06	
Chandler's,	1.5	2 11	
Coatesville,	3.2	2 20	
Gallagherville,	5.3	2 36	
Downingtown,	1.5	2 43	
Oakland,	4.1	2 55	
Steamboat,	3.2	3 04	
West Chester Int.,	3.8	3 15	
Paoli,	1.8	3 21	
Eagle,	4.1	3 33	
Morgan's Corner,	2.8	3 41	
White Hall,	3.1	3 50	
City Avenue,	4.8	4 04	
West Philad'a,	4.8	4 17	
BALTO. DEPOT,		4 30	P. M.

SPECIAL NOTICE.—A Pilot Engine will precede the Special Train, running ten minutes ahead of it.

GEO. C. FRANCISCUS,
Supt. Philad'a Division.

ENOCH LEWIS,
Gen'l Superintendent.

Benedictine University collection

side of it, in silent respect.

The village of Middletown, Pennsylvania, was reached at about 11:45 a.m. Large crowds had gathered. Here the first mention of a memorial arch over the railroad is made. The arch being achieved just before entering a train shed. The funeral arch was made of evergreens and spanned over the tracks. National flags draped in mourning were reported during a brief memorial stop. It is said that large crowds had gathered here in 1861 to greet Lincoln on his way to Washington.

At Elizabethtown, a brief stop was made at 12:15 p.m. A large flag was suspended from the depot, to which was affixed the motto, "We Mourn a Nation's Loss." Gathered crowds made a rush over trackside piles of wood to catch a glimpse of the coffin. The scene was described as more animated than mournful. By 12:30 p.m. the train was under way, passing crowds of mourners at Mount Joy, Landisville and Dillerville.

Near Wheatland, west of Lancaster, the home of ex-president, James Buchanan, was pointed out to the reporters on the train. The home was about two miles in the distance. The *New York Tribune* made a reference to the home. "James Buchanan and his house are visible as we approached the city. No flag, no emblem of mourning indicating patriotism and sorrow, could be detected on the house, nor, perhaps was any expected." Other less favorable remarks were made in the article. Buchanan, had gone to Lancaster to pay his respects to Lincoln. He was at trackside near the station in his carriage when the train stopped.

To the west of Lancaster, Congressman Thaddeus Stevens was standing at trackside, reportedly in a tunnel, as the train passed. He lifted his hat in respect to the slain President.

In five minutes, the next scheduled stop at Lancaster, Pennsylvania, was reached. It was an industrial town governed by a group largely known as "Copperheads." The April 21, issue of the Lancaster newspaper, *Intelligencer* announced the train would stop in the city at 2:19 p.m. Late that Friday evening after the paper had closed for the night, it was learned the train's schedule had been changed and it would arrive one hour earlier. The change of time was posted on the paper's public bulletin board. All businesses were requested to close at 10:00 a.m., in observance of mourning, some did not honor that request.

All churches held memorial services at noon, apparently in contest with the Copperhead ceremony, which got under way at 11:00 a.m. The *Intelligencer* gave only the briefest description stating; "The whole address was full of the bloodthirsty vindictiveness of the fanatical crew now ruling the country. Our readers would not thank us for reporting the windy harangue in full."

In preparation for the coming of the train many buildings, public and private were heavily draped in emblems of mourning. Fourteen churches observed their ritual symbols of mourning by decorating the church buildings accordingly. The Pennsylvania Railroad station and facilities were extensively decorated, both inside and out. Drapery was festooned with American flags at all high points of the

An example of the mourning badge worn by many during the passage of the train. Style and complexity changed from town to town along the route. -- *National Park Service collection*

ties. The highlight was a large portrait of Lincoln with a placard proclaiming; "ABRAHAM LINCOLN, the Illustrious Martyr of Liberty! The Nation Mourns His Loss. But Though Dead, He Yet Liveth!" Lincoln stopped here in 1861, to the shouts and cheers of throngs of well-wishers. The streets were draped with flags and crowded. He stepped from the train to address the crowds from a balcony at the Caldwell House Hotel before departing for Harrisburg.

At an early hour on the morning of April 22nd, thousands of people started to gather at the station. When the train arrived at 1:05 p.m., the crowds were so dense, it was almost impossible to get the train through. Crowds were estimated at 20,000 to 40,000 people waiting at the station. As the train arrived, people began surging in every direction. The funeral car attracted their attention, and they began pressing toward it. One lady fainted and a voice was heard to shout, but the crowd continued forward. Another shouted, "Grant is on board!" electrifying the crowd even more. Crowds pushed both directions in the sea of people looking for him. Someone in the funeral escort came out onto the platform of a car to calm the crowds and request they remain in their places, and the crowd calmed.

A floral memorial was to be placed on the coffin by a select group of seven ladies, Patriot Daughters. They were inside the station waiting room, but their approach to the train was nearly impossible. A man had to help clear a path. They were momentarily lost in the crowd, until they neared the funeral car. Entry was finally gained and the wreath of white camellias and roses was laid, to join the florals received at earlier stops.

Departing town the train passed the Norris Locomotive Works, a major manufacturer of steam railroad locomotives, needed for the war effort, was working this day. They shut the plant down to honor the late President. Extensive preparations were made to acknowledge the deceased. Their shop buildings were draped in suspended festoons, and looped between windows with red, white and blue ribbons. A large flag was draped around the pole at the top of the main building. As the train was announced, all workmen, estimated at from 400 to 600 men, left their jobs to stand on the nearby freight cars, locomotives, tenders or at track side, silently drawn up in line with uplifted hats in respect to the remains. Many family members joined them, most wearing mourning badges.

After the train departed Lancaster, the Copperhead meeting reassembled, and more equally distasteful speeches were espoused in, "the bloodthirsty vocabulary of the radical fiends ... which was full of froth and fury, signifying nothing."

The assemblage broke up late in the afternoon and the newspaper went on to state that many persons had become disgusted with the proceedings and left before the closing of the meeting. The actions of the people through their presence at trackside cancelled any opinions the newspapers may have tried to portray.

As the train continued east, it was observed that near the tracks in many places old men had been carried down in their chairs. Women with infants held them up to witness the cortege's passing. And so it was with all the towns and villages this day. Everything had come to a virtual stop and people crowded to see the funeral train pass, manifested by grief, many dropping to their knees, with heads bowed, tears streaming down their cheeks.

Noticeable on this leg of the journey, was the strewing of flowers in profusion on the tracks by the school children at many places. John Miller, the locomotive engineer, later commented, "...it was with difficulty the engine passed through, as the wheels in crushing the flowers, became so slippery that the train almost stalled more than once."

Strasburg Junction, later known as Leaman Place, a junction with the Strasburg Railroad, was a stop for the train. A brief memorial ceremony was conducted. This site was a place frequently used by locomotives needing water, and may have been a scheduled stop for that reason. There was quite a concourse of countrymen present. The short-line railroad ran several special trains to bring mourners to the junction. While the funeral train was stopped, it allowed those from the rural area to honor the martyred president. In a nearby siding stood a Harrisburg bound passenger train, the passengers standing adjacent in the fields, with heads uncovered, solemn silence about until the train passed by. Lincoln's 1861 train stopped here for water, and he appeared briefly on the platform to let the trackside crowd see him. He passed some humorous remarks and Mrs. Lincoln appeared on the platform as well.

The train passed through Penningtonville at 2:05 p.m. to a large crowd of people, heads bowed, prayers whispered and tears of sorrow streaming in the warm spring sun.

The *Philadelphia Inquirer* stated, "At Parkersburg [2:15 p.m.] we found the whole country at the railroad station, but the train ran so swiftly by that there was barely time for them to catch a glimpse of the funeral car, toward which all eyes were strained." People had collected on the steps of homes, in windows or doorways on railroad cars and lining fences to catch a glimpse of the train.

The forges at Coatsville were silent, every place closed and the residents stood silently at the depot and along the tracks to pay homage to the President. A reporter on the train wrote of this place: "Men and women bowed in grief with reverent awe. The sorrow and anguish of an afflicted nation is best seen in a silent people." In 1861 flags and banners draped the tracks as local people showed their support for the president-elect.

A fuel and water stop was planned for the train at the historic colonial city of Downingtown, in the Brandywine Valley. Amid the gently rolling hills and colonial roots of Southeastern Pennsylvania, the train arrived at 2:50 p.m. Large crowds of mourners had gathered at the depot. It was described as a quiet and somber gathering. Many quietly asked in which car was the President? Around the car they gathered, many on tiptoe, seeking a glimpse of the coffin. Heads were uncovered and bowed in prayer during a memorial service. Men hand loaded cords of split wood on the locomotive tender, and the tender tank was replenished with water during this stop. Soon the locomotive whistled and they resumed their journey. The train passed by a public house near the tracks, where another large collection of people gathered, with festoons hung and a picture of the late president on display. Lincoln's train stopped here in 1861 for water and he may have appeared on the platform to greet well-wishers during the brief stop. Slowly the funeral train moved on toward Philadelphia, the cradle of American independence.

The April sun shown brightly as the train passed through Oakland, Walkertown and Steamboat. Hundreds of people stood at trackside, holding flags draped in mourning, heads bowed in prayer as the train passed by. Near this area another passenger train was being held in a siding, its occupants also silently standing at trackside with heads uncovered until the Funeral Train had passed.

Groups of people stood along the margins of the railroad at Westchester Intersection, all the men lifting their hats in respectful homage to the memory of the deceased as the train passed by. Poles had been set and rope strung from which were displayed flags. Similar scenes were repeated at Paoli. Passing through the suburbs of Philadelphia, and into the Delaware River Valley, many observed the tastefully draped private homes, and the eagerly growing assemblages.

At Eagle Station, amid a group of mourners, a woman held in her arms a child, probably not over three years of age. The child wore a dark sack with a mourning scarf across his shoulder, waving a flag trimmed in crape. This minor incident found ready appreciation by all who witnessed it from the passenger cars and in the crowd.

Newspapers reported that from the time they left Harrisburg until they reached Philadelphia, not a person in sight was engaged in labor. Ploughs were left in their furrows, shops were closed and a Sabbeth quiet prevailed.

The train came into Mantua, then West

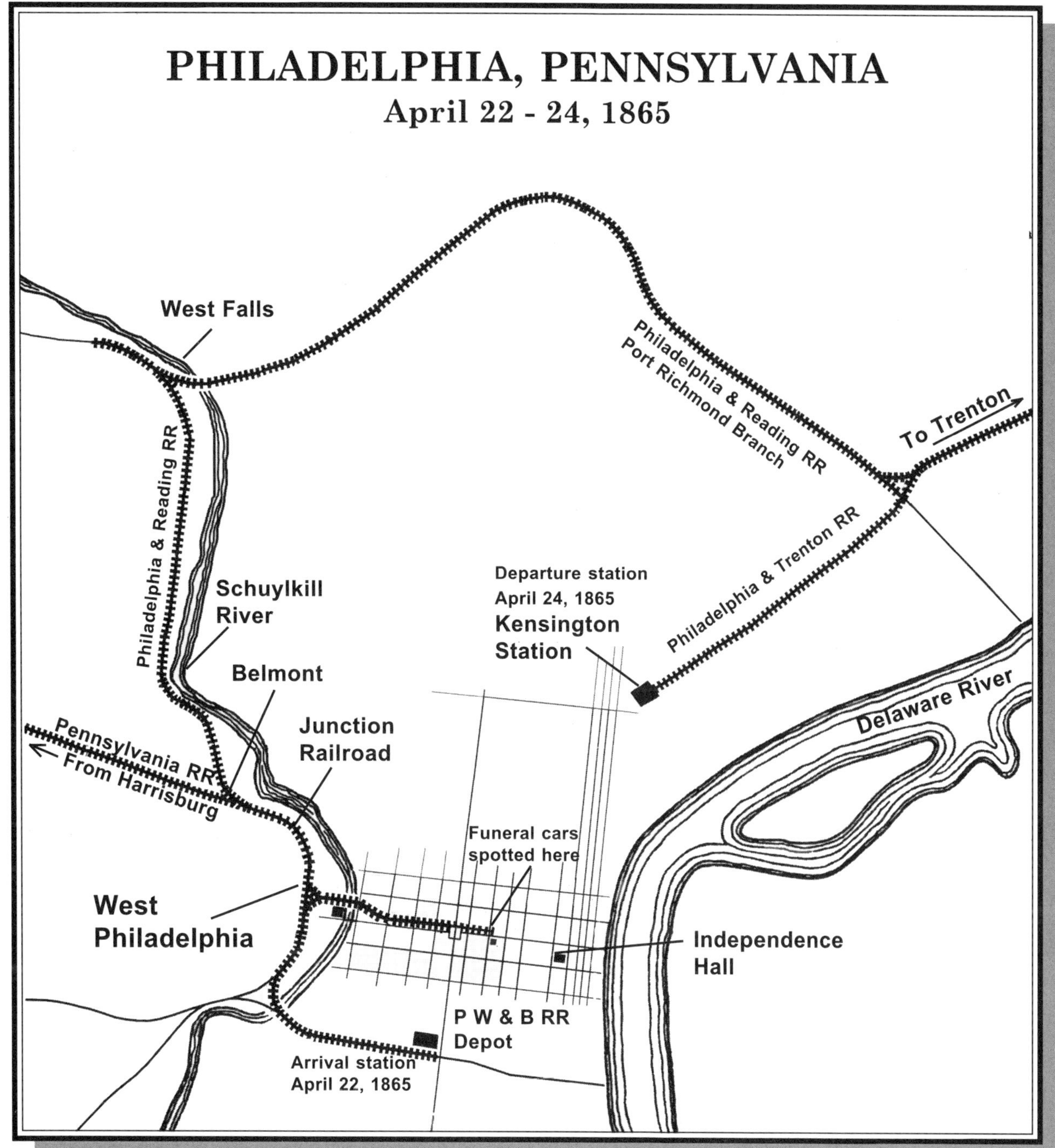

Philadelphia over the "Main Line" of the Pennsylvania Railroad. Crossing over the Schuylkill River, the train passed onto the track of the Junction Railway and then the Philadelphia, Wilmington and Baltimore Railroad for the last mile to the depot at Broad and Prime Streets.

The logistics at Philadelphia were a greatly magnified version of the events at Baltimore. Independence Hall, on Chestnut Street was within two blocks of the Pennsylvania Railroad's Market Street trackage, but there was a serious problem. To have brought the cars into the station at Eleventh and Market Streets, normal practice was to detach the cars from the locomotive near the Schuylkill River and move them one car at a time, east into central Philadelphia via mule teams. This would not work for the entire train.

The only solution to get the entire train into town was to utilize the massive Baltimore Depot of the P W & B Railroad at South Broad and Prime (Washington Avenue), over 1.5 miles south of Independence Hall. This facility had been built in 1852 in order to get steam powered trains nearer to the central business district. For the train it meant crossing the Schuylkill River farther south.

Though the train was scheduled for arrival at 4:30 p.m., it did not arrive until twenty minutes later. Almost simultaneously with its entrance into the depot building, the report of a cannon announced it to the entire city, and the firing of minute guns was continued during the entire progress of the procession. Some time during the evening, one of the men attending one of the cannons was killed when the barrel exploded, apparently from overheating. His was the first of two deaths that was reported to a person paying honor to the deceased President.

The Philadelphia Escort or guard of honor went into the station to meet the car containing the body as it was removed from the train. Forming two lines, between which passed the Veteran Reserve Guard of Escort with the coffin and the guard on either side, the Escort fell in behind and followed with bare heads and solemn steps to the hearse, which was waiting in front of the station building.

The scene out front and over much of central Philadelphia was described as a sea of people. The hearse took Mr. Lincoln's coffin through Philadelphia's jam-packed streets to Independence Hall.

The April 24th edition of the *Philadelphia Inquirer* wrote: "A grand, emphatic and unmistakable tribute of affectionate devotion to the memory of our martyred chief was paid by Philadelphia on the arrival of his remains on Saturday evening. No mere love of excitement, no idle curiosity to witness a splendid pageant, but a feeling far deeper, more earnest, and founded in infinitely nobler sentiments, must have inspired that throng. The multitudinous waves like a swelling sea, surged along our streets from every quarter of the city, gathering in a dense, impenetrable mass along the route prescribed for the procession. The myriads of expectant faces gathering around the depot at Broad and Prime Streets, and lining the route of the procession for hours waited for the funeral train's arrival. The various civic associations marching in orderly columns with banners draped in mourning, waited to take their assigned places. The bands leading such associations, and making the city vocal with strains sweet but melancholy music could be heard. The folds of sable drapery drooping from the buildings, and the half-masted flags, with their

The Lincoln funeral train on the Junction Railroad at West Philadelphia, Pennsylvania, on April 22, 1865. It arrived here about 4:00 PM on April 22, 1865. The train still had to cross the Schuylkill River and enter the tracks of the Philadelphia, Wilmington and Baltimore Railroad for its destination at South Broad and Prime Streets.

The Baltimore Station of the Philadelphia, Wilmington and Baltimore Railroad at South Broad and Prime Streets in Philadelphia, Pennsylvania. The Lincoln funeral train arrived here about 4:50 PM on April 22, 1865. It was nearly 1.5 miles over Philly streets to Independence Hall. There were railroad tracks within two block of Independence Hall, but they could not handle steam locomotives or fully coupled trains at this time.

mourning borders all were striving to express the same emotion. It was this which gave them interest or significance.

"Between 3:00 p.m. and 4:00 p.m., the military escort, under Brigadier-General O. S. Ferry, arrived at the depot, and formed in line along Broad Street. On the right were three regiments of infantry, and next to them two batteries of artillery, and below them was the City Troop of Cavalry, mounted on their chargers, conspicuous afar off by their brilliant uniforms and fur-crowned helmets. Below these, in a long succession, were the various civic associations, all drawn up in line along the east side of the street, and waiting to fall into their places in the column as the procession moved by, constantly swelling in its progress."

The City of Philadelphia had assigned 600 policemen to help with crowds, and some believed it was not enough. All day trains and boats brought people to the city so they could have a glimpse of the martyred Lincoln.

Many civic associations displayed tasteful and appropriate banners. As the time for the arrival of the train approached, the throng in the street grew rapidly. The eagerness of the people to obtain positions from which a good view could be obtained, rendered it necessary for the police to use considerable exertion to keep clear the space necessary for the passage of the pallbearers and escort from the door of the building to the hearse. The Committee of Arrangements was at the station in readiness to receive the remains and the party accompanying them on behalf of the city. They also waited for the special escort of military and naval officers detailed by order of General Cadwalader as a special guard of honor.

The hearse, especially constructed for the occasion, was an imposing structure well adapted for its purpose, which was to display as prominently as possible, the coffin. It was drawn by eight black horses, with silver-mounted harnesses.

At 5:15 p.m. the hearse, followed by the special city guard of honor on foot, and the carriages bearing the funeral party and members of the Philadelphia Committee, commenced to move. The military escort took its place in advance, keeping time to the slow, solemn music of the bands and the melancholy tolling of the bells. It was near dark as the procession stepped out onto the streets.

The Philadelphia Committee on Preparations had realized after the outpouring of people at Baltimore and Harrisburg, and the disappointment by many, they had to lengthen the procession route. During the afternoon of April 21, an expanded parade route was announced. The procession would proceed north on Broad to Walnut, west to 21st Street, north on 21st to Market, east on Market to 3rd Street, south on 3rd to Walnut, entering Independence Square from the south. At this date Independence Hall was used as Philadelphia City Hall.

The procession was ordered in eleven divisions. When the hearse reached Broad and Lombard Streets, the procession remained halted for some time. A choir of about 100 voices was stationed at the corner, and began to sing hymns. Those in the area were moved to tears. At two other locations along the procession route other choirs also sang during the passage of the hearse.

It was nearly 8:00 p.m. when the hearse arrived opposite the southern main entrance to Independence Square. The Union League Association had been detailed to receive the body at that point, and superintend the work of having it placed in its proper position in Independence Hall. A band was placed in the Independence Hall steeple, and prior to the arrival of the remains performed a number of dirges.

When the hearse reached the main entrance to the Square, the coffin was removed and taken within the enclosure, when the line of procession was formed. The members of the Union League stood with uncovered heads. The band in the steeple performed a mournful dirge. The Square was brilliantly illuminated with Calcium Lights, about sixty in number, composed of red, white and blue colors, which gave a peculiar and striking effect to the melancholy spectacle. A Philadelphia resident, Rubens Peale, wrote of that experience, "The corpse arrived this afternoon from Harrisburg and it was dark, and although the square was brilliantly illuminated with Greek lights each side of the great walk Red, Blue & White, which made a most brilliant appearance and lighted up the wholes square & Streets even yet much of the procession near lost to us. The crowd was so dense [sic] in Walnut Street that police could scarcely keep the crowd back."

Amid a breathless silence, broken only by the slow and mournful strains of the band, grief-stricken citizens standing uncovered, sorrow was depicted on every countenance. Amid the tolling of bells and the sound of minute guns fired in the distance, the coffin of the murdered Executive was conveyed within the classic shades of Independence Hall.

The body was placed on an oblong platform in the center of the Hall, covered with black cloth. He lay north and south, the head toward the south, and directly opposite the Liberty Bell. The lid of the coffin was removed far enough to expose the face and breast of the deceased. An American flag, the one used to cover the coffin during the funeral procession, was thrown back at the foot of the coffin, and a number of wreaths of exotic flowers lay on it.

THE TRAIN AT PHILADELPHIA

Once the coffin and funeral escort had departed from the P W & B Depot, the train was moved back out to the West side of Philadelphia, at the facilities of the Pennsylvania Railroad. According to S. M. Sener, a witness to the Philadelphia ceremonies, and whose father was in the employment of the Pennsylvania Railroad, the *United States* and Officers' car was uncoupled and taken down the Market Street line, where they remained during most of the ceremonies. The rail journey from the Schuylkill River bridge to the center of the city was not by steam railroad locomotive, but with mule teams, the standard way to move railroad cars over the streets of Philadelphia at this time. The two cars were spotted at the Pennsylvania Depot at 13th and Market Streets.

The *United States* remained guarded, where the coffin of young Willie remained for the entire journey. Selected guests, though greatly restricted, were granted special visitation rights to enter the car and pay their

The *United States* and officers car with Pennsylvania Railroad locomotive Number 331 at West Philadelphia, Pennsylvania, on the Junction Railroad on April 23, 1865. These two cars had been taken to the PRR Market Street Station near Independence Hall. It appears they were being moved out to Kensington Station to join the rest of the funeral train for its April 24 journey to New York City.

respects to the young son of Lincoln.

PUBLIC VISITATION AT PHILADELPHIA

The circumstances of public visitation at Baltimore and Harrisburg could hardly have been a predictor of the overwhelming outpourings of sympathy at Philadelphia. The great man who had shown mercy and compassion, the leading advocate of peace, who reconciled a nation though over 600,000 had died fighting for the cause, and much of the south lay in ruin, was now honored by each individual. The goodness and generosity of his outstretched hands had been deeply received. It was the manifestation of public grief and popular appreciation, which stood among ordinary observances of the death of this Statesman. The sting of his death humbled a nation until all was mercifully changed, and largely forgiven.

At 10:00 p.m., the doors of the Hall were opened to those holding an admission card. From that hour until midnight an unbroken stream of people passed through the building into Independence Square. They entered the room where the body lay in state by the southern door, and passed out by steps erected over a window at the south end of the room. During the two hours a band, stationed near the Hall, performed a great number of dirges and other funeral selections.

A cordon of police, under the charge of High Constable Harry Clark, were stationed from the outer door of Independence Hall, to the balustrade that surrounded the coffin. Through the avenue formed by the police, visitors passed to view the remains; Mayor Henry occupied a position at the head of the coffin, surrounded by the committee having the body in charge. The visitation was closed at midnight, and remained closed until 6:00 a.m. on Sunday, when unrestricted public visitation was begun. Philadelphia was the other city en route to close the remains from public visitation during the night.

So great was the anxiety of the citizens to view the body of their beloved Chief Magistrate that hundreds of them remained around Independence Hall all night, waiting patiently for the doors, or rather the windows, to be again thrown open. Long lines of the general public began forming by 5:00 a.m. At its greatest, the double line was three miles long and wound from the Delaware to the Schuylkill Rivers. Philadelphia officials estimated 300,000 people tread the dusty streets to pass by Mr. Lincoln's open coffin. The wait was up to five hours. So many people wanted to view Mr. Lincoln's body that police had difficulty maintaining order in the lines.

From 6:00 a.m. on Sunday until 1:00 a.m. on Monday morning, the public was admitted. As soon as the day began to break, people from all parts of town began to flock to the neighborhood of Fifth and Chestnut Streets. The crowd had become most dense, and when the doors were opened, a double line of mourners was formed, extending as far west as Eighth Street, and east to Third Street. The residents of West Philadelphia flocked across the Market Street Bridge by the hundreds, while the Camden ferryboats apparently brought across the Delaware about one-half of the population of New Jersey.

The entrances were through two windows in Chestnut Street, and the exits through the windows facing on Independence Square, temporary steps having been placed in position for that purpose. By this arrangement two lines of spectators were admitted at a time, passing on either side of the coffin. The *Philadelphia Inquirer*, in its report of the scenes of the memorable day, said: "Never before in the history of our city was such a dense mass of humanity huddled together." Hundreds of persons were injured from being pressed in the mob, and many fainting females were extricated by the police and military and conveyed to places of security.

A correspondent for the *Gazette*, described the events. "About noon [Sunday] there was great excitement around the Hall, many women and children having fainted. The police and the guards seemed helpless to stay the rush. Large ropes had been fastened to the street corners to keep back the moving surging masses. Over these ropes hundreds of women were dragged by policeman and the guard to save them from being injured. The soldiers with bayonets fixed, strove to drive back the crowd, but it was useless. The policemen became exhausted in their useless endeavors to keep order. Governors, Senators and prominent military men spoke to the vast crowds from the Windows of Independence Hall, and counseled patience, but their voices were either lost by the din and bustle of the huge throngs. Women shrieked when one of their sex fainted, and little girls and boys cried and struggled to get out of the great jostling masses, where they had become wedged like brick. This wild, reckless excited mass of humanity looked and acted like anything else than a vast assemblage who had come to pay respect to the honored dead. Perhaps nobody else is to blame for the great disorder. The police seemed to be doing all in their power, as were the guards to allay excitement and counsel patience, but what could they do with the hundreds of thousands who

Independence Hall at Philadelphia, Pennsylvania, where Lincoln's remains lay in state from April 22 to April 24, 1865. The crowds were so great here that near riots resulted. - *Electronic illustration by author*

TRAVEL LOG

April 22, 1865 106 miles

VIA Pennsylvania Railroad		Gap	
Harrisburg	DEPART 11:15 a.m.	Christiana	
High Spire		Penningtonville	
Middletown	11:45 a.m.	Parkersburg	2:15 p.m.
Branch Intersection		Chandler's	
Conewago Siding		Coatsville	2:30 p.m.
Elizabethtown	12:15 p.m.	Gallagrerville	
Kuhnz's Siding		Downingtown	2:50 p.m.
Mount Joy		Westchester Intersection	
Landisville		Paoli	
Kauffmann's Siding		Eagle	
Dillerville		Morgans Corner	
Lancaster	1:05 p.m.	White Hall	
Bird-in-Hand		City Avenue	
Gordonville		Mantua (Zoo)	
Leaman Place		West Philadelphia	
Kinzers		Philadelphia	ARR. 4:50 p.m.

were actually wild to get a look at the ashes [sic: body] of the republic's best beloved servant.

"Many women lost their bonnets, while others had nearly every particle of clothing torn from their persons. Notwithstanding the immense pressure and the trying ordeal through which persons had to pass in order to view the remains, little disorder prevailed, everyone apparently being deeply impressed with the great solemnity of the occasion. After a person was once in line, it took from four to five hours before an entrance into the Hall could be effected. Spectators were not allowed to stop by the side of the coffin, but were kept moving on, the great demand on the outside not permitting more than a mere glance at the remains, which were under military guard."

At one time excitement in front of the Hall was intense, and severe pushing in the crowds was reported. A number of women and children who reached within a few yards of the doors would be compelled to step out of the line from the effects of the pushing they had undergone. Small children would be lifted overhead and passed from hand to hand until out of harms way. Several small boys were seen crawling over the heads of those collected in the sea of humanity, until they finally fell to the ground. While this restlessness was going on, pickpockets were plying their trade, much to the disgust of those who discovered they had been relieved of their money or other valuables.

Ozias Hatch, on the train as part of the Illinois Delegation wrote his wife: "... joined the train at Harrisburg - could not get to Washington on time. About Philadelphia - At the entrance the crowd was so immense that hundreds were injured. The sight was the most fearful I ever saw."

The crowds continued coming from all parts of New Jersey, Delaware and Pennsylvania, to view the remains. They came by boat, horse, buggy, train and on foot. Never had anyone anticipated this overwhelming outpouring. The real importance of Abraham Lincoln's ways of mercy and compassion were being manifested.

APRIL 24, 1865
PHILADELPHIA - NEW YORK

The funeral train had been prepared to move out for New York City, during the visitation at Independence Hall. In that same time while the *United States* was in Philadelphia, Honor Guard officers, Lieutenants Joseph Durkee and Edward Murphy, set about the task of restoring the emblems of mourning to the *United States*, water soaked from the rains between Washington and Harrisburg. Fabric festoons and drapings were replaced, and the silver fringe restored. Philadelphians contributed materials, and the two spent most of the night of April 22nd, rehanging the entire car.

Sometime during the late evening of April 23rd, a refreshed *United States* and Officers car was moved from the Pennsylvania Depot at 13th and Market Streets via mule power back to the Schuylkill River, where it was met by a locomotive and moved to the Philadelphia and Trenton Railroad via an early and circuitous route around Philadelphia.

Departing West Philadelphia, the train ran a short stretch on the Junction Railroad, which connected the Pennsylvania Railroad to the Philadelphia and Reading Railroad, (formerly the state-owned Philadelphia and Columbia Railroad at "Belmont," near the present ZOO junction). Belmont was at the west end of the Columbia Bridge. At Belmont, the train proceeded straight onto the P & R main line moving west along the Schuylkill River to West Falls. Here the train reversed direction and ran onto the P & R's Port Richmond Branch, which looped around the north side of Philadelphia to the coal terminals at Port Richmond. The Philadelphia and Reading crossed the Philadelphia and Trenton Railroad. The train was switched to a connecting track and was backed south to Kensington Station,* on the north side of Philadelphia.

COMING ONTO THE TRAIN

General John A. Dix and Staff at Philadelphia. Governor Joel T. Parker of New Jersey came on board at the State line, at Morrisville, with his staff, consisting of
Adjutant-General R. F. Stockton,
Quartermaster-General Perrine, and others. They were accompanied by United States Senator John P. Stockton, Rev. D. Henry Miller, and Colonel Murphy.

There was also upon the train a committee from Newark, consisting of the Mayor, Joseph P. Bradley, Esq., the President and other members of the Newark Council.

The shortened train of the two through cars was reassembled with seven cars of the Camden & Amboy Railroad at Kensington, to bring the train back to nine cars. It was held in ready to continue the journey over three short railroads from the north side of Philadelphia to Jersey City, New Jersey. Locomotives of the Camden & Amboy Railroad were decorated in emblems of mourning to draw the train to New Brunswick. C & A locomotive No. 72 had charge of the funeral train while C & A No. 24 pulled the pilot train.

The train included a single baggage car, six coaches, the *United States* and the Officers' car. A description of the cars indicates the baggage and six coaches were a bright yellow, the *United States* a chocolate color, more of a maroon at this time because chocolate was not the brown color it has today. The Officers' Car was a crimson color.

The *Newark Daily Advertiser* makes a fascinating revelation about the baggage car in the train, "[with] - a restaurant, specially fitted up for the purpose, immediately in the

* Kensington Station at Philadelphia, Pennsylvania, and Kensington Junction, Illinois, are not to be confused. Kensington Station was a point of origin for the train on April 24, 1865. Kensington Junction, Illinois, was the place south of Chicago, Illinois, where the train passed from the tracks of the Michigan Central Railroad over to the Illinois Central Railroad on May 1, 1865, on the way to Chicago.

NEW JERSEY

April 24, 1865

Jersey City
New York City
Newark
Elizabeth
New Brunswick
Princeton Jct.
Morristown
Trenton
Bristol
Philadelphia, Pennsylvania

Railroads used:

Philadelphia to Trenton -- Philadelphia and Trenton Railroad
Trenton to New Brunswick -- Camden and Amboy Railroad
New Brunswick to Jersey City -- New Jersey Railroad & Transportation Co.

Jersey City to New York City -- Ferry boats

rear of the locomotive ...." This is the only mention of on-train dining provision* over the entire journey. The baggage car had been modified to serve food. It is doubtful food was prepared on the train, but rather, was prepared trackside and put on the train at Trenton for serving.

At 1:00 a.m. on Monday morning, April 24th, public viewing ended. Because of the masses of people who passed by the remains, the undertaker was required to remove much dust, which had collected upon it, and to make other necessary preparations for proper departure of the body. By 2:00 a.m. the coffin was closed and preparations begun for the departure procession to Kensington Station. The funeral procession began its long march from Independence Hall around 3:00 a.m. The escort consisted of the 187th Pennsylvania Infantry, city troops, guard of honor, a detachment of soldiers to guard the body, Perseverance Hose Company, and the Republican Invincibles.

The procession left Independence Hall heading north on 5th Street, proceeding to Oxford, where it turned east, then north on Front Street to Kensington Station of the Philadelphia and Trenton Railroad. A band of music played dirges on the long march. On the way thousands of citizens joined. The procession reached Kensington Station near 4:00 a.m.

When General Townsend arrived at the station, he issued the following telegraph to Edwin M. Stanton. "We start for New York at 4 o'clock. No accident so far. Nothing can exceed the demonstration of affection for Mr. Lincoln. Arrangements most perfect. E. D. TOWNSEND, Asst Adj-Genl."

After the coffin was removed to the train, the hearse was taken back to Independence Hall where, even though the viewing was over, thousands of people passed through the empty Hall as a gesture of mourning. The hearse was set out front for the public to observe.

DEPARTING KENSINGTON STATION

In the predawn hours of Monday, April 24, the Lincoln Funeral Train departed Kensington Station, Philadelphia, just after 4:00 a.m. headed toward New York, an 86-mile trip. From Philadelphia to Trenton, the tracks ran parallel with the Delaware River. General John A. Dix* and staff came onto the train at Philadelphia, carrying responsibility for security of the coffin and the train until the train was out of New York State.

This day the train started over the tracks of the Philadelphia and Trenton Railroad. The pilot locomotive carried a telegrapher and two signal men. The two signal men were to ride on the rear of the locomotive tender. Accounts indicate this pilot locomotive pulled no other cars. This is the only recorded time no cars were attached to the pilot engine. On this railroad the locomotive tenders were covered with a type of canopy known as a "gig top." One of the brakemen sat on the back of the roof, which was a covered seat for the brakeman, who worked the tender brake by a large foot pedal. He maintained look-out duties also.

The pilot engine had explicit orders to pull up to each station along the tracks and

*The first recorded instance of the operation of a dining car was in 1862 on the Camden and Amboy Railroad. It was a baggage car that had been converted into a diner of sorts In addition to a small kitchen, the car contained an oblong counter around the four sides of which patrons ate while seated on high stools. From the inside of the oblong counter food was served by waiters in white jackets. It is unknown whether this could have been the baggage car used on the Lincoln Funeral Train.

* General John Adams Dix, was 67 years old at the time of the Lincoln Funeral. He had been appointed a cadet during the War of 1812, and served in the United States Army until 1828, having attained the rank of captain. He practiced law in Coopertown, New York, and was involved in politics. Assistant Treasurer of the United States at New York 1853; Appointed postmaster of the city of New York 1860-1861; Appointed Secretary of the Treasury by President James Buchanan 1861. Reactivated to military service and served in the Union Army as Major General 1861-1865. He later returned to political life as Governor of New York 1873-1875. Dix was involved heavily in the blossoming railroad industry in the 1850's and 1860's, having served as president of the Rock Island Railroad in the late 1850's and also elected president of the Union Pacific Railroad in 1863, while he was actively involved in the Civil War process. He declined the position.

stop to await a telegraph message from the last station, that the funeral train was passing by. Mr. R. S. Van Rensselaer oversaw operation of the train as far as New Brunswick. Most of the early miles departing Pennsylvania were made on tracks that paralleled the Delaware River. This is the first time the train operated in the darkness of night for any distance. The journey took about six hours to run over the 86 miles of trackage to Jersey City.

Bristol, Pennsylvania, 26 miles from Philadelphia, was reached shortly after 5:00 a.m. to the firing of guns and bonfires. The train made its first stop here to masses of mourners and a brief ceremony. In a few minutes it started on. At Morrisville, Pennsylvania, just short of the New Jersey State Line, at the Delaware River, a place locally referred to as the Durdeng Line, the train stopped to receive New Jersey Governor Joel T. Parker and staff, the Newark delegation and others who were invited to join the escort. Departing town, the tracks crossed the Delaware River and the Pennsylvania - New Jersey State Line.

At Trenton, New Jersey, in 1861, Mr. Lincoln stopped on his way to Washington, visiting both Houses of Legislature. He then moved on to Philadelphia, speaking at Independence Hall. The visit this date was scheduled only for a thirty minute stop, instead of

NEW JERSEY RAILROAD & TRANSPORTATION CO.

SPECIAL ARRANGEMENT

FOR THE TRANSPORTATION OF THE REMAINS OF THE LATE

PRESIDENT ABRAHAM LINCOLN

OVER THE NEW JERSEY RAILROAD

On Monday, April 24, 1865

UNDER INSTRUCTION FROM THE WAR DEPARTMENT

A Pilot Engine will precede the Special Train, leaving each Station 10 minutes in advance of that train

THE SPECIAL TRAIN WILL BE RUN AS FOLLOWS:

STATION	TIME	SPECIAL INSTRUCTIONS
Leave New Brunswick at	7:55 A.M.	No train or Engine (except the Pilot Engine) must enter on the main line Track for New York, or leave any Station within 20 minutes in advance of the Special Train.
Leave Metuchen at	8:07 A.M.	
Leave Rahway at	8:35 A.M.	No Train or Engine must enter on the main track, or leave any station until 20 minutes after the Special Train has passed.
Lcave Elizabeth at	8:55 A.M.	
Leave Newark at	9:20 A.M.	No Train or Engine must pass over Posaic Bridge, either way, between 9:05 A. M. and 10:00 A. M. unless both the Pilot Engine and Special Train have passed.
Arrive at Jersey City	9:50 A.M.	
Due at New York (by Ferry Boat) at 10:00 A.M.		Telegraph Operators must be at their stations and report the arrival and departure of the Special train to all stations.

A Pilot Engine will precede the Special Train, leaving each Station 10 minutes in advance of that train.

F. WOLCOTT JACKSON, Gen'l Sup't.

J. W. WOODRUFF, Ass't Sup't.

Reproduction of New Jersey Railroad Special Timetable for April 24, 1865

ADJUTANT-GENERAL'S OFFICE,
April 19, 1865.

Major-General Dix,
Commanding Department of the East,
New York City:

You will meet the remains of the late President Abraham Lincoln upon their entry within your lines and escort them to Buffalo, N.Y., keeping guard over them under the orders of this Department while they remain in your command. The ceremonies and public honors to be paid them while in your command will be in conformity with the directions of the executive of the State, to whom you will report. Acknowledge receipt.

By order of the Secretary of War:
E. D. TOWNSEND,
Assistant Adjutant-General.

Orders for General John S. Dix to escort the funeral train from New York City to Buffalo, New York. Dix departed with the train at Philadelphia on April 24, and stayed with the train until it stopped at the New York - Pennsylvania line on April 28, 1865.

the one day stop at the other six state capitals on the route. It was determined its close proximity to Philadelphia would warrant people to travel there, or to New York City.

Early in the dark hours crowds began assembling at the Clinton Street station of the Camden & Amboy Railroad, in hopes of having a gaze upon the funeral train. Every hilltop on the line of the road and other advantageous points, including a nearby bridge were occupied by throngs of spectators. At 5:00 a.m. the bell at City Hall commenced tolling. The Trenton band and 200 soldiers of the Reserve Corps were on the platform to give some order and respect to the expected train.

At just after 5:30 a.m. the train pulled into the station to a crowd estimated at well over 5,000 people. This was a planned breakfast stop for the escort. Food was apparently put onto the train, opposed to the funeral escort, getting off to take the meal, as was the custom at this date. A detachment of the Reserved Veteran and Invalid Corps, drawn up in line on the platform gave the customary funeral honors. Minute guns commenced firing, when the train came into sight.

The crowds surged forward and they became difficult to control as the train pulled into the station platform. The guards were nearly driven from their posts. At 5:45 a.m. the train came to a halt, when Major Newton's command presented arms and drums beat out their muffled chant.

General Edward Townsend, stepped from the train and was received by Trenton Mayor Mills and a Committee of Citizens. The Mayor offered brief remarks, and they were responded to by Townsend in appropriate terms. At that conclusion, the train moved slowly along the length of the station platform, stopping at intervals for all to see the funeral car. The pressure of the crowd at times was so excessive that many found it difficult to keep their places. General Townsend granted permission to selected people to enter the car, and it is thought a committee of ladies entered the car to lay a wreath on the coffin.

The bells of the town continued to toll. Breakfast was reportedly served to the funeral escort while at the station. Food was likely brought onto the train prepared, and placed in baskets, then served from the baggage car to the funeral escort, details remain hidden. Records speak of the train being stopped for some thirty minutes. Emblems of mourning were prominent everywhere. Music was performed by Lischer's Band.

The reporter for the *Daily True American* noted: "One of the cars contained a large number of wreaths, which had been presented by ladies on the route."

Additional state representatives boarded, and at about 6:15 a.m. the train commenced on at a slow rate, amidst a profound silence, while the band performed a solemn dirge. After the train had passed out of sight the military and citizens formed in a procession and marched to the State House where there was a presentation of arms and the ceremony at the State Capitol ended.

From Trenton the new line (relocation) of the railroad was used to Dean's Pond, where the tracks returned to the original alignment. It ran parallel with the Raritan Canal to near Princeton Junction, over the Camden & Amboy Railroad. Passing Princeton, New Jersey, at 6:45 a.m. crowds of students from Princeton University, and townspeople, displayed mournings. Many of the university students had made signs to express their feelings toward the martyred President.

Nearing New Brunswick crowds of anxious onlookers lined both sides of the track. More than 5,000 people greeted the train upon its arrival at the New Brunswick Station. Minute guns were fired, and every respect was shown to the martyred remains during a ceremony. The stay here was reportedly nearly an hour.

NEW BRUNSWICK LOCOMOTIVE CHANGE

The New Jersey Railroad and Transportation Company took over operation of the train at New Brunswick. Mr. F. Wolcott Jackson, Superintendent of the New Jersey Railroad oversaw operation of the trains into Jersey City. This stop was for a required change of locomotives, and marked the first of several locomotive changes en route during the journey. Two locomotives of the New Jersey Railroad were assigned. The Number 40 locomotive handled the Funeral Train while the *H. R. Remsen,* took the role as pilot engine for the short run into Jersey City. No public explanation for this locomotive change has been discovered, however, in this distance the locomotives would have required fuel and water, and it may have been quicker to just change the locomotives.

Leaving town, the two trains crossed the Raritan River for the short remaining 25.5 miles. Continuing on, the train passed through Rahway at 8:34 a.m. and Elizabeth at 8:45 a.m. Here a group of school children stood trackside holding banners expressing their sorrow.

On April 22, officials at Newark revealed the train would make a brief stop in their city. It was however, the wish of the Common Council to have the train stay for one-half hour for a more formalized memorial service. Application was made to Secretary of War Stanton, who telegraphed a reply the timetable could not be altered.

Young and old, child and adult, without distinction of color or religion, crowded along the margins of the tracks, filled the highways, streets and depot grounds to witness the train. They expressed in every way possible their sorrow and reverence demonstrating a deep sense of public loss and appreciation for the virtues of this fallen leader. Many stood silent with heads bowed in silent prayer, others knelt, many wept. Hymns and appropriate music were sung, salutes fired, floral immortales presented, bells tolled as a New Jersey expressed the intensity of their love and veneration for Lincoln's memory along the railroad tracks.

At Newark, tens of thousands of people gathered along the tracks on Railroad Avenue. Crowds filled every space by 9:00 a.m., when the police, Common Council, clergy and Veteran Reserve Guards removed the crowd back to a safe distance. The train pulled into the Newark Market Street Station for a brief station stop at 9:15 a.m., just seven miles from its Jersey City destination. This was the hometown for Captain James McCamly, who was in charge of the late President's honored men, the Veteran Reserve Guard of Escort on the train.

Only a brief few minutes was spent at the station, heads were bowed with reverence, many persons weeping. Many convalescents were at the platform from the United States Military Hospital. Those who could stand, stiffly saluted. Those patients not so fortunate, in wheel chairs and on crutches made every attempt to salute. It was at this site when the menfolk removed their hats to honor the deceased. The ladies in turn removed their bonnets. The brief stop ended in a few minutes. The train started slowly on, past Center Street and East Newark Stations, where crowds had also gathered.

Thomas Brady, the engineer later observed, "hundreds of people tossed flowers onto the tracks as the train approached." At every place there was the unmistakable evidence of universal grief.

Several reporters noted that among no class was the deep-felt sorrow more apparent than in the Negroes gathered to witness the passing of Lincoln's remains, whom many considered their friend and deliverer.

THE HUDSON RIVER FERRY MOVE

Immense crowds had gathered in Jersey City, and around the depot grounds in anticipation of the arrival of the funeral train at an early hour. At this date the station stood at the corner of Montgomery and Hudson Streets, with normal ferry service offered to a slip at Cortland Street in lower Manhattan, across the river. All rail traffic was suspended at 9:00 a.m. in anticipation of the train. The city requested all businesses to close in respect for the dead. As the trains approached the station, the thunderous boom of field artillery rapped across the horizon, announcing the arrival of the trains. General John A. Dix had charge of the depot at Jersey City. It was sealed from general access to all excepting those with passes and members of the press.

Coming down Railroad Avenue, the train arrived at the immense train station and shed at Jersey City at 10:03 a.m., but some 13 minutes off the scheduled time. It entered on the northern track of the handsome structure, built in 1857. The station had been draped in poignant symbols of mourning and festoons. On the west wall of the concourse, the huge clock had been frozen at 7:22, the approximate time of Mr. Lincoln's death. On the front of the immense structure hung a banner reading "Be still and know that I am God." Lincoln had spoken from inside the massive waiting room of this station in 1861. Now his arrival was met by silence and expressions of sorrow.

Upon arrival of the train at the station, the Hoboken German Singing Societies sang the fitting ode *Integer vitas* (A Man of Upright Life). The Veteran Reserve Guard of Escort shouldered the coffin from the car, following behind was the procession of dignitaries who marched to the east end of the depot on one platform, then countermarched to the west entrance on another platform, where they exited onto Exchange Place. The coffin was placed in a hearse drawn by six gray horses, draped in a black pall. The hearse was taken onto the ferry boat *Jersey City*, where the New York Common Council took formal possession of the remains.

New York Governor Reuben H. Fenton did not receive the remains, as had been expected. Instead, Chauncey M. DePew, Secretary, State of New York, and later railroad magnate of the New York Central Railroad, received it on behalf of the Governor. Newspapers reported the Governor unavoidably detained at a session of the New York legislature in Albany.

Once loaded onto the ferry boat *Jersey City* it lifted anchor and slowly sailed across the Hudson River to New York. The distance across the river was approximately one mile. When the coffin left the slip, it also left the State of New Jersey. This completed the shortest visit to any state on the entire funeral route, lasting just over four and one-half hours.

The flags of all the ships in the harbor area were lowered to half-mast in honor of the slain president. It was received at Desbrosses Street Slip on the New York side at 10:50 a.m. The funeral escort came across on the ferry with Lincoln's coffin, along with the German singing societies who sang an ode.

The logistics of getting the funeral cortege and an estimated 300 escorts across the Hudson River presented a bit of a challenge. At this time New York and New Jersey were not connected by any bridge or tunnel. At this river crossing, the first of two, Mr. Lincoln's coffin was taken off the train and ferried across the river. The funeral escort was also ferried across on possibly two more boats. A total of five ferry boats were required for funeral duty.

No mention is made how all the baggage, suit cases, uniforms and personal effects were taken off the train and ferried across, or how far they had to be transported to reach the waiting train on the Hudson River Railroad. Another consideration is the barging of the two passenger cars across the river. Wood cut illustrations show the car positioned across the hull of the ferry, which one might consider opposes the order of other ferries used a few years later to transport railroad cars across rivers. Cars were normally positioned parallel with the line of the ship's hull and carried within the hull deck. The wooden framework on the ferry this day supporting the rails appeared to be a temporary arrangement, suggesting that the movement of the passenger car was not a routine service at this time.

While the two cars waited their lightering, the Sentinels of the Veteran Reserve Guard of Escort remained on guard duty at the cars.

While the ceremonies now focused on the New York City visitation, four more ferry boats awaited the two railroad cars to be taken off their tracks and lightered across the Hudson River. With the New Jersey crowds moving out, the *United States* and the Officers' car were switched out and taken down to the ferry slip, where first the *United States* was lightered (floated) across the river, followed by the Officers car'.

It appears the cars were ferried to a wharf near Christopher and Barrow Streets at West Street on the New York side of the Hudson River, then pulled south to their destination at the Chamber Street Station of the Hudson River Railroad.

The rest of the passenger coaches were returned to Philadelphia with the members of the escort who were not proceeding north of New York City.

The funeral train entered the great railway station at Jersey City, where the remains were off-loaded, and carried to the ferry slip for tranfer across the Hudson River to New York City. The masts of sailing ships can be seen over the roof tops in the back ground.

GENERAL ORDERS No. 31.
HDQRS. DEPARTMENT OF THE EAST,
New York City, April 21, 1865.

I. The major-general commanding, having, in obedience to the instructions of the War Department, conferred with the governor of the State in respect to the reception of the remains of the late lamented President of the United States, hereby announces that the public honors to be paid to them in this city will be in conformity to arrangements in progress, under the direction of the common council, the details of which will be hereafter published.

II. The military ceremonies will be conducted by Major-General Sandford, commanding the First Division of New York National Guards, under whose orders the Seventh Regiment will be designated as the escort and special guard to the remains while they are in this city.

III. All general and field officers in the service of the United States in this city are directed, and officers of the Navy of equivalent rank are requested, to report at these headquarters for the purpose of officiating as a guard of honor to the remains while at the City Hall.

IV. Major-General Robinson, U.S. Volunteers, will provide a proper escort at Albany and Buffalo, and will confer with General John F. Rathbone of the New York National Guards at the former city, and with the general in command of the National Guards at the latter, both of whom have already received the necessary instructions from the governor of the State.

By command of Major-General Dix:
D. T. VAN BUREN,
Colonel and Assistant Adjutant-General.

TRAVEL LOG

April 24, 1865 86 miles

Via Philadelphia and Trenton Railroad
Camden & Amboy Railroad
New Jersey Railroad and Transportation Co.

Philadelphia DEPART	
Kensington Station	4:00 a.m.
Bridesburg	
Wissinoming	
Tacony	
Holmsburg	
Penny P.O.	
Pierson's	
Torresdale	
Bories	
Andalusia	
Cornwell's	
Eddington	
Schenck	
Bristol	5:00 a.m.
Old Spring	
Tully Town	
Wheat Sheaf	
Penn Valley	
Morrisville*	
Tenton Jct., N.J.*	ARR 5:45 a.m.
	DEPART 6:15 a.m.
Lawrence Station	
Princeton Jct.	6:40 a.m.
Plainsboro	
Monmouth Jct.	
Dean's Pond	
Millstone Jct.	
New Brunswick*	7:35 AM
Piscataway	
Metuchen	
Union Town	
Houghtonville	
Rahway	8:34 a.m.
Linden	
Elizabeth	8:45 a.m.
Waverly Park	
Newark	9:15 a.m.
Jersey City*	10:03 a.m.
via ferry boat New Jersey to New York City,	
New York City	ARR 10:50 a.m.

APRIL 25, 1865
NEW YORK - ALBANY

Arrival of the remains at the ferry slip on DesBrosses Street in New York City, April 24, 1865. This was the first of two ferry crossings of the Hudson River. -- *Obsequies of Abraham Lincoln in the City of New York, 1866*

Up and down the river the banks and wharves were filled with people. Thousands thronged to the extreme edge of the piers and watched the movements of the *Jersey City* as she neared her destination. All hands on boats and other ships stood silent, some up in the rigging to pay their respects to the slain president. The scene was described as peculiarly impressive as the *Jersey City* slowly crossed. All the ships had emblems of mourning prominently displayed. In several cases the vessels' sides were draped in mourning colors, the masts wreathed in black muslin, while all persons who happened to be on board stood with uncovered heads as the boat moved past. The guns were silent, the bells ceased to ring out, the only sounds were of the paddle wheels smacking the still water as the ferry boat tread across the river.

When the boat was within a few hundred yards of the dock, at the foot of Desbrosses Street, (also spelled Debrosse Street) the German Societies commenced a funeral ode from the First Book of Horace, which produced a thrilling effect upon all who heard it. The solemn notes of the song as they burst forth from nearly one hundred voices gave touching inspiration to the sorrow of the moment. When they reached the Manhattan dock, the boat was moored. Generals Dix and Sandford left the boat, when the hearse, together while those composing the procession, followed. The firing of guns and the tolling of bells commenced to announce the arrival of the cortege in New York.

The scene at the foot of Desbrosses Street

Funeral car *United States* being ferried across the Hudson River to New York City. April 24, 1865. Unique here, the car is sitting across the boat's hull. The officer's car was brought over in the same manner and set on tracks in New York City. -- *Obsequies of Abraham Lincoln in the City of New York, 1866*

could not fail to make a lasting impression upon the thousands who were congregated on the housetops and awnings for several blocks on each side of the ferry. Every available spot was occupied along Desbrosses Street, from West to Hudson Street. Hours before the arrival of the body, masses of people had been gathering in the City Hall Park, along Broadway and Chatham Streets. They gathered in and on the buildings overlooking the plaza in front of the City Hall. More than twenty thousand citizens were assembled where the ceremony of receiving the body was to be witnessed.

The window sashes of all the houses were removed in order that the occupants might have an unobstructed view of the procession. As far as the eye could see there was a dense mass of heads protruding from every window in the street. The fronts of the houses were tastefully draped with mourning, and the national ensign was displayed at half-mast from almost every housetop.

The remains were carried up Hudson Street, to Broadway then to City Hall. The procession guarding the body filed into the park at 11:30 a.m. The hearse, drawn by six horses and guarded by two companies of the Eighth Regiment, New York State National Guard, stopped before the door of the Hall. The coffin was immediately taken from the hearse, and carried up the circular staircase under the rotunda. The coffin was then placed on a black velvet dais, amid a solemn dirge, played by the German Liederkranz band. The several German singing clubs, of the Liederkranz Society, and numbering nearly a thousand voices, sang several solemn dirges.

For the second time on this date General Townsend made a telegraph report to Secretary of War Stanton. "We have arrived here safely. Demonstrations of deep feeling and respect all along the route. Minute guns fired and bells tolled. The car nearly filled with flowers sent in at every stopping place. Reached Jersey City at 10 AM exactly. E. D.

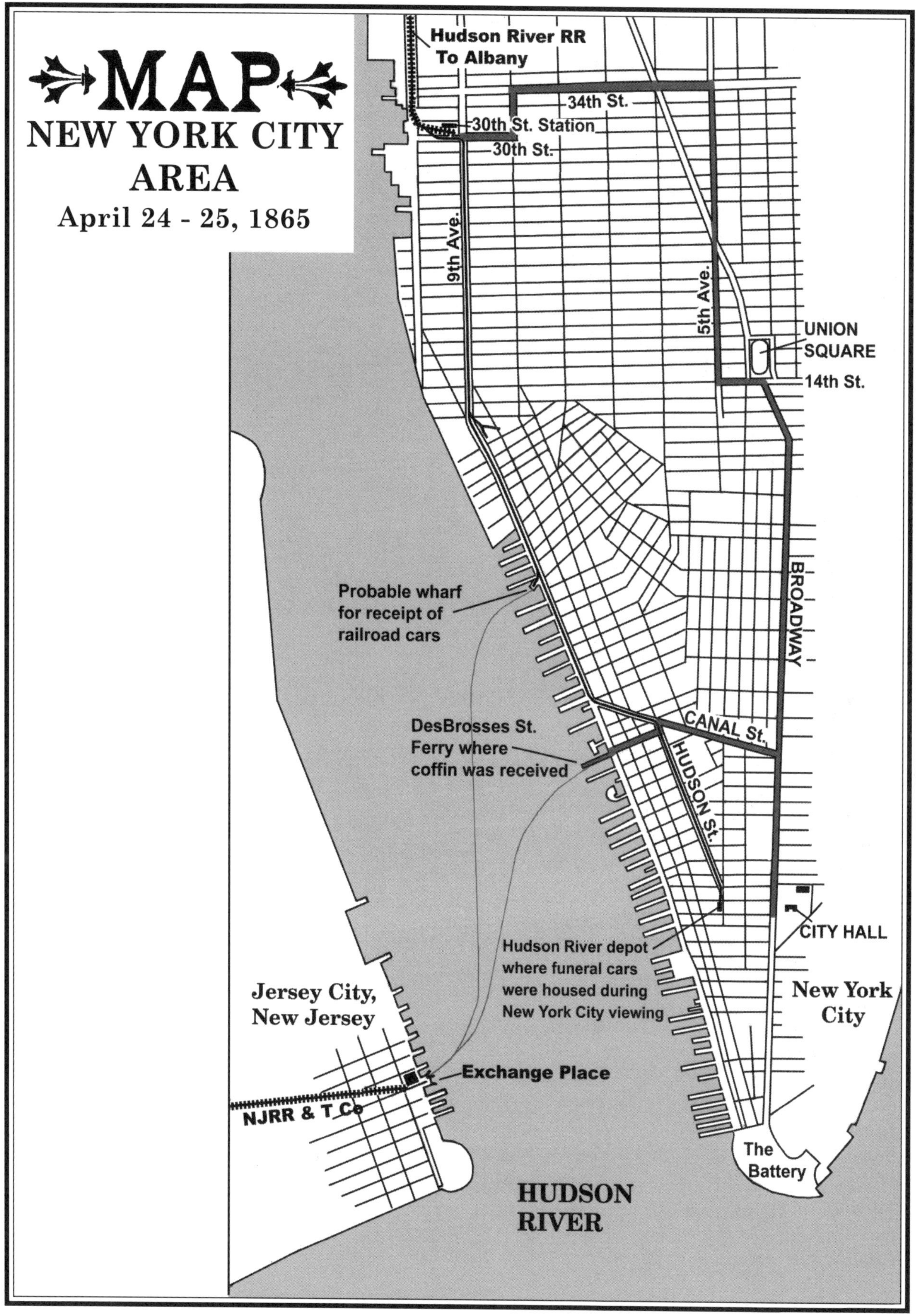
MAP
NEW YORK CITY
AREA
April 24 - 25, 1865
Hudson River RR
To Albany
34th St.
30th St. Station
30th St.
9th Ave.
5th Ave.
UNION
SQUARE
14th St.
BROADWAY
Probable wharf
for receipt of
railroad cars
DesBrosses St.
Ferry where
coffin was received
CANAL St.
HUDSON St.
CITY HALL
Hudson River depot
where funeral cars
were housed during
New York City viewing
Jersey City,
New Jersey
New York
City
Exchange Place
NJRR & T Co
The
Battery
HUDSON
RIVER

TOWNSEND." The telegraph was received in Washington at 12:30 p.m.

MASSES MOURN IN NEW YORK CITY

The public was admitted to City Hall after 1:00 p.m. From distant points throughout the state, remote from the line of travel which took the President to his last bourne in Illinois, thousands of people flocked to the city in the hope of gaining a view of his bier. From Brooklyn, Jersey City, Williamsburg and neighboring localities, there was throughout the day a constant stream of people, crossing in the ferryboats, many of whom joining in the line remained for several hours, until at last they reached the goal of their desires. The steamboat *Granite State*, from Hartford, Connecticut, brought down over three hundred passengers. They marched from the boat to the City Hall for the viewing. One of the passengers placed a cross, two feet in length, upon the coffin.

At one point more than 500,000 people waited in line to view the remains of Mr. Lincoln. Less than one-third got to pass by the coffin. Pickpockets worked the evergrowing crowd, much to the chagrin of the police. Several newspapers complained the arrangements for viewing the body were very bad. The public was compelled to enter through the east basement, up to the main corridor, then file through a narrow passage and up a spiral stair case in the Hall building.

One newspaper complained that from the time the corpse was deposited in City Hall, until removed, the appearance indicated that the embalming had not been perfect; "discoloration is daily increasing, and it is thought the coffin cannot be opened after leaving this City."

On this day a photograph of Mr. Lincoln in death was taken by New York photographer, T. Gurney & Sons. Exposure of the single wet plate took 25 minutes. Thought to have been destroyed on orders of Secretary of War Stanton, one of the prints was found in a file in 1952.

Throughout the night the crowds did not slow. As the dawn broke on April 25th, the lines were still forming, even though many knew they could not get in to see the remains before the closing. Two ladies tried to kiss the corpse but were prevented. The masses came silently up the stairs, with tears streaming down their face, some women wept bitterly. Old and young, rich and poor, all passed in rapid review. One poor Irish woman laid a small cross at the foot of the coffin, with the words inscribed, "God preserve your soul." The immediate crowds were visibly affected.

One of the festoons in front of City Hall caught fire during the morning, causing great excitement as the cry of fire was made. The presence of mind of a police officer, who tore down the burning drapery, saved a rush in the crowd, and injury to bystanders. During the public hours people were admitted at the rate of nearly one hundred a minute. More than one hundred and fifty thousand persons saw the body.

During the morning Governor Fenton and Legislative Committee arrived by boat to accompany the remains to Albany. At 11:40 a.m., the doors of admission were closed to the general public and the remains prepared for removal. All the foreign Consuls dressed in their diplomatic uniforms, Governor Fenton, General Dix, accompanied by his staff, and several distinguished Generals were present. When all was in readiness the order was given and six of the Veteran Reserve Guard of Escort raised the coffin upon their shoulders. A sergeant at each end steadied it to prevent the possibility of an accident. The coffin was

SPECIAL ATTENDENTS ON THE TRAIN THROUGH THE STATE OF NEW YORK

Judges Davies and Porter, of the Court of Appeals; Hon. Chauncey M. Depew, Secretary of State; Generals. Alex. W. Harvey and George S. Batchellor; E. Merritt and S. E. Marvin, Staff Officers; Colonel L. L. Doty, of the Military Bureau; George Dawsoni, of the Albany Journal, Wm. Cassady, of the Argus and Atlas. Gov. Fenton himself only rode the train from New York City to Albany.

borne slowly down the spiral staircase and out of the City Hall.

DEPARTURE FROM NEW YORK CITY

At about 2:00 p.m., Mr. Lincoln's coffin was placed on a magnificent 14 foot long funeral hearse. It was drawn by a large hitch of 16 horses wearing long blankets. A massive funeral procession began that went up Broadway to Fourteenth Street, over to Fifth Avenue, up Fifth to Thirty-fourth Street, and across Thirty-fourth to Ninth Avenue then down to the Hudson River Railroad Depot at Thirtieth Street and Tenth Avenue. More than 75,000 citizens marched in the huge procession through New York's jam-packed streets. Windows along the route reportedly rented for up to $100 a person.

The head of the massive procession reached the Hudson River Railroad Depot at 3:00 p.m. The columns halted and formed in line facing to the west, to allow the hearse and escort of mourners to pass. At 3:30 p.m. the approach of the hearse was made known by solemn refrains of bands. The rear of the procession was some 28 blocks back at 14th Street and 5th Avenue.

Regiments brought their arms to a present, officers saluted with their swords, and colors draped in the badges of mourning were lowered.

While the public viewing was under way the *United States* and the Officers' car were ferried across the river, set upon Hudson River Railroad tracks and moved to the main passenger station at the junction of Chamber and Hudson Streets in lower Manhattan. This is where the coffin of Willie Lincoln was guarded while in New York City. The Hudson River Railroad made available seven of their best passenger cars for the train. These cars were reported as "new." The required festoons of mourning were tastefully attached to the cars. This was not the starting point for the funeral train. The cars were moved a few miles north to Thirtieth Street Station where the train would receive the remains of the deceased President and depart the city.

At this time, the track was laid through Hudson, Canal, and West Streets, to Nineth Avenue, which it followed to the upper city station, at Thirty-fourth Street. Over this part of the route the rails are laid even with the street surface. Normal practice was to move the cars by what was known as a steam dummy or a "dumb engine." It is quite probable the train was separated into a few cars each, so these small steam dummies could draw the cars through the streets, whereby the corporation regulation of the City of New York, the larger steam locomotives were not allowed to run. The engines for this unique application appeared very much like an ordinary freight car, or even a small street car. The machinery (drive rods on the locomotive wheels) was almost entirely hidden out of sight. The boilers were designed to attempt to consume its own smoke. While passing north through the city, the cars were preceded by a man on horseback, who gave notice of its approach by blowing a horn.

The pilot locomotive *Constitution* was assigned to lead the cortege. It was a last-minute selection, the original locomotive selected having been replaced; *D. T. Vail*. The locomotive *Union* pulled the nine car funeral train. The two locomotive engines were most beautifully and appropriately decorated under the direction of Mrs. Cushing, and her sister. They were variously described as exquisitely tasteful with mourning symbols for the occasion. The *Poughkeepsie Eagle*, gave a brief description; "The tender was heavily hung with black cloth, looped up with silver eagles and ... the whole surrounded by white and black satin ribbon. On each side of the engineer's house [locomotive cab] was a portrait of Abraham Lincoln, shrouded with crepe and black and white satin. The brass railing and stanchions were also heavily draped. Silk American flags were placed on each side of the smoke stack, completely enveloped in crepe. On the front end of the cow catcher was a flag staff with a flag attached, on which was the word 'Union' also shrouded in crepe. The engineer was Mr. William Buchana, Master Mechanic at 30th Street. The head lights on both engines were shrouded in black."

TIME TABLE

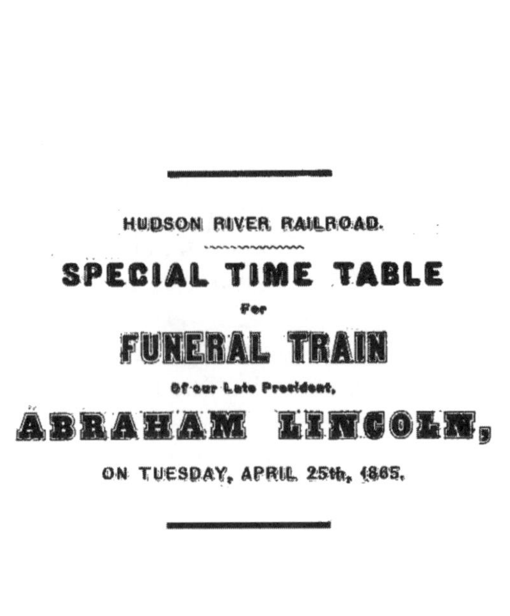

HUDSON RIVER RAILROAD.

SPECIAL TIME TABLE

For

FUNERAL TRAIN

Of our Late President,

ABRAHAM LINCOLN,

ON TUESDAY, APRIL 25th, 1865.

Leave	New-York, (29th Street)	4.00 P.M.
"	Manhattan	4.20 "
"	Yonkers	4.45 "
"	Dobbs' Ferry	5.00 "
"	Irvington	5.07 "
"	Tarrytown	5.15 "
"	Sing Sing	5.30 "
Arrive	PEEKSKILL	**5.57** "
Leave	PEEKSKILL	**6.00** "
"	Garrison's	6.26 "
"	Cold Spring	6.33 "
"	Fishkill	6.50 "
"	New Hamburgh	7.06 "
Arrive	PO'KEEPSIE	**7.25** "
Leave	PO'KEEPSIE	**7.40** "
"	Hyde Park	7.56 "
"	Staatsburgh	8.08 "
"	Rhinebeck	8.24 "
"	Barrytown	8.40 "
"	Tivoli	8.52 "
"	Germantown	9.10 "
"	Catskill	9.27 "
Arrive	HUDSON	**9.38** "
Leave	HUDSON	**9.41** "
"	Stockport	9.52 "
"	Coxsackie	10.00 "
"	Stuyvesant	10.07 "
"	Schodack	10.26 "
"	Castleton	10.35 "
Arrive	EAST ALBANY	**10.55** "

Copy of Hudson River Railroad Special Time Table for April 25, 1865. A third page in the time table gave the following special instructions. "Train has right of track over all other trains bound in either direction; and trains must reach stations at which they are to meet, or let special pass, at least 10 minutes before special is due. A 'pilot' engine will leave New York 10 minutes in advance of special,running 10 minutes ahead of published schedule to East Albany. Pilot engine has same rights as special, and at stations where trains meet or pass it, they must wait for special. The special will run at a slow rate of speed through all towns and villages. Train No. 10 will, this day, leave Thirtieth St. at 4:15 p.m. All station masters, trackmen, drawbridge tenders, switchmen, and flagmen will be governed by the general rules of the company." -- *Benedictine University collection*

The *Union* conveyed the President from Albany to New York, while on his first triumphal progress from Springfield to Washington, in 1861. Mr. William Raymond was the engineer for the train, and Mr. J. M. Toucey, assistant superintendent of the road, acted as conductor, assisted by a carefully selected staff of brakemen. As soon as possible, the train was taken to the Thirtieth Street Station to await the arrival of the funeral party that afternoon.

The word was given, and the parties who were to accompany the remains entered the cars assigned to them. New York Governor

Wood-cut illustration of the Lincoln Funeral Train departing Hudson River Railroad's Thirtieth Street Station behind locomotive *Union*, April 25, 1865. The artist who cut this drawing shows the funeral car as second from the locomotive, when it was actually at the opposite end of the train. On the right the funeral procession comes down 30th Street. -- *Obsequies of Abraham Lincoln in the City of New York, 1866*

Ruben Fenton was accompanied by his staff. At 4:00 p.m. the depot bell rang alerting all to the impending departure. At approximately 4:15 p.m. to 4:25 p.m. the train began its 141-mile journey to Albany through the Hudson River Valley.

Leaving the station, the train moved over trackage laid in Eleventh Avenue, up to 60th Street where the tracks entered their own right-of-way.

The train would pass through spectacular scenery as it paralleled the beautiful Hudson River. In the next 74 miles it would pass through seven tunnels and deep valleys, of nearly 700 feet. From Poughkeepsie north, the valley opened into fertile rolling country.

ELABORATE PUBLIC DISPLAYS OF MOURNING HEIGHTEN

As the train passed slowly down the station platform, everyone standing upon it removed their hat. Outside of the gate of the depot yard, on Tenth Avenue, the immense throng of mourners there gained a very brief glimpse of the coffin. The usual hoarse clangor of the engine bell was deadened by the tongue being muffled.

It had been five days since the train left Washington, D.C., and by this time many of the communities the train would visit had enough time to plan elaborate displays and pageantry. Newspapers were carrying the wire stories submitted by reporters riding the train. Many of these accounts gave a great deal of detail on certain scenes witnessed from the train, accounts of the public demonstrations and displays along the route.

As the train entered the Hudson River Valley, into an area known as the Palisades, large crowds of spectators were gathered along the tracks to witness the trains passing. It was observed that the hills, woods, railroad crossings and even the boats on the river were filled with people. An estimated 4,000 people were trackside at Manhattan to witness the trains.

The roads leading to the station at Mount Saint Vincent were jammed with mourners as the train neared. People there made a large black flag with white letters expressing their feelings, "We Mourn Our Nations Loss." Yonkers erected an arch near the tracks with the words, "Yonkers mourns the loss of the President." Thousands of people lined the tracks as far as the eye could see. As the train slowly passed by, every man raised his hat and ladies removed their bonnets. At Dobbs Ferry, the station was so heavily draped in emblems of mourning it was almost not visible. Irvington, where many of the New York merchants reside, spared no expense in making visible expressions of mourning. Seven thousand people gathered at the beautifully draped station and along the railroad to witness the train.

At Hastings, twenty miles out, and the home of Commodore Farragut, famous for his declaration, "Damn the torpedoes! Full speed ahead!" a striking memorial was erected near the depot. It consisted of a four columned arch draped with mourning and flags, and bearing the following inscription: "We will cherish the memory of Abraham Lincoln by supporting the principles of free government, for which he suffered martyrdom."

Beyond Irvington, the trains passed through an area known as the Highlands over the next 24 miles, through Tarrytown, Sing-Sing and Peekskill.

Tarrytown had painted the side wall of a building near the railroad as an American flag, and erected an arch over the tracks adorned with drooping flags. Young ladies stood on the station platform, dressed in white, heads bowed, holding hands in line. One reporter noted, "The large crowd looked

Funeral arch at Sing-Sing, New York, over the tracks of the Hudson River Railroad. The arch was constructed with public subscriptions of goods and labor. It features the double pillar and the Goddess of Liberty at the top. The view looks north, probably taken mid-afternoon April 25, 1865. This is the view members of the funeral cortege would have seen as they neared the station on the left. The train passed here about 5:30 p.m.- *Ossining Historical Society collection*

sad and mournful."

At Sing-Sing the train passed through the yard of the New York State Prison, directly to the rear of the main building. The track was several feet below the yard. Two arches of brick, twenty-four feet of span and six hundred feet in length, were, one on each side of the yard for the purpose of rendering it secure. The towns' people had gathered in the days before to plan a massive memorial arch through which the train would pass. It was constructed by public subscription of goods and labor near the station The town's arch twenty-five feet high, was adorned with black and white cloth and evergreens. A statue of the Goddess of Liberty was displayed at the top, along with several banners having inscriptions, and a large black and white banner proclaiming, "We Mourn a Nations Loss." It appears the train made a brief memorial stop at this location.

The crowds were especially large near the depot. A group of cadets were drawn up in line. Next to them stood a long row of men, who removed their hats for the passing of the train. A number of ladies dressed in white with black sashes stood on the station platform.

Sing-Sing also marked the place where the railroad crossed a bay at the junction of the Croton and Hudson Rivers. A draw bridge here was guarded for the trains.

The citizens of Peekskill, the fire department, and cadets of Peekskill Academy assembled in the town square about 5:00 p.m., and in procession, marched to the depot of the railroad to await the approach of the train. The train arrived shortly thereafter and halted. A memorial service of about 10 minutes was conducted. The *Highland Democrat* reported; "The train stopped about ten minutes at the depot, and was witnessed with uncovered heads and solemn faces, and sorrowful hearts by the multitude. Minute guns were fired ... and a solemnity never before experienced in Peekskill hung like a thick cloud over the place.

"The utmost order prevailed ... and the solemn hour was generally observed as an expression of sorrow at the terrible calamity and the nation's loss." The train continued on.

At one place along the tracks a hundred school girls, dressed in white, came down to the trackside and witnessed the train. Thousands of people crowded the margins of the railroad, stood at road crossings and at stations to do reverence to the remains of Lincoln. Many knelt as the train passed by, with heads bowed, perhaps in silent prayer.

THE SCENE AT WEST POINT

Garrison's Landing, a station opposite West Point, on the Hudson River, was reached at 6:20 p.m. The depot building had been elegantly decorated in crepe and flags. Three companies of gray-clad cadets, numbering one thousand and a detachment of the cavalry from the United States Military Academy, led by General Cullum ferried across the river by boat earlier. They were drawn up in line as the train arrived for a brief memorial service. Wearing appropriate badges of mourning, all presented arms in impeccable formation. The officers stood in formation separate from the cadets with heads uncovered. The Academy fired salutes from cannons at their post on the west side of the river, while the train was at the station. Two bands played fitting music. The Eastman National Business College performed during the military service. The United States Military Academy Band, standing to the front of the train played appropriate funeral music during the stop. Existing reports suggest select Officers and/ or Cadets entered the funeral car: Charles King, West Point Class 1866 writing in *Illustrated Sunday Magazine* July 10, 1910, states: "A few days later we formed lines parallel with the railway over at Garrisons and with our drums and colors draped in black, stood at the present, as the day was dying and a long funeral train rolled slowly by. On the platforms and at the car windows, were generals famous in song and story, but we had eyes for only that solemn pile on which was laid all that was mortal of him who had become immortal, whose works and whose wisdom gain in worth and power with every added year, the inspiration of a reunited people so long as the flag shall float and the nation live."

The sun was setting low over the Hudson Valley and while here the colors of a brilliant sunset lit the train until darkness slipped over the hills. Bonfires, torches and lanterns were used from this point to light the train and the night.

As the train prepared to start on, the Eastman band again boarded. Starting on through the hills, the funeral train passed through a 900-foot tunnel at Phillips Hill, this the fifth and longest tunnel on this route. Emerging from the tunnel the train crossed over an inlet on a trestle nearly a mile long.

The entire village of Cold Spring was at the tracks as the funeral train passed by. A huge portrait of the president was hung on the depot and arch was visible with a live scene depicting the Weeping Goddess of Liberty. A young lady knelt upon a dais, in sorrowing attitude, one hand grasping the flag whose folds, clad in transparent black, fell by her side. The other hand rested upon and held fast to a floral anchor. Before her, on the same dais, was a small monument, deeply and darkly clad, inscribed simply "Abraham Lincoln." This was the first of three such symbols along the route.

Fishkill was reached at 6:55 p.m. Spectators were evident in large numbers throughout this area. On the bank opposite Newburg, was where George Washington made his headquarters during the Revolutionary War, a flag was draped in mourning from the house. The station had been tastefully decorated in mourning with a banner across it reading, "In God We Trust."

THE POUGHKEEPSIE DINNER STOP

At Poughkeepsie, extensive preparations had been made for a planned meal stop. An estimated 25,000 people were at trackside to meet the cortege of the pilot train and funeral train as it arrived. The second meal stop was made here to refresh the approximately 200 honored members of the funeral escort. Brigadier General, A. B. Eaton, Commissary General of Subsistence was in charge of food arrangements at this location.

Providing the feast were the three Johnston Brothers, local farmers, who operated a lunch counter inside the station. They were noted for their topmost point of excellence. A large meal was prepared and served inside the station.

The Johnston's raised their own chickens and cows, and at this time Civil War troops dreamed of having their train stop for a quick ham sandwich, cruller, pie or glass of milk with a thick layer of cream. Mrs. Williams was the cook, and her talents were given regard equal to that of the highest railroad official. At this time the Johnston's served food across a counter in the station. There were no tables or chairs for the patrons' use. Preparations for this important meal had to be made including, tables, chairs and table service, not to mention waitresses to serve it.

The special timetable called for a standard 15 minute meal stop, arriving at 7:25 p.m. and departing at 7:40 p.m. The newspapers suggested the meal stop would take up about 40 minutes. The actual arrival time was 7:10 p.m., but departure was much later 8:10 p.m.

The Eastman National Business College of Poughkeepsie provided a band for musical accompaniment having departed with the train from New York. An impressive memorial service was conducted while the train was at the station. Eight selected ladies laid floral wreaths on the coffin of the President. Refreshments were offered following the memorial ceremony. Thirty Provost Guards protected the train while the escort was in the restaurant. Eastman's band rejoined the train to continue on to Albany, as a participant in the memorial ceremonies there.

It appears the locomotives were serviced at this stop with fuel and water. The Albany delegation also boarded the train during this stop. Resuming the journey, it being dark, torches at each station lit up the scene for the throngs who stood by, and bonfires blazed from jutting rocks at many points. The train was constantly illuminated by bonfires and torchlight along the route.

Crowds greeted the train at Hyde Park. What was described as a beautiful circle of light and a large assemblage greeted the train at Staatsburg. A band stationed on the veranda of a nearby hotel, playing appropriate airs paid their deepest respects at Rhinebeck. Barrytown honored the lamented president with a torch light procession and banners. Reporters described people gathered in large groups at Tivoli. The depot was draped in drooping flags. Some of the finer residences, it was noted, were handsomely illuminated and festooned in flags. Germantown and Catskill illuminated the tracks with large bonfires.

Hudson was reached at 9:45 p.m., and great crowds of people were standing in mourning as the train came to a stop. It is described that elaborate preparations had been made. The Hudson House and American Hotel were handsomely draped in mourning and illuminated. Entering the station area, an arch of evergreen with black and white crepe had been constructed. A dais below depicted a live scene, the Weeping Goddess of Liberty. A group of young ladies dressed in white sang a dirge, two others dressed in black entered the funeral car, placed a beautiful floral arrangement on the president's coffin, then knelt for a moment and quietly withdrew. The whole area was lit by torches, changing night into day.

Departing a few minutes later, the train passed through Stockport then Stuyvesant, Schodack, and Castleton. Crowds, lined the track holding torches and having great bonfires to catch a glimpse of the train. Men removed their hats and ladies removed their bonnets in a demonstration of respect.

Such crowds standing in the dark along the tracks would become the standard for passage of the train over most of the balance of the journey.

ARRIVING AT ALBANY

Late on April 19th word was received that the Funeral Train would make an 18-hour stop over in Albany. The Albany *Atlas & Argus*, gave public notice on April 22, just three days before the planned arrival. "The Body of the deceased President will lie in state in the Assembly Chamber on Wednesday. The body embalmed preserves its naturalness and life-like look. This will be the only opportunity afforded for citizens within a circle of many hundred miles to view all that remains of the late Chief Magistrate. The Funeral Cortege will not stop on its way from New York, nor on its passage to Buffalo, long enough for this purpose, except in this city.

"We presume that tens, nay hundreds of thousands of citizens of Massachusetts and Vermont, of Northern New York, and of counties within reach of Albany, will pour into the city on Tuesday and Wednesday. The military display and torchlight procession on Tuesday night, when the remains are received, will afford a spectacle alone sufficient to attract an immense crowd.

"Our citizens, and especially the hosts of our public houses, must provide for the exigency."

All day Tuesday residents had been busy at the East Albany station and grounds drap-

WAR DEPARTMENT,
Washington City,
April 20, 1865—11 p.m.

Major-General Dix,
New York:

A small escort of honor, consisting of nine general officers, a captain, and twenty five privates accompany the remains from Washington to Springfield, but while at New York, Albany, and Buffalo a larger escort should be provided by you. The number of troops, &c., to be assigned for that duty is left to your discretion.

EDWIN M. STANTON

Headquarters, 9th Brigade. N. G. S. N. Y
Albany, April 24, 1865

Special Order No. 27

I. Special Order No. 198, General Headquarters, have assigned to this Command the sad but honorable duty of escorting and guarding the remains of the late President of the United States during their passage through the city. The Brigade is favored in being able, by this last tribute of respect to the earthly remains of our Chief Magistrate, to express in common with their fellow citizens its sense of fearful loss which our country has sustained.
II. Companies A and F Tenth Regiment, Company C Twenty-fifth Regiment, under the command of Major J. R. Harris, are hereby detailed to meet the remains on their arrival at East Albany to escort them to the Capitol; and to guard the same until the procession moves on Wednesday.
These Companies will form precisely at 10:00 p.m. on Tuesday evening the 25th inst. on State street, the right resting on Pearl.
Major Harris will report in person for further instructions to the General Commanding.
III. The Twenty-fourth Regiment N. G. N. Y. S. having accepted an invitation to form part of the funeral escort, will be met on their arrival in this city, and escorted to their proper position in line by two companies of the Twenty-fifth Regiment, which are hereby ordered to be detailed for such service by Col. Walter S. Church, commanding.
IV. The Brigade line will be formed promptly at 12 m. on Wednesday, 26th inst. on the East side of Eagle Street, the right resting on Steuben. The Tenth Regiment will form on the right of the line. The Twenty-forth Regiment on the left of the Tenth and the Twenty-fifth Regiment on the left of the Twenty-forth.
V. Regimental, Field and Staff Officers will parade dismounted.
VI. Commanding Officers of Regiments will see that appropriate badges of mourning are worn in accordance with the provisions regulating such occasions.
Company A Tenth Regiment, will accompany the remains to Buffalo.

By order of
Brig. Gen. JOHN P. RATHBONE
B. F. Baker, Brigade Inspector

A copy of the military orders for the National Guard, State of New York while the Lincoln Funeral Train was at Albany, New York. Similar orders were issued by the military at various stops along the route. Some were quite extensive instructions. -- *Albany Argus & Atlas April 24, 1865*

ing the station in elaborate festoons of mourning. A torchlight funeral procession was planned to escort the coffin of the President across the river by ferry boat.

Dark had long settled over the Hudson River Valley. As the train neared the station, the tolling of church bells could be heard, as well as the firing of a cannon to announce the trains arrival. According to orders issued by Mayor Eli Perry, the bells and guns were to be sounded from the time the coffin was removed from the train until it enter the Capitol building, about two hours.

The trains arrived at the Hudson River Station of East Albany, at 10:55 p.m., opposite Albany. At this date there was no bridge across the Hudson River. According to timetables, passengers were ferried across to the station grounds. A railroad bridge did exist about six miles north at Troy, but the time required to move the train there, then across the river and down the west side to Albany was probably excessive.

The remains were received at the depot by the appointed committees. The Veteran Reserve Guard of Escort removed the coffin from the *United States* and deposited it in the hearse. It was drawn by six gray horses draped and plumed. Carriages were in attendance to receive Governor Fenton and the Joint Committee. City officials, many citizens of distinction, and members of the Legislature, were also present to join in the procession. The night was starlit, still and pleasant.

From the depot the cortege moved to the steam powered ferry boat, *New York*, Seth Green, Captain, and crossed to the west side of the Hudson. This was the last time Lincoln's body was on a boat and moved over the water.

Twelve Albany fire companies had assembled at the ferry landing bearing their torches to light the way across the river. It was described that night had been turned into day. The entire party crossed the river and was guided by torch lights. Dense crowds had lined the river banks, wharves and boat docks, and stood silently as the ferry made its way across the river. The black waters of night were reflecting the yellow glow of the hundreds of torches lighting the way. Beyond the sounds of the paddle wheels splashing water as the boat tread across the river, the only other sounds were those of the church bells as they pealed and cannons thundered a voice of solemn commemoration.

The funeral procession was guided through throngs of people and to the capitol by a ribbon of torch light. The procession formed at the Albany ferry landing being led by Scrieber's Band and Eastman's College Band playing the *Dead March*. Governor Fenton and committee, with the other attending mourners in carriages, followed the hearse. The Guard proceeded and followed the hearse, while the firemen, making a flanking line on either side, comprised the order of the procession up the State Street hill to the Capitol. Three companies of militia from the Tenth Regiment, and one from the Twenty-fifth, were in attendance as escort.

Massive crowds filled the streets, quiet and sorrowful. The streets were thronged as they had never been before. Describing the procession, the *Atlas & Argus* said; "... a sad procession moved through our streets to and from the Capitol. Aside from the slow tread of this procession, not a sound was heard in the streets." The smoke and glare of the torchlights, the silent tramp and the perfect hush of the people, as the cortege moved on its way through the capital of the State, was very impressive.

Mr. Lincoln had stopped here in 1861 to address the Legislature on his way to be inaugurated as President.

With the funeral party safely across the river, the train was taken up-river nearly six miles to Troy, New York, where a railroad bridge existed. The *United States*, the Officers' Car, and possibly one other car with baggage was uncoupled from the coaches and the shortened train moved onto the Rensselear and Saratoga Railroad and crossed the Hudson River to West Troy.

On the west side of the river it traveled back to Albany, on the Rensselear and Saratoga Railroad. It was halted near the ferry landing. At Albany servicing of the through cars took place. The New York Central added coaches and sleeping cars to the train. The body of young Willie was guarded by the Veteran Reserve Guard of Escort sentinels while the cars sat near the station.

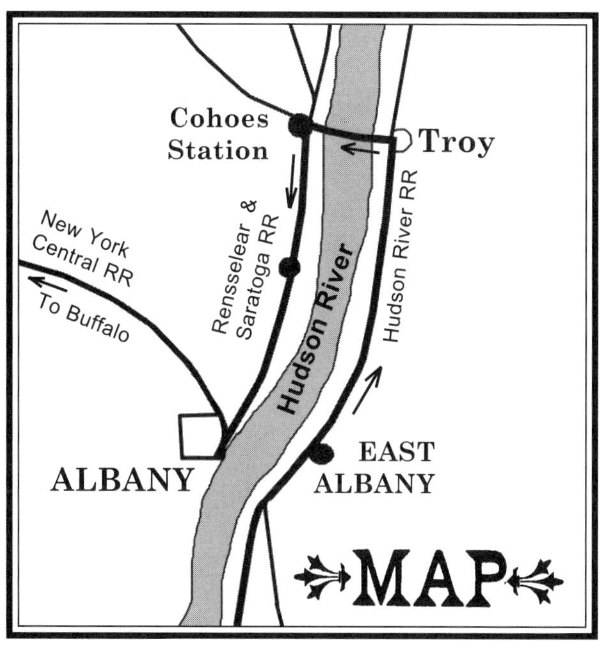

EMPTY TRAIN MOVE AT ALBANY, NEW YORK

The Lincoln funeral train halted at East Albany, on the Hudson River Railroad, where the coffin and funeral cortege were off-loaded. The empty train with the coffin of Willie Lincoln, proceeded six miles north on the Hudson River Railroad. At Troy, New York, the train was switched to tracks of the Rensselear & Saratoga Railroad. It moved west over the railroad bridge to Cohoes Station, than south about six miles to the Albany riverfront where it was switched to the New York Central Railroad for the journey to Buffalo, New York.

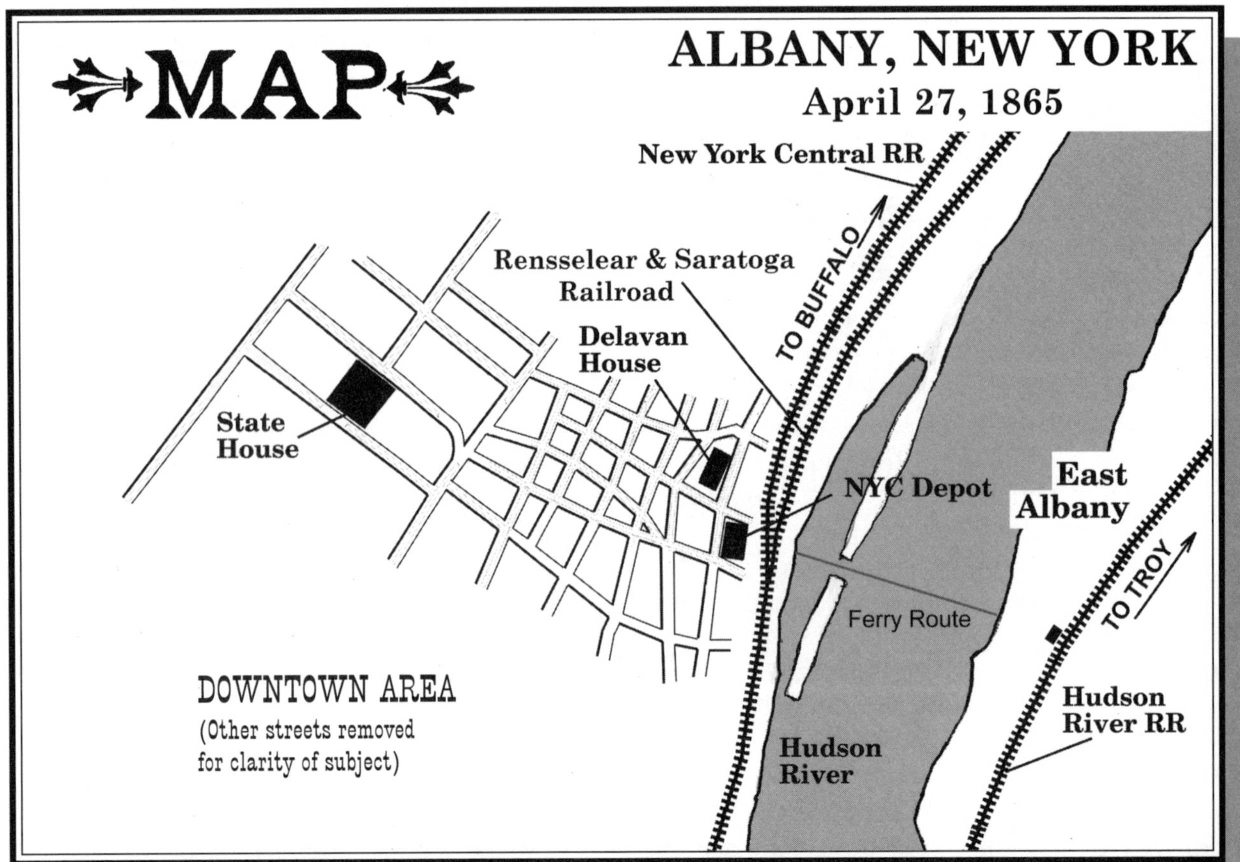

ALBANY MEMORIALS

The Committee for Reception at Albany, planned to have the coffin open for public viewing from 4:00 a.m. to 12:30 p.m. The New York City newspapers were reporting the body was in an advanced state of decomposition as the remains left there, and the coffin would not again be opened until the train reached Springfield. The errant report did not deter the masses from coming. The Albany *Atlas & Argus*, published a short notice: "We have received the following note from the Legislative Joint Committee: 'The remains will be exposed to view in the Capitol from 6 a.m., to 1:30 p.m.'"

Throughout the previous day trains from all directions came in heavily loaded with mourners from as far as 200 miles away. They came from the river cities and villages, from the important city of Boston, from Vermont as well as other sections of New York State. Every hotel accommodation and sleeping space was taken in just a few hours. By afternoon the streets of Albany were thronged with people. The rain of the previous week ended, yielding a pleasant day. Albany residents were busy repairing the damaged mourning drapery on public buildings. By evening many of the restaurants were asked to stay open all night, "... an arrangement absolutely necessary, because of the large number of strangers that had already arrived in the city, many of whom could not find any hotel accommodations." Hundreds spent all night in the streets.

By Wednesday morning the Rensselear and Saratoga Railroad resorted to using freight cars to transport the masses of mourners. It was without sufficient passenger coaches to meet the overwhelming demand for transportation to Albany.

Arriving passengers found a profusion of sable drapery prevailed at the depot, on the boats, and at every point along the route, from the landing at Albany to the platform where the remains lay in state in the Capitol Assembly Chamber.

A contingent of officials from nearby Troy, New York, departed both by train and on the river boat *C. Vanderbilt* on the 26th. On the train were the Mayor, Common Council, Board of Supervisors, Board of Fire Commissioners and Loyal Order of Odd Fellows. On the boat was the 24th Regiment New York State National Guard. The troops arrived at the Columbia Street Wharf at 10:30 a.m. and promptly disembarked to form a line nearly 700 men strong, and march up State Street to City Hall, where all were received by the Albany Mayor Perry.

General John F. Rathbone of the National Guard, State of New York, established a Guard of Honor to stand at the coffin while in was in the Capitol. The guard was set up for a first watch from 12:00 midnight till 3:00 a.m. Second watch from 3:00 a.m. to 6:00 a.m. Third watch from 6:00 a.m. to 9:00 a.m. Fourth Watch form 9:00 a.m. till noon. The last watch was from noon until the closing at 2:00 p.m.

At 1:00 a.m., on the morning of April 26th, the coffin was opened. The President was exposed for view in the Capitol of New York. The coffin rested upon a simple platform, covered with black velvet, trimmed with silver bullion. A silk flag of the Union was wound around it.

The Assembly Chamber was simple but tastefully draped in mourning. One inscription, in black relief, extended over the Speaker's desk, in the words of Lincoln--; "I have sworn a solemn oath to preserve, protect and defend the government."

The doors were opened and people were admitted, passing the corpse in two unbroken lines. Throughout the time of viewing the utmost quiet and decorum prevailed in the chamber. A reporter who witnessed the tribute the people paid to the memory of Mr. Lincoln at the Capital of the Empire State, said: "All day the streets have been crowded with people to see the remains of the late beloved President. They reached from the Assembly Chamber at the Capitol to the foot of State Street, in a prolonged and patient line four deep. However enthusiastic and earnest the feelings kindled in the great cities through which the funeral procession had passed, its approach through the State to the great masses of the rural population of the interior indicates a power of feeling and unanimity of sentiment which must present permanent results in the public opinion of the country for generations."

At one point the lines were over a mile long, estimated at over 50,000 people. As dawn broke sunny and clear, the lines did not diminish. The sun bore down and by noon women fainted by the dozens, and had to be carried out of the crowd. So desperate were people to gain access to the capitol the *Troy Daily Press* gave an account. "Hundreds of women forfeited their sense of propriety to curiosity, and actually 'scaled' the high iron fence around Capitol Park, frequently meeting with mishaps in the dangerous undertaking, which caused the more modest of their sex to blush, and the other sex to laugh and jeer." All day extra trains and excursion boats brought masses of people to pass by the coffin in a gesture of sorrow. The *New York Times* reported, "The city gave evidence of its sincere sorrow, not only in the deep mourning drapery that covered every building, both public and private, but in the quiet bearing and sad countenances of the people. Never before was such a multitude gathered at the capitol; and what was everywhere noticeable, everybody seemed to fully participate in the solemnities of the occasion."

The plan to have closed the Capitol doors after reception of the remains, then begin public viewing at 6:00 a.m. quickly vanished as the crowds swelled awaiting arrival of the train. Once the doors were opened at 1:00 a.m., they stayed open to the throngs of mourners until 1:30 p.m. the next afternoon.

With the crowds attending the Statehouse, pickpockets were busy lifting watches and wallets from the unsuspecting. Some in the crowd suddenly found three and four empty wallets in their coat pockets, deposited by the thieves to hide the crimes. Newspapers reported hundreds had been victimized by the pick pockets. While many were downtown, burglars were at work in their vacant homes and many returned home to discover they had been relieved of their valuables, adding to the heartbreak and sadness. Some of the thieves were caught and jailed. Several had followed the train from New York City.

The Washington escort and the Veteran Reserve Guard of Escort stayed at the Delavan House during the evening, knowing this would be the last night they would rest in a hotel during the night hours until they reached Chicago on May 1st. The next five nights would be spent on the funeral train as it moved toward Springfield.

The New York City newspapers carried articles about photographing the remains, against the wishes of the Lincoln family. By noon on April 26th, General Edward Townsend was being called to accountability by Secretary of War, Edwin Stanton. "As Admiral Davis was not responsible there is no occasion to find fault with him. You being in charge, and present at the time, the sole responsibility rests upon you; but having no other officer of the Adjutant General's Department that can relieve you and take your place you will continue in charge of the remains under your instructions until they are finally interred. The taking of a photograph was expressly forbidden by Mrs. Lincoln, and I am apprehensive that her feelings and the feelings of her family will be greatly wounded. EDWIN M. STANTON, Secretary of War"

General Townsend sent two responses to Stanton, and left Albany at 4:00 p.m. on the train for the longest night's journey. "Hon. E. M. Stanton: Your dispatch just received. I was not aware of Mrs. Lincoln's wishes, or the picture would not have been taken with the knowledge of any officer of the escort. It seemed to me the picture would be gratifying, a grand view of what thousands saw and thousands could not see. Leave here punctually at 4 p.m. Townsend."

The telegraph was received in Washington, D. C. at 6:30 p.m. Before the train left Albany, one more telegraph of explanation went from Townsend to Stanton. "General Dix, who is here, suggests that I should explain to you how the photograph was taken. The remains had just been arranged in state in the City Hall, at the head of the stairway, where the people would ascend on one side and descend on the other. The body lay in an alcove, draped in black, and just at the edge of a rotunda formed of American flags and mourning drapery. The photographer was in a gallery twenty feet higher than the body, and at least forty distant from it. Admiral Davis stood, at the head and I at the foot of the coffin. No one else was in view. The effect of the picture would be general, taking in the whole scene, but not giving the features of the corpse. Townsend."

A number of telegraph messages went to Washington in following hours from the photographer, T. Gurney & Sons, H. J. Raymond,

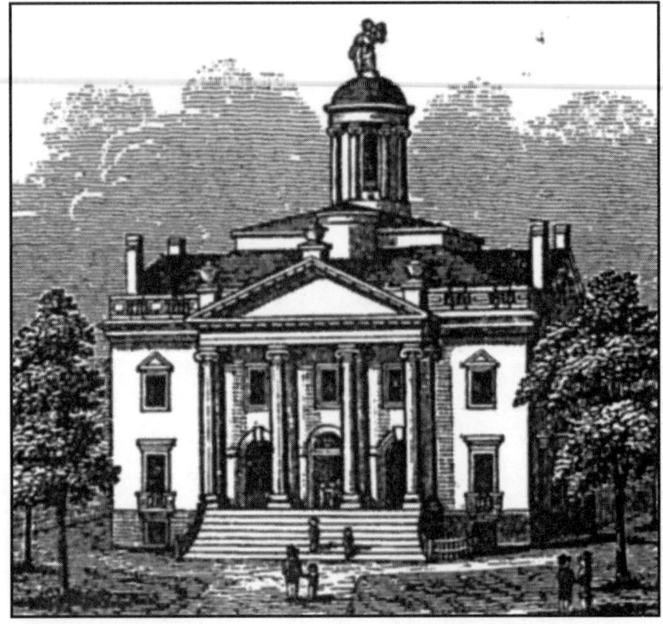

New York State House at Albany, New York, where Lincoln's remains lay in state on April 26, 1865. The reception room was the assembly chamber. Albany was the second of three stops across the State of New York. -- *Historical Collections of the State of New York, John W. Barber and Henry Howe, 1844*

and Henry Ward Beecher, all asking for postponement of the destruction of the negatives. Late that evening an order was issued to General Dix to seize the glass plate negatives and destroy them.

Not known to Stanton or the military officers, Gurney had already made several prints. While he may have surrendered all to General Dix, one was not destroyed, and was discovered in some of Lincoln's Secretary's records in 1952.

While the fussing about the photograph was going on a more important event was unfolding at Port Royal, Virginia. John Wilkes Booth and David Herold were tracked down. Booth was shot in the back of the head. In the early morning sun the assassin expired. News of Booth reached the train by the time it arrived at Buffalo.

PREPARING TO DEPART ALBANY

Public viewing ended at 12:30 p.m. and for the next hour members of the Legislature and Common Councils viewed the remains. At 1:30 p.m. the viewing ended and the lid was closed. In a few minutes the Veteran Reserve Guard of Escort removed the coffin from the Hall of Representatives and placed it in the hearse drawn by six gray horses. At 2:00 p.m., the procession having been formed under Grand Marshal Franklin Townsend, commenced to move over the prescribed route. It was composed of the 10th and 25th Regiments of Albany, the 24th and the Light-Horse Battery of Troy, the State and city authorities, the Fire Department, and a large number of civic societies. The Common Council of Albany along with the Common Council from the City of Troy, officials of neighboring cities and citizens participated. Political groups and individuals were invited to attend, but to refrain from showing any political affiliation.

Under a pleasant sunny day the procession moved from the Capitol, east on State Street, to Dove, down Washington Avenue and State to Broadway, and Broadway, to the railroad crossing, altogether a distance exceeding a mile. The streets were densely packed during the march to the train. Such a mass of human beings, estimated at approximately 60,000 was never before seen on the streets of Albany. A young boy sustained a broken arm in the crowd and was carried to help by Alderman Sullivan.

There were four bands, including Doring's Band and Perkin's Drum Corps, in line; and as the procession moved down the hill, the bands playing "Love Not," "Auld Lang Syne," "Come and Let Us Worship," the effect was described as thrilling. All the buildings along the route were draped with mourning. Among the most touching mottoes on house fronts were the following: "The heart of the Nation throbs heavily at the portals of the tomb." "Let us resolve that the Martyred dead shall not have died in vain." The *Troy Daily Times* gave a description as the procession was moving. "Thus on, still onward, through streets crowded but quiet, moves the mournful caravan. Thousands witness its slow progress, as it marches under of drapery and almost endless inscriptions. It seems as if every great utterance of the lamented dead had been transcribed for this occasion."

At 3:30 p.m. the procession arrived at the joint New York Central - Boston and Albany Union Depot, at Broadway. The appropriately draped funeral train was drawn up to receive the remains. The Veteran Reserve Guard of Escort removed the coffin from the hearse and placed them directly on the awaiting *United States*.

Members of a greatly enlarged funeral escort accompanying the remains to the west then left their carriages and entered the train. It took 15 minutes for everyone to board the train, including Ex-Governor Seymour and Utica Mayor Butterfield. Delegates for Syracuse, Rochester and Buffalo also boarded the train.

From this station, the train turned west across New York State. Now every mile the train progressed would bring it closer to Springfield, Illinois.

The funeral hearse was immediately moved for public exhibition at the new fire house of Engine Company No. 8 in Albany. It was described as a beautiful piece of workmanship, truly gorgeous and costly, displaying admirable taste in every point. Its designer, Mr. James Allen, Undertaker, was given praise in the local papers for his efforts. Few realized his efforts were last-minute. The Albany Committee on Arrangements had planned on using the grand hearse from New York City. At the last moment those plans were cancelled.

TRAVEL LOG

April 25, 1865 141 miles

Station		Time
Via Hudson River Railroad		
New York City	DEPART	4:15 p.m.
Fort Washington		4:25 p.m.
Yorkville		
Mount St. Vincent		
Manhattan		
Harlem		
Spuyten Duyvel Creek		
Yonkers		4:55 p.m.
Hastings		
Dobbs Ferry		
Irvington		5:15 p.m.
Tarrytown		5:20 p.m.
Sing-Sing (Osining)		5:30 p.m.
Oscawana		
Crugers		
Peekskill *		5:55 p.m.
Garrison's Landing * (opposite West Point)		6:20 p.m.
Cold Spring		6:40 p.m.
Fishkill-on-the-Hudson		6:55 p.m.
North Hamburg		
Poughkeepsie *	ARR	7:10 p.m.
meal stop	Depart	8:10 p.m.
Hyde Park		
Staatsburg		8:18 p.m.
Rhinebeck		8:35 p.m.
Barrytown		8:40 p.m.
Tivoli		8:52 p.m.
Germantown		
Catskill		9:35 p.m.
Hudson		9:45 p.m.
Stockport		10:07 p.m.
Stuyvesant		10:23 p.m.
Schodack		10:37 p.m.
Castleton		10:45 p.m.
East Albany	ARR.	10:55 p.m.
Empty train move over Hudson River bridge		
Nail Factory		
Troy - cross Hudson River		
West Albany		

NEW YORK STATE

April 24 - 28, 1865

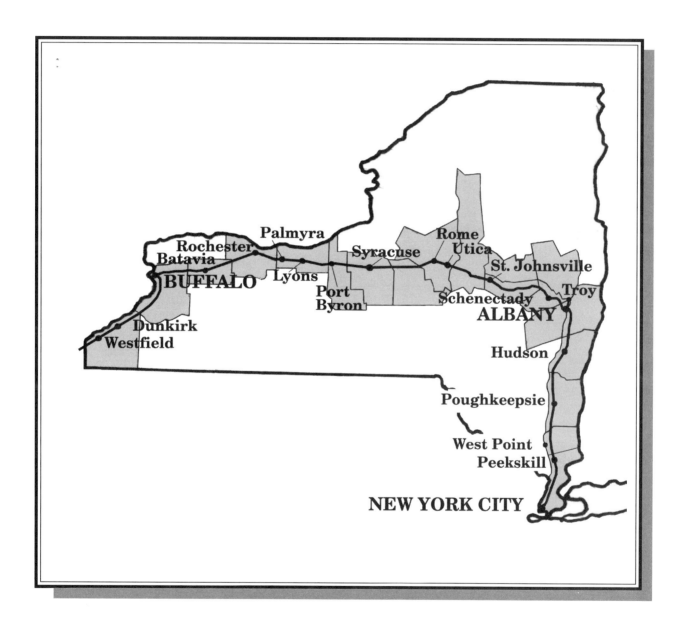

Railroads used:

New York City to Albany -- Hudson River Railroad
Albany to Buffalo -- New York Central Railroad
Buffalo to Erie, Pa. -- Buffalo and State Line Railroad

APRIL 26 - 27, 1865
ALBANY - SYRACUSE - BUFFALO

At Albany, the funeral train was prepared with eight festooned cars of the New York Central Railroad being added with the *United States* and the Officers Car. The train now ten cars, made up of a baggage car, two coaches and five "new" sleeping cars furnished by the New York Central Railroad, and under the Superintendence of Webster Wagner. Wagner was a highly successful businessman who rivaled upstart George Pullman, in the sleeping car business. The cars were in charge of sleeping car conductor Mr. Chamberlin.

Sleeping cars were a relatively new element to railroad travel and suggested privilege, first-class and luxury. It was well above the accommodations offered in the standard coach, and surely proper for the members of the funeral escort who would spend fifteen hours aboard the train on this night.

Decoration of the cars was carried out under the direction of Joseph Jones, Master Carpenter and Superintendent of the Car Department for the New York Central at West Albany. The coaches were brand new, never having been run out of the shop. They were described as, "elegant and elaborate, and featured carpeting expressly for the occasion." Designs for decorating the cars were created by Mr. J. F. Lyons. The decorations required 700 yards of alpaca fabric and the requisite amounts of white bunting. Great skill was displayed in decorating and adorning the cars. The pilot locomotive on the first leg of the night's journey was the *Chauncey Vibbard*, decorated by its engineer Harvey Henry. Leading the funeral train the first leg was the locomotive *Edward H. Jones*, decorated by the Master Mechanic for the railroad of the same name. At the time this was considered the most powerful locomotive on the railroad, and one having pulled the visiting European heads of state over the railroad. The engineer was Peter Arthur.

The decoration and art of the train was described as, "... the most perfect specimens of artistic skill, being elegant and neat, yet far removed from inappropriate showiness or gaudy display. The [New York] Central indeed spared no pains to do all that lay in their power to render the seven passenger cars, which they furnished, both neat and attractive. Their entire interior was fitted up handsomely. Between each window, upon the exterior, the panels were draped in black, and three stars arranged on each panel at appropriate distances. Other mourning emblems also added to heighten the somber effect."

Over the next 298 miles, the railroad had prepared no less than eight locomotives, and complementing crews to handle the train without difficulty. A car repairman was sent along with many tools needed to make immediate repairs to the cars if needed. The telegraphic department sent along two telegraphers, one in the pilot train and the other on the funeral train with "novelty" telegraph instruments designed to be portable, carried in the pocket and easily attached to the line-side telegraph wires in case of an emergency.

The journey from Albany to Buffalo was the longest leg of the funeral journey, covering 298 miles in 15 hours, mostly at night. This was the first of six nights journey on the route to Springfield. Neither the escort, nor the citizens along the route were prepared for the massive turnout of people along the tracks, nor the overwhelming expressions of sympathy offered.

The train was now clearly in territory of deep mourning. General Edward Townsend later recalled, "As the President's remains went farther westward, ... the people more especially claimed him as their own, the intensity of feeling seemed if possible to grow deeper."

On the journey west from Albany, New York, Governor Reuben H. Fenton, did not accompany the train. Press accounts state he had to stay behind and attend business with the New York legislature. Chauncey Depew, took the honor of representing the Governor. As an elderly gentleman, in 1909, speaking of his journey that night across New York, he said: "The hostile hosts of four years before were now standing about the roadway with bared heads, weeping. As we sped over the rails at night, the scene was the most pathetic ever witnessed. At every crossroads the glare of innumerable torches illuminated the whole population from age to infancy, kneeling on the ground, and their clergymen leading in prayers and hymns."

THE RIBBON OF FLAMES

At four o'clock in the afternoon the funeral train departed Albany, headed for Utica, Syracuse, Rochester and Buffalo, a 298-mile trip via the New York Central Railroad. Great crowds gathered in anticipation of the passing of Lincoln's funeral train on its way west.

This leg of the journey would be through the Mohawk River valley and paralleling the famous Erie Canal, crossing it five times en route to Buffalo.

At 4:45 p.m. the train arrived at Schenectady, for a brief memorial stop, reported at about a one minute stop. A funeral procession had been held there on April 19, before it was known the train would pass through the city. A memorial was also held at the First Dutch Church. A clerk in a State Street store, suggested to have had Copperhead, pro-Southern, tendencies, made a slurring remark against the martyred President and he was very effectively dealt with, being compelled to leave town summarily after being practically "cuffed to a peak."

Multitudes of people were gathered along the railroad, and many buildings were festooned in mournings to show their reverent respect as the train passed by. The mechanics of the railroad shops stood in line at the track with heads uncovered, a strange silence prevailed, broken only by the constant exhausts of the working locomotive. The signal men along the railroad yards bore in their hands white square flags, bordered with black.

The village of Amsterdam was passed at 5:25 p.m. The village had been established in 1793, and boasted a population of 5,135 at this date, most of whom were at trackside. Residents constructed an arch over the track, decorated with red, white and blue draped cloth along with other evidence of mourning. Village bells tolled from the time the train came within hearing distance until it had passed from the area.

As the sun set low across the Mohawk Valley, a second arch was encountered over the tracks at Fonda at 5:45 p.m. This arch was hung with draped flags. A large concourse of citizens had gathered to pay their respects. The station and homes near the railroad were all draped in mournings, and minute guns were fired in salute as the train passed.

Near Palatine Bridge, the funeral escort observed a white cross had been erected on a grassy mound robed in evergreens and mourning. To each side of the cross was posed a woman in an attitude of prayer. In back stood a man with his head uncovered. On the cross was the inscription: "We have prayed for you; now we can only weep."

Palatine Bridge, was reached at 6:25 p.m., and a brief stop was made to accommodate the great crowds gathered along the tracks. Minute guns were fired as the train passed and a band played solemn dirges at track side. The crowd stood in silence, showing sincere respect as a band played appropriate music. Palatine Bridge was important to the region. It was the first bridge west of Schenectady over the Mohawk River, having been built in 1788.

Palatine Bridge, was also the home of Webster Wagner, who worked for the New York Central Railroad between 1843 and 1860. He quit to start a sleeping car business on the New York Central Railroad. Wagner was founder of the Wagner Palace Sleeping Car

TIME TABLE

NEW YORK CENTRAL RAILROAD.

SPECIAL TIME TABLE

FOR

FUNERAL TRAIN, CONVEYING THE REMAINS

OF OUR LATE PRESIDENT,

ABRAHAM LINCOLN,

FROM

ALBANY TO BUFFALO.

WEDNESDAY, APRIL 26, 1865.

ALBANY TO SYRACUSE.

		Pilot Engine.	Funeral Train
Leave	ALBANY	3.50 P. M.	4.00 P. M.
"	Schenectady	4.35 "	4.45 "
"	Hoffman's	4.58 "	5.08 "
"	Cranesville	5.08 "	5.18 "
"	Amsterdam	5.15 "	5.25 "
"	Tribes Hill	5.30 "	5.40 "
"	Fonda	5.45 "	5.55 "
"	Yosts	5.58 "	6.08 "
"	Palatine Bridge	6.15 "	6.25 "
"	Fort Plain	6.22 "	6.32 "
Arrive	ST. JOHNSVILLE	6.37 "	6.47 "
Leave	ST. JOHNSVILLE	6.50 "	7.00 "
"	East Creek	6.57 "	7.07 "
"	Little Falls	7.25 "	7.35 "
"	Herkimer	7.40 "	7.50 "
"	Ilion	7.46 "	7.56 "
"	Frankfort	7.52 "	8.02 "
Arrive	UTICA	8.15 "	8.25 "
Leave	UTICA	8.35 "	8.45 "
"	Whitesboro	8.45 "	8.55 "
"	Oriskany	8.53 "	9.03 "
"	ROME	9.05 "	9.15 "
"	Green's Corners	9.17 "	9.27 "
"	Verona	9.28 "	9.38 "
"	Oneida	9.40 "	9.50 "
"	Wampsville	9.48 "	9.58 "
"	Canastota	9.55 "	10.05 "
"	Canaseraga	10.04 "	10.14 "
"	Chittenango	10.15 "	10.25 "
"	Kirkville	10.26 "	10.36 "
"	Manlius	10.33 "	10.43 "
Arrive	SYRACUSE	11.05 P. M.	11.15 P. M.

This Pilot Engine and Train will have the right to the track over all other trains, and no train will run within **thirty minutes** of their time.

E. FOSTER, Jr., } Ass't Supt's.
Z. C. PRIEST, }

H. W. CHITTENDEN,
General Sup't.

On the longest leg of the funeral journey the New York Central Railroad issued this timetable to members of the funeral escort. Two public timetables were also issued. Those two were larger handbill style. -- *Benedictine University collection*

Company, and three of his "Wagner Cars" were added to the train this night. These cars went all the way through to Indianapolis, Indiana.

The village of Fort Plain was passed at 6:32 p.m. The depot was draped in mournings, a large crowd of people had gathered at trackside to watch as the train passed by. The scholars from a local academy, with their teachers were arranged in line at the depot to honor the lamented dead. It is reported the ladies sat in carriages, slowly waving flags.

TIME TABLE

SYRACUSE TO BUFFALO.

		Pilot Engine.	Funeral Train.
Leave	SYRACUSE	11.20 P. M.	11.30 P. M.
"	Warners	11.44 "	11.54 "
"	Memphis	11.50 "	12.00 A. M.
"	Jordan	12.04 A. M.	12.14 "
"	Weedsport	12.16 "	12.26 "
"	PORT BYRON	12.30 "	12.40 "
"	Savannah	12.50 "	1.00 "
"	Clyde	1.05 "	1.15 "
"	LYONS	1.25 "	1.35 "
"	Newark	1.40 "	1.50 "
"	PALMYRA	2.05 "	2.15 "
"	Macedon	2.17 "	2.27 "
"	Fairport	2.41 "	2.51 "
Arrive	ROCHESTER	3.10 "	3.20 "
Leave	ROCHESTER	3.25 "	3.35 "
"	Cold Water	3.45 "	3.55 "
"	Chili	3.58 "	4.08 "
"	Churchville	4.10 "	4.20 "
"	Bergen	4.20 "	4.30 "
"	West Bergen	4.30 "	4.40 "
"	Byron	4.40 "	4.50 "
"	BATAVIA	5.08 "	5.18 "
"	Crofts	5.25 "	5.35 "
"	Corfu	5.40 "	5.50 "
"	Alden	5.53 "	6.03 "
"	Wende	6.01 "	6.11 "
"	Town Line	6.06 "	6.16 "
"	Lancaster	6.20 "	6.30 "
	Forks	6.27 "	6.37 "
Arrive	BUFFALO	6.50 A. M.	7.00 A. M.

This Pilot Engine and Train will have the right to the track over all other trains, and no train will run within **twenty minutes** of their time.

W. G. LAPHAM, J. TILLINGHAST, } Ass't Supt's.

H. W. CHITTENDEN, *General Sup't.*

THE ST. JOHNSVILLE MEAL STOP

The third scheduled meal stop for the funeral train was made at St. Johnsville, New York. This town was a relative newcomer in the Mohawk Valley, having been established in 1838. Its importance to the railroad was a trackside railroad restaurant, known simply as Colonel Cook's. Because on-train dining was still a novelty, and largely relegated to the pots of grub and coffee served from box cars on civil war troop trains, all regular passenger trains made periodic stops for the refreshment of passengers, the arrangements generally limited to a counter or small stand for the patrons.

Colonel Cook's served from 300 to 400 meals on a typical day. When the train schedule from Albany to Buffalo was laid out, St. Johnsville became a meal stop scheduled for 15 minutes.

The funeral cortege arrived at 6:47 p.m. Brigadier General, A. B. Eaton, Commissary General of Subsistence, and Captain Penrose, Commissary of Subsistence, were in charge of food arrangements at this location. Well in advance of the trains coming, they had arranged for the food and its preparation. A large meal was served to 125 in the funeral train cortege inside the restaurant. Twenty-four young ladies from the most wealthy and refined families of the village and surrounding area acted as hostesses and served the meal.

The details of the meal stop are told by Mrs. Emma Randall Taboer, in a recollection of the event in *The Syracuse Herald* in 1914.

"One day an order came to serve dinner to the officers who were on President Lincoln's funeral train. This order caused much excitement in our little village, everyone wishing for a sight of the great men.

"Our wish was granted by Mr. Cook, inviting several of the young women to assist in serving the guests. We were asked to wear white dresses and black sashes, and of course each one tried to look her very best. The train arrived ...., I was assigned to serve five generals, and you may be sure I put forth my best effort to serve them well. During the dinner one of the generals asked my name, wishing me to write it down for him, which I did, and thought no more of it. At the close of the dinner a message came saying that the young women who had served the guests so well were invited to go through the funeral car.

"This was considered a great honor, and we were escorted through a guard of soldiers to the car. Just inside the car was a small casket and when I asked one of the officers about it he said it contained the remains of Willie Lincoln, who died in 1862. We passed on into the center of the car where, surrounded by several of his faithful generals who looked sad and careworn, was the casket containing the body of our beloved president. The car was draped in black, festooned with silver stars. It was too dark for me to read the

TIME TABLE

NEW YORK CENTRAL RAILROAD.

Time Table of Special Train & Pilot

WITH THE

REMAINS OF ABRAHAM LINCOLN, LATE PRESIDENT OF THE UNITED STATES,

Wednesday, April 26th, 1865.

	Pilot Engine.	Funeral Train.
Leave Albany	3.50 P. M.	4.00 P. M.
" Schenectady	4.35 "	4.45 "
" Hoffman's	4.58 "	5.08 "
" Cranesville	5.08 "	5.18 "
" Amsterdam	5.15 "	5.25 "
" Tribes Hill	5.30 "	5.40 "
" Fonda	5.45 "	5.55 "
" Yosts	5.58 "	6.08 "
" Palatine Bridge	6.15 "	6.25 "
" Fort Plain	6.22 "	6.32 "
Arrive St. Johnsville	6.37 "	6.47 "
Leave St. Johnsville	6.50 "	7.00 "
" East Creek	6.57 "	7.07 "
" Little Falls	7.25 "	7.35 "
" Herkimer	7.40 "	7.50 "
" Ilion	7.46 "	7.56 "
" Frankfort	7.52 "	8.02 "
Arrive Utica	8.15 "	8.25 "
Leave Utica	8.35 "	8.45 "
" Whitesboro	8.45 "	8.55 "
" Oriskany	8.53 "	9.03 "
" Rome	9.05 "	9.15 "
" Greens Corners	9.17 "	9.27 "
" Verona	9.28 "	9.38 "
" Oneida	9.40 "	9.50 "
" Wampsville	9.48 "	9.58 "
" Canastota	9.55 "	10.05 "
" Canaseraga	10.04 "	10.14 "
" Chittenango	10.15 "	10.25 "
" Kirkville	10.26 "	10.36 "
" Manlius	10.33 "	10.43 "
Arrive Syracuse	11.05 P. M.	11.15 P. M.

This Train and Pilot will have the right to the track over all other trains, and no train will run within thirty minutes of their time.

E. FOSTER, Jr., Z. C. PRIEST, } Ass't Supt's.

H. W. CHITTENDEN,
General Superintendent.

Public timetable issued for the funeral train between Albany and Syracuse. -- *Benedictine University collection*

inscription on the casket but one of the generals read it for me, 'Abraham Lincoln, sixteenth president of the United States,' etc.

As we left the car someone called my name and upon turning I found it was the general who had asked for my name at dinner. He gave me a small package and upon opening it I found one of the silver stars which had been among the decorations in the car."

It appears while the meal was being taken the locomotives were serviced with fuel and water.

From this stop onto Batavia, New York, the train operated under the cover of night, most of it in rain showers. Various recollections conclude along most of this route it appeared as though the demonstrations of respect were continuous. The bonfires and torchlights illuminated the night for nearly the entire distance. The people would not allow Lincoln to pass into an eternal darkness. Minute guns were fired at so many places it seemed almost continuous. Because of the close proximity of the many towns and villages along the route, it is also reported that the music of bands and choirs was so numerous that, after passing a station, the sound of a dirge or requiem would scarcely die away in the distance, until it would be caught up at the next station they were approaching.

Through the long wet hours of the night the funeral cortege received almost continuous honors of respect for Abraham Lincoln.

From the beginning the train had orders allowing it to add two or more sleeping cars for the repose of those on-board during night travel. These cars were first attended at Albany and the same sleeping cars stayed with the train all the way to Indianapolis, Indiana. Other cars were used on the Indianapolis, Chicago and Springfield legs. It is amazing that anyone could sleep in view of the many public demonstrations made throughout the nights of travel.

At Little Falls, New York, a brief station stop was made. A cannon heralded the approach of the train. Mournful dirges were played by a band on the station platform. A committee of ladies of Little Falls boarded the funeral car long enough for a wreath and other floral displays to be placed on the coffin.

The committee of presenters included; Mrs. S. M. Richmond, Mrs. E. W. Hopkins, Mrs. Powers Green, Mrs. J H. Bucklman, Miss Mine Hill, Miss Helen Brooks, Miss Maria Brooks, Miss Mary Shaw. The band performed a dirge during the brief stop. Their tribute was printed in several newspapers. "The ladies of Little Falls through their committee present these flowers. The shield as an emblem of the protection which our beloved President has ever proved to the liberties of the American people. The cross, of his ever faithful trust in God, and the wreath as the token that we mingle our tears with those of our afflicted nation."

Herkimer had plannned a brief memorial ceremony and passed out handbills announcing the forthcoming stop. The train was greeted by a crowds of mourners and a group of thirty-six ladies dressed in white with black sashes. On their head were a wreath of flowers, and each was holding a miniature national flag draped in crepe. The local delegation turned out with floral wreaths. As the train approached there was no call for "brakes" from the engineer. It was suddenly realized the train was not going to stop. The wreaths of flowers were thrown onto the open platforms of the passenger cars. Disappointed, the crowd left the station as the train disappeared into the west.

Moving on toward Utica, the train passed through Ilion. There they were greeted by a torch-light procession of the people. Just to the side of the tracks the Remington gun factory was brilliantly illuminated as a show of respect for the President.

"OLD SARATOGA" SOUNDS AT UTICA

There was a scheduled stop of ten minutes in Utica to change locomotives. This afforded the local residents time for a memorial service. A Utica delegation, including Mayor Butterfield, and twelve other prominent citizens went to Albany to accompany the funeral train west as part of the official escort.

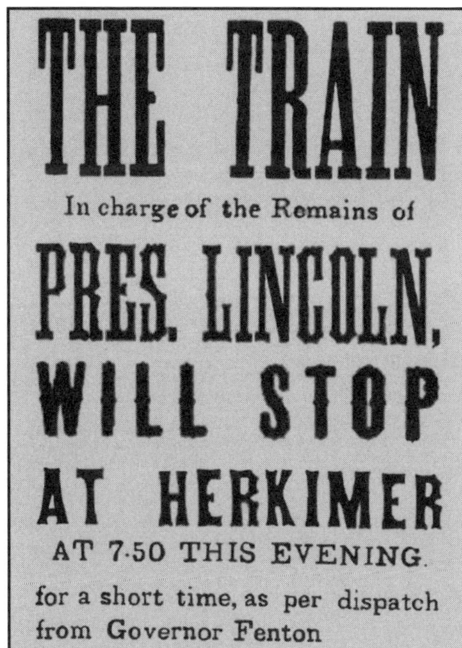

THE TRAIN

In charge of the Remains of

PRES. LINCOLN,

WILL STOP

AT HERKIMER

AT 7.50 THIS EVENING.

for a short time, as per dispatch from Governor Fenton

Herkimer, New York, handbill dated April 26, 1865, advising residents of a planned stop of the Lincoln Funeral Train. The train did not stop according to press accounts.

Throughout the day, elaborate efforts had been underway to appropriately decorate the station in emblems of mourning. The front of the depot (facing the tracks) was draped with flags from the eves and under the roof, gracefully festooned from pillar to pillar, and looped with rosettes. They were draped with ribbons of black and white cloth. Both the express and telegraph offices were also draped in crepe, while upon the roof floated two flags at half-mast. The entire area was outfitted with locomotive headlights and other lamps rendering sufficient light for the train to be discernible at considerable distance.

Hours before the scheduled arrival of the train masses of people began to arrive at the railroad depot. A crowd estimated at 25,000 people anxious to catch a glimpse of the train lined both sides of the track. The 45th Regiment of the National Guard was pressed into duty to form a line on either side of the tracks. They were stationed, a few arms apart, with weapons visible for crowd control. They were not required this night.

"Old Saratoga,' a rather large cannon was moved to Miller's Bridge, about a half-mile away, to announce the coming of the train. As the time neared, rain gently began to fall. Immense crowds had filled all the space around the station, every house top, railroad car and roof. The pilot train entered the depot area at about 8:10 p.m. About ten minutes later, "Old Saratoga" thundered the coming of the funeral train. There was silence as the train entered the station area. The Old Utica Brass Band, perched upon a box car roof played, *Dead March in Eaul.* The train entered the station area at 8:20 p.m. and was met by tolling of City bells. The trains were in station an estimated 20 minutes while locomotives were changed. The Mendelssohn Club sang mournfully while the train remained halted. No specific mention is made of any formal wreath-laying ceremony, however, a Mrs. E. M. Gilbert sent a white wreath of flowers to lay upon the coffin.

While the memorial service was under way, the locomotives were changed. The No. 4 replaced the *Chauncey Vibbard*, pulling the pilot train. The engineer for this next leg was T. Harrett. The locomotive *Major Priest* replaced the *Edward H. Jones* on the funeral train with engineer J. Vrooman at the throttle. The funeral train whistled-off and departed into the raw chill of a wet spring night at about 8:40 p.m.

At the small towns of Whitesboro and Oriskany, crowds had gathered to watch the train slowly pass, many buildings around the railroad were draped. At Rome, the depot and railroad house opposite it, were draped with emblems of mourning. The rain fell heavily, but did not deter the great crowd present to witness the train. It appears a brief stop was made. The small towns of Green's Corners, and Verona, were passed through with crowds gathered along the track and with bonfires.

Oneida was reached at about 9:50 p.m., where a brief stop was made. A great crowd of men and women were assembled with their heads uncovered. A fire company stood in line with torches, surrounding the funeral car as soon as the train had stopped. Just beyond was an arch festooned with flags and decorated transparent lamps. While the train was in the station, minute guns were fired, and a brief memorial was conducted. Wampsville, and Canastota, had large assemblages of people and bonfires to greet the train. Canaserga, Chittenango, Kirkville, and Manlius were passed through as a near continuous line of people gathered along the tracks, many waving torches or flags in tribute to the dead.

THE SYRACUSE STOP

On April 21, six days before arrival of the train, newspapers were reporting a tentative route across New York, though advertised, it was still shaky. A telegraph was received on the morning of April 19, stating the train would pass through Syracuse and central New York State. In the afternoon another telegraph was received stating the train would be routed over the Pennsylvania Central Railroad. Later that night, 11:00 p.m., yet another telegraph was sent by Edwin Stanton, Secretary of War, to Major General John Dix. reconfirming the route: "It has been finally concluded to conform to the arrangements made yesterday for the conveyance of the remains of the late President Abraham Lincoln, from Washington to Springfield, viz: by way of Baltimore, Philadelphia, Harrisburg, New York, Albany, Buffalo, Cleveland, Columbus, Indianapolis, and Chicago to Springfield."

Meanwhile a local committee had been formed to organize a proper reception for the funeral cortege. The depot in Vanderbilt Square had been elegantly decorated during the afternoon, and presented a grand and imposing appearance. From the rafters, stained by wood smoke, [from the steam locomotives] hung flags draped in mourning. Crossing and twining along the whole length of the building were drooping festoons of black and white.

That night, characteristic of April, was showery. Long before the time the train was to arrive, the station and the streets were thronged with people. Crowds promenaded along Railroad Street admiring the display made by the illumination and decorated houses on either side.

Syracuse, was reached at 11:05 p.m. The train passed through a tunnel about a mile east of town, making its way toward the "shed-like" enclosed passenger station. A few minutes before the appointed time, the pilot engine arrived. It is reported that by looking behind the pilot train the bright gleam of the headlight of the funeral train could be seen following in the distance. The pilot train, consisting of the locomotive and a coach, passed through the cavernous station shed without stopping.

Slowly, quietly, amid the booming of the minute guns, the tolling of bells and the strains of the death march, the train bearing the President's body came chugging into the station through the crowds estimated at nearly 30,000 people.

One after another, the cars appeared in black, glided by, brakemen on the platform cranking down the brakes. Soon a coach came in, whose peculiarly somber yet rich decor identified it as the car in which the remains were lying.

While the cars were standing in the station, a chorus sang an anthem appropriate to the solemn occasion, and when they finished, a band again played the dirge.

One Mrs. Pitch, many years later gave an interview of her recollections of that night. "I well recall the passing of Lincoln's funeral train, said Mrs. Pitch. The Hon. Dennis McCarthy invited my mother and myself to accompany him to the depot, as 'twas' called. When, as mayor he paid official tribute to the beloved President. One thing occurred which transcended all others; a marvel, many termed it, and so it still seems to me, a most beautiful thing yet, puzzling-with its mystery; and significance.

"In the dark old shed-like structure many doves found homes aloft among the smoked stained rafters. These were, for the most part gray and at night particularly sought seclusion high above. Around the funeral car which stood well toward the eastern end near Warren Street were gathered those invited to look upon Lincoln's face. It was a goodly throng and the Mayor and his party held a place in the front. Suddenly as we waited in full view outside of the flower-strewn casket within, a dove, perfectly white came sailing in graceful circles from the rafters and poising over the car dropped slowly down until it lighted gently upon the car-roof directly over Lincoln's head. Its head was dropped as its eyes would pierce the boards to search beneath for something they could see.

"As this occurred half-breathed expressions of astonishment were heard and they wondered at the omen. I never was so affected in my life. To cap all, that one white dove in all the flock, when it rose, sought lodgment on two-crossed American flags marking the station's eastern entrance, thereon to perch until the funeral train it watched had vanished on its Western way."

While the train was yet standing in the station, a small bouquet was handed to the delegate from Idaho (Hon. W. H. Wallace), upon which were the appropriate words - *The last tribute of respect from Mary Virginia Raynor, a little girl of three years of age. Dated Syracuse, April 26, 1865.* It was laid on the President's coffin by General Aken. Shortly thereafter the train started on.

Unknown to the local papers, a hometown fellow was on board the train. First Sergeant Addison Cornwell, Co. I, 7th Veteran Reserve Corp. (formerly 134th New York Volunteer Infantry) was one of the 29 honor guards to accompany Lincoln's body all the way to Springfield for burial.

A STRANGE TELEGRAPH MESSAGE FROM SYRACUSE

On April 28, 1865, the Syracuse *Daily Journal*, inserted a small story shining some light on the poor quality of reporting on the

The white dove incident while the train is stopped in Syracuse, New York, depot shed April 26, 1865. On the back platform General McCallum, meets local dignitaries as the crowd gathers around. -- *Electronic illustration by Author*

progress of the train by the *Associated Press* news agency. This group was authorized to report activities of the funeral escort on the train:

"The following dispatch was sent from this city by one of the agents of the *Associated Press* on board the funeral train:--

'*Syracuse, Wednesday, April 26.*

The funeral cortege arrived at Syracuse at 11:50 P.M. Thus far no accident has occurred. Although it is raining, there are at least thirty-five thousand people witnessing the passage of the train at this place. The firemen are drawn up in line, and their torches and numerous bon fires light up the scene solemnly. Bells are tolling and cannons booming.'

The blunders in this beautiful telegraphic effusion average somewhat less than one a line. The cortege reached here, not at ten minutes before twelve, but at five past eleven; it was not raining at the time of the arrival; there were not thirty-five thousand people witnessing the passage of the train; the firemen were not drawn up in line; there were no torches; and there were no bonfires. The reporters of the Associated Press, during the stay of the train in this city, were comfortably slumbering on the soft couches of the new sleeping cars, and knew about as much of the ceremonies here as they did of contemporary transactions on the planet Saturn."

The Editors of the *Daily Journal* were quite displeased with the miscarriage of public trust and false journalism for such an important event. It is echoed at other locations, if not in actual words, for the lack of words published.

The purpose of the stop at Syracuse was a change of locomotives. From here to Rochester, the Pilot Train locomotive was Number 202, engineer R. Simmons. The Funeral train was led by Number 248, engineer John H. Brown.

The train departed, following the ribbon of flame across New York. The rain did not seem to deter anyone at this hour. Mourners assembled at the stations of Warren, Memphis, Jordan and Weedport, holding torches and lanterns, with their heads uncovered as a sign of respect. A brief stop was made at Port Byron, where a large assemblage of people stood about the railroad with torches and bonfires. As soon as the train stopped, they flocked around it, trying for a glimpse of the coffin.

At 1:25 a.m., the train made its next stop at Lyons. Pulling into the station, the train was met by another large assemblage of people silently holding torches or standing near bonfires. As soon as the train stopped, they flocked around the funeral car.

Palmyra was reached about 2:15 a.m., for a ten minute stop and memorial service. The station was about a mile from town, most people walked out to meet the train in the dark and rain. As the train came to a stop it was met at the depot grounds by crowds, the salute of minute guns, a band playing dirges, and tolling of city bells. The details of this ceremony have largely been lost to history. The *Palmyra Courier*, on a page three article the next day reported: "The train stopped at this station ten minutes, and a large number of our citizens (including a few ladies) were at the depot. Of course there was nothing to be seen but the hearse and nine cars, heavily draped, which were viewed with solemn interest."

The remains of Lincoln would not be allowed to pass into the darkness of night, or an eternal darkness. Even at the villages of Macedon and Fairport, crowds carried torches, sang hymns and wore badges of mourning as signs of respect and sorrow for the deceased President.

THE *Dean Richmond* PULLS THE TRAIN

The funeral train arrived at Rochester, on Lake Ontario at 3:20 a.m., to the salute of minute guns, tolling of city bells and massive crowds, estimated in the thousands of people. The train remained in the station for a fifteen minute ceremony while locomotives were again changed. The military formed on the north side of the railroad depot to receive the train. This guard, drawn up in line, consisted of the Fifty-Fourth National Guard State troops, First Company of Veteran Reserves, hospital soldiers, a battery attached to the Twenty-Fifth brigade, and the first company of Union Blues. The Independent and New Marines Regimental Band played a funeral dirge.

On the south side was the Mayor with twenty-five members of the common council of Rochester, together with Gen. John Williams and staff, Major Lee, commander of the post, with his corps of assistants, and Gen. Martindale and staff. A brief ceremony was held with the appropriate prayers, and the laying of a wreath by selected ladies of the community.

Rochester had been the boyhood home of General Daniel C. McCallum, General Manager of the United States Military Railroads during the Civil War, and the man who had the responsibility and authority for this train. This was the town where his family settled after immigrating from Scotland.

The locomotives selected to pull the trains from Rochester to Buffalo had been picked by Mr. Upton, Master Mechanic of railroad. Locomotive Number 79 was selected to pull the pilot train. The locomotive *Dean Richmond*, which drew the inaugural train for Lincoln in 1861, was selected to pull the funeral train. The Rochester *Daily Union & Advertiser* described the decoration and uniquely, the talent who decorated the locomotives. "In the front [of the locomotive] was a portrait of the deceased President trimmed with crepe. Over it were American flags festooned, and about the sides black and white rosettes and other emblems of mourning. The work of decorating was neatly executed by the ladies under Mr. Upton. Hundreds of ladies went to the Round House yesterday and provided their services to assist in this work."

The Buffalo Morning Express gave a similar description of the *Dean Richmond*. "It had a full length portrait of the President underneath the head lights in front, which was surrounded by the graceful folds of two national flags thrown over the upper part of the engine, each were trimmed with black and white crepe. Two exquisite bouquets took the place of the engine flags and another still surmounted the sandbox. The hand rails were neatly adorned with festoons of black and white tasteful rosettes. The cab was draped with the national colors."

According to the news accounts, the train left on-time, headed for Batavia, about a two-hour journey to the west. En route it passed through several small towns. Dr. Adonis of the *Chicago Tribune* wrote: "Since leaving Rochester we have passed through Coldwater, Chili, Churchville, Bergen, and Byron. At all these places were groups of villagers and country people who had come to honor the dead. The stations were becomingly draped with drooping flags and other mournful decorations."

Awaiting the funeral train at Batavia was the Reception Committee from Buffalo, which included Honorable Millard Fillmore. The Committee left from Buffalo's Exchange Street Station at 6:00 p.m. Wednesday, April 26, by a special passenger car provided for their accommodation by the New York Central Railroad. The party passed the night at Batavia awaiting the funeral train.

BATAVIA STOP AT DAYBREAK

At 5:18 a.m., the funeral train arrived at Batavia, where it was received by an immense concourse of people. The assemblage had begun with the very dawn, when the firing of the minute guns awoke the village from its slumbers and hastened the steps of pilgrims from the surrounding country side. Before the train appeared, it had grown to the proportions of a throng. The multitude stood with their heads bowed, silent, sorrowful and reverent, paying that sincere homage to the dead which had everywhere been so memorable and remarkable. The depot was handsomely draped with a conspicuous portrait of the President enveloped in black and white cloth streamers with rosettes of velvet. A huge flag was hung from the station. A band played appropriate music and a choir sang dirges to the dead. Many reported the immense crowd acted in a solemn and religious manner during the presence of the cortege.

The pause of the train was for ten minutes, during which the committee from Buffalo took their places in the car reserved for them. The funeral party had been increased by the addition of ex-President Fillmore, and Messrs. J. A. Verplank, J. Gallasten, James Sheldon, S. S. Jewett, Henry Martin, Philip Dorsheimer, J. P. Slivens, E. S. Prosser, John Wilkinson, Henry Morrison, N. P. Hopkinson, on behalf of the Mayor of Buffalo.

From Batavia to the destination of Buffalo, there were no more intermediate stops made. Several hundred people were standing along the margins of the railroad at Alden, Craft and Corfu. By now the dawn had broken and the fires and torches were not required. At every station and almost continuously the train passed between long lines of people, who had come to catch but a fleeting glimpse of what bore the remains of their beloved President. Everywhere they bowed, with uncovered heads, in afflicting bestowment of their little passing tribute of solemn reverence.

Near Lancaster, a group of young children, bundled against the raw air, were seen sitting in a wagon near the farm houses, waving white flags toward the trains.

ARRIVAL AT BUFFALO

The funeral train arrived in Buffalo at 7:00 a.m. on April 27, 1865, at the Exchange Street Depot. The longest single leg of the funeral journey was over. During the length of this night's journey, it had taken a total of eight locomotives to bring the two trains from Albany to Buffalo.

Exchange Street Depot was handsomely draped in a style appropriate to receive the remains. *The Buffalo Morning Express* was at the station to report the unfolding events.

"With the gray light of morning, people here were astir to prepare for the reception of the funeral train on its arrival as preliminary and unfinished arrangements were completed by the authorities for the carrying out of the program as previously arraigned. The time for the arrival of the train was 7:00 o'clock, but long ore that hour, the streets in the vicinity of the depot were filled with the eager and expectant multitude. At ten minutes before seven, the pilot engine, properly decorated for the use to which it had been assigned, arrived to announce the approach of the funeral train. Punctually to the time, the latter came slowly in - so slowly and silently that it announced in its very manner the solemnity of its nature. The crowds received it with uncovered heads and every mark of respect. The depot had been elaborately draped as also was the Wadsworth House, Bloomer's Dining Saloon and other buildings in the vicinity. On the arrival of the train in the depot, the burial party was shown into Bloomer's Railroad Dining Saloon, where they were entertained in Bloomer's best style.

"The train which bore the remains and the funeral party was a grand affair and attracted much attention. The cars of which the train was made up were also draped with exquisite taste.

"The chief attraction of all was the funeral car which has borne the remains thus far from Washington, and is designed to bear them to the hero's welcome home. Black curtains have been placed at all windows. Inside and out, the car is robed in black. A deep silver flange also hangs from the edge of the roof and the festoons of crepe are looped over each window with a silver star and large silver tassel."

At 8:00 a.m., the procession was formed in front of the depot. Crowds were forced back. The Veteran Reserve Guard of Escort removed the remains of the eminent deceased from the *United States* and borne it to the funeral hearse in front of the depot on their shoulders. The coffin was placed on the funeral hearse, which was drawn by six magnificent white horses, draped in a black cloth of mourning to their feet. The line of the procession was up Exchange Street to Main; up Main to Niagara; Niagara to Delaware; Delaware to Tupper; Tupper to Main and

Main to Eagle.

An immense number of people along the line of march, filled all the available spaces. The business places were all closed. Every window and housetop was filled and covered with a mass of human beings.

Massive crowds gathered around St. James Hall. The crowd was both restless and anxious to testify to the respect and sorrow for the deceased. It was described as an orderly but intense anxiety to get one look at the corpse. The *Chicago Tribune* wrote: "Men, women and children were constantly expressing their wishes ... [to get one look at the corpse.] Could they only get one look, they thought they would be satisfied for a life time, and to be debarred of this holy privilege seemed an irreparable loss. Of course there were hundreds upon hundreds who did not realize this uppermost and absorbing wish."

As the procession moved up the streets toward the Hall, immense crowds nearly blocked every street. There was a rush for the entrance. There were no reported serious mishaps, except several cases of fainting of ladies who were not able to stand the severe pressure brought upon them. Finally the throng was loosened and matters so arranged that free passage was given.

At a few minutes before 10:00 a.m., the procession arrived at the St. James Hall (Young Men's Association Building). The coffin was taken from the hearse and borne into the hall on the shoulders of the Veteran Reserve Guard of Escort, through the Main Street entrance. The coffin was placed upon a double dais erected for that purpose, the upper one inclined to an angle of perhaps twenty degrees, and the whole richly draped in black velvet with silver fringe and rosettes. As the remains of the deceased President were placed upon the dais, the St. Cecelia Society, sung the solemn dirge, "Rest, Spirit, Rest," with impressive effect. General Dix and others requested it be repeated after the coffin had been opened for exhibition.

John Harrison Mills, one of the local guards for the coffin later recalled of his experience: "... I was early at St. James Hall, where a canopy and dais were being finished for the reception of the precious dead. I keenly remember an opening being made out on to Washington Street, and that over the sidewalk from Eagle Street south an incline was built to a platform over the basement windows, which admitted four abreast. After the procession the body was brought in from Main Street at 8 o'clock, and from that time up to 10 o'clock, when the crowd of men poured in from Washington Street, and of ladies and children from Main Street, I was at liberty to sketch the beloved face, so calm in death."

"After my return from the war I plunged into both artistic and literary occupations, and my hair was worn long in the fashion of all artists of that period. As I stood at the head of the coffin in my faded soldier suit and fatigue cap, with my gun on my shoulder and my crutch against a pillar, looking neither to right or left, I heard a whispered, 'Mills, you ought to have got your hair cut. You don't look like a soldier.' I shall never forget the sensation made upon me, who had been for hours in the seventh heaven, as this mundane suggestion was directed at me from my friend George Gibson, also a long-haired artist. I landed on earth again, and after that was keenly alive to the eager mass of humanity which surged past the immortal dead up to 8 o'clock that evening, when the lying in state was over ...."

The *Buffalo Morning Express* offered a description. "The corpse was dressed in plain black and the face wore that same kind, benignant look that characterized the 'People's President' when alive. The face was slightly discolored, but not as much as many had been led to expect. The lifelike expression of the features were surprising. The thought would arise as we gazed upon the quiet face that he had found the rest for which he must have so often sighed."

The choir was apparently behind a curtain as the remains were prepared for viewing. Their chorus was reported as, "... the sweet strains of melody seemed, indeed, angelic."

While the newspapers were reporting a near normal appearance, it must have been a great concern to the embalmer as to whether the remains would hold up for all the requirements of the journey through May 6, the original date for burial. Telegraphs between the Illinois Committee on the train and the Springfield Committee on Arrangements tell a different story with great concerns.

RECEPTION ARRANGEMENTS

President Millard Fillmore acted as honorary chairman for the Citizen's Committee on Observance of the Day of Obsequies at Buffalo, on the 19th. He and the other Committee members, (Nelson K. Hopkins, J. A. Verplanck, J.C. Masten, F. P. Stevens, Henry Martin, Jas Sheldon, E. S. Prosser, P. Dorsheimer, S. S. Jewett, John Wilkeson, and S. H. Fish) decided to restage the mourning processional when they learned the train would stop at Buffalo on the 27th. The arrangements for reception of the remains were of a most complete character.

The appearance of the Hall, as prepared for the occasion, was grandly impressive. It was in the form of an immense indoor pavilion, sable and somber, but adorned in the most exquisite perfection of art. The walls of the pavilion were richly and tastefully decorated and wreathed with black and white crepe, lace and fringe. Large bows of crepe also decked its sides. Eight columns, elaborately draped with wreaths, rosettes and festoons, were placed in position around the inner line of the apartment. There were three arched entrances, or passageways, with the folds of the drapery looped up with rosettes and ties of white and black. The whole was set off by a magnificent chandelier suspended from the center, directly over the dais and remains.

After removal of the body for Cleveland, the Hall was kept open for the inspection of those who did not have an opportunity to pay their respect to the deceased.

THE CROWD IS ADMITTED

As soon as the doors were thrown open, people began to pour into, and pass through the hall.

There was but a single purpose; to view all that was mortal of the great man. All day long they passed by the coffin in uninterrupted lines. Persons of all ages and conditions came to pay their respects to the man whom they had so much admiration and loved.

It was estimated the number of people that passed through the Hall was from eighty to one hundred thousand people. There was not the slightest incident to mar the decorum of the occasion. The place was oppressively silent, save the constant tramp of the multitude. The arrangements for the passing of the people was admirable. The main entrance was on Eagle Street, near Washington, up which they came four abreast. Upon entering the hall, they divided, two passing to the right and two passing to the left, only to reunite on the other side of the coffin. They then marched down and out of the entrance on Eagle, near Main Street.

At noon the Buffalo Common Council, Mayor Fargo, the Common Council of Rochester, New York, and Rochester Mayor Moore, filed through the Hall to pay their respects. Throughout the day many Canadians came over to view the remains. The Canadian Railways granted special permits allowing their employees time to view the remains.

Large delegations of clergymen from all denominations availed themselves of the opportunity to look upon the remains of the highest regarded Christian Ruler of modern times.

A SCHEDULE CHANGE

Up through departure from Albany, it was planned for a May 3rd arrival in Springfield, and a May 6th burial. During the April 27th, ceremonies in Buffalo, telegraph messages were sent between the Illinois Delegation on the train and the Committee on Arrangements at Springfield. The following announcement was the result: "Springfield, April 27. After further consideration, the Committee of Arrangements agreed to deliberate upon changing the day of the funeral, and thereupon corresponded by telegraph with the Illinois delegation accompanying the cortege. The answers received have induced the committee to change the day, and, much as they regret the fact, they feel that uncontrollable conditions require that change. We therefore respectfully announce that the funeral of our late president will take place on Thursday, May 4th, at 12 o'clock, M. The programme will, of course, be changed to suit the shorter time, but ample opportunity will be given to all to view the remains until 9 o'clock, A.M., on Thursday, May 4th. J. T. STUART, Chairman, J. C. CONKLIN, Secretary."

It was at this point the media started to emphasize the many florals being brought to the train and at the places where the remains lay in state.

While the remains were in Buffalo news was received of a great disaster on the Mississippi River just north of Memphis, Tennessee. The river boat *Sultana* blew up in the early hours of April 27 with 1,900 on board. Early estimates put the death count at 1,700. A number of the men were Union prisoners of war, just released from their confederate captors. Details of the disaster were carried in newspapers right next to the stories of the Funeral Train.

This vew of the interior of the funeral car *United States* with the coffin of President Abraham Lincoln appeared in the *Philadelphia Inquirer* April 25, 1865. The view is from the opposite end of the room as the one on page 42. Note the lack of a flag over the coffin, added is the heating stove and the arrangement of the window dressing. Also missing in this view is the honor guard. This view also shows the florals, not seen in the other view-- ***Philadelphia Inquirer, April 25, 1865***

TRAVEL LOG

April 26 - 27, 1865 298 miles

Via New York Central Railroad

Albany	DEPART	4:00 p.m.	Kirkville		10:36 p.m.
Schenectady*		4:45 p.m.	Manlius		
Crainesville			Syracuse*		11:05 p.m.
Hoffman's			Canton		
Canajoharie			Jordon		
Amsterdam		5:25 p.m.	North Weedsport		
Akin			Clyde		
Fonda		5:45 p.m.	Memphis		Midnight
Yost			Cross Erie Canal		
Sprakers			Port Byron		12:40 p.m.
East Creek			Lyons		1:25 p.m.
Palatine Bridge		6:25 p.m.	Cross Erie Canal		
Fort Plain		6:32 p.m.	Newark		
St. Johnsville			Palmyra		2:15 a.m.
meal stop		6:47 p.m.	Meriden		
Little Falls*		7:35 p.m.	Fairport		2:50 a.m.
Herkimer		7:50 p.m.	Brighton		
Ilion		7:56 p.m.	Cross Erie Canal		
Frankfort			Rochester*		3:20 a.m.
Utica	ARR	8:20 p.m.	Coldwater		
	DEPART	8:40 p.m.	Chili		
Whitesboro			Churchville		
Oriskany		9:03 p.m.	Bergen,		
Rome		9:10 p.m.	West Bergen		
Cross Erie Canal			Batavia*		5:18 a.m.
Green's Corners			Crofts		
Verona			Oakfield		
Oneida		9:50 p.m.	Corfu		
Wampsville			Alden		6:03 a.m.
Canastota		10:05 p.m.	Wende		
Canaserga			Town Line		
Cross Erie Canal			Lancaster		6:30 a.m.
Chittenango			Buffalo	ARR	7:00 AM

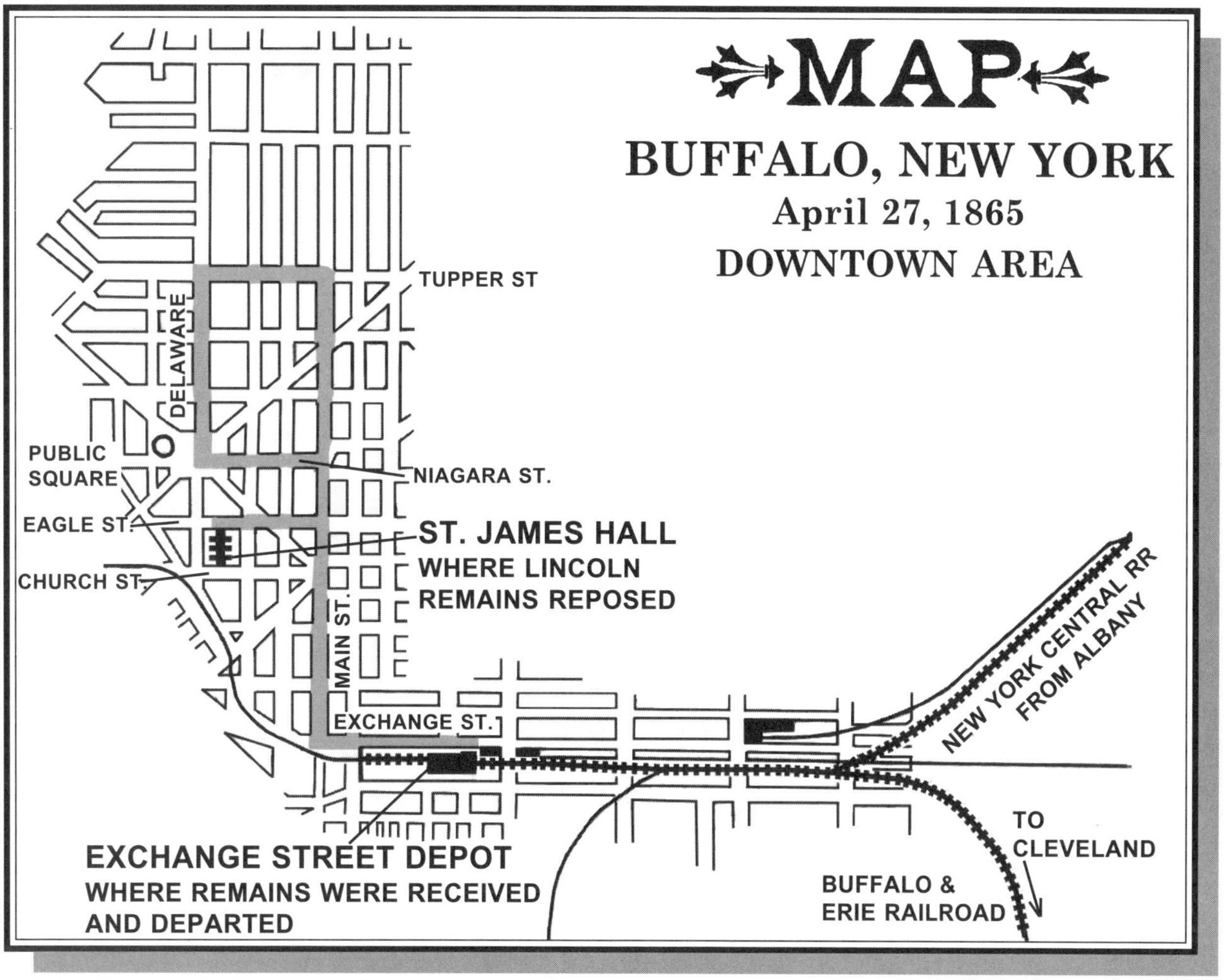

MAP

BUFFALO, NEW YORK

April 27, 1865

DOWNTOWN AREA

TUPPER ST
DELAWARE
PUBLIC SQUARE
NIAGARA ST.
EAGLE ST.
ST. JAMES HALL
WHERE LINCOLN REMAINS REPOSED
CHURCH ST.
MAIN ST.
EXCHANGE ST.
NEW YORK CENTRAL RR FROM ALBANY
EXCHANGE STREET DEPOT
WHERE REMAINS WERE RECEIVED AND DEPARTED
TO CLEVELAND
BUFFALO & ERIE RAILROAD

The *United States* and Officers' Car thought to be at Buffalo, New York, April 27, 1865 -- *Buffalo and Erie County Historical Society*

APRIL 27 - 28, 1865
BUFFALO - ERIE - CLEVELAND

At 8:15 p.m., the coffin was closed and arrangements begun to escort the remains to Buffalo's Exchange Street Depot. The Veteran Reserve Guard of Escort carried the coffin on their shoulders to the awaiting hearse. Crowds of mourners stood in mournful respect as bands played solemn dirges. With the darkness of the night, all was wrapped in the deepest sorrow. A large body of citizens followed the procession to the last point at the depot and watched as best they could, straining to see the coffin be put aboard the *United States.*

Just prior to starting toward Cleveland, the ladies of the St. Cecelia Society placed upon the coffin a beautiful harp, woven of flowers and evergreen. The ladies of the Unitarian Society presented an elegantly worked anchor of flowers and evergreens. Numerous other floral tributes were also bestowed upon the coffin. Only after the final flowers were set upon the coffin did the masses turn their footsteps homeward.

To the melodic notes of a band, the funeral cortege and escort boarded the funeral train, departing on their sorrowful way to the west over the Buffalo and Erie Railroad. The locomotive moved out at 10:10 p.m.

Many of the New York Central passenger cars stayed with the train as it departed Buffalo, and continued through to Indianapolis.

The Buffalo Morning Express made an observation as the train departed: "The solemn spectacle has passed. The body of the great martyr has been borne through our hushed streets and onward to its rest. We have looked upon the immortal face and a sacred memory is in our hearts. We have hallowed a shrine in our midst forever, the touch of the dead man's bier. The procession of cities and States has swept on to the west, and the funeral dirge which wailed upon us from the ocean a week ago is dying along the lakes. What a journey of the dead we have seen! What a nation's performance of the funeral rites of a nation's Chief! What a nation's great testimony of love and grief! We have borne our part. In the majestic spectacle we have paid our tribute of honor to the illustrious dead; we have done it lovingly and well. The remembrance of the great solemnity is made forever grateful to us by the perfect harmony and decorum of its every circumstance. Our city has done honor to itself in the method and the manner of Abraham Lincoln."

Part of this night's 183 mile journey would be within sight of Lake Erie. About 10:50 p.m. the train passed Hamburg, New York. Many farm families stood around great bonfires, with heads uncovered in silent respect to their fallen leader. Similar scenes were repeated at North Evans and Angola.

The first reported stop west of Buffalo was at Silver Creek, where a brief stop was made, the details of which are not recorded. At 12:10 a.m. on April 28, Dunkirk, New York, was reached along the shores of Lake Erie. As the train stopped, it was greeted by a large crowd. At the station thirty-six young ladies dressed in white, knelt with a flag in the hand of each, greeting the train. The station was artistically decorated with festoons of mourning. A band played a requiem in a moving scene as the train came to a stop and the crowds gathered around for a brief memorial. The ladies entered the funeral car to place a wreath of evergreens and flowers on

COMING ONTO THE TRAIN

At the New York - Pennsylvania state line, Erie Mayor F. F. Farrar, George W. Starr, F. B. Vincent, E. P. Bennett, J. T. Walsher and Capt. F. A. Roe, U.S.N.

DEPARTING FROM THE TRAIN

Major-General Dix and staff.

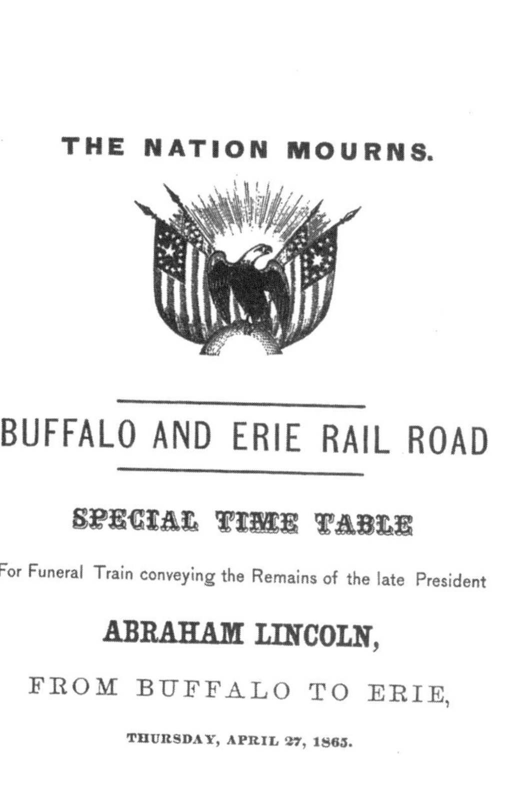

THE NATION MOURNS.

BUFFALO AND ERIE RAIL ROAD

SPECIAL TIME TABLE

For Funeral Train conveying the Remains of the late President

ABRAHAM LINCOLN,

FROM BUFFALO TO ERIE,

THURSDAY, APRIL 27, 1865.

BUFFALO TO ERIE.

	Pilot Engine.	Funeral Train.	Remarks.
Leave BUFFALO,	10.00 P. M.	10.10 P. M.	
" HAMBURGH,	10.30	10.40	
" NORTH EVANS,	10.45	10.55	
" ANGOLA,	11.03	11.13	
" FARNHAM,	11.18	11.28	
" IRVING,	11.25	11.35	
" SILVER CREEK,	11.35	11.45	....Wood and Water.
" DUNKIRK,	12.00	12.10 A. M., 28th.	
" BROCTON,	12.20	12.30	
" PORTLAND,	12.25	12.35	
" WESTFIELD,	12.50	1.00	....Wood and Water.
" RIPLEY CROSSING,	1.05	1.15	
" RIPLEY,	1.14	1.24	
" STATE LINE,	1.22	1.32	
" NORTH EAST,	1.35	1.47	
" MOREHEADS,	1.47	1.57	
" HARBOR CREEK,	1.55	2.05	
" WESLEYVILLE,	2.04	2.14	
Arrive ERIE,	2.20 A. M.	2.30 A. M.	

This Pilot Engine and Funeral Train will have EXCLUSIVE RIGHT TO THE TRACK over all other Trains upon the line.

A. T. WILLIAMS,
Ass't Sup't.

J. LEWIS GRANT,
Gen'l Sup't.

the coffin of the president. Many stood in respectful silence. An undisclosed number of the New York dignitaries departed from the train at this stop.

Westfield, a scheduled fuel stop was reached at 1:00 a.m. This town was a favorite to Lincoln during his run for the presidency. It was from this town twelve-year-old Grace Bidwell, had written a letter to advise President-elect Lincoln to grow a beard. She stepped forward in 1861 and greeted Mr. Lincoln during his inaugural journey to Washington. There is no record of her presence on this mournful night.

While the locomotives were receiving fuel and water, five young ladies boarded the car and laid a floral cross and a wreath on the coffin. The train then commenced on.

The last station passed in New York was Ripley, at 1:24 a.m. Crowds had gathered around the depot and bonfires blazed. Eight minutes later the train passed State Line, Pennsylvania, marked with a bonfire and drooping flags hanging from temporary poles.

THE ERIE, PENNSYLVANIA SITUATION

North East, Pennsylvania, was reached at 1:47 a.m., and the train stopped briefly to allow the New York delegation to disembark. General John A. Dix, and staff also got off the train here, their job about finished, and in preparation for General Joseph Hooker to take over the train ahead in Ohio. At this date Hooker was in charge of the Army of the Northern Ohio, including the states of Ohio, Indiana, Illinois and Michigan. The small Pennsylvania delegation came on board as the train prepared to enter the State of Penn-

NORTH EAST, PA.,
April 28, 1865—1 a.m.

Hon. E. M. STANTON,
Secretary of War:

I met the late President's remains at Philadelphia, Pa., and have been constantly with them. They just passed beyond the line of my department. Everything has been most satisfactory.

JNO. A. DIX,
Major-General.

sylvania for the second and last time. This is the only state to have hosted the Funeral Train twice.

While at the station stop, twelve-year-old Leonora Crawford entered the funeral car and placed a bouquet of roses formed in the shape of a cross on the coffin. After the funeral train left, General Dix caught the eastbound passenger train back to New York.

At just after 2:00 a.m., the train passed Harbor Creek, Pennsylvania, A number of farmers and their families stood at the station, draped in drooping flags and illuminated by bonfires, paying final respects to the president.

The Pennsylvania delegation this time was headed by Erie, Pennsylvania, Mayor F. F. Farrar. Citizens of his town made suitable arrangements to honor the remains as the train was to stop at the station. Through some misunderstanding, alleged to have originated with railroad officials, it was supposed that the delegates of the funeral escort had made a special request that no public demonstration be made in order to give them the opportunity for sleep. It appears this rumor was started on April 27, with a scant comment in the Erie newspapers falsely indicating a stop was not planned. The train arrived at Erie, Pennsylvania, at 2:50 a.m. some 20 minutes off the advertised schedule. A change of railroads and locomotives was made here.

The *Erie Observer* gave a description of the abbreviated ceremony. "On the arrival of the train on Thursday, the bells were tolled and minute guns fired. A large concourse of our citizens were assembled at the depot, but owing to the insufficient time, very few were able to obtain a view of the remains. Those in charge were obliged to restrict the number

CUSTOM-HOUSE, DISTRICT OF ERIE, COLLECTOR'S OFFICE
Erie: Pa., April 22, 1865.

Hon. JOHN BROUGH:

DEAR SIR:

I see by the printed programme that the remains of ex-President Lincoln will remain in Buffalo from 7 a.m. to 10 p.m., a period of 15 hours, when the train will leave for Cleveland, arriving there the next morning. By this arrangement the funeral train will pass through Erie at midnight. Our citizens having had the pleasure of a meeting with Mr. Lincoln when he was on his way to Washington: desire to pay his remains the tribute of honor and respect which they have felt for him as President, and desire me to address you and ascertain whether by reducing the time at Buffalo a few hours they could not have the privilege of doing so. We feel as if it would be just to the citizens of this part of Pennsylvania to allow them the few hours that would enable them to pay their last respects to him, especially as such a long detention will occur at Buffalo and Cleveland, on both sides of our city and State. If it may be in your power to modify the time arranged between Buffalo and Cleveland, and which will not interfere with any other part of the route, please advise me by telegraph, and very much oblige,

Yours, very truly,
M. B. LOWRY,
State Senator, Erie and Crawford Counties.

who passed through the funeral car, to ladies and those who accompanied them. Owing to a misapprehension on the part of the citizens, the demonstration was scarcely in keeping with the size of the city."

When the morning newspapers for April 29, came off the press they read of a disinterested Erie. The *Toledo Blade* printing the "News by Telegraph" stated, "Erie, 2:50 a.m., - There was no particular demonstration at this place."

The honorable Mayor of Erie, F. F. Farrar, issued a telegraphic message to most major newspapers, apparently feeling humiliated for how his esteemed city was perceived to lack of a formal demonstration and expression of mourning was made during the brief stop.

COMING ONTO THE TRAIN

At Wickliffe, Governor Brough, on behalf of Ohio, received the funeral party. At that point his staff joined him, consisting of General B. R. Cowen, Adjt.-General; General Merrill Barlow, Q. M. General; General R. N. Barr, Surgeon General; Col. Sidney D. Maxwell, Aid-de-Camp; Lt.-Col. John T. Mercer, Asst. Adjt.-General; F. A. Marble, Esq.,Private Secretary.

Major-General Joseph Hooker, commanding the Northern Department of the Ohio, joined the funeral party at Wickliffe, under orders from the War Department, to accompany the President's remains to Springfield, with his staff, including Col. Swords, Asst. Q. M. General; Lieut. Simpson, U. S. Engineers; Lieut.-Col. Lathrop, Assist. Inspector-General; Major Bannister, Chief Paymaster; Major MacFeely, Commissary, U. S. A.; and Capt. Taylor. United States Senator Sherman, Hon. S. Galloway, Hon. Octavious Waters and Major Montgomery, also met the remains at Wickliffe; together with a number of the prominent citizens of Northern Ohio, who had been appointed at Cleveland a committee to attend the fineral procession from the State line to that city.

"Erie, Pa. May 2

While acknowledging with profound humiliation the absence of a proper demonstration of respect on the part of this city to greet the remains of President Lincoln on their arrival here last Friday morning, justice to our citizens who have ever delighted to honor the lamented patriot while living, and who are second to none in heartfelt devotion to the memory of the distinguished dead, requires publicity of the fact, that in the midst of preparations for the mournful occasion they were informed by a Superintendent of the Cleveland & Erie Railroad that the funeral escort had made a special request that no public demonstration be made at this place, in order that their committee might have a rest and repose. Acquiescing with this unauthorized request is therefore the true cause of the apparent national discredit attributed to this city.

Signed F.F. Farrar, Mayor"

Locomotives were changed at Erie as were the railroads in charge of the train. There was a special feature about the running of the train from Erie to Cleveland. As far as possible, everything connected with the train was the same as on the occasion of Mr. Lincoln's journey over that road in 1861. The locomotive *William Case*,* was the same. The engineer of 1861, William Congden, was deceased, and the locomotive was run this night by John Benjamin. The fireman in 1861, George Martin, was at this date an engineer himself, but asked and obtained the privilege of again acting as fireman on the train. The same conductor, E. D. Page, was on hand in that capacity. Superintendent Henry Nottingham, as before, had the complete management. The pilot engine, *Idaho*, which preceded the train by ten minutes, was run by engineer J. McGuire, and fireman Frank Keehen. Issac Morehead was the conductor and Superintendent Grant oversaw the op-

* Some Cleveland accounts state the locomotive was named, "*L. Case.*"

eration of the train.

When the train resumed its travels at Erie, some 95 miles of track lay ahead in obtaining Cleveland, Ohio, the next scheduled town to host an official viewing of the remains.

Over the next 40 minutes the last towns in Pennsylvania were passed; Mill Creek, Swanville, Fairview, where the train crossed Walnut Creek. Girard and Springfield Station all acknowledged the passing of the train. At about 3:30 a.m. on April 28th the fourth state of seven on the route was exited in pine forests just a few miles from the shores of Lake Erie.

ENTERING OHIO

On April 24, General McCullum sent a telegram to Colonel Anson Stager from Albany, New York. "The remains of the late President will be exposed to the public in Cleveland." It was about to become reality as the train entered the Buckeye State. At the state-line the train needed only cover 70 additional miles to reach Cleveland. The usual practices of a formal ceremony for reception of the remains and for the train at the Ohio - Pennsylvania line was but a brief ceremony at Conneaut, the first station in Ohio.

Conneaut, a considerable lake port, was reached at 3:47 a.m. and the train was welcomed by a large crowd on the platform. A brief memorial ceremony was conducted, possibly wood and water may have been taken while the trains were here. A meet was scheduled with eastbound Fast Freight No. 3 at this station. The freight train was held in the siding while the funeral train was given full rights on the main line.

Kingsville, seven miles west, was slowly passed with crowds on the station platform, the depot itself draped in emblems of mourning.

The train reached Ashtabula, just 13 miles from Conneaut, at about 5:00 a.m. running thirty minutes late. The firing of minute guns heralded the approach of the train. Local citizens had decorated the station in appropriate emblems of mourning as an expres-

In this illustration, depicted is a trackside scene repeated many times along the hundreds of miles along the route. Crowds lined the tracks with torches, lanterns and stood by bonfires in order to see the Funeral Train passing in the night. -- *Illustration by Author*

TIME TABLE

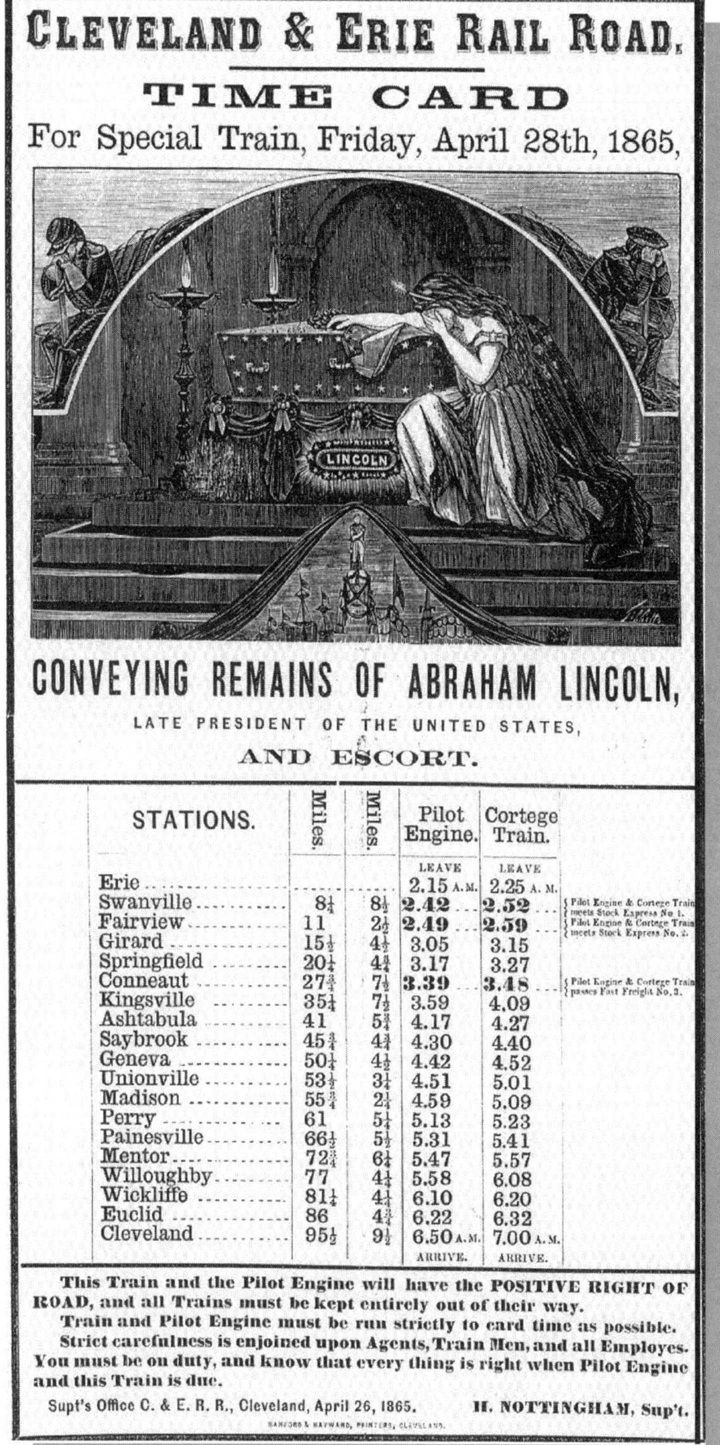

CLEVELAND & ERIE RAIL ROAD.

TIME CARD

For Special Train, Friday, April 28th, 1865,

CONVEYING REMAINS OF ABRAHAM LINCOLN,

LATE PRESIDENT OF THE UNITED STATES,

AND ESCORT.

STATIONS.	Miles.	Miles.	Pilot Engine.	Cortege Train.	
			LEAVE	LEAVE	
Erie			2.15 A. M.	2.25 A. M.	
Swanville	8¼	8½	**2.42**	**2.52**	Pilot Engine & Cortege Train meets Stock Express No 1.
Fairview	11	2½	**2.49**	**2.59**	Pilot Engine & Cortege Train meets Stock Express No. 2.
Girard	15½	4½	3.05	3.15	
Springfield	20¼	4¾	3.17	3.27	
Conneaut	27¾	7½	**3.39**	**3.48**	Pilot Engine & Cortege Train passes Fast Freight No. 3.
Kingsville	35¼	7½	3.59	4.09	
Ashtabula	41	5¾	4.17	4.27	
Saybrook	45¾	4¾	4.30	4.40	
Geneva	50¼	4½	4.42	4.52	
Unionville	53½	3¼	4.51	5.01	
Madison	55¾	2¼	4.59	5.09	
Perry	61	5¼	5.13	5.23	
Painesville	66½	5½	5.31	5.41	
Mentor	72¾	6¼	5.47	5.57	
Willoughby	77	4¼	5.58	6.08	
Wickliffe	81¼	4¼	6.10	6.20	
Euclid	86	4¾	6.22	6.32	
Cleveland	95½	9½	6.50 A. M.	7.00 A. M.	
			ARRIVE.	ARRIVE.	

This Train and the Pilot Engine will have the POSITIVE RIGHT OF ROAD, and all Trains must be kept entirely out of their way.

Train and Pilot Engine must be run strictly to card time as possible.

Strict carefulness is enjoined upon Agents, Train Men, and all Employes. You must be on duty, and know that every thing is right when Pilot Engine and this Train is due.

Supt's Office C. & E. R. R., Cleveland, April 26, 1865. **H. NOTTINGHAM, Sup't.**

SANFORD & HAYWARD, PRINTERS, CLEVELAND.

sion of sorrow to the deceased President. The train passed under a large flag formed to shape an arch, then stopped where a brief memorial ceremony was held with the presentation of appropriate floral tributes. An estimated 2,000 people were at the station to witness the train as the first streaks of gray awakened the morning sky in Ohio.

At the little towns along the shoreline of Lake Erie, the depots were draped in emblems of mourning as thousands of people gathered in the same manner as had been witnessed over the 700 prior miles. Saybrook, Geneva, Unionville, Madison, and Perry Station, had crowds along the track to witness the passage of the train. It was reported men stood with their heads uncovered while ladies waved white handkerchiefs. The geography of the land changed in this area. Here the pine forests that had framed the surrounding lands was left behind as the area broke into an agricultural region. The land now becoming spotted with hardwood trees. At Painesville, 29 miles out, the Grand River was crossed. Just a few miles away, at Kirtland, was the site of the first western Mormon Temple. Mentor, and Reynolds were passed as the gray light of day broke over northern Ohio.

The train passed slowly through Willoughby, at 6:08 a.m., 21 miles from Cleveland. Hundreds of people lined the margins of the tracks to witness the train. A number of aged gentlemen were noted at trackside, leaning on their staffs, heads uncovered in respect to the fallen President. The Chagrin River was crossed here, the tracks being some two to three miles inland from the shore of Lake Erie.

At 6:20 a.m., the train stopped at Wickliffe, fourteen miles east of Cleveland. The official reception committee of twenty select people for the Ohio Reception Committee boarded the train. They included Ohio Governor John Brough, and staff.

Nine miles from Cleveland, at Euclid, a final stop was made to take on additional citizens for the reception committee. General Joseph Hooker and staff entered here. He was in charge of the Army of the Northern Ohio. Hooker had military charge of the train for the balance of the trip to Springfield, Illinois. Here the tracks dropped into the valley on the approach to Cleveland. The brakemen were probably busy keeping the train under control. Three miles east of Cleveland, the tracks swung toward the shores of Lake Erie, and remained there until the train had entered the Union Depot.

As the train came in the Lake Shore track, newspapers reported a very beautiful incident took place. "Miss Fields, of Wilson Street, had erected an arch of evergreens on the bank of the Lake near the track, and as the train passed appeared in the arch as the Goddess of Liberty in mourning. The sight as it passed down the Lake Shore track was impressive, and was witnessed by a great crowd of people on the bank."

Dr. Adonis writing for the *Chicago Tribune* observed of the train's arrival: "It is indisputably asserted that as the cars were coming in from Buffalo this morning a line of people five miles long was voluntarily formed

In this illustration, depicted is the removal of Lincoln's coffin from the *United States*. Becaus e of the length of the coffin, it required the officers car be uncoupled and moved back so the coffin could be carried through the door and handed to the pallbearers on the ground. -- *Illustration by Author*

from that part of the city [along the tracks] away out beyond the suburbs, so eager were they to get a gaze at the funeral cortege and especially at the car which enveloped the dust of the fallen."

At 7:00 a.m., the funeral train pulled to a stop in the great shed of the Cleveland Union Depot. On reaching the depot, locomotive Number 40, named *Despatch*, of the Cleveland and Pittsburgh Railroad, tastefully draped in emblems of mourning, coupled onto the rear of the train, took it in its reversed position and drew it to the Euclid Street Station, on the east side of Cleveland, arriving there about 7:20 a.m. As the train moved up, a national salute of thirty-six guns was fired.

On arriving at the Euclid Street Depot, it was greeted by throngs of people. The train was stopped so that the funeral car lay nearly across the road. The depot was heavily draped with mourning and flags. A draped flag hung from a line stretched directly across the road.

The crowd around the station was exceedingly large, but owing to the excellent police arrangements and the orderly character of the people, there was no trouble or confusion. The large space reserved was kept perfectly clear. When the coffin was brought from the car, so great was the anxiety of the people to see it, that a number of them, mostly women, got under the train and remained there until warned off by the police to save their lives.

The Veteran Reserve Guard of Escort disembarked and were immediately drawn up around the funeral car, eight of them being ready to carry the coffin, while the others formed in line on either side with drawn swords presented as the sentinels. The Guard of Honor stood on one side, and Governor Brough and staff, with the leading members of the Committees and the Pallbearers, on the other. The Camp Chase Band stood in front of the depot, and the hearse was drawn up a few yards distant.

The Chief Marshal, Col. James Barnett, and his valuable assistants, Col. J. P. Ross, Silas Merchant, Col. O. H. Payne, Amos Townsend, George H. Burt, Maj. W. P. Edgarton, Major S. Race, and Capt. B. L. Spangler, formed and conducted the long procession with the most perfect order. There was no confusion, no noise, and all the different societies and bodies fell into the places in the procession allotted to them on time and with the precision of clockwork.

The hearse was surmounted with large black and white plumes, and the national colors draped. The hangings were of black velvet, with heavy silver fringe and silver tassels fastened up with crepe rosettes, each with a silver star in the centre. A beautiful wreath of flowers hung at the head of the hearse, and the bed on which the coffin was to rest was strewn thickly with white blossoms.

At a signal, the band played a solemn dirge, and the coffin was taken out of the car and borne to the hearse on the shoulders of the Veteran Reserve Guard of Escort, the sentinel guards marching by its side with drawn swords, attended by the pallbearers and Guard of Honor. On the head of the coffin was a cross of white flowers, and a wreath of similar flowers at the foot.

The hearse, surrounded by the Veteran Reserve Guard, with the Pallbearers on either side, the Guard of Honor, mounted, following, and preceded by the band playing a dirge, passed up Wilson Avenue. The 29th Ohio National Guard was drawn up in line, and saluted the cortege as it passed. The Civic Guard of Honor met the hearse on Prospect Street, and saluted it, when the cortege turned, and went back to Euclid Street, where the procession was formed according to the program.

The scene when the procession started was very solemn. A slight rain fell, dripping like tears on the remains of the good man in whose honor the crowd had gathered, but not enough to be heeded by the people assembled. The street was lined with a continuous wall of people, and the yards and houses were also crowded.

After the procession started from the depot, it moved slowly and solemnly, without stop or detention, until it reached the Square. As it neared the western end of Euclid Street, the number of people began to increase until the sidewalks and far into the street became a solid mass; but there was no noise or confusion in the crowd that lined the streets on the line of march. All seemed impressed with the deep solemnity of the occasion.

The Courthouse, City Council Hall, the Government Building, and other places around the Square near the pavilion in which the remains reposed during the day, were all tastefully and appropriately dressed in mourning.

There were reportedly over 6,000 people in the procession of organized societies. After the main procession passed a given point, the citizens fell in behind and followed it to the pavilion, in the same good order as characterized the proceedings.

There was a considerable crush at the entrance gate on Superior Street, but no boisterous actions. The admirable arrangements of the committee for preserving order in the neighborhood of the building where the remains were to be placed prevented confusion. The procession entered the enclosure by the East gate, and after the removal of the body to the building, filed out at the Rockwell Street gate.

A salute was fired on the arrival of the remains at the Square, and another at sunset. Half-hour guns were also fired during the day by the 8th Independent Battery, Ohio National Guard. Five large and beautiful flags, draped in mourning, drooped wet from the staff in the park all day.

The 29th Ohio National Guard occupied positions inside the enclosure, and were stationed as sentinels at numerous points. The hearse was driven up to the south side of the pavilion, and the coffin borne on the shoulders of Veteran Reserve Guard of Escort to the place prepared for it under the canopy. As the body passed the band played a dirge. As soon as the coffin was placed on the dais, a committee of ladies advanced and placed on it a number of floral ornaments and evergreens wreathed in the forms of crosses and coronas.

The embalmer and undertaker opened the coffin and looked over the remains. The Right Reverend Charles Pettit McIlvaine, Bishop of the Diocese of Ohio, advanced to the coffin and read from the Burial Service of the Episcopal Church:

"I am the resurrection and the life, saith the Lord; he that believeth in me, though he were dead, yet shall he live; and whosoever livith and believeth in me shall never die.

"We brought nothing into the world, and it is certain we can carry nothing out. The Lord gave, and the Lord hath taken away; blessed be the name of the Lord.

"Man that is born of a woman, hath but a short time to live, and is full of misery. He cometh up, and is cut down, like a flower; he fleeth as it were a shadow and never continueth in one stay.

"In the midst of life we are in death; of whom may we seek for succor, but of thee, 0 Lord, who for our sins art justly displeased?"

The passages would be repeated as harmonized vocal chants at Indianapolis two days later. The Bishop then offered an eloquent prayer, in which he prayed that this great affliction may be of good to the people. He prayed for blessing on the family of the deceased, and for health and blessing on Secretary Seward, whom the assassin tried, but failed to destroy. For President Johnson he asked that he might be led to follow the great example set him by his illustrious predecessor.

The religious services being concluded, the procession filed through the Pavilion, passing along both aisles. Many were affected to tears. The invalid soldiers from the military hospital, were drawn up inside the inclosure previous to the arrival of the procession. Many a bronzed veteran's eyes were wet as he gazed upon him who had laid down his life for his country. After the procession had passed through, the public was admitted, and thousands poured in a steady stream, without haste or confusion.

The heavy rain which continued to fall from the start of the procession seemed to have no effect in damping the determination of the people to take a last look at the remains of their beloved President.

After the funeral procession departed Euclid Street Station, the train was returned to the shelter of the Cleveland Union Station, on the lake front. While here the cars were cleaned and serviced. The coaches were switched out in preparation for the next leg of the journey. If the official symbols of mourning draping the cars were changed, it occurred while under the shelter of the station shed. The coffin of Willie was guarded and there are indications that selected individuals may have been granted permission to enter the car while the train was in waiting. Meanwhile, a very tired funeral escort sought the comforts of sleep at the Governor's home and Weddell House. General Townsend later recounted how a stranger had offered the use of his hotel room to the General, who reported he had to catch up on his sleep after the prior 15 hours.

PREPARATIONS AT CLEVELAND

When it was learned the funeral cortege would stop in Cleveland, a local committee for arrangements was formed to rapidly set forth a plan. The Local Committee on Location of Remains found no room or building, in which to place the remains suitable to accommodate the vast crowds that would be present to take the last look at their late President.

The Cleveland Committee decided to construct a Reception Building or funeral structure in the east side of the park near downtown. The Committee of Arrangements authorized the erection, and the building. Architects J. M. Blackburn and Koehler undertook immediate design, upon presenting it. Immediate approval was given. Work was commenced on Monday, April 24, with Mr. Blackburn personally superintending the workmen. The work was almost continuous, and late on Thursday night April 27, was completed, with Mr. F. R. Elliot providing the proper floral and detail gestures to the posts. This was the only location along the route to construct a reception building exclusively for repose of the remains and public viewing.

It was an oblong structure, open sided, twenty-four by thirty-six feet, and fourteen feet high. The roof was pagoda shaped, and over the centre of the main roof was a second roof, raised about four feet, and forming a canopy over the catafalque. The sides and ends of the building were open above the low breastwork, which was covered with black cloth. The roof was supported by pillars shrouded in black and white, and the open sides were elegantly draped with festoons of white and black, looped up with rosettes of white and black. The roof was of white canvas, the ribs supporting it being shrouded in black.

The ends of the building were heavily draped with black cloth. Over each end of the building was a large golden eagle with the national shield. The sides supporting the second roof were covered with black cloth on the outside, on which were fastened beautiful evergreen wreaths and floral devices. At the east end of the building, where the procession entered, were six splendid regimental flags of silk. Eight immense plumes of black crepe surmounted the sides of the building. Slender flag poles bearing crepe streamers and mourning flags were arranged along the top of the building. Evergreen and floral wreaths were used to loop up the drapery and crown the capitals of the columns. Directly over the upper roof was a streamer stretched between two flag poles, bearing the inscription from Horace: "Extinctus amabitur idem" (Dead, he will be loved the same).

The inside of the building was in admirable keeping with the exterior decorations. Heavy drapery of black cloth, festoons of evergreen, and floral wreaths and bouquets completely shrouded the pillars and roof. In the center was the catafalque, a raised dais, twelve feet long, four feet wide, and about two feet high to the underside of the coffin. The floor and sides of the dais were covered with black cloth and velvet. The floor was so inclined that on entering the building the visitors were able at once to see the remains and keep them in sight until nearly leaving the building. From the corners of the dais sprang four slender columns supporting a canopy draped in black cloth with silver fringe. The corners of the canopy hung with silver tassels. The capitals of the pillars were wreathed with flowers. At the head and foot of the dais were several seats covered with black cloth, designed for the use of the Guard of Honor.

The floor of the building was covered with thick matting, so as to deaden every sound. The building was well lit with gas lamps at night. The people entered from the east and passed through the broad passages on each side of the dais. They exited out on the west side.

Colonel H. L. Robinson, the advance representative for the train stated, "[he] has seen nothing equal to it in beauty and taste, in any of the cities in which the remains have been exposed." Cleveland was the only place on the route of the funeral cortege where a special building had been erected for the reception of the remains.

MOURNERS JOURNEY TO CLEVELAND

While rapid construction of the Pavilion was under way, a route for the funeral procession had to be finalized. A plan had been considered up through April 24, to off-load the train at the Union Depot on the lake front and travel the short distance to the Public Square. After reconsidering the route and the dramatic outpourings elsewhere, it was decided to move the train to the east side of Cleveland, off-load there and greatly extend the length of the funeral procession route along Euclid Street.

Much of the region was planning a journey to Cleveland. A delegation of two hundred came from Meadville, Pennsylvania, under the marshalship of Capt. Derrickson. They wore a large badge upon the lapel of the coat with the word "Meadville." A delegation of about five hundred came from Detroit, to do honor to the memory of the President. Two bands, the Detroit City and the Light Guard, escorted them. Other mourners came aboard trains and lake ships. Delegations from western Pennsylvania, and even an advance delegation from Chicago, were heading for Cleveland.

Every train that arrived on the railroads during April 27, was filled; all the hotels were crowded, and hundreds of persons were unable to procure even a sleeping place upon the floor.

Sailing ships arrived at portside bringing delegations from Michigan and Canada. Mourners were greeted with the symbols of mourning. Men, women and children of all classes and conditions, wore some mourning badge or symbol of sorrow. Toward evening of Thursday the citizens on Superior, Euclid, Prospect, Bank and other streets, around the Public Square, commenced to drape their dwellings and places of business.

Along the line designated for the passing of the procession, the hanging of emblems of mourning was very elaborate, tasteful, and almost universal.

At daybreak on Friday morning, the citizens were startled from their slumbers by a salute of artillery, and in a very short time the whole city was astir. By 6:00 a.m. the streets were crowded with people, some winding their way down to the Union Depot, to the park, or to other advantageous positions on the line of march. Throngs of people started for the Euclid Street Depot, from which the procession was to start. Thousands of people from the country and from other cities had arrived during the preceding days, and all night the streets had been crowded. The weather was gloomy and threatened rain, and by the time the train arrived the rain began to fall steadily but not heavily.

The city could not have looked better, in spite of the rain, as the dust was laid, and the partly opened foliage, with its delicate green tint, lent beauty to the elegant dwellings and grounds along the avenues through which the procession was to pass.

The importance and solemnity of the occasion was evidently appreciated by every one. Dense crowds lined the streets from the Euclid Street Depot to the Public Square. The heavily draped buildings, the uniform stillness and the decorum of the immense gathering of people, testified to the respect and love borne to the deceased by the people of Cleveland and the surrounding country.

As the procession moved down the streets toward the reception building, the immense crowds who came to witness the solemn events nearly blocked every street. A boisterous mirth of unnecessary noise came as a rush for the entrance through the guard on Superior Street. There were no reported mishaps, "...except for the fainting of a couple of delicately constituted ladies."

THE PUBLIC IS ADMITTED

It was at this site, on April 14th in Cleveland, where a massive celebration was conducted and thanks given for the ending of the Civil War. Now, 14 days later, on this exact spot lay the remains of the assassinated president. In the crowds were thousands of people who had been there two weeks earlier celebrating when the first telegraph arrived with the horrible news that the President had been shot and was not expected to survive.

All day long an endless procession of mourners stood in the rain for the privilege of marching past the coffin. The immense crowds were hourly added to by the trains and steamers arriving from different points.

The crowds seeking admission were formed into a column four deep. The line separated into two columns, each line of two abreast, and marched through on either side of the catafalque, passing along.

The military guard of officers stood at the foot of the coffin and at the corners. One of the guard of honor or general officers stood or sat at the head of the coffin. The civic guard of honor were arranged along the sides of the building, to pass the visitors through in proper order. A squad of the 29th Ohio National Guard was stationed at different points in the enclosure.

The most reverent silence and deep feelings were exhibited by all who passed through. The passageways being ample, there were abundant facilities for obtaining a good view of the remains. The position of the coffin was such that the spectator got a close full view. According to newspaper accounts, the features of Lincoln were but slightly changed from the appearance they bore when exposed in the Capitol at Washington. Other papers disagreed stating that Lincoln's face was haggard, and much discolored. The *Cleveland Daily Leader* offered, "... the process of decay had defied the art of the embalmer, and that indeed death had set its everlasting seal upon once benign and thoughtful countenance, but so short a time since radiant with homely humor, and joyful in the realization of an early return of the Nation to peace and Union."

During the afternoon, several bands from the region and those belonging to Cleveland, were stationed on the balconies of the hotels and other prominent buildings, near the Public Square. They played dirges, adding to the solemnity and impressiveness of the occasion.

At different times during the day an

Public Sqaure at Cleveland, Ohio. In the center of the photo is the reception building, constructed just for the memorial. The hearse and teams of white horses are visible on the right. Lincoln's remains lay in state here on April 28, 1865.- *Cleveland Public Library collection*

accurate count of those passing through was taken. It was reported that in the first four hours the rate was nine thousand per hour; then it fell to between seven and eight thousand, and increased in the evening. When night fell, and the lamps were lit. The crowds increased rather than diminished. Until evening the visitors were nearly all from the surrounding region. The city people held back on their visiting to give those a chance who would have to leave by the evening trains. So vast were the crowds, and anxious to gratify their desires to pay a last act of homage to the dead, they were willing to endure standing in long lines in the rain and mud, a most uncomfortable situation. The elements with all their adversity, did not seem to abate the desire or determination of the mourners. Wet, tired and cold, they did not seem to mind standing in the rain or stepping through the mud. At 10:00 p.m., when the gates were shut, more than one hundred thousand people had visited the remains.

THE FLORALS

One of the most distinguishing expressions of sympathy noted along the miles of track were the ongoing offerings of flowers. Cut flowers were strewn on the tracks at many places. Others offered elaborate floral arrangements in the form of wreaths, shields, crosses and floral blankets. In the history of American funerals, it is doubtful whether florals have ever been offered to the measure witnessed with the passing of the Lincoln Funeral Train. Reporters started noting the massive quantity of florals in the funeral car at the time the train was passing through northern New Jersey.

By the time the train reached Cleveland, on the eighth day, florals were very evident in the memorial acknowledgments and being offered en masse by ordinary citizens.[1]

Cleveland distinguished itself in two ways during the stay of the train there. The most distinguishing feature of the ceremonies and testimonials of the day was the

[1]Distinguished Poet, Walt Whitman wrote an exceptional poem, *"When Lilacs Last in the Dooryard Bloom'd"* and in it he expressed his sorrows and his gestures of acknowledgement to Lincoln with cuts of blooming lilacs. General Townsend makes two acknowledgements of other simple floral offerings in his memoirs, one north of Columbus and a second at Columbus. The importance and funeral ritual of floral offerings as immortelles was clearly established in America with the Lincoln Funeral Train.

Locomotive *Nashville*, used to pull the Lincoln funeral train from Cleveland to Columbus, Ohio. This view was taken at the Cleveland, Columbus and Cincinnati Railroad roundhouse, probably on the afternoon of April 28, 1865. The train was kept inside Cleveland Union Station during the Cleveland ceremonies. At the appropriate departure time the train was pulled down to Vineyard Street Station where the escort and Lincoln's coffin was loaded for departure. -- *Library of Congress*

profusion and beauty of the floral decorations and floral offerings. Besides the great number of flowers woven into the decorations of the Pavilion, a large number of beautiful floral immortelles were lain on the coffin. Among them were the floral offerings made by the ladies of the Soldiers' Aid Society of Northern Ohio, consisting of an anchor of white roses, azaleas, and other white flowers. Each fluke of the anchor was made of magnificent calla; a cross of beautiful red blossoms; and a wreath of blue flowers. The ladies decided to place the anchor in charge of Lieutenant-Colonel Simpson, U. S. Engineers, for presentation to Captain Stephen Champlin, one of the survivors of the Battle of Lake Erie. The cross and wreath accompanied the remains from Cleveland. Some accounts state that at various intervals the coffin was covered with fresh flowers. At Columbus, similar exercises in floral tributes were made, and High Street was covered with flowers.*

THE FORMAL INVITATION ON THE PART OF THE CITY OF CHICAGO

Traveling to Cleveland to meet the train was Charles L. Wilson, Editor of the *Chicago Journal*, and Chairman of the Committee of One Hundred Citizens appointed by the Chicago City Council to receive the remains for the City of Chicago, at Michigan City, Indiana, on May 1st.

By invitation of Ohio Governor John Brough, Mr. Wilson and the Illinois Delegation on the train plus the general officers of the escort paid him a visit at his Cleveland residence. Mr. Wilson formally extended the hospitalities of the City of Chicago to the funeral escort. He assured the delegates that at least 25,000 people had pledged to participate in the funeral procession at Chicago.

* There is some opinion the increased presence of florals, especially west of Buffalo, was to mask some apparent odor that may have been starting to emanate from the remains. There is no discovered evidence to lead to a conclusion. There is also some indication the train may have taken ice at certain stops, perhaps to keep the remains cold, and extend preservation? No clear evidence has been discovered.

Locomotive *Nashville*, used to pull the Lincoln funeral train from Cleveland to Columbus, Ohio. This view was taken at entrance to Cleveland Union Station, probably on the afternoon of April 28, 1865. The train was kept inside the massive train shed during the Cleveland ceremonies. At the appropriate departure time the train was pulled down to Vineyard Street Station where the escort and Lincoln's coffin was loaded for departure. -- *Library of Congress*

TRAVEL LOG

April 27 - 28, 1865 183 miles

VIA Buffalo & State Line Railroad	
Cleveland & Erie Railroad	
Cleveland & Pittsburgh RR	
Buffalo, New York DEPART	10:00 a.m.
New Hamburgh (Hamburg)	10:50 p.m.
North Evans	
Lake View	
18 Mile Creek	
Derby	
Evans Centre	
Angola	11:13 p.m.
Farnham	
Irving	
Silver Creek	11:45 p.m.
Sheridan Station (Lackawanna)	
Dunkirk	12:10 a.m.
Van Buren	
Salem	
Brockton	
Portland	12:35 a.m.
Westfield*	1:00 a.m. fuel
Ripley Crossing	1:24 a.m.
Quincy	
State Line	1:32 a.m.
North East, Pa	1:47 a.m.
Harbor Creek	2:05 a.m.
Erie Cleveland & Erie RR	2:50 a.m.
Mill Creek	
Swanville	
Fairview	
Girard	
Springfield	3:27 a.m.
Conneaut, Ohio	3:47 a.m.
Amboy	
Kingsville	
Ashtabula	4:27 a.m.
Saybrook	
Geneva	4:52 a.m.
Unionville	
Madison	5:09 a.m.
Perry	
Lane	
Painesville	5:41 a.m.
Heisley	
Mentor	
Reynolds	
Willoughby	6:08 a.m.
Rushroad	
Wickliffe*	6:20 a.m.
Euclid	6:32 a.m.
Noble	
Nottingham	
Collinwood	
Coits	
Glenville	

Cleveland ARR 7:00 AM at Cleveland Union Depot. Move via reverse move over Cleveland & Pittsburgh Railroad to: Euclid Street Station

APRIL 28 - 29, 1865
CLEVELAND - COLUMBUS

During the day, while the funeral train was at Cleveland Union Station, it received cars of the Cleveland, Columbus & Cincinnati Railroad, in addition to the sleeping cars of the New York Central Railroad, going through to Indianapolis. The highly decorated locomotive *Nashville* was pulled from the round house for official photographs during a brief appearance of the sun.

Around 10:00 p.m., the Sentinel Guard boarded the empty train. It was moved about a half mile south to the Vineyard Street Station of the C C & C Railroad to await the arrival of the funeral procession.

At 10:00 p.m. the coffin was closed. A stream of people passed through the Pavilion until the very last moment. At 10:30 p.m., the coffin, covered with florals, was taken from the Pavilion on the shoulders of the Veteran Reserve Guard of Escort and placed in the hearse, preparatory to being conveyed to the Funeral Train.

About the time the remains were being removed from the Pavilion the heavens broke and rain poured down in torrents. The streets along the whole length of the line of march were crowded with people soaked by the storm.

Leaving the reception building the es-

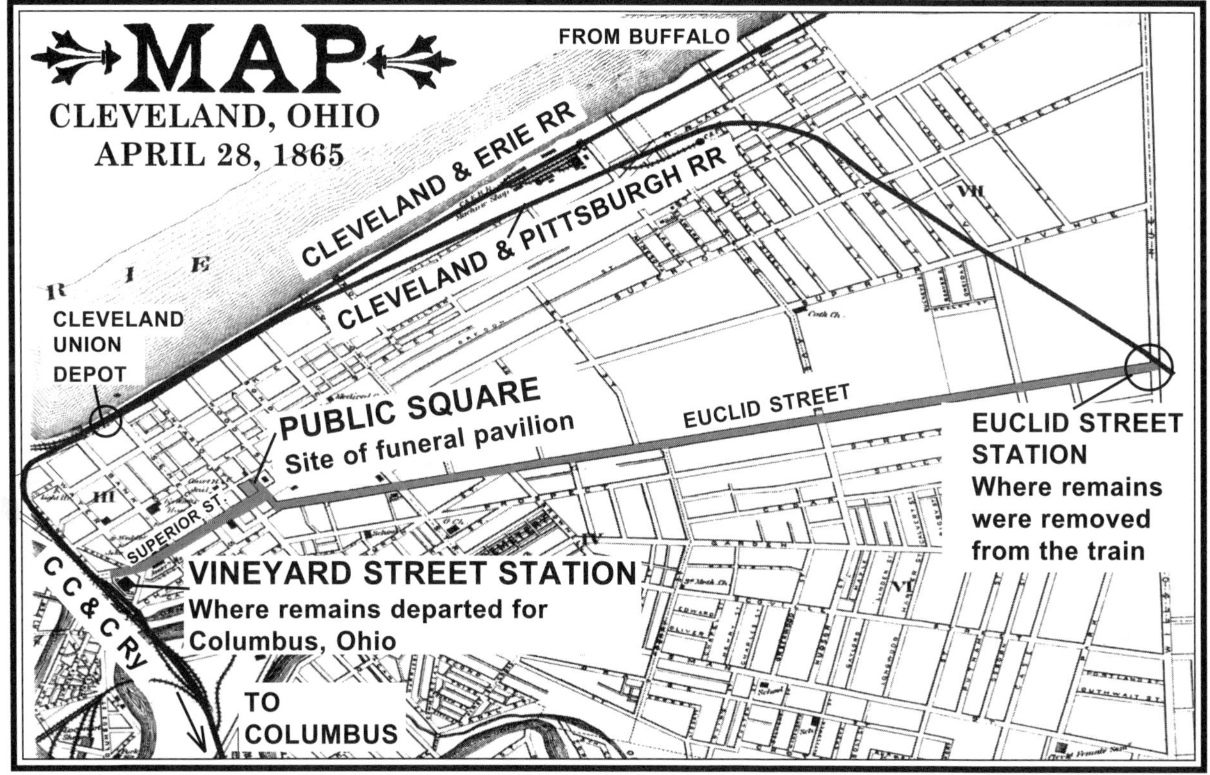

Cleveland, Ohio, also saw funeral train arrive on rail lines near the public square. It stopped at the Union station, then was pulled backwards on the Cleveland & Pittsburgh Railroad to Euclid Avenue station. An elaborate parade was planned to the public square, near the Union Station. When the funeral train left Cleveland, the body was taken a few blocks to the Cleveland, Columbus and Cincinnati Railway station near the Cuyahoga River to resume it journey to Columbus. -- 1868 Ohio Atlas

TIME TABLE

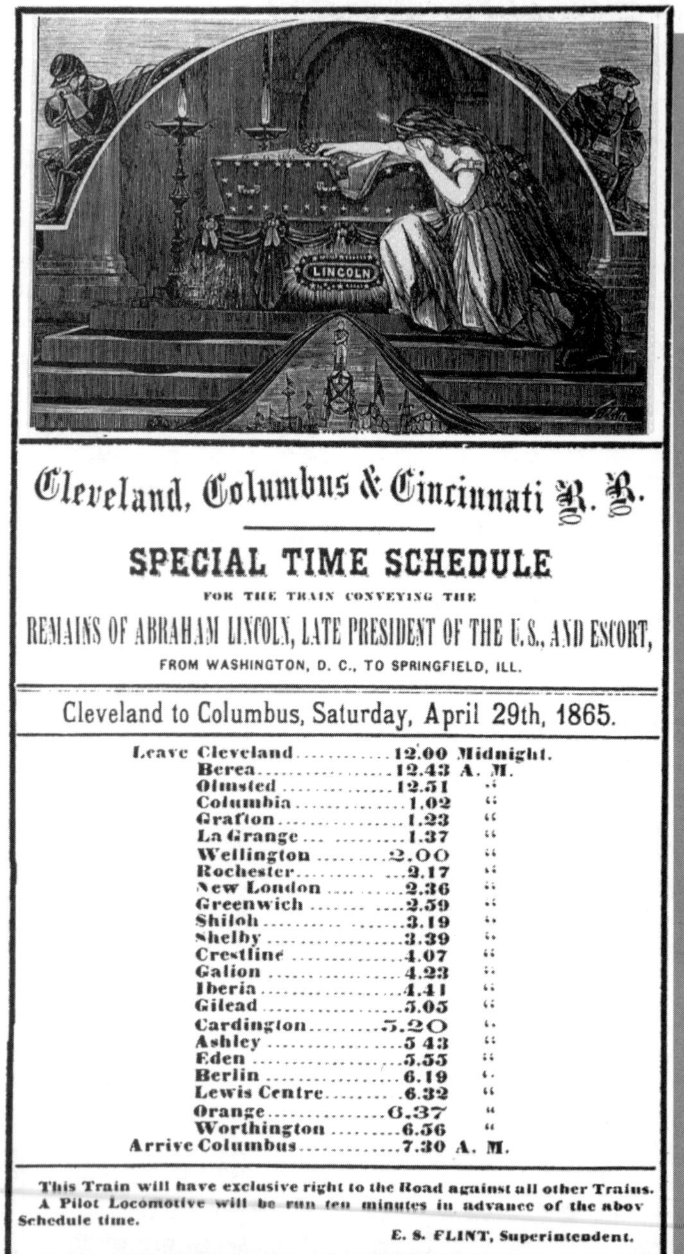

Cleveland, Columbus & Cincinnati R. R.

SPECIAL TIME SCHEDULE

FOR THE TRAIN CONVEYING THE

REMAINS OF ABRAHAM LINCOLN, LATE PRESIDENT OF THE U. S., AND ESCORT,

FROM WASHINGTON, D. C., TO SPRINGFIELD, ILL.

Cleveland to Columbus, Saturday, April 29th, 1865.

Leave	Cleveland	12.00	Midnight.
	Berea	12.43	A. M.
	Olmsted	12.51	"
	Columbia	1.02	"
	Grafton	1.23	"
	La Grange	1.37	"
	Wellington	2.00	"
	Rochester	2.17	"
	New London	2.36	"
	Greenwich	2.59	"
	Shiloh	3.19	"
	Shelby	3.39	"
	Crestline	4.07	"
	Galion	4.23	"
	Iberia	4.41	"
	Gilead	5.05	"
	Cardington	5.20	"
	Ashley	5 43	"
	Eden	5.55	"
	Berlin	6.19	"
	Lewis Centre	6.32	"
	Orange	6.37	"
	Worthington	6.56	"
Arrive	Columbus	7.30	A. M.

This Train will have exclusive right to the Road against all other Trains.

A Pilot Locomotive will be run ten minutes in advance of the abov Schedule time.

E. S. FLINT, Superintendent.

cort procession was lead by a platoon of Cleveland policemen carrying lanterns, followed by the Detroit City Band and the 29th Regiment Ohio National Guard, the General Committee of Arrangements; the Military Guard of Honor in carriages; the Civic Guard of Honor bearing lanterns then the funeral hearse lead by four white horses; the Father Mathew Temperance Society; the Eureka Lodge of Masons, and large numbers of men and women who joined them. The elaborate procession moved just a few blocks down Superior Street to the station. Heavy rain continued falling as the cortege with three bands playing a dirge, moved down Vineyard Street, at the foot of which the funeral train had been placed. The Veteran Reserve Guard of Escort shouldered the coffin and placed it in the funeral car as the official escort boarded the cars. Precisely at midnight the train started for Columbus, under the direction of Superintendent E. S. Flint, with Charles Gale as Conductor.

The Funeral Train was preceded, between Cleveland and Columbus, by the pilot engine, *Louisville*, in charge of Assistant Superintendent Blee and Master Mechanic W. F. Smith, with E. Van Camp as the Engineer and C. Van Camp as the Fireman. The engine of the Funeral Train was the *Nashville*, with George West as Engineer and Peter Hugo as Fireman. Mr. T. J. Higgins, the Superintendent of Telegraph, accompanied the train with necessary telegraph instruments, to be used in case of an accident. General McCullum, who had temporary military possession of all the railroads from Washington to Springfield, had an efficient aid in Captain J. P. Dukehart, of the Baltimore and Ohio Railroad, who carried out his superior's orders, as to the time of starting with a fidelity which commanded general admiration.

Departing Cleveland and the Cuyahoga River Valley, the first seven miles to the west, was an uphill struggle for the train, until it crested near Rockport. Berea, just 12 miles west of Cleveland was reached at 12:43 a.m. A scheduled stop and a memorial service was conducted as heavy rains continued to fall. Here the railroad crossed the East Branch of the Rocky River over a beautiful stone arch bridge, with a falls just below the bridge.

Olmstead, on the Rocky River also had a stone arch bridge to carry the tracks away from Lake Erie and toward the heart of Ohio.

Crowds of people endured all the harshness of spring weather, and the downpour of rain at the small stations of Columbia, Grafton and LaGrange to demonstrate their reverent respects and personal tributes to the fallen President.

Wellington, a scheduled memorial stop 36 miles from Cleveland, and 99 miles from Columbus, was heralded with the whistle of the approaching train at 2:00 a.m. This stop may have been necessary to replenish fuel and water consumed by the locomotive during the climb out of the Cuyahoga River Valley.

Many people were gathered at the small stations of Rochester, New London, and Greenwich, even as the heavy rain continued to fall. The funeral cortege observed many bonfires continued to blaze and mourners stood with heads uncovered even in the worst weather conditions of the raw, cold, wet spring night. One reporter suggested the crowd looked "sad and thoughtful."

At Shelby Junction the train stopped briefly. Many in the crowd were carrying lanterns, instead of the torches seen on previous nights journey. They quickly gathered around the funeral car in hopes of a glimpse of the coffin. At Vernon many came to pay their respects, having been at the trackside for hours in the raw cold and rain of spring, and the dark of night. Their sole purpose perhaps was in saying thanks for a son returned from the war, or in some other personal expression of sorrow.

Vivid evidences of grief were manifested along the entire line between Cleveland and Columbus. The people gathered at the depots and at other points in throngs, eager to pay tribute to the memory of him whom they had loved. The rain fell in torrents from the time the train left Cleveland until it reached Crestline. The glow of bonfires, torches and lanterns was common. Principal buildings along the route were draped in emblems of mourning, bells tolled and rain soaked flags drooped at half-mast. People turned out en masse sorrowing. They stood in groups, heads uncovered and with saddened faces gazing with awe upon the train as it moved slowly by. Most of the coach and sleeping car lamps were extinguished, but the funeral car was fully lit. The yellow glow of the lamps streaming out the windows and piercing the night as it passed by. The funeral escort observed badges of mourning everywhere along the route. The blustery rain had not prevented residents from assembling along the way.

A fuel stop was made at the important junction city of Crestline at 4:07 a.m. This was the site for the shops and locomotive service facilities of the C C & C. During the stop a brief ceremony was held at the handsome depot. A large crowd was gathered to witness the train, many having come over the Pennsylvania Railroad west of Crestline, such as Lima, Ohio, and Fort Wayne, Indiana. Many came from the east over the Ohio and

Pennsylvania Railroad, for an opportunity to make their expressions of sorrow.

Galion, 78 miles from Cleveland, a small railroad junction town was passed at around 4:20 a.m. as the train moved deeper into Ohio. A large number of people gathered at the station, many holding lanterns. They stood with a quiet and reserved air as the cortege passed.

The small villages of Iberia (St. James) and Gilead (Edison) greeted the train as the colors of dawn broke over the train for the second day in Ohio. Cardington, a planned stop, saw an immense crowd of citizens assembled, estimated at over 3,000 mourners. Bells were tolled upon approach of the train, and minute guns were fired. The station was tastefully festooned with a large national flag draped with rosettes of crepe hanging from either end of the depot. In front and over the doors and windows was a white banner on which was inscribed "He sleeps in the blessings of the poor, whose fetters God commanded him to break." When the train stopped, the crowd flocked about it with reverential tread in hopes of catching some brief view of the coffin, then the train moved on.

Ashley was passed at 5:43 a.m. and as at many other villages vivid displays of respect and immortelles were exhibited. Sadness and mourning, deep and solemn, prevailed in every town and hamlet along the tracks. Crowds stood silent, in deep sympathy and merciful for the efforts of the President. The train did not pass through the college town of Delaware, on the cut-off, but rather over the main line a few miles to the east. The town was not included in the official timetable.

The passing miles presented a pitiful scene of uncomely and muddled gatherings of folks in wet clothes, standing about the margins of the railroad in the rain with bared heads, weeping. The scene was most sad. At every crossing the blaze of bonfires and torches illuminated the whole crowd, kneeling on the wet ground, or standing, their clergymen leading in prayers and hymns as the train slowly passed. It was the only way left to demonstrate their grief and show reverent respect and compassion for the departed President.

Passing through Eden at 6:00 a.m., reporters noted the skies had cleared. The morning sun shown near Delaware, south to Columbus.

Passing through Delaware County, the train was coming into the home region for many of Andrews Raiders.* John Reed Porter, who managed to escape the Confederate capture several times after the raid, was raised a few miles away.

Crowds stood at trackside through the small villages of Eden (Leonardsburg), Berlin, Lewis Center, Orange and Flint in a fresh morning sun, raising the spirits as the train passed.

At Worthington, passed at 6:56 a.m., lines of people had assembled on the station platform, men removing their hats as the train approached. Many were farmers who came to show reverence to the dead. South of Worthington, beside the track, about five miles above Columbus, stood an aged woman bare headed, her gray hairs disheveled, tears coursing down her furrowed cheeks, holding in her right hand a sable scarf and in her left a bouquet of wild flowers, which she stretched imploringly toward the funeral car, her most sincere tribute to the memory of the slain President.

AT THE CROSSING

Reflect on what the rural and small town crowds gathering at trackside might have witnessed. In many places, villages, and even at clusters of farm homes, people congregated for the respectful honor of glimpsing the passing of the Funeral Train. Accounts state that groups assembled at schools, churches and

*Anndrew's Raiders were 22 Union Army soldiers under the command of James Andrews. They were mainly from Ohio. On April 12, 1862, they were attempting to disrupt Confederate supply lines and burn rail bridges on the Western and Atlantic Railroad between Atlanta, Georgia to Chattanooga, Tennessee. After being discovered, an extended chase ensued using railroad locomotives. They Union men were captured by the Confederates soldiers, and some were hanged as spies. Their story soon became a legend.

even in town squares, then walked en masse to the local railroad depot, or to the nearest railroad crossing and waited, sometimes for long hours of a raw, chilly spring day or night. Sometimes they stood in the rain for the honor of being a witness to the first national funeral of a United States President.

For the group who assembled at their church, and walked to the railroad crossing, accounts of witnesses state that at the passing of the Funeral Train, such groups stood and sang hymns. Others knelt with heads bowed in prayer, led by a clergyman.

There were no paved roads, A large portion of the route was muddy, and people knelt in the mud in prayerful or silent contemplation. Many were soaked in the rain, but they stayed just the same. Bonfires were built to light the night and make the train visible. These also provided warmth for the gathered souls.

Perhaps this is the scene replayed at thousands of rail-road crossings during the passage of Lincoln's Funeral Train. -- *Electronic illustration composed by author*

Consider that a young family might have gathered at a rural crossing with neighbors to bare witness to the train, bundled in clothes to withstand the brisk weather of spring. The bonfires kept away the bone-chilling dampness of the rains. Perhaps they carried a small basket of food, and maybe a bible or other testament of their faith. If there was wood, a fire was made near the tracks as the children played, or complained about the dampness. Stopping their activity just long enough to watch the passing of a freight train or the passenger train, still hours in advance of the coming funeral train. At night, maybe the children were bundled into blankets in a wagon, and covered with a tarp to keep the rain away. A local soldier or deputy, posted to guard the crossing kept an eye on the people so no one was hurt or any trouble arise to possibly interrupt the train.

Then in the distance after long hours of waiting and small talk, came the sounds of shrill whistle and the constant pant of a nearing locomotive, not moving exceptionally fast. It was first visible as a plume of white smoke and exhaust steam in the distance. Looking down the tracks shimmered the golden glow of a dancing oval star of light. (If perhaps during the day, the distantly fuzzy form of a nearing locomotive, highly decorated in yet undefined ways.) Maybe the cold and rain were forgotten, then the locomotive approached, nearer, looming larger and larger, the sounds of flags and bunting flapping in the breeze. The locomotive bell sounded and the repeated screeching of the whistle piercing the air bringing a sudden silence over the gathered crowd. Suddenly the image prominently displayed on the front of the locomotive comes into focus; a portrait of the lamented dead president, framed in florals and evergreen.

As the drive rods of the passing locomotive slid up and down on the spoked wheels of the locomotive, people looked up and in their minds were suddenly burned the notion that in the next few minutes they would express and experience emotions that would never occur again. Then the Pilot Train was gone, in the coach sat people important to this moment in time, although most are not known to history. One might be aware of the odor of wood smoke lingering behind the train, and the noise of the constant patter of rain drops striking the ground, a bird in the distance or the crackle of the nearby bonfire. Then the whistle and exhaust of the first train disappears up the track, and a strange silence overcomes the crowd.

Down the line the distant sounds of a harder working locomotive seem to catch the attention of all. Everyone comes to a silent pause, standing huddled, looking in the direction of the sounds. Someone is on a roof top or in a tree, keenly straining to catch the first glimpse. Then he yells, "here it comes!" Maybe a clergyman is asking for all to join in a prayer, or a few ladies spontaneously starting the whisper of a hymn, and one by one, more voices joining. As history has indicated, some knelt and bowed their heads in prayer, right in the middle of a muddy road, or in a pasture, or at a small town railroad depot.

In the distance came the sounds of a different whistle and the constant pant of the nearing locomotive, working harder to pull several cars, not moving exceptionally fast, and maybe giving a whistle order to the brakemen for "brakes down" to respectfully pass the gathered crowd at a slower speed. The chill ceased to make itself felt in the new focus.

The Train was visible at a considerable distance as a plume of white smoke marked its coming. Then they saw the golden glow of a dancing oval of the distant headlight. (If perhaps during the day, the distantly fuzzy form of a nearing locomotive, highly decorated.) Everyone focused on one thing as the locomotive approached, nearer and nearer, looming larger and larger, the sounds of flags and bunting flapping in the breeze the locomotive bell was sounding and the repeated blasting of the whistle piercing the air could be heard as the sound of prayer or hymns rose from the gathered crowd. Suddenly the image prominently displayed on the front of the locomotive came into view, a portrait of the lamented dead president.

At many places people tossed cut flowers onto the tracks in front of the locomotive, marking the sacred path in floral tribute. At night many held torches creating the effect of a ribbon of flame to guide the way.

The flapping of the flags was noticed in those first moments as the drive rods of the passing locomotive slid up and down, pushing the spoked wheels of the locomotive ever onward. People looked up and in their minds were suddenly burned the image of men leaning out of the locomotive, then came each car decorated in emblems of mourning; yellow, blue or orange cars, with black crepe hung along the sides, and of faces in the windows, governors, senators, congressmen and generals; important men. The sound of wheels clicking over the joints of the rail was barely noticed. Some held small flags, draped with black ribbons, someone held a banner. Soldiers were drawn up at attention, perhaps tears streaming down their cheeks.

The menfolk at trackside removed their hats, and perhaps many bowed their heads as the funeral car came into view. Its chocolate color and black crepe drew the attention of all. For those on the ground, it was with the knowledge that the coffin of the deceased president was inside. Maybe one could get a glimpse of the Honor Guard standing over the coffin through the windows ... and then one last car passed by.

The train was slipping into the distance, and it could not be stopped, nor could the events of the moment be changed. A second pall of smoke drifted from the train as the exhausts picked up. Then the expressions of sorrow ended, the prayers were over and men took their families in arm and slowly started toward home, tears in their eyes, and sorrow in their hearts

No greater mercy could be shown by the silent majority who came to pay their respects. Now the train rolled ever closer to its destination.

THE NEW ROUTE

From Cleveland, Ohio, to Indianapolis, Indiana, the train passed over trackage new to any Lincoln rail journey and the funeral train. For the next 322 miles, the only thing common to the train was the two cities in which it would stop for day-long memorial services at Columbus and Indianapolis.

By the time the funeral train left Cleveland, it was quite apparent that a shortage of passenger coaches existed to meet the demands of moving the citizens to ceremonies in Ohio. Many special trains were planned for the Columbus stop, in order to facilitate the many who planned on attending the ceremonies there. Several Ohio newspapers had announced that a shortage of coaches existed. They said it might be the railroads could not run additional cars on their passenger trains, and few extra trains would be operated to Columbus.

The C C & C offered to run one train from Springfield to Columbus, if a minimum of 200 passengers could be obtained. The fare for the round trip was $3.00. This train did operate, departing Springfield about 5:30 a.m. on April 29, and arrived at Columbus via Delaware, Ohio, at 9:30 a.m., following the route of the funeral train from Delaware down to Union Station in Columbus.

The other railroads radiating out of Columbus also operated at least one extra train for mourners along their lines.

Trains had to be parked at Columbus wherever space allowed. The last trains from Cincinnati and Dayton, on the Columbus and Xenia Railroad unloaded at 6:00 a.m., and all other trains were held out until at least 8:00 a.m. to allow for the procession to move from the station to the Statehouse.

The special train's evening departure from Columbus was scheduled for no later than 6:00 p.m. to allow for the return of the escort and remains to the train. As dawn broke over the city, the towers, gable, offices, baggage rooms and lamps of the Union Depot displayed the symbols of mourning heavily draped. The nearby office of the Little Miami Railroad Company and the nearby Columbus & Indianapolis Central Station were also decorated in the respectful symbols of respect.

An immense crowd had been in Columbus most of the night, and every sleeping space was filled. By 6:00 a.m., they had gathered on High Street between the station and the State House in anticipation of the coming trains. At 7:15 a.m. the pilot train pulled into the Union Depot shed on High Street, amid the ringing of muffled bells.

Guards were stationed along the margins of the tracks to prevent the crowds from stepping onto the tracks. A hushed silence drew over the throngs of people as the whistle of the funeral train could be heard in the distance announcing its coming. At precisely 7:30 a.m. the train pulled through the great shed of the Union Station and stopped so that the funeral car lay nearly across High Street. An immense crowd of spectators was congregated in the immediate vicinity. Bands of music assembled with the military in procession, played solemn dirges while the coffin was taken from the car and laid in the hearse by eight Veteran Reserve Guard of Escort. The other Veteran Reserves marched by its side with drawn sabers, attended by the pallbearers and military guard of honor.

As soon as the procession was clear of the train, it pulled away from the station, being spotted near the C & I C roundhouse to the west, where an honor guard was established to protect the train and the remains of little Willie. Thousands visited the train throughout the day, and only a few privileged were allowed to enter. The day was clear as the ceremonies took place at the Statehouse. While viewing was under way, the train was serviced and prepared for its next journey of 188 miles. James Ovid Wellford Smith a mechanic in the roundhouse, was the second of Andrews Raiders to be in the area.

COLUMBUS, OHIO,
April 29, 1865

Hon. E. M. STANTON:
The funeral train has arrived here safely.

E. D. TOWNSEND,
Assistant Adjutant-General.

THE COLUMBUS MEMORIAL

An immense crowd of spectators was congregated in the vicinity of the depot. Bands of music played solemn dirges while the coffin was taken from the car and laid in the hearse by the Veteran Reserve Guard of Escort, the other Veteran Reserves marching by its side with drawn sabers, attended by the pall bearers and military guard of honor.

The procession formed according to the program, and was the most imposing and most impressive. The slow measured tread of the troops, the muffled drum, the dead march, the enshrouded colors, told their own tale of the solemn occasion on which they were passing in review before the assembled thousands.

The funeral procession moved promptly from the depot at 8:00 a.m., south on High Street to Broad, east on Broad to Fourth, south on Fourth to State, east on State to Seventh, south on Seventh to Town, west on Town to High, north on High to west front of the capitol.

A mounted cavalry force was stationed at all the intersections of High Street north of Town Street, for the purpose of preventing all vehicles from entering on High Street-that it must be kept clear during the movements of the procession.

The hearse was the center of attraction. All along the line of march it was preceded and followed by hundreds, striving to keep as near as possible to the somber structure.

Every window, housetop, balcony, and every inch of the sidewalk on either side of High Street was densely crowded with a mournful throng, assembled to pay homage. In all the enormous crowds a profound silence reigned. Conversation was carried on in whispers.

Along the entire line of march, dwelling houses, shops, stores, and other places of business, and all public buildings, were tastefully and solemnly decorated.

The columns at the west front of the Capitol were tastefully draped in spiral turns of mourning cloth from top to bottom. Immediately over the entrance (west front) was placed the inscription, "God Moves in a Mys-

This illustration at Columbus, Ohio, on the morning of April 29, 1865, depicts the reception processional turning east onto Broad Street from High Street. The soldiers to the front of the hearse are the 88th Ohio Volunteer Infantry. Behind the hearse are the carriages for the pallbearers'. The procession moved in five divisions. After several additional blocks, the procession came up in the background on High Street where the crowds pose. The coffin was carried into the Ohio State House for the seventh day of public viewing en route to Springfield.

terious Way," and over the cornice of the columns was placed a quotation from President Lincoln's last inaugural address: "With Malice toward none; with Charity for all." Each of the windows in the west front was heavily draped.

At about 9:00 a.m. the head of the procession arrived at the west entrance of Capitol Square. The 88th Ohio Volunteer Infantry acting as special escort, passed in immediately, forming lines in two ranks on each side of the passageway from the gate to the steps of the capitol. Slowly and solemnly the escort, headed by General Hooker and staff, and Governor Brough and staff, passed to the Capitol entrance, and reverently, the coffin was lowered from the shoulders of the Veteran Reserve Guard of Escort to the flowery bed of the catafalque awaiting it. The officers named, with their attendants, Major-General Hunter and staff, the General officers in charge of the corpse from Washington, General Wager Swayne, staff, and pall bearers.

Mrs. Hoffner, representing the Horticultural Society of Cincinnati, the only lady present, stepped softly forward and placed at the foot of the coffin an anchor composed of delicate white flowers and evergreen boughs, a wreath of the same upon the breast of the dead, and a cross at the head.

The Rotunda of the Capitol, was transformed into a gorgeous tomb. The column of light streaming down from the dome made distinct and impressive each feature of the solemn scene.

The entrance ways and the corresponding panels were uniformly draped with black cloth, falling in heavy folds from the arches to the floor. In the panels, the drapings were gathered to the sides equidistant from arch to floor, and then allowed to fall in full volume, and closing at the bottom as at the top. In three of these central spaces thus formed, were grouped the war-worn battle flags of veteran Ohio regiments.

On a platform was placed the dais for the reception of the coffin. This platform, tastefully carpeted, the rise of each step dressed in black, was ornamented with emblematical flowers and plants in vases so arranged as to present, with their impression of beauty, the sorrow for the dead.

The impressive solemnity with which the ceremonies were conducted, continued without interruption. The officers on duty firmly but courteously enforced every rule for the visitors.

It was estimated that more than eight thousand passed in and out every hour from 9:30 a.m. to 4:00 p.m. Estimates set a viewing number at over fifty thousand people.

Many scenes during the day were impressive. All felt the sorrow. Thousands of persons stood in line on High Street, four abreast; the lines extending in either direction, north from the west gateway to Long Street, and south from the west gateway to Rich Street, patiently awaiting their opportunity. For more than six hours a steady stream of humanity poured through the channel, all desiring a glimpse at the martyred President on his bier.

General Townsend later recounted a touching incident. "While at Columbus I received a note from a lady, wife of one of the principal citizens, accompanying a little cross made of wild violets. The note said that the writer's little girls had gone to the woods in the early morning and gathered the flowers with which they had wrought the cross. They desired it might be laid on little Willie's coffin, they felt so sorry for him."

The hour for the removal of the coffin from the rotunda had nearly arrived. A majority of the people who had listened to the 3:00 p.m. funeral oration quietly wended their way toward High Street, which was densely thronged, until the cortege was reformed and moved to the depot.

At 6:00 p.m. the doors of the Buckeye State Capitol were closed, the bugle sounded assembly, the soldiers took arms, and the procession began reforming for the final escort back to the depot. As the body was being borne out to the hearse at the west gateway of the Capitol grounds, a national salute of cannons was fired. Soon after, the procession moved north on High Street, and the remains of the President were transferred to the funeral car at the depot of the Columbus and Indianapolis Central Railway.

The committee superintending the catafalque in the rotunda, recognized the profound sorrow of the citizens and determined to allow it to remain until the remains of Mr. Lincoln were consigned to the tomb at Springfield. It is recorded as a memorable deed for the citizens of Columbus, and every morning until that of the 4th of May, fresh flowers were placed around the dais where the President's coffin had rested. Thousands of men, women and children visited and revisited the catafalque.

In February 1861, Mr. Lincoln had been given the most enthusiastic reception ever bestowed by the people of Ohio upon a citizen of the Republic in this capitol building.

Union Station at Columbus, Ohio, circa 1865. This view looks northeast across High Street, where the remains of Abraham Lincoln, were received on the morning of April 29, 1865. Later that day the train departed on the tracks of the Columbus & Indianapolis Central Railway for Indianapolis, Indiana. Those tracks are visible to the left and just above the Union Station structure. -- *Pennsylvania Railroad collection via the author*

TRAVEL LOG

April 29, 1865 135 miles

Station	Time	Station	Time
Via Cleveland, Columbus and Cincinnati Railway		Shelby Jct.	3:39 a.m.
		Vernon	
Cleveland DEPART	Midnight	Crestline	4:07 a.m.
West Park		Galion	4:23 a.m.
Berea	12:43 a.m.	Iberia (St. James)	
Olmstead		Gilead (Edison)	
Columbia		Cardington	5:20 a.m.
N. Eaton		Ashley	5:43 a.m.
Grafton		Eden (Leonardsburg)	6:00 a.m.
LaGrange		Berlin	
Wellington	2:00 a.m.	Lewis Center	6:45 a.m.
Rochester		Orange	
New London	2:30 a.m.	Flint	
Greenwich	2:57 a.m.	Worthington	6:56 a.m.
Shiloh		Columbus ARR.	7:30 a.m.

OHIO
April 28 - 30, 1865

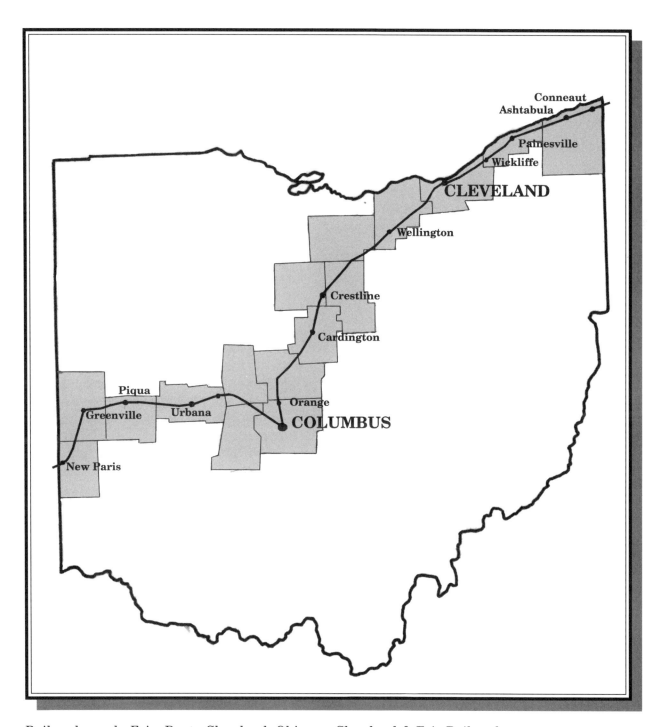

Railroads used: Erie, Pa. to Cleveland, Ohio -- Cleveland & Erie Railroad
Cleveland to Columbus -- Cleveland, Columbus & Cincinnati Railroad
Columbus to Indianapolis, Indiana -- Columbus & Indianapolis Central Railway

APRIL 29 - 30, 1865
COLUMBUS - RICHMOND - INDIANAPOLIS

THE ALTERNATE ROUTE

Abraham Lincoln went to Washington in 1861, and his route between Indianapolis, Indiana, and Columbus, Ohio, was via Cincinnati, Ohio. This was not the case with the 1865, funeral train route. A much less populated corridor was chosen, one via the Columbus & Indianapolis Central Railway on what was then known as the Piqua route, 90 miles north of Cincinnati. There were three officially announced stops on the 188-mile route, although several additional stops were made.

Cincinnati city officials voiced protests that their town was being passed-by. Those in charge encouraged the City of Cincinnati to send a delegation to Columbus, to be a part of the official service and to escort the remains to Indianapolis.

The reasons for skipping Cincinnati remain somewhat clouded. Two explanations have been discovered. The first was that a Cincinnati stop would consume an additional day and they felt Lincoln's remains would not withstand the additional time. A second explanation is found in a simple article in the *Dayton Journal* from April 19, 1865. "The *Cincinnati Inquirer*, Copperhead organ of Ohio, and the favorite paper of Kentucky rebels and which, with other Copperhead papers of the north, has proclaimed, during the past four years, that the south could never be conquered, has hung out the white flag." Cincinnati had long been a stronghold for southern sympathizers and was known to be a hot bed of volatility. It was apparently felt to be a security risk for the appearance of the train. Ohio Governor John Brough, and his committee selected the route through Ohio, being aware of the Cincinnati problems. A Cincinnati delegation made the trip to Columbus, for the funeral ceremonies, along with delegations from neighboring towns of Covington and Newport, Kentucky. They rode a special train following the same route Lincoln took in 1861 via Xenia, on the Little Miami and the Columbus & Xenia Railroads, arriving in Columbus on Friday, April 28, amid masses of people coming to attend the official ceremonies.

Governor Brough apparently decided not to use the Dayton and Western line which followed a portion of the 1861 inauguration route from Columbus to Xenia, then switching to the Dayton & Western rails through Dayton to New Paris, Ohio, into Indiana. The reason is found in an 1859 advertisement for the railroad where it mentions a lack of stations between Xenia, Ohio, and Richmond, Indiana. Not many people would have seen the train.

A Dayton delegation was also formed to attend the funeral ceremonies. There was no public opposition to the lack of consideration for the passage of the train through their town. On April 25, the delegation met at the Montgomery County Courthouse and made plans to travel to Columbus via a special train on April 29, to be a part of the memorial ceremony. One hundred prominent Dayton men were selected to attend, and by special train made the journey some 60 miles to the east.

When Lincoln's train passed along the selected route later that night no reporter from the Dayton papers and only the *Cincinnati Gazette* reported the passage of the train.

The *Richmond Palladium* provides a clue as to the train's makeup for the journey from Columbus to Indianapolis. "The funeral train which brought the remains of President Lincoln from Columbus to this City consists of nine cars, eight of them furnished by the New York Central, Cleveland and Buffalo and

Cleveland, Columbus and Cincinnati Railroad lines. The ninth car, containing the body, is the 'President's car' built for the convenience of the president and other dignitaries in traveling over the United States Military Railroads." No mention is made of the locomotives. The balance of the train were sleeping or parlor cars.

The train made at least twelve stops during its journey from Columbus to Indianapolis. This was an unusually high number considering stops made elsewhere along the train's route. An opinion at the time expressed complaints had been heard during the funeral cortege's travel across New York and the northern half of Ohio, that it had not made enough stops for public expressions of mourning. This may hold some merit since no published schedule for the train over this leg of the journey has ever been discovered. The times indicate at least one hour was planned for locomotive fueling, and a second hour was planned for two scheduled stops. Local opinion has long held that the train may have run slightly over its advertised speed in order to accommodate trackside petitions to

Columbus was reached via the Cleveland, Columbus and Cincinnati Railway. They operated into a Union Depot north of the State House on High Street. When leaving for Indianapolis, the cortege followed the same parade route in reverse. On the west side of High Street at the C & I C Railway, was a small station, not on the map. The coffin was loaded on the train to resume its journey over the Great Central Route of the Columbus & Indianapolis Central Railway, decided upon in order to avoid Cincinnati. The west end of the line near the Ohio - Indiana line had only been open for rail traffic a few weeks. A perferred route via Dayton was not considered. - *1868 Ohio Atlas*

stop briefly for brief memorials.

PASSAGE VIA THE COLUMBUS & INDIANAPOLIS CENTRAL RAILWAY, "THE GREAT CENTRAL RAILWAY" INTO INDIANA

The operation of the trains and schedules was controlled by the military with a high degree of precision being reported.

Orders to each railroad required posted guards at all high locations and strategic places, such as curves, bridges, tunnels and crossings with other railroads. All switches were spiked in place to safeguard against a possible derailment. The Funeral Train held rights over all other trains, requiring them to halt one hour before the special train's arrival. A pilot locomotive, which by the time the train arrived in Ohio, was pulling a car of special delegates and railroad employees, ran ten minutes ahead of the train to alert people of the coming approach of the funeral train.

This new route of 188 miles was through the rural farm lands of western Ohio and eastern Indiana. The region was dotted with small villages, settled before Ohio was a state. To get to the Ohio-Indiana line, the trains would have to traverse five major river valleys.

By the time the train reached Columbus every newspaper in western Ohio was full of stories describing the assassination of Lincoln, as well as accounts of the funeral services at Philadelphia, New York and Albany. Every church held a memorial service at its Sunday services, many of which were also recounted in the newspapers. While the large cities enjoyed daily newspapers, the outlying rural communities were left to a weekly newspaper. Many local newspapers printed extra pages to cover the importance of this tragic event.

James Gormley, the engineer from Columbus, Ohio, was assigned the duty of running the locomotive pulling Lincoln's funeral train from Columbus to the west. Twenty-six year- old Gormley had been promoted to locomotive engineer in 1861. Gormley, was born in Mullingar County of West Meath, Ireland, January 9, 1839. He immigrated to the United States as a boy and settled in Columbus, Ohio, by 1851. At age 12, he was hired by the Columbus, Piqua and Indiana Railroad to wipe down the steam locomotives. This was dirty work. By the age of 21, he had worked himself up to the job of a locomotive engineer, running the fast passenger trains, between Columbus and Piqua, Ohio, a distance of 73 miles.

With a great deal of pride he climbed into the cab of the tastefully decorated locomotive to do his part in the proper funeral procession for Lincoln.

DEPARTURE FROM COLUMBUS

The funeral procession left the Ohio Statehouse just after 6:00 p.m., not returning the eight or so blocks until "after dark." The train had been brought back to Union Depot where it received Lincoln's remains, and the members of the funeral escort.

At 7:50 p.m. the pilot train with the Cincinnati delegation on board departed, as rain started to fall. As soon as the coffin was secured and the funeral party was back on the train, the whistle sounded, brake wheels were loosened and the locomotive began its rhythmic panting as the train left the station. In the background, the patter of rain falling seemed constant. The noises of the crowd faded, as the chugging and the shrill whistle of the locomotive can be heard as it moves into the distant valley. Rolls of thunder in the background faded away as guns were fired in a final salute to the fallen President.

A strangeness filled the air as it departed the station on High Street, just a few blocks north of the Ohio Capitol Building. Lincoln's funeral train traversed the tracks of the Columbus & Indianapolis Central Railway, departing Columbus, Ohio, station grounds on High Street the evening of April 29, 1865, via the new route that took it through Urbana, and Piqua, to the interchange of Union City Junction, later renamed Bradford Junction, a small railroad village, eleven miles

West of Piqua. There it would take the newly completed line via Greenville and New Madison, on its way to Indiana.

The funeral train left Columbus at 8:00 p.m. D. E. Smith, Esquire, President and J. M. Lunt, Esquire, Superintendent of the Columbus & Indianapolis Central Railway, accompanying it, giving personal attention to the wants and wishes of 300 or so passengers in the delegation. They had with them Messers, Blemer and Cummings, chief track men, and William Slater, telegraphic operator, with all of the implements for immediate repair in the event of a breakdown, or track failure. S. A. Hughes, Esquire, as Conductor, and Mr. James Gormley, Engineer, were in charge of the train. Leaving Columbus, the train crossed the Olentangy and Scioto Rivers, entering the open Ohio country.

The first village on the line was Hilliard, nine miles to the West. It had been named for one of the officials of the railroad. Pleasant Valley, later renamed Plain City, 16 miles West of Columbus, was passed at 8:45 p.m., bonfires lit up the country for miles. The train slowed to the prescribed speed and was met by a large concourse of citizens assembled around the depot. Two American flags, draped in mourning, were held in hand by two ladies.

Watches read 9:00 p.m. as the train passed the small berg of Unionville. About two hundred people were present, most of them sitting in wagons' - the people having come from the surrounding countryside. Anguished faces greeted the train as it passed by. Young children and babies were held up so they could witness the solemn passage. At Milford an assembleage of people was gathered around large bonfires. Four or five hundred people waved flags and handkerchiefs slowly. About two miles from that place a farmer and his family were standing in a field by a bonfire waving a flag. The train slipped into sparsely populated country.

The cortege proceeded through Milford, crossing the Springfield, Mount Vernon & Pittsburgh Railroad, the first of four lines between Columbus and Piqua. The telegraph key clicking off an "O S" message to Woodstock that the train was on the way.

A brief stop was made at the small village of Woodstock, 35 miles west of Columbus, for a memorial ceremony by the crowd of mourners. At 9:46 p.m. the train stopped for about five hundred people who greeted the train. The ladies presented bouquets; one by Miss Villard, Miss Lucy Kimble and Miss Mary Cranston, on the part of the ladies of Woodstock; another by Mrs. G. Martin and Miss Delilah Beltz, two sisters. These ladies were permitted to enter the funeral car and strew the florals on the coffin. The Woodstock Cornet Band, Warren U. Cushman, leader, played a dirge and hymn-*Dreaming, I sleep, Love* and *Playl's Hymn*. The Village bells slowly rang; men stood silent with uncovered heads.

Continuing to the west, Cable was reached at 10:13 p.m. where a very large crowd assembled around large bonfires. A soldier stood in the center of an assemblage, holding a flag. All men stood with heads uncovered.

A scheduled water stop was probably made at Brush Lake, three miles West of Woodstock in eastern Champaign County. There is no mention of this stop in the accounts. Either the locomotives were taking on water at the other station stops or this unimportant event was not worth mentioning.

The miles west of Columbus presented scenes of folks gathered in the rain and dark, soaked in wet clothes, standing about the margins of the railroad. The scene was most sad. At every crossing the blaze of bonfires and torches illuminated the whole countryside. Small crowds huddled together, maybe holding a lantern or a torch, possibly kneeling on the wet ground, bared heads bowed, some uttering prayers or singing hymns as the train slowly passed. All were demonstrating their expressions of grief for the departed President.

The train started down the long grade of the Mad River Valley, an area of gently rolling hills, rich black bottom land covering gravel of the highest quality. Continuing toward Urbana, crews were anticipating a planned stop and possibly some fuel for the locomotives while a memorial service was held at the station grounds. Other trains on the railroad were held in sidings while the two trains were in the wide Mad River Valley, a distance of nearly 24 miles.

On April 26, the *Urbana Union* carried a one paragraph announcement that the train would reach Urbana between 10:30 p.m. and 11:00 p.m. The paper picked up the New York City pronouncements which the newspapers there stated, "*... the remains will not again be exposed to public view, until the arrival at Springfield, Ill.*" Because of this, many residents had planned to travel to Columbus to view the earlier procession and ceremonies there. At least one special train was put on to take mourners to Columbus.

*Urbana, 44 miles west of Columbus was reached at 10:40 p.m.. A ten minute stop was made for a public memorial at the joint depot grounds. In the heart of this rich Mad River Valley, land of Simon Kenton, not less than three thousand people had gathered at the joint depot grounds. The grounds were lighted by bonfires.

The pilot train arrived ten minutes earlier. It was not without problems. A beautiful arch of evergreens and flowers made by the ladies of Urbana, and erected across the railroad earlier in the evening proved too narrow for the passage of the train. It had to be hastily removed to the disappointment of many.

As the train came into town its whistle was sounded to apply brakes. On the station platform was a large cross, entwined with circling wreaths of evergreen, which was worked under the direction of Mrs. Milo G. Williams, President, Ladies Soldiers Aid Society. From the top of the cross, and shorter arms, were hung illuminated colored transparencies. On the opposite side of the track was an elevated platform, on which were forty gentlemen and ladies, who sang with patriotic sweetness the hymn, "*Go to Thy Rest.*" The singers represented the Methodist, Baptist, Episcopalian and Presbyterian Churches. Large bonfires made the night as light as day. Minute guns were fired in salute to the fallen president. Ten young ladies entered the car and strewed flowers on the martyr's bier. One of the ladies was so affected that she cried and wept in great anguish. The imposing appearance could not fail to make a lasting impression upon the minds of all who witnessed it.

Departing, the trains exited the station shed, crossed the Mad River & Lake Erie Railway, and the broad gauge Atlantic and Great Western Railroad. Military guards stood watch on the railroads. The next thirteen miles of railroad were the most difficult with heavy grades and sharp curves, not usually found in the flat lands of western Ohio. To the west could be heard whistles of the pilot train calling for brakes on its distant climb out of the fertile valley.

Just nine miles north was called home for Wilson Wright Brown, another of Andrew's Raiders. Brown was a railroad engineer at the time of his 1862 military assignment. Further north in Hardin County, the very first Medal of Honor winner, also one of Andrew's Raiders resided, Jacob Parrott. His medal was awarded on March 25, 1863.

As the train departed, the brakemen were positioned out on the car platforms, ready to act on the brake wheels as the train started up the long grade toward St. Paris. This most treacherous grade had accounted for several runaway trains and had taken a number of lives in derailments. People along the western rim of the Valley could tell the location of the train by the whistle signals.

The train passed Rice, near the Mad River and ran across the flat black earth of the richest kind for a couple miles. At Westville Station, also known as McGrew, crowds from the west side of the Mad River Valley were gathered to pay respect to the dead president as the train departed from the west side of the fertile farm valley and made the assault on

*Local lore suggests the planned stop at Urbana was to add a second locomotive to aid in lifting the train over 3% grades to the west. If this is so, the locomotive likely stayed with the train for the next 25 miles to Piqua where the roundhouse was located. No records have come to light confirming local lore.

the Blue Hill. The trains had to climb steep grades for eight miles. The barks of the locomotive exhausts were sharp and the echoes bounced off the hills alerting all to the passage of the train, as did the engineers whistle signals for brake application or release. After reaching the summit of the hills at St. Paris, the train stopped briefly near Springfield Street for a public memorial. Just up the street from the station was the school house where Marion Ross, one of Andrews Raiders had taught. It stood as a silent reminder to the real cost of the Civil War. Mr. Ross was captured by the Confederates and executed for crimes against the Confederate government. He was later awarded the Medal of Honor posthumously.

There were brilliant illuminations, by which could be seen a number of drooped flags. A large assembly was present, and stood in silence as they looked at the passing train.

As the funeral train pulled in, everyone stood in silence, men with their heads bared, looking at the train. Selected citizens were allowed to enter the president's car with a floral tribute. In St. Paris, a lady and man were selected to jointly place the wreath on the coffin. Mr. Christian McMorran and Mrs. Rachel Furrow, were selected to carry out this sacred duty. They solemnly entered Abraham Lincoln's funeral car carrying the beautiful creation made by a Mrs. Stourenmeyer, and placed upon Lincoln's coffin. The large bouquet was a most artistic one.

Continuing on just four miles west at the small Miami County village of Conover, a long line of people two deep stood in file; on the right boys and girls, then young men and women, and on the left elderly people. In the center, supporting a large American flag, were three young ladies, Miss Eliza Throckmorton, Miss Nora Brecount, and Miss Barnes. A patriotic religious song, with a slow and mournful air, was chanted by the flag bearers. Forty-two men had volunteered to fight in the War from the Conover and Fletcher area, several of them were there to honor their hero.

A DILEMMA AT PIQUA

Citizens of Miami County and the surrounding Miami Valley region were alerted to the coming of the Lincoln Funeral Train through small announcements in the local newspapers on April 27. Two aids of the United States Military Railroads, Robinson and Wyman had alerted the citizens of Piqua to the planned coming of the train and their desire for a public memorial in prior days. It appears the stop was planned to take on fuel and water. Personal friend of Lincoln and local Civil War hero, the Reverend Colonel Granville Moody* of Piqua was honored, being selected to head up plans for the track side memorial service. Local committees were formed and as the time approached, plans were made public.

Thousands of people gathered along the margins of the railroad in the raw and chilly night to honor the lamented dead. Six miles east, the train passed through Fletcher, near the site where the Indians had worked out the details for the Greenville Treaty. Bonfires lit up the night sky as the train passed through the village and started down the long grade. A telegraph message was sent to Piqua. The train's brakemen again manned the brake wheels as the train dropped down a seven-mile grade into the Miami River Valley, passing through the small stop of Spring Creek en route.

It rattled over the Dayton and Michigan Crossing, at eastern edge of the Miami River,

*Reverend Colonel Grandville Moody, a Methodist preacher, had become friends with Lincoln during anti-slavery struggles. He was regarded as a warm personal friend of President Lincoln, and it was he whom Lincoln pledged to issue the Emancipation Proclimation. Reverend Moody held pastorates in Piqua, Ohio, twice. On Easter Sunday, April 16, 1865, he first preached a sermon on the death of Lincoln, at Piqua, then traveled to Columbus and gave great oration about Lincoln to crowds gathered there in mourning. Moody was known as the great "Fighting Parson." He was a Colonel in the 74th Ohio Regiment, and was wounded four times at the Battle of Stone River. He was known for his eloquence, enthusiasm, personal magnetism and unflinching loyalty to God and right. He regarded these as elements of power and success. Many considered him a true patriot.

overlooking the town. The engine crew noticed the glow from torches against the rainy sky as they entered the long covered bridge spanning the Miami River, two blocks east of the station grounds. At twenty minutes past midnight, in the early morning hours of Sunday, April 30, 1865, the train reached Piqua, 73 miles west of Columbus.

As the train exited the covered bridge over the Great Miami River and Miami-Erie Canal, its whistle was sounded to apply the brakes. Wheels began to squeal under the grip of the tightening brake shoes. A large crowd of mourners greeted the train as it crossed Main Street, then Wayne Street, easing to a stop at the station grounds.

The train was met with tolling church bells, bands of music, and a torch lit procession. Plans called for a splendid arch illuminated with gas jets to span the tracks. This item was apparently scratched at the last minute. The station was decorated in American flags and hung with Chinese lanterns. The station stop was made at Wayne Street depot grounds. Not less than ten thousand people crowded around the train. A great desire was expressed to see the President, and many ladies inquired if , “Little Willie” was along. When answered in the affirmative they exclaimed: “O, I wish I could see him!”

The Troy and Piqua Bands played appropriate music, after which a delegation from the Methodist Churches, under Rev. Granville “Colonel” Moody, sang a hymn. Rev. Moody repeated the first line, it was then sung by the entire choir. Thirty-six ladies in white, with black sashes, stood on a draped platform, and sang a plaintive tune. As they closed, the band followed with a touching dirge. Local accounts suggest the effect of these ceremonies at midnight baffled description.

A great number of people came down from Sidney. Fearing that all present would not have a chance to pass along the car, William Barber, held up Clay Carey and his brother, also many others to look at Lincoln’s coffin through the window of the car.

While the train was stopped, workmen from the nearby roundhouse went about the task of locomotive requirements and seeing to any supply needs, including wood and water. The telegraphic agent sent a message to stations further west announcing the arrival of the train, and its departure.

About 35 miles north another of Andrews Raiders, William Bensinger, worked on the railroad at Lima. Eventually he worked for the newly organized Lake Erie & Louisville Railroad, helping with its construction to the west via St. Marys and Celina.

The funeral trains departure to the west was immediately challenged by steep grades for three miles, lifting the train out of the Miami River Valley.

The following Saturday, May 6, a scath-

Piqua To-Night

The funeral train of cars with the several committees of escort and other attendants, having in charge the remains of our country's much beloved murdered President, will pass through Piqua about 12 o'clock to-night. The citizens of that place propose a demonstration on that occasion, and request us to extend an invitation to the citizens of Troy and vicinity, to meet with them and join in paying a last tribute of respect to the remains of the honored dead.

The programme is as follows:

1. There will be torches held a few paces apart along the line of railroad through the city.
2. An arch will be arranged over the Wayne Street crossing, to be suitably trimmed and lighted.
3. Music thirty-six young ladies dressed in red, white and blue, with badges, will chant a funeral dirge.
4. The bells of the churches and City Hall will be tolled while the remains are in the city.

Text of *Miami Union* newspaper announcement and invitation at Troy, Ohio, April 29, 1865. The next week this newspaper was laced with editorials sharply criticizing the City of Piqua over its lack of follow-through on announced memorial plans for the Lincoln Funeral Train. -- *Troy (Ohio) Historical Society collection*

ing editorial appeared in the *Miami Union*, a Troy, Ohio, newspaper sharply critical of the City of Piqua's lack of preparations. "On invitation, quite a large number of people from this part of the county went up. But instead of finding the advertised arrangements, they ... had the mortification of finding that no preparations had been made for the occasion. The people were there, but that was about all. No 'guns' were fired - no 'torches' were lighted - no 'church bells' were tolled - no 'bonfires' were kindled - no 'illuminated' arches appeared on the track of the road. A few tunes were played by the band and a hymn sung by some ladies and gentlemen under the direction of Colonel Moody-that was all. We do not know who was to blame for the failure, but certainly it was a failure-at least it is so regarded by all who have conversed about it."

Elsewhere in that same paper were editorials about the alleged ill-treatment of certain "most prominent" Troy citizens by the proprietor of a Piqua hotel while they were awaiting the arrival of the Funeral Train. The funeral escort apparently were unaware of any failure of any special service at Piqua.

THROUGH THE CHILLY NIGHT

Just a few miles west of Piqua, the train slipped into the Stillwater River Valley at Covington, slowing for the crowds. It passed through another covered bridge over the river, through a cut and swung into a long gentle curve toward Union City Junction.

Drooping flags and other evidences of mourning were displayed at Covington and Union City Junction. (Union City Junction, one of many early names given to Bradford, the junction switch to continue its trip to the South toward Richmond, Indiana.) There were a large number of people around huge bonfires. The funeral train stopped briefly to replenish fuel and water. Selected mourners were admitted to the car to pay their last respects as part of the service. The railroad saw mill had been busy sawing firewood for the locomotives. Legend has it that one of the laborers sorted out the best wood in the ricks to help ease the journey for the train.

This was the junction town of the railroad. The Second Division tracks were followed to the southwest.

This line of railroad had been opened but a few weeks and represented the newest line of track over which the train passed. The tracks followed gently rolling hills of the finest gravel deposits.

The train passed through Gettysburg, in Darke County, at 1:10 a.m. A large number of people stood around bonfires as the train pressed on in the dark and rain. The only memorial in Darke County was at Greenville, the site of the signing of the Greenville Treaty many years prior. Thirty-six young ladies dressed in white slowly waved the Star Spangled Banner which greeted the cortege from the station platform. *Lafayette's Requiem* was sung with thrilling effect by a number of ladies and gentlemen. About five hundred people congregated about the station, which stood at the crossing with the Dayton and Union Railroad. Company C, 28th Ohio Infantry, was drawn up in line, with fire arms reversed. The depot was tastefully decorated. On the other side of the depot were two bonfires fifteen feet high, which shed most brilliant light all around the train and depot.

The people had been notified of the coming train through a simple article in the *Greenville Democrat* on April 26. The small article stated the train would pass through the village between 1:00 a.m. and 2:00 a.m. in the morning. The paper went on to apologize for the lateness of the hour, encouraging all the town residents to turn out. It stopped at the station at 1:36 a.m.

As the trains passed through the tiny villages of Weaver's Station, New Madison, and Wiley's Station, it was observed hundred's of mourners from the rural area were gathered in reverent respect along the newly finished railroad track. Local journals indicate the railroad had been opened less than two weeks with the passage of this train.

At New Paris, the last station in Ohio, another railroad junction was encountered. If this railroad had been selected, it would have followed the 1861 Lincoln train from Columbus to Xenia, then switched to the Dayton and New Paris branch.

Great bonfires lit up the skies around the depot at New Paris, on the Ohio-Indiana line. A crowd was gathered about, who stood in the rain with uncovered heads. A beautiful arch of evergreens was formed above the track, under which the train passed at 2:41 a.m. The arch was twenty feet high and thirty feet in circumference. The train crossed the switch to the Dayton line, crossed the road and whistled to a stop at the depot. The pilot train continued into Indiana with the Cincinnati delegation on board.

A portion of the Indiana delegation was received in a brief ceremomy before continuing on to the first town in Indiana, Richmond. The Ohio delegation stepped off the train to make room for the Indiana representatives. No mention is made how the Ohio delegation returned to Columbus. It is believed that a special train returned them.

THE TRAIN ENTERS INDIANA

Official Indiana delegation efforts to greet the funeral train commenced at Indianapolis, Indiana, early in the evening of April 29. Governor Oliver P. Morton* and a large contingent of official Indiana representatives and newspaper reporters departed at 8:00 p.m. on a special train for Richmond, 69 miles east. They were received at the Union Station depot grounds in Richmond about 11:30 p.m. En route they observed the preparations being made to honor the funeral train at the stations. Some preparations had been under way all day, and perhaps a few days prior where arches and other large displays were involved.

Some time after midnight the Indiana dignitaries preceded five miles east of town to the railroad junction at New Paris, Ohio, just across the state-line to await the arrival of the funeral train. It is reported that Governor Morton and a portion of his party stayed in Richmond to officially receive the train.

The Funeral Train appeared from the north. The scheduled stop was made to take on board all the Indiana delegations. Turning west, the train crossed the state line and entered Indiana, the land where a youthful Lincoln had lived from the time he was seven until he was eighteen. The Hoosier State received Lincoln in the silence of death. Indianians welcomed the remains in sorrow and prayerful silence.

At 2:00 a.m., the bells of Richmond were tolled, calling all to the station grounds in preparation for the memorial services. For hours, thousands of people had gathered at the station grounds near "E" Street and Fort Wayne Avenue. Special trains brought masses of people to participate in the memorial service. Richmond was known as a Quaker town and many broad rimmed hats and Quaker bonnets were observed in the growing crowd. At about one hour before the arrival of the train, section hands spiked all the track switches to prevent a derailment. This was a considerable task considering the number of tracks in the vicinity of the station grounds.

At this time Richmond was a regional railroad hub with six lines radiating out from the station. It was the only town short of Indianapolis with the rail facilities capable of handling the many trains.

Throughout the day a massive effort was put forth to properly festoon the depot grounds in mournings appropriate for this solemn occasion. Buildings were draped in black, and an evergreen wreath was placed at the droop on each trimmed with flags. An arch, estimated at 25 feet high and 30 feet across, with two pillars, was constructed by employees of the Chicago & Great Eastern Railroad under the direction of Abe Brandt. It was

*Governor Oliver P. Morton was known as "the Soldiers' friend" and stood solidly with Lincoln in the Union effort during the Civil War. He was considered a patriot by many in recruiting troops for the war, and for the favorable treatment of returning soldiers. Morton's legs became paralyzed in 1864. Although handicapped, he traveled to Washington, D.C., to attend Lincoln's National Funeral then toured the war torn south before returning to Indiana. He personally received the remains of Lincoln on behalf of the State of Indiana and saw to the utmost honors while within the State. He went on to be a United States Senator from Indiana.

hoisted up in front of the depot, elaborately trimmed with symbols of mourning and evergreen, topped by a canopy of flags and a portrait of Lincoln. The *Palladium* describes the arch. "Upon the sides of the arch were American Flags, arranged in triangles, and transparencies alternately red, white and blue, together with festoons hanging from the summit. About 18 feet above the track was a platform draped in mourning and supporting a coffin, at the side of which sat Miss Mary McClelland, and representing the Genius of Liberty crying. She was accompanied by mourners in the characters of the Army and Navy. Above this group arose another triangle of evergreens and velvet studded with roses and rosettes. At the ends of the platform were Flags in drooping folds."

As the train approached, on a sweeping curve from the east, a scene not unlike that of Baltimore, Maryland, was encountered. The church bells were ringing, as well as those of the adjacent railroad locomotives. They* had been tastefully decorated in mourning and were lit with revolving lamps. Coaches were lit and bonfires around the station grounds provided additional lighting.

* No specific mention is made of a locomotive change at this station. There is evidence to suggest a change was made. The time in station of 30 minutes is typical of the time required for a locomotive change, and the notation of decorated locomotives standing in the yard is the other indicator. The mileage would suggest a locomotive change was made at Richmond.

More than 15,000 mourners awaited the train as it entered the station. This was more than the population of the entire town, even though the time was 3:00 a.m. A Committee of Ladies of Richmond, consisting of three ladies, Mrs. S. R. Lippincott, Mrs. Nannie Vaughan and Miss. Annie Vaughan, prepared two beautiful wreaths of flowers, and with permission granted by General Hooker, entered the car and deposited them on the coffins of the President and his son. Flowers for the arrangements were donated by local greenhouses.

The train remained at the station for approximately 30 minutes while memorial services were conducted and the remains of Lincoln were received by the State of Indiana. Upon their conclusion, the funeral cortege moved slowly away to the music of a solemn dirge, and onto the great trestle over the Whitwater River just a quarter mile to the west. The Governor's special stayed at the station, under orders, for about one hour before commencing its journey west.

Near Richmond, the last of the regional home to any of Andrews Raiders was encountered. E. A. Mason was born near Richmond.

The train continued on to Indianapolis over the tracks of the C & I C Railway, where it passed through Centerville, the former home of the Honorable Oliver P. Morton, Governor. The depot was splendidly festooned in mourning with two chandeliers at either end of the station platform, brilliantly

The Weeping Goddess of Liberty, a scene repeated variously and depicted on some of the public timetables was a coffin, at the side of which sat the Goddess of Liberty, and representing the Genius of Liberty weeping. She was accompanied by mournes in the characters of a soldier and sailor, weeping. A live scene was played out at Richmond, Indiana, on April 30, 1865.

INDIANA

April 30 - May 1, 1865

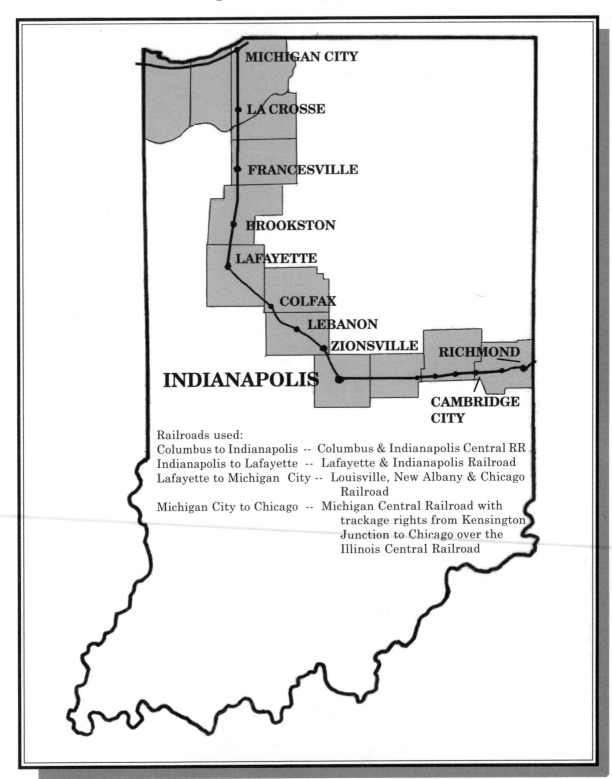

MICHIGAN CITY
LA CROSSE
FRANCESVILLE
BROOKSTON
LAFAYETTE
COLFAX
LEBANON
ZIONSVILLE
RICHMOND
INDIANAPOLIS
CAMBRIDGE CITY

Railroads used:
Columbus to Indianapolis -- Columbus & Indianapolis Central RR
Indianapolis to Lafayette -- Lafayette & Indianapolis Railroad
Lafayette to Michigan City -- Louisville, New Albany & Chicago Railroad
Michigan City to Chicago -- Michigan Central Railroad with trackage rights from Kensington Junction to Chicago over the Illinois Central Railroad

lit. Over 2,000 people had gathered along the margins of the track to show their reverent respects. There is some evidence to suggest the train may have made a brief stop, departing at 3:41 a.m.

CAMBRIDGE CITY STOPS

The train passed through Germantown about 25 minutes later, reaching Cambridge City at 4:15 a.m. Three unscheduled stops were made in this small town according to a small article in *The Cambridge City Tribune* for April 26, 1928. The article is related by a witness to the plans, F. C. Mosbaugh: "Cambridge City was favored with three stops of the Lincoln Funeral Train. J. H. Banbenthumson, local railroad telegraph operator, also conducting a news and periodical stand in his office in the depot, the writer was in his employ and two days before the train was scheduled to pass through, I overheard a conversation in the telegraph office, between the local yardmaster and the engineer who was detailed to pull the train from Columbus to Indianapolis. In this conversation they planned that upon arriving at Capitol Hill Park, where the artillery was placed, on signal by the yardmaster, the train was to stop for five seconds in front of the homestead of and complimentary to General Sol Meredith, a great personal friend of the departed president. The second stop of 15 seconds was at the local station that the car in which Lincoln's remains lay was spanned by the large and beautiful arch reaching across two tracks and built by the patriotic citizens of this place. The third and last stop in this city was the railroad crossing in the west end of town. The schedule so planned was carried out, I believe in every respect."

"Not withstanding the cold, misty rain that fell throughout the preceding day and that night, people gathered from near and far and by midnight the crowd began to increase rapidly. At the time the train arrived about 4:15 [a.m.] it is estimated that fully three thousand people were assembled and bowed their heads in respectful silence."

Here the railroad crossed the bridge for the Whitewater Canal as the first streaks of gray in the dawning eastern sky appeared.

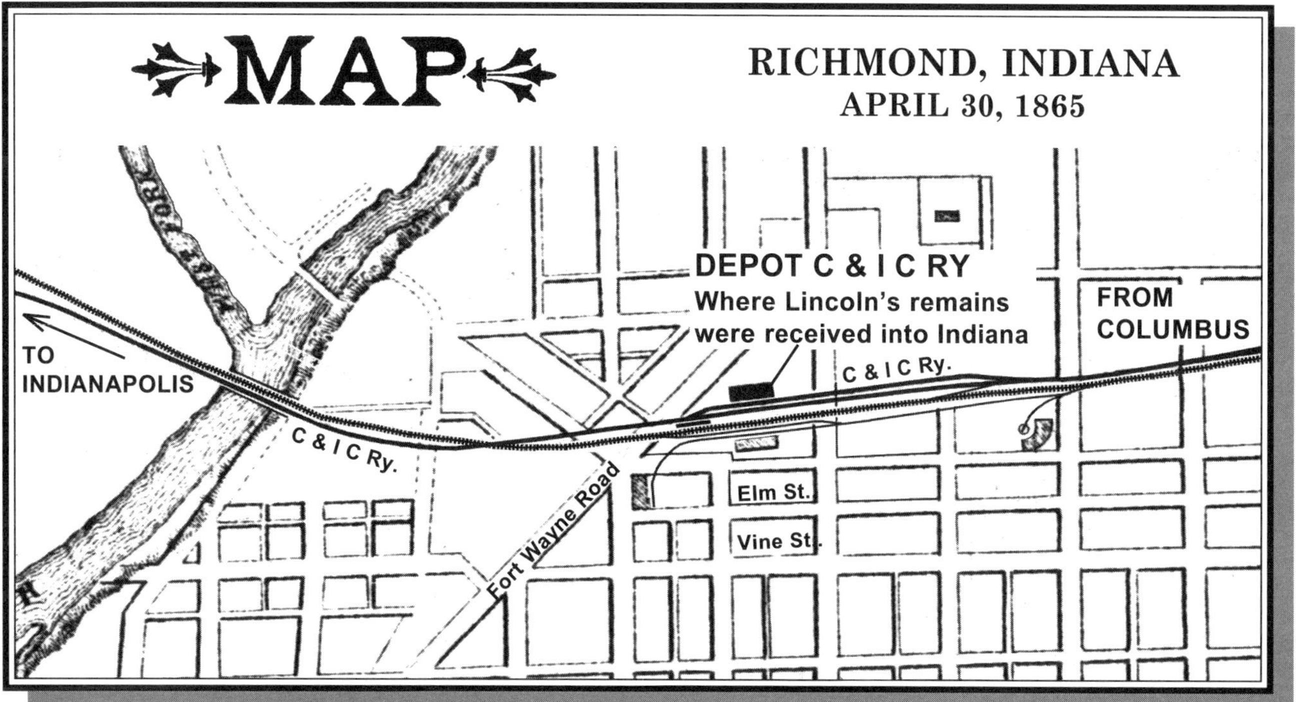

Richmond, Indiana, was an important stop for the Lincoln Funeral Train. It was the first station west of the Ohio-Indiana line where the remains were recieved into the state on April 30, 1865

As the cortege passed through the town, salvos of artillery were heard. Town citizens had constructed an arch over the railroad, beautifully decorated and draped in mourning. At this station, Bengal lights were used to illuminate the train during its brief stop.

This first 26 miles into Indiana demonstrated clearly the heartfelt sorrow of the Midwest. Various papers suggested this demonstration of sorrow had excelled anything that had been witnessed prior in both taste and appropriateness.

The terrain of Eastern Indiana, was quite flat; the train had little challenge of grades, and accounts suggest that the glow of bonfires could be seen at a considerable distance.

Dublin, 51 miles from Indianapolis, was reached at 4:27 a.m. A beautiful arch was constructed over the tracks, entwined with evergreens, mourning emblems and other displays of their deep grief. Portraits of Lincoln, Grant, Morton, Sherman and Sheridan were displayed and night was turned into day by large bonfires. People gathered around them in silence to witness the trains passing.

The area from Richmond to Dublin, had been largely under the Quaker beliefs since the region's settling. It was a strong abolitionist territory and overwhelmingly voted for Lincoln in his 1864 run against McClellan for President.

At Lewisville, a scheduled stop, nine miles west, a delegation entered the train to pass out memorial cards containing the sentiments of its people.

> **LINCOLN:**
>
> The Savior of his Country; the Emancipation of a Race, and the Friend of
>
> **ALL MANKIND!**
>
> Triumphs over Death, and mounts Victorious upward, with his old familiar tread.

It was nearly 5:00 a.m. when the train slowed for Knightstown. The train was welcomed with two arches over the tracks. The depot building was tastefully decorated in festoons of mourning. Mourners lined the margins of the tracks as a choir sang appropriate hymns.

Charlottesville was reached at 5:40 a.m., 30 miles east of Indianapolis. The reporter for the *Indianapolis Daily Journal* made comment. "This little village had not forgotten that the honored dead was a friend of the oppressed, and chief among the procession at the depot was quite a large body of colored people. How fitting and sublime seemed the gospel declaration, as the Great Emancipator's coffin passed through a file of free men, 'Of one blood made He all nations of men.' The brightest star in the immortal diadem that encircles the brew of Abraham Lincoln, in his fist to his country: 'Be ye indeed free.'" Many of the rural towns the train passed through over the prior 150 miles had links to the underground railroad.

A SMALL TRACKSIDE CEREMONY

At Greenfield, the scene was not so somber as expected. Folks were on the tracks at several spots, some in front of the passenger depot, and others scattered here and there as overflowing extensions of the crowd. Across the tracks a little knot of three boys, hands in pockets, were chattering with each other, pacing up and down. Two older fellows were standing together, each arm around the other and probably soldiers remembering what it means to be a comrade. There were many on the platform of the station. The women in their long dresses were not busily conversing any longer, nor the men in the almost universal black color of the group. From atop the station a lone sentinel was perched to keep a sharp eye for the coming funeral train from the east.

The telegraph station in Charlottesville, wired it just passed through town and was heading for Greenfield. The word spread throughout the crowd quickly.

People stood around suddenly silent, some weeping. One fellow was heard to say, "Well we know the train won't stop here, but we still can remember Abraham Lincoln." And so those gathering at the station decided to have a memorial for the martyred President as the funeral train approached. Capt. Reuben Riley was asked to speak. Riley's hair turned white in the Civil War, but he was otherwise young-looking even after his return from the conflict. His black mustache covered his upper lip and tipped out to points at each end remained the young black of his pre-Civil War service. Speaking so matter of factly and forcefully he said: "Folks, want me to read from his Second Inaugural Address while we are awaiting for the train?"

From Lincoln's address. "On the occasion corresponding to this four years ago, all thoughts were anxiously directed to an impending civil war. All dreaded it—all sought to avert it. While the inaugural [sic] address was being delivered from this place, devoted altogether to saving the Union without war, insurgent agents were in the city seeking to destroy it without war—seeking to dissole [sic] the Union, and divide effects, by negotiation. Both parties deprecated war; but one of them would make war rather than let the nation survive; and the other would accept war rather than let it perish. And the war came. One eighth of the whole population were colored slaves, not distributed generally over the Union, but localized in the Southern part of it. These slaves constituted a peculiar and powerful interest. All knew that this interest was, somehow, the cause of the war. To strengthen, perpetuate, and extend this interest was the object for which the insurgents would rend the Union, even by war; while the government claimed no right to do more than to restrict the territorial enlargement of it. Neither party expected for the war, the magnitude, or the duration, which it has already attained. Neither anticipated that the cause of the conflict might cease with, or even before, the conflict itself should cease. Each looked for an easier triumph, and a result less fundamental and astounding. Both read the same Bible, and pray to the same God; and each invokes His aid against the other. It may seem strange that any men should dare to ask a just God's assistance in wringing their bread from the sweat of other men's faces; but let us judge not that we be not judged. The prayers of both could not be answered; that of neither has been answered fully. The Almighty has his own purposes.

"Woe unto the world because of offences! for it must needs be that offences come; but woe to that man by whom the offence cometh!" If we shall suppose that American Slavery is one of those offences which, in the providence of God, must needs come, but which, having continued through His appointed time, He now wills to remove, and that He gives to both North and South, this terrible war, as the woe due to those by whom the offence came, shall we discern therein any departure from those divine attributes which the believers in a Living God always ascribe to Him? Fondly do we hope—fervently do we pray—that this mighty scourge of war may speedily pass away. Yet, if God wills that it continue, until all the wealth piled by the bond-man's two hundred and fifty years of unrequited toil shall be sunk, and until every drop of blood drawn with the lash, shall be paid by another drawn with the sword, as was said three thousand years ago, so still it must be said "the judgments of the Lord, are true and righteous altogether.

"With malice toward none; with charity for all; with firmness in the right, as God gives us to see the right, let us strive on to finish the work we are in; to bind up the nation's wounds; to care for him who shall have borne the battle, and for his widow, and his orphan—to do all which may achieve and cherish a just and lasting peace, among ourselves, and with all nations." *

After the reading many in the crowd wept. Many veterans came to the depot wearing their uniforms of the Civil War. These men felt they were agents of an angry God who struck through time to destroy slavery.

To everyone's surprise the train paused briefly at Greenfield. Reverend Manner's son, a Disciples minister, asked for prayer, and said, "Thank you God for the life of Abraham Lincoln. You give us an America for those thirsting. Let us offer our waters. If penni-

* Lincoln's Second Inaugural Address was read at several stops enroute from Washington to Springfield.

less, let us say, come, buy and eat. Incline your ear and allow us this grace. Give the soul of America life as we remember your sure and steadfast love for Abraham Lincoln. We heard you say, Behold, I made him a witness to the peoples, a leader and commander for the peoples. Behold, you shall be a light to all nations that you know not, and nations that knew you not shall run to you because you have a Patriarch agreeable to the Familyhead, God, and the Holy One of this New Israel. Amen." The mourners at the depot took off their hats, some wept anew. All were reverent as they watched the ten-car funeral train continue slowly to the west beyond Greenfield.

The train arrived at Indianapolis Union Station, a sheltered structure over the tracks at 7:00 a.m. Upon arrival of the train, D. E. Smith, President of the C & I C Railway issued the following telegraph: "The funeral train arrived here precisely on time. There was a perfect torchlight along the whole route. Every farm house had its bonfire in order to see the train. Urbana, Piqua, Greenville and Richmond turned out their entire population. Nearly every town had arches built over the track."

Even though it was raining, the train was housed in the massive shed of the station. By ceremony the coffin was removed to a hearse drawn by the same horses that had pulled his carriage through the city on February 11, and 12, 1861, when he made a speech from the balcony of Bates House on his way to Washington.

WASHINGTON, D.C.
April 22, 1865.

Adjutant-General TERRELL,
Indianapolis, Ind.:

The Secretary of War directs that the funeral ceremonics in each State will be under direction of the governor. The body will lie in state in the Capitol on Sunday. I authorize you, General Stone, Major Lozier, and the State officers to confer with the mayor and the citizens and arrange the programme. I will be there. Let the programme befit the great occasion and the character of the State.
O. P. MORTON.

TRAVEL LOG

April 29 -30, 1865 188 miles

Columbus DEPART	8:00 PM
Scioto (Grand View)	
Mounds	
Marble Cliff	
Hilliards	
Bronson's (Hayden)	
Pleasant Valley (Plain City)	8:45 p.m.
Unionville	9:00 p.m.
Milford Center	9:19 p.m.
Woodstock*	9:46 p.m.
Fountaine Park	
Brush Lake	
Cable	10:13 p.m.
Hagenbaugh	
Urbana*	10:40 p.m.
Rice	
Westville (McGrew)	
St. Paris*	11:24 p.m.
Lena	
Conover	11:50 p.m.
Fletcher	12:00 Midnight
Spring Creek	
Jordan	
Piqua*	12:20 a.m.
Summit	
Covington	
Union City Junction (Bradford)*	1:10 a.m.
Gettysburg	
New Harrison	
Greenville	1:36 a.m.
Weavers Station	
New Madison	
New Paris*	2:41 a.m.
Richmond, Indiana*	3:00 a.m.
Centreville	3:41 a.m.
Harvey's	
Germantown	4:05 a.m.
Cambridge City	4:15 a.m.
Dublin	4:27 a.m.
Straughn's	
Lewisville*	4:38 a.m.
Coffin's (Dunreith)	
Ogden	
Rayville	
Knightstown	
Charlottesville	5:40 a.m.
Cleveland (Riley)	
Greenfield	
Philadelphia	5:57 a.m.
Cumberland	6:30 a.m.
Engine House (Thorne)	
Indianapolis ARR.	7:00 a.m.

APRIL 30, 1865
INDIANAPOLIS

FUNERAL HONORS

ON RECEPTION OF THE REMAINS OF

ABRAHAM LINCOLN,

Late President of the United States.

Header of public hand bill announcing the funeral honors for Abraham Lincoln at Indianapolis, Indiana. Due to the heavy rains the funeral procession had to be cancelled. A parade was held May 1, after the body had left for Chicago. The hand bill dates April 29, 1865. -- *Charles Huppert collection*

The funeral cortege arrived at Indianapolis Union Station at 7:00 a.m. Extensive preparations had been made for receiving the remains in a manner due the distinguished character of the deceased, consistent with the dignity and reputation of the State of Indiana. The massive Indianapolis Union Station was draped in festoons and other appropriate gestures of mourning. Thousands had gathered from every part of the state to pay their last tribute to the lamented President.

Along the entire route of tracks in Indiana, the people testified their sympathy in the most demonstrative way. Passing every station, preparations had been made to acknowledge the remains in a most appropriate manner, as seen with saddened faces, the playing of solemn music, and the deep hoarse raps of the artillery testified to the deep grief that prevailed everywhere.

In the predawn hours of April 30, many special trains from the region arrived, bringing delegations to the Indianapolis ceremonies. The *Indianapolis Daily Sentinel* described it as, "a sorrowful pilgrimage." Trains arrived on seven different lines, each being met at the Union Station by an Assistant Marshall to conduct each special delegation to their assigned positions for participation in the funeral procession. As the rains resumed all of the station bunting and other decorations of mourning were soaked.

The streets to the Statehouse were packed with humanity, having come in on many trains to catch a glimpse of the remains. The military was drawn up in open order, facing inward, forming a line on either side of the street, with bayonets extended. The guard extended five blocks from Illinois up Washington Street to the State House doors.

The general arrangements were under the direction of Major-General Alvin P. Hovey, commanding the District of Indiana. The corpse was taken in charge by the local guard of honor, under command of Colonel Simonson, and conducted from the train to the hearse. The Indianapolis City Band played a sad and sorrowful dirge, called *"Lincoln's Funeral March,"* composed expressly for the occasion by Charles Hess, of Cincinnati. A least three other musical arrangements were written for the funeral journey. The procession was lead from Union Station by Governor Oliver Morton and General Joseph Hooker on horse back. The coffin was carried to the Indiana State

INDIANAPOLIS, INDIANA

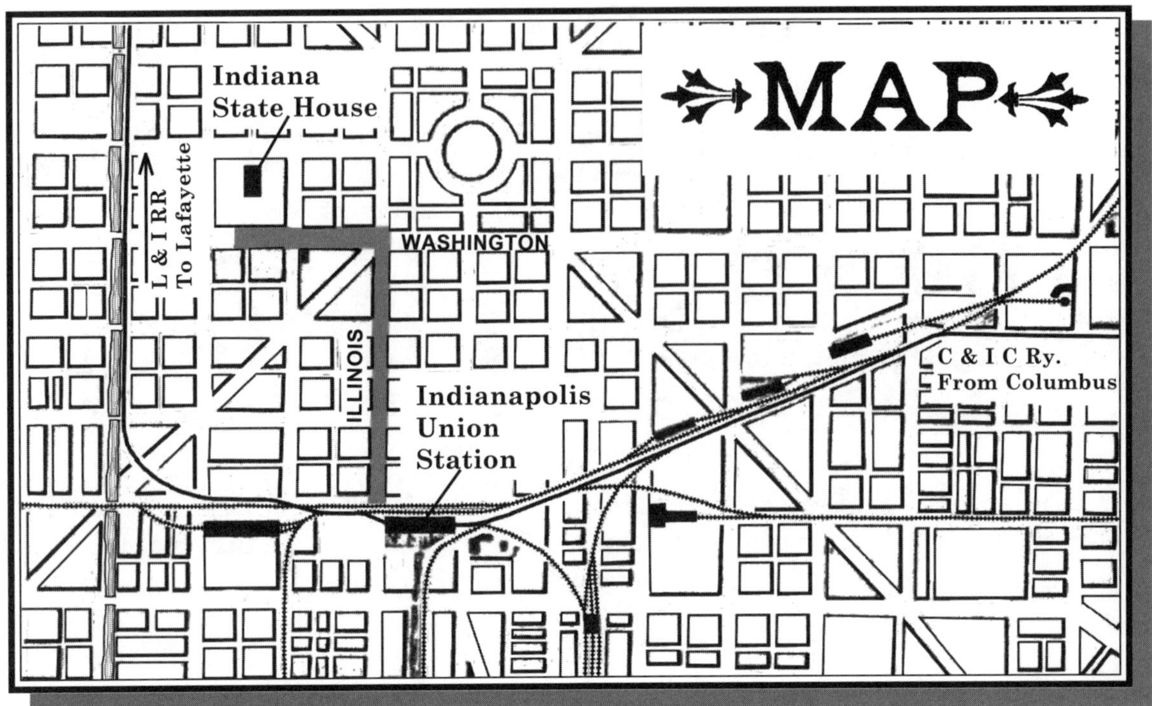

Indianapolis had planned an elaborate parade to honor the lamented president. It rained so hard the parade was cancelled and a much shorter, and direct route was taken from the Union Station up Illinois Street to the Indiana Statehouse on Washington Street. This visit to Indianapolis was also noteable since this station was the first joint line Union Station in the United States. -- *From an 1867 Map of Indianapolis, Indiana*

Indianapolis Union Station depicted at the time of the Lincoln Funeral Train's departure for Chicago on April 30, 1865. This is a view of the west end of the massive structure. The funeral train would have come in from the back of this massive building earlier in the day. -- *Electronic illustration by author*

House in a hearse topped by a silver-gilt eagle, drawn by six white horses with black velvet covers, and each bearing black and white plumes. Although rain had been almost an everyday occurrence on the journey, it was so heavy in Indianapolis that the giant procession was canceled and the entire day devoted to viewing.

INDIANAPOLIS MEMORIALS

The rain which had fallen early in the night stopped and sometime after midnight the skies cleared to reveal a starlit sky for the coming of the train. By the break of day the crowd began to gather en masse about the massive Union Station, and at 6:00 a.m. all the streets and avenues leading to it were packed with people who had come to pay their last tribute of respect. The clouds had also returned and opened with a pelting rain just about the time the train arrived. It was a near repeat of the weather events at Harrisburg, Pennsylvania, which greeted the arrival of the train there.

At 7:00 a.m. the long awaited funeral train arrived in the massive shed of the first joint Union Station in America, just five blocks from the Statehouse.

The heavy rain quickly forced cancellation of plans for a larger procession. In a much abbreviated ceremony the remains were taken directly to the State House.

Order and sobriety was observed by the crowds. With arrival of the train, minute guns were fired, city bells chimed and the Indianapolis City Band, at track side in the station played appropriate dirges. Once the Veteran Reserve Guard of Escort had shouldered the coffin, the procession moved to the waiting hearse. The hearse left the great shed where the procession commenced.

Through the open ranks of soldiers standing at a "present arms," the procession took up its line of march to the State House. Even though the rain was falling heavily, on either side, amid the sound of tolling bells, all along the entire line of march the citizens thronged the sidewalks, balconies and housetops. The streets quickly turned into a sea of mud, adding to the difficulties of endurance for the people.

During his 1861 journey to Washington, Lincoln gave an address, not to the convened Indiana State Legislature, but rather from a balcony of Bates House, just down the street from the Statehouse. He was greeted by a rousing reception of well-wishers. This was probably the town where he learned his election to office was important to the people. On

Indiana State House at Indianapolis, Indiana, where Lincoln's remains lay in state, April 30, 1865. The canopy building was constructed especially for the memorial services. --*Indiana Historical Society, Bass Photo collection*

this date sorrow and grief greeted the coffin. The funeral cortege stayed at Bates House while the coffin laid in state at the state capitol.

Indianapolis spared no expense in giving proper honors to the deceased President. All the merchant shops and business offices bore expressive badges and emblems of mourning. Washington Street was reported to have presented superior displays. At all the intersecting streets were triple arches, adorned in part with evergreens and national flags, arranged in the most tasteful and beautiful manner.

State House Square was hung with wreaths of arbor vitae. At each corner on Washington Street small arches trimmed with evergreen had been erected. The white fence all the way around the capitol grounds had been whitewashed.

During the prior week, an extensive canopy had been constructed from the main entrance of the State House out to Washington Street. The structure was of considerable size. Underneath was a carriage way and a six-foot passage way on either side. The sixteen pillars supporting the oak structure were fifteen feet high. Portraits of General Grant, General Sherman, Admiral Farragut and Governor Morton were suspended from the pillars.

On the pedestals at the top rested handsome busts of Washington, Webster, Lincoln and Clay. The entire structure was beautifully shrouded in black and white crepe, relieved by evergreens, with a display of flags. At the north side a simple Gothic arch, decorated with the usual draping, had been erected. The pillars of the south front of the Capitol were spirally covered with alternate white and black cloth, the latter edged with evergreens, while the coat of arms of the State was placed in the pediment.

> As it will be necessary to prepare a large number of rosettes, and a large amount of other needle work will be required for the decorations on Washington street, as many ladies as can do so are requested to come to No. 113 West Washington street, as early as 9 o'clock A.M., this morning, and those who cannot come in the morning, are requested to come at 2 o'clock.
>
> By request of the committee.

Article in the *Indianapolis Morning Journal* for April 29, 1865, requesting ladies to volunteer their efforts in the preparation of needlework for the mourning emblems at Indianapolis. All emblems were ruined the next day by the rains.

During the performance of a funeral dirge, the tolling of bells and the sound of cannons, the coffin was conveyed to the interior of the State House in the presence of the military and civic escort.

The decorations in the Hall, had been superintended by Colonels Fryburger and Sturm in the prior week, reflecting much credit upon those who designed and arranged them. The work was described as elaborate and finely executed. Along the walls hung wreaths of evergreen set off by white roses and hung with portraits of Washington, Lincoln, Johnson, Seward, Sheridan, Hovey, Morton, Douglas, Sherman, Grant, Colonel Dick O'Neill, and Edward Everett. The portraits were trimmed in white and black crepe interwoven with leaves of laurel. Garlands of myrtle and evergreen, fastened with black crepe neatly tied and woven with white rosettes and diminutive flags were profusely hung about the walls. The floor was carpeted with a black matting to prevent the sounds of treading feet. Busts of Washington, Lincoln, Jackson, Webster, Clay and Douglas were placed at intervals, their brows bound with laurel.

Mr. W. H. Lommis, suggested dressing the portraits of those dead in white crepe, trimmed with leaves of camellia, jasmine, myrtle or passion vine. Portraits of the living were dressed in black crepe relieved with white. The portrait of Lincoln was shrouded in white crepe with groups of camellia leaves at intervals, fastened with silver stars. Over the top was a coronet of white crepe with silver stars. A portrait of Washington was artistically adorned with white crepe and trimmed in the rare passion vine.

From the conservatory-greenhouse of Mr. Lommis came all of the floral and evergreen decoration used as the interior decorations of the Statehouse. The coffin of Lincoln was decorated with white camellias and roses, orange blossoms, white lilies, callas, alyraium, myrtle, geraniums, and passion flowers. The newspaper noted the flowers were prepared in a solution of gum arabic, to protect them from the action of the atmosphere. After the coffin was removed, the flowers were collected, sewn into a white satin and placed in glass cases at the State Library.

A bust of Lincoln, by T. D. Jones, of Cincinnati, stood on a pedestal at the head of the coffin, its brow encircled with a laurel wreath.

The hall was curtained with black, and brilliantly lighted with numerous chandeliers. The catafalque, on which the coffin rested, was covered with black velvet, and trimmed with silver fringe. The crowning glory of the interior decorations was the canopy overhanging and surrounding the catafalque. It was constructed of black material, in pagoda shape, with white cords and tassels. The ceiling was studded with golden stars. The coffin, as it rested upon the dais, tilted toward the south entrance. It was surrounded with flowers, and when the Veteran Reserve Guard of Escort placed the coffin there, white wreaths and floral crosses were laid upon it. A choir of sixty voices under the direction of Professor Benjamin Owen sang a funeral hymn from the burial service of the Episcopal church.

While the coffin was being prepared for public viewing, eight rosebuds were noted, having been placed there while in New York. General Hooker gathered them and presented them to Mrs. Willard, with a request they should be shared with Mrs. Lommis, Mrs. Colonel O'Neill and Mrs. Grosvenor, who had arranged the new flowers on the coffin. The ladies prized the buds.

At 9:00 a.m., the doors of the State House were opened, and the people, who had patiently waited for hours, were permitted to view the corpse. The Sabbath Schools of Indianapolis formed in procession on Washington Street and near the early hour passed in order by the remains.

Far down the west side of Washington Street, reaching east to Illinois, the sidewalk was closely packed with people, holding their places, frequently through great personal discomfort. Old men and young men, women with children in their arms, black people and white, indiscriminately associated. They were animated by the same motive, not the gratification of a morbid curiosity, but an earnest, loving desire to gaze for the last time on the features of a great and good man, to whom they were grateful, doubly endeared by the atrocious act which destroyed his life. The touching solemnity of the Guard of Honor, were arranged in solemn silence about the coffin. Sorrowful faces of the passing multitude, turned to catch one last glimpse of the features of the dead President, upon all who witnessed it, ineffaceably impressed the sadness of this scene. Lincoln was described as, "... a good deal discolored and emaciated -- wearing a haggard and careworn look, but otherwise rather natural."

Not withstanding the forbidding weather, a constant stream of people passed through the State House. It was estimated that 155 people per minute passed by, and that more thann 100,000 viewed the remains in the course of the 13 hours of viewing.

The colored Masons, in regalia, and colored citizens generally, visited the remains in a body. They formed a very respectable procession, at the head of which was carried the Emancipation Proclamation and at intervals banners bearing the following inscriptions: "Colored Men, always Loyal." "Lincoln, Martyr of Liberty." "He Lives in our Memories." "Slavery is Dead."

Elaborate preparations had been made for a civic and military procession, but the rain fell so heavily that at about noon, General Hovey announced the afternoon procession was cancelled* on account of the heavy rains, and instead the viewing would be continuous. This was quite a disappointment to

* The mourners did not want to leave Indianapolis. A mock funeral procession was held on Monday May 1, with an empty coffin placed in the funeral hearse. The emblems of mourning were left in place at the Statehouse for 30 days for public viewing.

many who had made extensive preparations for the procession. The *Indiana Journal* justly said: "The unpropitious weather prevented the funeral pageant, but an offset to the disappointment of the people in this, was the increased facility given to view the remains as they lay in state at the Capitol. Every Indianian may feel that the honor of the State has been rather brightened than compromised by their reception of the remains of President Lincoln, and that the State where he passed some years of his youth, has rendered her full quota of honor to him as the Savior of his Country."

The rainy weather made walking on the gravel streets terrible walking and rendered any public display futile. It was suggested the intended procession would have eclipsed anything seen excepting that at New York City.

All the hotels in town were filled and yet the trains continued bringing more people during the day to view the remains. The streets were densely packed with people, willing to sacrifice fine apparel to the ongoing rains and the mud streets in order to behold a glimpse of the deceased President. The fine bonnets and gorgeous dresses of many ladies were, as one paper reported, "sacrifice was most reckless," and many ladies demonstrated a bravery and persistence thought not to have been possessed by the fairer gender.

The *Indianapolis Daily Sentinel* special reporter offered an observation of those waiting in the cold rain of Spring for a glimpse of the remains. "All in all the multitude presented the most grotesque and ridiculous appearance we have ever witnessed. The elements with all their conspiring, did not seem to abate the zeal or quench the inordinate desire of sight-seeing which had, apparently, usurped the dominion of reason. Wet, tired, cold and famished, bedaubed with mud and filth, they presented a sorry sight indeed. No more inclement and uncharitable day could have been, and no more enthusiastic mass of sightseers could have possibly been collected together."

While the crowds filled the streets and stood in the rain and mud, for a glimpse at the remains, pickpockets worked the crowds.

THE INDIANAPOLIS STREET RAILWAY DISPLAY

The days of horse drawn street railway had come upon Indianapolis at this early date. The small four-wheel horse cars were quite the feature in the demonstrations for Lincoln's procession of respect to the Statehouse. The cars had been tastefully decorated for the occasion. Each car carried draped flags, and festoons of black and white, gracefully arranged. Each horse was decked with similar emblems of mourning. Each car had an appropriate motto upon the side of the car, with black letters on white muslin, stretched from one end of the car to another. They are as follows:

Car No. 10 -- *Sorrow for the Dead, Justice for the living, Punishment for Traitors.*

Car No. 11 -- *He has gone from Works to his Reward.*

Car No. 12 -- *East, West, North and South Mourns, for the greatest friend of suffering humanity is gone.*

Car No. 13 -- *Fear not Abraham! I am thy Shield. Thy reward shall be exceedingly great.*

Car No. 14 -- *Justice, not Revenge.*

Car No. 15 -- *With Malice towards none, With Charity for all.*

Car No. 16 -- *Too good for Earth, To Heaven thou art gone, and left a Nation in tears.*

Car No. 17 -- *The joy of our heart has ceased, Our dance has turned into mourning.*

Car No. 18 -- *Peace thou gentle Spirit, Souls like thine with God inherit Life and Love.*

Car No. 19 -- *The tear that we shed, though in secret it rolls, shall long keep his memory green in our souls.*

Car No. 20 -- *Thou art gone and Friend and Foe alike appreciate thee now.*

Car No. 21 -- *A Nation's heart was struck April 15, 1865.*

Car No. 22 -- *There is no crime beneath the roof of Heaven that stains the soul of a man with more infernal hue than damned Assassination.*

In the evening the front of the street railway office was brilliantly illuminated with lanterns representing the American flag, with the motto inscribed on each, "Our Union Forever."

The displays were significantly lessened because of the pelting rains.

Sunday evening witnessed the closing of the public viewing at the Indiana Statehouse. It had rained solidly all day, but that did not deter the crowds. At about 9:00 p.m. the crowds diminished, allowing those who came to take a long look at the remains. After nightfall many bonfires were lit, illuminating the streets between the Statehouse and Union Station, casting a lurid glare on the buildings as the time to return to the train approached.

Sometime during the day General McCullum advanced the time for departure of the train to 11:00 p.m. The ceremonies closed at 10:00 p.m. with a procession of the Marshals around the coffin, after which the Guard of Honor and the Veteran Reserve Guard of Escort filed in and took charge of the remains. At a few minutes past ten, while the band played the solemn air "Old Hundred," the coffin was lifted from the dais to the shoulders of the Veteran Reserve Guard of Escort, and carried out to the hearse.

At 10:00 p.m. the soldiers again formed lines on either side of Washington Street and Illinois Street from the Statehouse to Union Station. The soldiers presented arms, each holding a torch. The procession headed out onto Washington Street and south on Illinois in solemn fashion. Several carriages followed the funeral car, along with the Indianapolis city band.

The procession, headed by the carriages of Generals Hooker and Hovey, and composed of the civic and military escort, attended by Senator Lane and Representatives Orth, Stillwell and Farquhar, moved, amid the tolling of bells and thousands of uncovered heads, to place the coffin of Abraham Lincoln upon the train prepared by the Lafayette and Indianapolis Railroad Company, for the journey to Chicago.

The *Indianapolis Daily Sentinel* gave a description of those who witnessed the procession. "This was the most solemn and imposing of all the pageantry that has attended the remains in this city. The wailing sadness of the music, the fitful glare of the lamps, the deep silence unbroken except by the heavy tramp of the soldiers and muffled rumbling of carriage wheels, made it the most impressive scene of all, in the mournful occasion. We cannot adequately describe the sensations experienced, as we witnessed the slowly moving cortege pass by."

The City Councils of Louisville and Cincinnati, and a delegation from Covington, together with Gov. Bramlette, of Kentucky, and a staff of thirty, were the guests of Indiana during the funeral ceremonies at its capital. They stayed at Bates House where Lincoln spoke in 1861. Adjutant General Terrill, General A. Stone, Colonel W. W. Frybarger and Colonel W. R. Holloway, of the Governor's staff, and C. P. Jacobs, General Mansfield, General Bennett and John M. Morton were detailed by Gov. Morton to accompany the funeral cortege from Indianapolis to Springfield.

THE UNIQUE TRAIN OPERATIONS

The Indianapolis - Chicago leg was the last of four legs of the journey to employ multiple railroads for the transportation of the funeral cortege. One unique detail of this leg of the journey, was that the managers of the principal railroad lines involved, met at Indianapolis to work out a timetable common to all. The three railroads involved included the Lafayette and Indianapolis Railroad; Louisville, New Albany and Chicago Railroad and Michigan Central Railroad.*

Train times were among the first problems to be worked out. At this juncture there

*History has stated the train also operated on the Illinois Central Railroad. It did run over 13 miles of the Illionis Central from Kensington to Chicago under a trackage rights agreement that existed between the Michigan Central and the Illinois Central. There were no special crews or other trains involved in this 13 mile run.

* The Michigan Central Railroad is reported to have operated its own sleeping car service since 1858. Evidence indicates the cars were those of Woodruff and Case Sleeping Car companies. Pullman did not affiliate with the Michigan Central Railroad until Spetember1865, some four months after the passage of the funeral train.

was no such thing as standard time zones, thus each railroad could and did select its own local time. The real problem being that even though two railroads might operate into the same town, their published times could vary by 15 to 20 minutes even though each could have a train pulling into adjacent tracks at the same instant.

The time problem arises at various times when a newspaper reporter observes his own local time, and not that of the railroad over which he is passing. The advertised schedule shows the common time as worked out.

During the journey, there were two planned locomotive changes and one fuel stop. Each railroad would provide its own locomotives, appropriately decorated. The LaFayette & Indianapolis locomotives pulled the train the first 65 miles to LaFayette. The next 90 miles saw the locomotives of the Louisville, New Albany and Chicago Railroad on the train. The final 54 miles into Chicago saw the train pulled by locomotives of the Michigan Central Railroad. The tracks of the Michigan Central Railroad did not enter Chicago proper at this time. They used trackage rights over 13 miles of the Illinois Central Railroad.

To each railroad fell the duty of decorating their own locomotives, selecting crewmen, and providing some cars for the train.

The operations on this leg of the journey were the most complicated since the 15-hour run across central New York State in days previous. All required a great deal of coordination to assure flawless operations.

North of Indianapolis the train maintained ten cars. While the remains were at Indianapolis, the *Cleveland Daily Leader* reported to its Cleveland readers, "Mr. R. N. Rice, Superintendent of the Michigan Central Railroad Company has furnished four elegant sleeping cars, one directors' car, two regular day cars, and a baggage car. These with the engine are tastefully clothed with mourning. He personally superintends the movement.*" Adding in the *United States* and the P W & B Directors' car, the train now expands to ten cars. By this statement, we find no passenger equipment provided by the LaFayette and Indianapolis Railroad, nor the Louisville, New Albany and Chicago Railroad. This is the first time since the train left Albany, New York, there had been a complete change of car equipment provided by the participating railroads.

The locomotives selected for the first leg of this night's journey were prepared with appropriate decorations and emblems of mourning at the railroad yards near St. Clair Street, several blocks north of the Union Station. The pilot train locomotive being the *Boon*, with Thomas Colien, engineer. The funeral train locomotive was *Stockwell*, Charles Lamb, engineer. The train was kept in the train shed at Indianapolis Union Station while train's emblems of mourning were touched up, the cars inspected, cleaned and lamps filled with oil for the coming night's journey. The *United States* was kept at Union Station and guarded.

INDIANAPOLIS,
April 30, 1865.

Hon. E. M. STANTON:

Governor Oglesby informs me you assented to Governor Bramlette, of Kentucky, and four of his staff, joining the funeral party here. I have no orders that seem to apply to him. Shall he have tickets?

E. D. TOWNSEND,
Assistant Adjutant-General.

WAR DEPARTMENT,
Washington City,
April 30, 1865—5 p.m.

Adjutant-General TOWNSEND,
Indianapolis and Chicago:

Governor Bramlette and staff were authorized to join the train. I have just got your telegram.

EDWIN M. STANTON.

RULES AND REGULATIONS

1. The figures in Table represent the time upon which the Pilot Engine is to run, and the FUNERAL TRAIN will follow, leaving each station ten minutes behind the figures of this table.
2. The funeral train will pass stations at a speed not exceeding five miles and hour, the engineman tolling his bell as the train passes through the station and town.
3. Telegraph offices upon the entire route will be kept open during the passage of the funeral train, and as soon as the train has passed a station the operator will at once give notice to that effect to the next telegraph station.
4. The pilot engine will pass no telegraph station without first getting information of funeral train having passed the last preceding telegraph station, coming to a full stop for that information, if necessary.
5. Upon the entire route a safety signal will be shown at each switch and bridge, and at entrance upon each curve, indicating that all is safe for the passage of pilot and train—each man in charge of a signal knowing personally such to be the case, so far as his foresight can provide for it. The signal from Indianapolis, until reaching broad daylight, to be a white light, and from that point to Chicago, a white flag, draped.
6. The engineman in charge of pilot engine will carry two red lights in the night, and an American flag, draped, during daylight, indicating that a train is following, and will also provide themselves with red lights, flags and extra men, to give immediate notice to the funeral train, in case of meeting with anything on the route causing delay or detention.
7. The enginemen in charge of the funeral train will keep a sharp lookout for the pilot engine and its signals.
8. The pilot and funeral train will have entire right to the line during its passage, and all trains of every description will be kept out of the way.
9. Each road forming the route will run its train upon its own standard time.

W. F. REYNOLDS
President. L & I R.R.

B. F. MASTEN
Sup't. L., N.A. & C. R.R.

R. N. RICE
Gen. Sup't. M. C. R. R.

To accommodate the uniform movement of the funeral train on its 210 mile journey to Chicago, the following special operating rules were issued jointly by the three railroads at Indianapolis.

MAY 1, 1865
INDIANAPOLIS - CHICAGO

The coffin was taken into the station and loaded back on the *United States*, under the shelter of the imposing roof. On the next track sat the pilot train, ready to move out on orders. It was ready to exit the west end of the structure and give advance notice that the mournful cortege was following.

At about 11:50 p.m., the pilot train, led by *Boon* departed. Ten minutes later the *Stockwell*, departed with the ten car funeral cortege, with the eight provided cars, furnished by the Michigan Central Railroad. It rolled over the LaFayette and Indianapolis Railroad, heading for LaFayette, Michigan City and Chicago.

The first 64 miles northwest of Indianapolis, was the only place west of Cleveland, Ohio, where the funeral train retraced any of the 1861, inauguration train route.

Departing Indianapolis Union Station the tracks turned north and ran parallel with the Central Canal for the first few miles, before crossing it. Within a mile of the canal the tracks crossed the White River and Crooked Creek. Augusta Station, the first village north of Indianapolis was passed at 12:30 a.m.

A correspondent with the *Indianapolis Journal,* riding on the Funeral Train, described its passage over the first 38 miles north of Indianapolis. "Zionsville, 15 miles from Indianapolis was reached at about 12:40 a.m. A large assemblage of people with lighted lamps and torches awaited at trackside for the train, which made a brief stop for a memorial in the rain. Upon learning in which car lay the President's remains, they flocked about it with the greatest anxiety, many endeavoring to get a look at the remains."

The train slowly passed the village of Whitestown, 21 miles north at 1:07 a.m. The funeral cortege was greeted with the now common bonfire and torches. "A number of young ladies are drawn up dressed in white with black sashes." An estimated one hundred people stood near large bonfires in the drizzling rain. The men remained with uncovered heads while the train passed.

Lebanon, county seat of Boone County welcomed the train at 1:30 a.m. for its second brief memorial stop. The newspaper reported, "... it seems as if both town and country were gathered together to honor the dead. Lamps, torches and bonfires send their brilliant light about the assemblage suspended from wires and transparent lights, behind which are drooped flags dressed in mourning. A beautiful arch of evergreens and roses was erected, under which the cars passed. This handsome structure was festooned with velvet rosettes, miniature banners and other decorations. Colored transparencies lent their attractions to make the embellishments more fairylike than real."

Hazlebrigg Station was passed about 1:40 a.m. Thorntown, some 38 miles north, marked the train's arrival at 2:10 a.m. A large number of people were standing at the depot and along the margins of the track. The men stood with uncovered heads as the funeral cortege passed. Bonfires lit the night. The community in and about Thorntown was composed principally of Quakers, and certainly their assembling thus to honor the dead is but additional testimony to their well known devotional life.

During the night, the trains passed through Colfax, a small junction village where it crossed the Logansport, Crawfordsville & Southwestern Railroad. At Clarks Hill, a crowd had assembled at the station, many carrying lanterns to illuminate their way. At 2:50 a.m., the train passed Stockwell. The *Chicago Tribune* reported a fine display with crowds surrounding the depot. Many bonfires and lamps were suspended along the way-

TIME TABLE

INDIANAPOLIS TO CHICAGO.

Miles.			Pilot Engine.
	Leave	Indianapolis	11.50 P. M.
10		Augusta	12.30 A. M.
15		Zionville	12.47 "
21		Whitestown	1.07 "
28		Lebanon	1.30 "
33		Hazelrigg	1.55 "
38		Thorntown	2.10 "
43		Colfax	2.25 "
48		Clarke's Hill	2.40 "
52		Stockwell	2.50 "
56		Culver's	3.00 "
63		Lafayette Junction	3.20 "
65		Lafayette	3.35 "
72		Battle Ground	3.55 "
78		Brookston	4.15 "
82		Chalmers	4.25 "
88		Reynolds	4.45 "
96		Bradford	5.08 "
104		Francisville	5.35 "
110		Medaryville	5.50 "
118		San Pierre	6.15 "
133		Wanatah	7.00 "
142		Westville	7.30 "
146		La Croix	7.40 "
155		Michigan City	8.25 "
168		Porter	8.55 "
176		Lake	9.20 "
188		Gibson's	9.55 "
196		Calumet	10.20 "
209	Arr.	Chicago (Park Place)	10.50 A. M.

side. Culver Station was acknowledged in scenes repeated along the route.

Lafayette Junction on the east side of the Wabash River, was the site where three rail lines met. This was the place where Lincoln's 1861 train moved from the Toledo, Wabash and Great Western Railroad, over to the Lafayette and Indianapolis Railroad on the journey to Indianapolis. It was also near the southern terminus of the Wabash and Erie Canal this night. The funeral train stopped at Lafayette Junction, ending the journey over the L & I. This was also the last duplicate mileage, where Lincoln had traveled during his 1861 journey to Washington, D.C.

One reporter in the funeral cortege described the scene at Lafayette at 3:35 a.m. "The houses on each side of the railroad track are illuminated and, as elsewhere, badges of mourning and draped flags are displayed; bonfires are blazing and bells tolling; Mournful strains of music are heard, and the people are assembled at all the stations to view the train." The crowd was described as very large and orderly.

LAFAYETTE, INDIANA

In Lafayette, the trains switched to the tracks of the Louisville, New Albany and Chicago Railroad. As the pilot train first arrived, the train halted south of the downtown, at or near Lafayette Junction. The L & I locomotive was uncoupled from the coach and run into a side track. A properly decorated locomotive of the Louisville, New Albany and Chicago Railroad, the *Rocket* backed down to the coach, and coupled on. Mr. Rhodes, engineer, then commenced the journey to the north according to the schedule. The same procedure was used to switch locomotives on the funeral train. The locomotive *Persian*, handsomely decorated, was in charge of Mr. A. Rupert. It is unknown whether a memorial ceremony was conducted at this site. At Lafayette, the tracks of the L N A & C ran up the middle of Fifth Street, through the middle of town where the station grounds were located.

The *Lafayette Courier* reported: "The funeral train passed through this city on time this morning. Not withstanding the positive announcement that it would stop a moment, there was a large crowd at Market space and along Fifth Street."

"Traveling at five miles per hour, the train passed through Lafayette to the tolling of church bells. The Silver Band, attached to the Combination Troop played a funeral dirge as the train passed through downtown Lafayette on tracks that ran on Fifth Street. Men stood uncovered and in respectful silence. Many were effected to tears."

Departing town, the railroad ran parallel with the Wabash and Erie Canal for about a mile, then crossed it about two miles on north. The train crossed the Wabash River about two miles further north. Passing through Battleground (City), an estimated 300 people lined the tracks, and waved flags. Brookston, and Chalmers, were passed as the hour of dawn approached. The train may have made a brief stop at Reynolds. It is reported a great many farmers and their families came to town from a distance of 20 miles to pay their respects. At this village tracks of the Toledo, Peoria and Warsaw Railway were crossed.

The small village of Francisville, a scheduled stop was reached at 5:45 a.m. The trains paused for fuel and water. A large crowd assembled around the *United States*, many straining on tiptoe to catch a glimpse of the coffin. While the locomotives were being serviced, a memorial was held, and a wreath laid on the coffin. The service was concluded with a group of ladies singing *Old Hundred*.

Medaryville saw the train pass at sun rise. A large number of people were present to satisfy their wishes to pay some gesture of respect to the dead. At San Pierre, the crowd was large, having waited throughout the night for the coming of the train. They had erected flags and many people were seen wearing mourning badges. North of town the train crossed over the Kankakee River, 120 miles from Indianapolis. Wanatah Station and Haskells were all the sites of crossings with other railroads, any of which could have handily taken the train directly into Chicago, none of which did.

More than 2,000 people were assembled at Westville. As the train neared the station, it passed under an arch, carefully spanning the tracks, and hung with emblems of mourning. A banner across the top read, "Though dead he yet speaketh." The funeral train stopped momentarily in order for the town's people to pay their respects to the late president and conduct a memorial ceremony. It was said that a more serious, thoughtful congregation had not been seen. A group of children were standing to the side, all carrying white mourning flags. At another place young women carried American flags with rosettes. A Mr. Wilkins sang a hymn, "The Departed" while the train was standing at the station.

The train passed through LaCroix (Otis), at 7:50 a.m. crossing the Lake Shore and Michigan Southern Railroad before entering into Michigan City. A demonstration of sorrow was made by the people congregated at the station.

Another long night of continuous memorials had passed. Indiana folk had demonstrated an unparalleled outpouring of sorrow. Tens of thousands of people stood in the rain, along the tracks, at road crossings, huddled around bonfires, to pay their respects of reverence to Lincoln. His way was not through a dark night, but lighted by thousands of torches and lanterns held by the common man. People bowed their heads in silent prayer and gave their public expression with hymns and mournful songs as the train passed through the state.

In this illustration, depicted is the Funeral Train passing under an arch decorated in emblems of mourning. This scene was repeated at many stations along the 1,700 mile route. It appears the most elaborate arch was at Michigan City, Indiana and Chicago, Illinois. -- *Illustration by Author*

At 5:00 a.m. the Chicago Committee of One Hundred met at the Michigan Central Station, in Chicago. There, a special train consisting of three first class coaches, plus a fourth car, likely a combination coach and baggage car were ready to depart for Michigan City to meet the Funeral Train. All the cars were neatly and tastefully decorated with alternate strips of black and white crepe, hanging, with festoons between the windows. The drapery was neatly ornamented with rosettes and small flags.

The Committee members boarded the train and at precisely 5:30 a.m., departed via the Michigan Central Railroad for the 54-mile run to Indiana. A breakfast had been prepared by the Tremont House, for those on the train. After the train departed, Mr. H. K. Sargent, General Agent of the Michigan Central Railroad extended an invitation to those on board. It was served in the baggage section of the train.

It was noted by Committee members there seemed to be little interest en route. The train reached its destination of Michigan City at approximately 7:45 a.m. It was greeted by a large crowd and the salute of a single cannon.

BREAKFAST AT MICHIGAN CITY

By dawn, the rains had stopped and the skies cleared. Upon reaching Michigan City, Indiana, the train was switched to the tracks of the Michigan Central Railroad, in preparation for the final leg of the journey into Chicago. The *Indianapolis Daily Journal*, described the arrival in Michigan City, on May 1. The reporter thought the change in weather was; "in harmony with the warm hearts and fervent patriotism of the men and women of Michigan City."

Michigan City, was a scheduled meal stop. This was the second planned breakfast stop on the route of the train. A locomotive change was scheduled before continuing the last leg of the journey into Chicago.

The funeral cortege bearing the remains of Lincoln pulled into the station. The train had to be turned. It is unclear whether it was turned on a wye track before hand, or whether it was turned while breakfast was being served. Upon arrival at the Louisville, New Albany and Chicago station, it passed under a triumphal funeral arch, made with great preparations by the ladies. Once stopped, the approximately 300 members of the funeral escort detrained to partake of the breakfast and to stretch. A white fish breakfast was served to them by many notable housewives who devoted their time to its preparation. They used their best linen and silver for a proper dining experience. Breakfast was served in the Louisville, New Albany and Chicago Railroad freight station house near the shores of Lake Michigan. Luther Bulock, one of the Veteran Reserve Guard of Escort on the train wrote in his journal: "At Michigan City stopped for breakfast and the table was spread with all that one could wish for."

While the feast was consumed, the trains were switched to the tracks of the Michigan Central Railroad, and locomotives changed for the final 54 miles of the journey. The pilot locomotive would be Michigan Central locomotive *Frank Valkenberg*, while the locomotive to draw the funeral train would be the *Ranger*. Both the pilot locomotive and Funeral Train locomotives were draped in black cloth, and bore in front of the headlight a portrait of the deceased President with a wreath of flowers and fruit, exquisitely done in wax. The sides of the locomotives were festooned with crape and black velvet, interspersed with rosettes.

When the Funeral Train was in station, the citizens of Michigan City were welcomed through the funeral car for a public visitation. This is one of three recorded times Lincoln's coffin was opened for public viewing while on the train. Preference was shown to the ladies. At first, eighteen ladies dressed in mourning stepped forward. They carried flowers wrought into wreaths, crosses, anchors, stars and shields, which were laid on the coffin. Then a group of 36 young girls and one more dressed as the Goddess of Liberty, had been selected to lay a cross of flowers on the casket. These girls wore long black skirts and white waists, and with uncovered heads they carried their offering to the funeral car where lay the remains of the martyred president. This cross was composed of trailing arbutus gathered from our native hills. The honor guards kept their watch over the mortal remains as the throngs of people came on board.

The crowd was held back by ropes. In a moment they surged forward in a near panic. Several had been knocked to the ground and trampled. So great was their desire to enter the car that confusion resulted. Several times it was announced the viewing would end as a method to rgain control of the crowds..

Upon the meeting of the committee sent out from Chicago to meet the funeral train, it was noted the officers in charge ... "were in full dress uniforms; the Chicago delegation was in black wearing heavy crepe on their arms." During the reception, the Chicago Committee and the Indiana officers in charge came forward to properly transfer the funeral cortege to their charge, and for the Illinois officers to receive the funeral cortege.

The reporters give a partial account of the scene in Michigan City: "... the train stopped at Michigan City, under a beautiful structure 12 feet wide, and the main columns 14 feet high. From these sprang a succession of arches in the Gothic style, 35 feet from the base to the summit. From the crowning central point was a staff with a draped national flag at half-mast. The arches were trimmed with white and black, and ornamented with evergreens and choice flowers. Numerous miniature flags fringed the curved edges, and portraits of the lamented dead were encircled with crepe. At the abutments and the ends of the main arch were the mottoes: 'The purposes of the Almighty are perfect and must prevail.' 'Abraham Lincoln, the noblest martyr to freedom; sacred thy dust; hallowed thy resting place.' On each side of the arch were

Michigan City, Indiana, May 1, 1865. The funeral train sits under the funeral arch constructed as the handiwork of the ladies of Michigan City. Note, the maidens in white blouses and black skirts standing in line near the arch. To the left background is the Louisville, New Albany and Chicago Depot where breakfast was served. It appears the car under the arch is one of the Michigan Central Railroad sleeping cars. By the position of the cars under the arch, it is probable the train is preparing to depart for Chicago. -- *Old Lighthouse Museum collection*

Michigan City, Indiana, where the Lincoln Funeral train escort had breakfast on May 1, 1865. It is believed the building where the white fish breakfast was served is the long white building in the top center of the map depiction. The scene looks south west. -- *Library of Congress*

the words 'Abraham Lincoln,' formed with sprigs of the arbor vitae, with the mottoes, 'Our guiding star has fallen;' 'The nation mourns,' and 'Though dead he yet speaketh.'"

The *Indianapolis Journal* reporter referred to the decorated arches as, "... the handiwork of the ladies of Michigan City ... most beautiful in execution and design." He commented: "In the brief moment we have to describe this wonderful piece of beautiful mechanism, it is impossible to do it justice. We have only to say that the women of Michigan City have reared a monument to the moral worth of Abraham Lincoln more lasting and enduring, more solid and substantial, than the laurels of warriors or crowns of kings - a cross of solid flowers."

The trains departed to the west at approximately 8:45 a.m. via the Michigan Central Railroad. Its departure was with eleven cars, having added one additional car, likely to carry the additional members of the Chicago Committee. This time the cortege consisted of three trains; the Pilot train, the Funeral train and the Chicago Committee train.

The trains passed Lake Station at about 9:30 a.m. The station had been draped in emblems of mourning. People gazing upon the train were described as having a most reverent look.

A minor incident occurred when notable personages from Washington were left behind at Michigan City. They were promptly put on a hastily gathered locomotive and dispatched toward the Funeral Train with the use of an "express engine." A telegraph message was apparently sent ahead to stop the Funeral Train. The stray members were reunited with the train at Porter Station, 13

PHOTO BELOW - Funeral car *United States* on the wharf at the Great Central Station in Chicago, Illinois, May 1 and May 2, 1865. - - *Library of Congress*

miles west of Michigan City.

The small whistle stop of Tollestone, was passed and at 10:05 a.m., Gibsons Station, Indiana, was passed as the train neared the Illinois border. Many people stood silently and reverently as the funeral cortege passed from Indiana, and slipped into Illinois

There was no triumphal return for Abraham Lincoln to the lands he called home. There were no stirring speeches and no cheering from the passing crowds. The Funeral cortege entered the state in silence, only interrupted by the sounds of the train, to tears and the awful silence of meeting death with merciful compassion.

At Kensington Junction, Illinois, near Lake Calumet, the train turned north for the final 13 miles into Chicago. It was reported near Lake Calumet, where the train entered the State of Illinois, many people had assembled, and squads of soldiers were seen on the hillsides, silently witnessing the cortege. A stop was made here while the arrangements necessary for the trains to safely enter upon the tracks of the Illinois Central Railroad were completed. While it was stopped, crowds gathered around the funeral car vainly trying to catch a glimpse of the coffin. This was the greeting of the nation's hero back to his homeland. There was little else other than sorrow, prayers and tears.

Kensington, Illinois, was an important junction on the route. It was at this place the Michigan Central Railroad tracks ended. The extension of the railroad to Kensington, Illinois, was completed in May 1852. At this same time trains were run to Chicago, Illinois, for 13 miles over the tracks of the Illinois Central Railroad. Crowds had silently assembled all along the route to witness the funeral train. They stood heads uncovered in respectful sympathy, and perhaps in thoughtful prayer or grateful appreciation for having sent a father, son or brother home from gruesome battle.

CHICAGO PREPARATIONS

On April 18th Governor Oglesby telegraphed citizens of Chicago, the remains of Abraham Lincoln would pass through Chicago, but the route and schedule were not confirmed. It was anticipated the train would travel via Cleveland and Toledo, along the Lake Erie shore, reaching Chicago about April 26. Word reached Chicago April 19, the train would stop for a state viewing on May 1 and 2. Immediately, the Common Council appointed a committee to superintend arrangements for the reception of the remains of the President. A second meeting on Friday, April 21, found several recommendations accepted and the plans announced. They generally included reception of the remains at Lake Park, opposite Park Row; A Committee of One Hundred Citizens be appointed to meet the cortege at Michigan City and conduct them to Chicago; The remains be deposited in Cook County Courthouse for viewing; An artist be employed to decorate the rotunda and Courthouse; A funeral arch be constructed at Park Row and a suitable catafalque be constructed to hold the remains. The planned route and order of procession were also recommended and approved.

The following Tuesday plans for the funeral arch, catafalque and hearse car were presented for final approval. Construction commenced immediately at the Park Row site. The architect of the arch, W. W. Boyington, personally oversaw construction.

The school teachers of Chicago were instructed that the children would take part in the reception procession on May 1st. The children were to report to their respective schools at 9:00 a.m. and conduct themselves to their designated site in body near Park Row at no later than 10:15 a.m. Upon conclusion of the ceremonies, the children were to be returned to their respective schools and dismissed until the resumption of classes on Wednesday. J. L. Pickard, Superintendent of Schools also stated: "Every precaution has been taken to guard against accidents, but all parents who are unwilling to trust their children with their teachers upon that day will please detain them at home." Each child was requested to carry a small flag draped in black crepe.

The horse drawn street cars were requested not to run east of the Chicago River on May 1 and May 2 because of the throng of people expected.

The funeral procession count on April 29, was over 25,000 expected participants. The hearse was finished in time and the arch received finishing touches at 10:30 a.m. on May 1.

THE CHICAGO FUNERAL OBSEQUIES OF ABRAHAM LINCOLN

Dawn broke over Chicago, gray and dreary with heavy clouds. Throughout the morning the clouds seemed to lift and as the Funeral Train neared Chicago the sun broke through. The train rolled through the southern suburbs of the city, and at every street the crowds of mourners increased, the men standing with heads uncovered. The brave boys of the Soldiers' Home of Fairview, some forty maimed heroes of the war, and a large representation from the troops on duty at Camp Douglas, gave the soldiers' salute and stood reverently in line as, with slackened speed, the train moved cityward. The Soldiers' Home was very beautifully decorated.

At every street crossing crowds had assembled. In every window and on rooftops people had gathered to silently witness the passage of the train.

At Weldon Station, about a half mile from Park Row, the salute of minute guns was fired and continued until the train reached its destination.

From before dawn people had begun filling the streets in the vicinity of the station, and now everywhere was a sea of humanity. Every place that could be used as seeing room was appropriated, including rooftops along Michigan Avenue to the water's edge. The limbs of trees were filled with people until they creaked and threatened to snap. Between 8:00 and 9:00 a.m. the newspapers described a mighty tide of people arriving in the area for reception of the remains. Every perch was occupied. A wooden fence near the platform collapsed under the weight of many people

Nearly ten thousand children, from the public and private schools, were at the reception area as spectators, and to march in the procession. Every organization, and society in Chicago was represented. In pursuance of orders issued by Brigadier-General Sweet, 400 members of the 15th Veteran Reserve Corps, 400 of the 8th Veteran Reserve Corps, and 400 of the 6th United States Infantry participated in the pageant, and detachments of the first two regiments performed guard duty during the afternoon and night. The 24th Ohio Battery was also in the city from Camp Douglas. One detachment served the minute guns at Park Row, while the remainder acted as mounted guards on the various parts of the line of march.

The *Chicago Tribune* described the still and clear surface of Lake Michigan as, "long ruffled by storm, suddenly calmed from their angry roar into solemn silence, as if they, too, felt that silence was an imperative necessity of the mournful occasion."

In the center of Park Row, near the railroad, a funeral arch had been erected. It was composed of one center and two side arches. The arch was designed and its construction supervised by W. W. Boyington. At the hour of 9:00 a.m., workmen were finishing the removal of scaffold and floral decorations were being added as masses of people began arriving.

Dwellings and business houses displayed symbols expressive of deep mourning, with many appropriate mottoes and tasteful devices.

In the vast crowd around the railway station there was no disorder. The crowd came to a deep silence as the pilot train arrived, and paused briefly near the arch, to unload its passengers. The locomotive *Frank Vkenberg*, was draped with black cloth and carried a large portrait of Lincoln under its headlight, with a wreath of flowers and fruit "exquisitely done in wax." The sides of the locomotive were festooned in crape and black velvet, interspersed with rosettes.

The Funeral Train arrived in Chicago at 11:00 a.m. It did not go the full distance to the Great Central Station, jointly used by the Michigan Central and Illinois Central Railroads. It stopped at the temporary platform built for this train at Park Row, nearly a mile south. The offloading platform was on the shore of Lake Michigan. When the train arrived at the temporary station near Park Row, guns were fired and the courthouse bell tolled.

On arrival of the pilot train the crowd fairly broke free from the barriers and made their way up the track to catch the first glimpse of the expected Funeral Train. With the firing of the minute gun to announce the trains approach, it came into view of the massive crowds from around the bend. The masses fell silent and all heads were uncovered as it pulled up to the temporary platform. The train uncoupled from the *United States* and the various escorts and committees stepped off the train and formed in line.

At 11:15 a.m., the coffin was lifted off the car and carried on the shoulders of the eight Veteran Reserve Guard of Escort to the dais on the funeral hearse sitting underneath the Funeral Arch. All uncovered their heads in reverence as the corpse passed by. The coffin was laid on the dais, and the mourners gath-

CHICAGO, ILLINOIS

CHICAGO RIVER
LAKE ST.
COOK COUNTY COURT HOUSE
GREAT CENTRAL STATION Funeral car spotted here while in Chicago
WASHINGTON ST.
MADISON ST.
CANAL ST.
MARKET
CLARK ST.
LAKE MICHIGAN
ILLINOIS CENTRAL RAILROAD TRESTLE
CHICAGO & ALTON DEPOT Departure site May 2, 1865, for last leg of the Lincoln Funeral Train
MICHIGAN AVE.
CHICAGO & ALTON RAILROAD
PARK ROW Arrival site May 1, 1865, for unloading Lincoln's coffin
TO SPRINGFIELD
GALENA & CHICAGO UNION RAILROAD

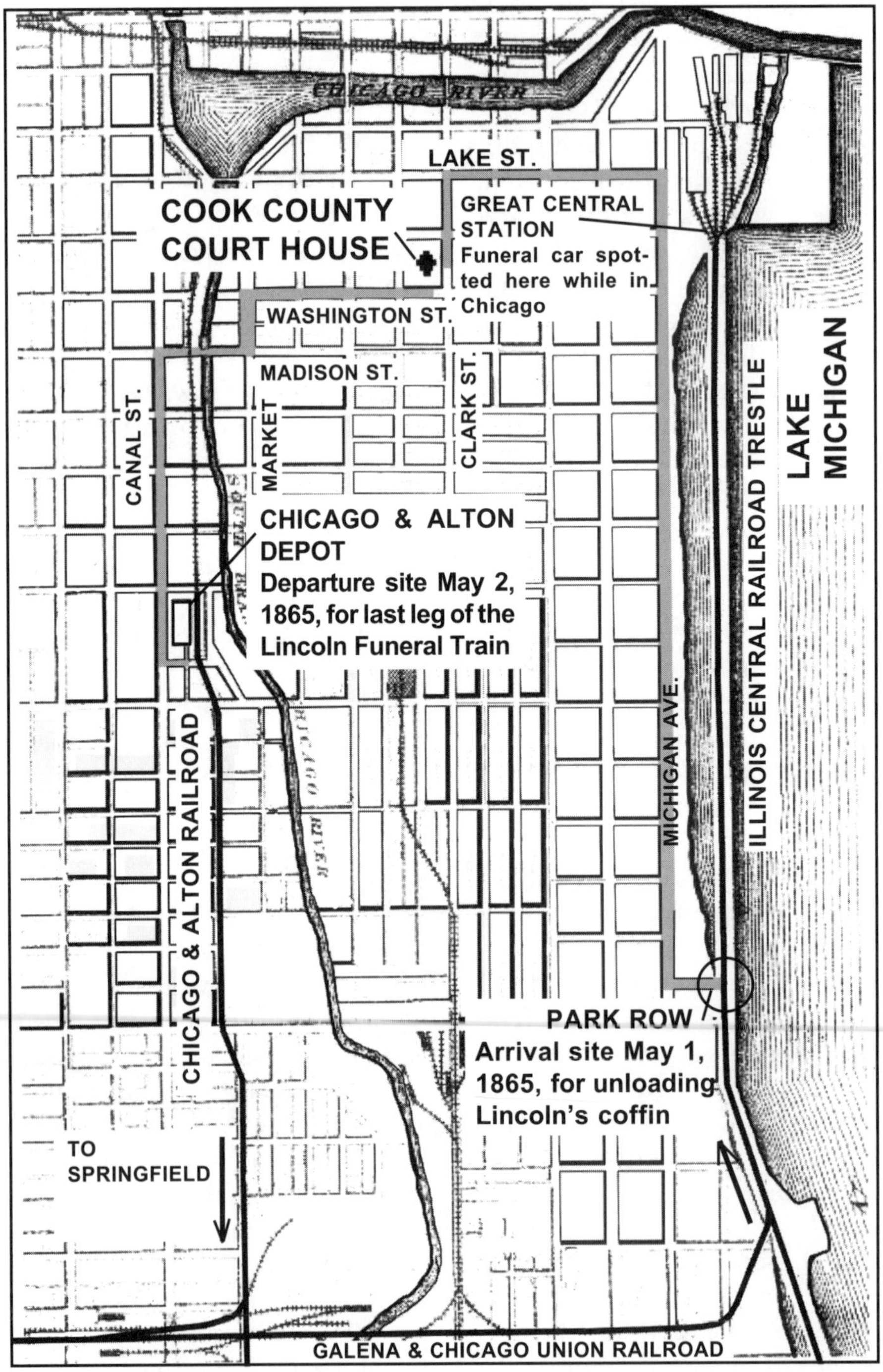

The Funeral train entered Chicago, over tracks of the Illinois Central Railroad. While the memorials were under way the empty train was transferred via the Galena & Chicago Union Railroad to the Chicago & Alton Railroad, where it departed for Springfield on May 2, 1865.

Locomotive *Ranger*, of the Michigan Central Railroad, sitting on the causeway trestle of the Illinois Central Railroad north of 12th Street in Chicago, Illinois, May 1, 1865. The first car behind the locomotive tender is the baggage car, next is a coach where the local delegates rode. A Michigan Central sleeping car is visible as the third car on the right of the photo. This is probably the most widely circulated photo of the funeral train. After the Great Chicago fire of 1871 this area was filled with the rubble and the shore moved well beyond the trestle.
-- *Illinois Central Railroad photo*

ered around it, the Great Western Light Guard Band took position in front and commenced the funeral march, "The Lincoln Requiem" composed by Vaas for the occasion. After a short pause, thirty-six young maidens dressed in white and banded with crape, came forward and walked around the bier, each depositing a floral immortelle on the coffin.

The *Chicago Times* reported on the maidens as 36 high school girls; "...this fair company of maidens had been the object of universal admiration and remark. [Before arrival of the train]. They were placed within the garden in front of one of the residences, where they awaited the coming of the train. Attired in snow white robes, with a simple sash of thin black crape tied with a rosette at the side, bareheaded and with a black velvet wreath over their brows, in front of which sparkled a single star, some with sunny ringlets hanging loosely round their shoulders; others with their hair arranged in neat plaits at the back--they looked the emblems of purity. It seemed as if a troop of snowy doves had suddenly fluttered down from heaven with messages of peace to men."

The hearse passed out of Park Row and onto Michigan Avenue: It was eighteen feet in length, with an extreme height of fifteen feet from the ground. It was drawn by ten black horses. Following the hearse came the military escort-the Veteran Reserve Guard of Escort and the delegations from Washington. They were succeeded by the Citizens' Committee of One Hundred, dressed in black, with crape hat bands and rosettes; the incoming and retiring Mayors of Chicago, and others.

The line of march was from Park Row to Michigan Avenue, along the avenue to Lake Street, down Lake to Clark, Clark to the east gate of the Courthouse square, and inside the square round to the south door of the Courthouse, in which the coffin was deposited.

The *Chicago Tribune* estimated citizens bordering the route of the procession, were not far from 120,000. The head of the cortege reached the Courthouse at 12:45 p.m. The military portion of the procession, under command of Brigadier General B. J. Sweet, was formed by regiments in the Public Square. As the hearse drew near the north entrance, they received it with a "present arms," and other military tokens of respect. General Hooker and his accompanying officers made a preliminary survey of the interior decorations of the Hall, and then returned to the north entrance. The coffin was borne into the Courthouse upon the shoulders of the Veteran Reserve Guard of Escort. While the coffin was being placed in position, a choir of 200 voices sang a dirge. The different parts of the procession filed through the Courthouse, past the corpse, and left by the north door.

The Courthouse was elaborately decorated. The north door was heavily draped in black, and a banner was suspended with an inscription, in black upon a white ground, "The beauty of Israel is slain upon her high places." On the south door was this inscription: "Illinois clasps to her bosom her slain and glorified son."

The catafalque stood in the center of the rotunda, directly under the dome. The canopy was draped with rich black. The roof of the catafalque, inside, was a plain flat top of heavy cloth, in which were cut thirty-six stars. Over these were placed a layer of white gauze, and over this several brilliant reflectors, which caused the light to shine through the stars, upon the body below, with a softened, yellow mellow radiance. The effect was new and solemn. Extending around the catafalque, about midway between the dais and the canopy, looped in elegant festoons, was a wreath of evergreens and camellias, no inconsiderable part of the decorations.

At 5:00 p.m., the remains were exposed to public view, and the announcement made that the public would be admitted. The crowd, which was anxiously waiting outside the Public Square, began to file into the Courthouse. Visitors passed through the rotunda without confusion, taking time only to glance at the revered remains, at the rate of 7,000 an hour

During the evening, dirges were sung, both solos and concerted pieces. Among others the following were performed: "Lord, I yield my spirit," and the choral, "Happy and Blessed are They," from the oratorio of St. Paul, "He that Endureth to the End," and "Farewell, Father, Friend and Guardian"-the last, words by L. M. Dawn, and music by George F. Root, composed expressly for the occasion. Root was also in charge of the music for the Chicago arrangements. At midnight the Germans, numbering several hundred, chanted a beautiful and impressive dirge. Drizzling rain began to fall about 9:00 p.m. It was long after midnight before there was any lessening in the crowds which sought to get a last look upon the dead President. They streamed through the rotunda in a constant line. It is estimated that up to midnight at least 40,000 persons had looked upon the remains of Abraham Lincoln.

Cook County Court House at Chicago, Illinois, where Lincoln lay in state May 1 and May 2, 1865. This was the only county court house to host the remains. The parade from the train to the court house was the largest parade ever staged in the western United States . Below is a view inside the Court House.

After midnight, persons anticipating the crowd of the forthcoming day, left their homes expecting to pass immediately into the rotunda where the corpse lay, but were disappointed, compelled to take their places with others, some of whom had waited for hours. At noon, on May 2nd, the line extended nearly a mile.

The *New York Tribune* said: "A part of day before yesterday, all of night before last, and all day yesterday, the remains of the President lay in state amid the imposing funeral surroundings in the Courthouse, and still there was not sufficient time for all who sought the privilege to look upon his face."

THE TRAIN AT CHICAGO

As soon as the remains and escort were off the train, it was moved north over the Illinois Central trestle, built nearly a half-mile from shore for access to the Great Central Station and train shed near the Chicago River. Photos indicate the train was held here for a portion of the layover in Chicago. At some point the *United States* and Officers' car were uncoupled and left on the platform. A guard was posted for the remains of Willie. The balance of the train was moved elsewhere, and new cars added in preparation for the final leg of the journey.

One of the *Associated Press* reporters wrote at Chicago, "Since leaving Washington on Friday, 21st of April, to this time, the 3d of May, twelve days, we have traveled 1,700 or 1,800 miles. The funeral cars which we started from Washington have come all the way without accident, even of a trivial character, having happened, so perfect have been the arrangements."

"Colonel Robertson [sic: Robinson], who is connected with the military railroads, now composes one of our party. The fatigue of the journey has been relieved by kind attentions everywhere, and the personal attentions and hospitalities profusely bestowed."

TRAVEL LOG

May 1, 1865 210 miles

Via Indianapolis & LaFayette Railroad
Louisville, New Albany & Chicago Railroad
Michigan Central Railroad

Times reported are those of the funeral train as it passed the listed stations

Station		Time
Indianapolis & LaFayette Railroad		
Indianapolis DEPART:		Midnight
Augusta Station		
Zionsville		12:40 a.m.
Whitestown		1:07 a.m.
Lebanon		1:30 a.m.
Hazlebrigg Station		
Thorntown		2:10 a.m.
Colfax		
Clarks Hill		2:40 a.m.
Stockwell		2:50 a.m.
Culvers Station		
Lafayette Jct.		
Louisville, New Albany & Chicago Railroad		
Lafayette		3:20 a.m.
Battleground (City)		3:55 a.m.
Brookston		
Chalmers		
Reynolds		
Bradford (Monon)		
Francisville		4:45 a.m.
Medaryville		
Sant Pierre		6:25 a.m.
La Crosse		
Wanatah		
Haskells		
Westville		7:40 a.m.
LaCroix (Otis)		
Michigan City*	ARR	7:45 a.m.
Michigan Central Railroad		
Michigan City	Depart	8:45 a.m.
Porter		
Lake Station		9:30 a.m.
Tollestone		
Gibsons Station		10:05 a.m.
Calumet		10:30 a.m.
Trackage rights on Illinois Central Railroad		
Kensington Junction		
Hyde Park		
Chicago ARR.		11:00 a.m.

MAY 2 - 3, 1865
CHICAGO - BLOOMINGTON - SPRINGFIELD

DEPARTING CHICAGO

After dusk, the funeral escort reassembled at the Cook County Courthouse. Public visitation ended and with proper ceremony the coffin was closed. Young ladies came to place upon it fresh flowers wrought into significant and touching emblems. The last dirge was chanted by the choir before leaving the Courthouse. The funeral escorts surrounded the bier, lifting the coffin upon the shoulders of the Veteran Reserve Guard of Escort. It was carried out of the Courthouse to the hearse between lines of flaring torches. Long after the gates of the public square had been closed, a long, dense column still waited in the vain hope of being admitted.

According to the *Chicago Times,* "Taken all in all, Chicago made a deeper impression upon those who had been with the funeral from the first than any one of the ten cities passed through before had done. It was to be expected that such would be the case; yet, seeing how other cities had honored the funeral, there seemed to be no room for more; and the Eastern members of the cortege could not repress surprise when they saw how Chicago and the Northwest came, with one accord, with tears and with offerings, to help bury this Duncan who had been so clear in his great office. The last of these tributes was the escort of torches to the funeral train, showing the cortege as it passed to thousands who were themselves wrapped in darkness."

The cortege was flanked by a thousand torchbearers, who marched parallel with it, and three feet from the sidewalk. The route of the procession was fairly short, compared to that of Philadelphia or New York City. It was along Washington and Market streets to Madison Street Bridge, and south to the depot of the Chicago and Alton Railway.

The torchlight display was the most beautiful ever witnessed in the west. When it reached the depot, the glare of its lights fell upon thousands of people who had taken a last look at the corpse in the rotunda of the Courthouse, and were unwilling to be absent when it departed from the city.

Escorting the hearse from the Courthouse to the Chicago and Alton Railway Station were hundreds of torchbearers, Chicago Common Council acting as pallbearers, and an array of military organizations headed by General Joseph Hooker. The bells of Chicago were tolled, as a choir sang a dirge, and several bands of music performed solemn airs.

The approach to the train was lined by soldiers to keep the crowds back some distance through which the escorts passed.

The escort consisted of the Guard of Honor, Illinois Delegation, the congressional delegation, military escort, and various citizens' committee. They were followed by the Chicago Common Council, and several women who joined the train as part of the Chicago Committee, dressed in black skirts with white waists. Women had been excluded from traveling on the train other than the short stretch of travel between Michigan City and Chicago. This night would present another first with both women and people of color on the train.

A MINOR ACCIDENT

While the train had been free from problems, the funeral procession was not. The procession was marching toward the C & A depot, when a wooden sidewalk near the corner of Washington and Market Streets gave way under the great weight of the spectators standing upon it. About a dozen people plunged into a trench about seven to eight feet deep, most receiving only scrapes and cuts.

A few minutes later at the corner of Madison and Market Streets another sidewalk also collapsed, throwing between 100 and 130 people into a trench filled with broken bottles, bricks and rubbish. Several of the torch bearers broke off from the procession to help with the rescue efforts. This time it was reported that nearly everyone thrown to the ground was injured, some quite seriously. There were reports of broken bones, a dislocated shoulder and contusions to the head. The *Chicago Tribune* later gave notice: "A large number of hats, caps, bonnets, etc., were taken from the scene of the accident by the police, and may be seen for identification at the Central Police Station."

As the funeral cortege prepared to board the train, Mr. Timothy B. Blackstone, the recently appointed President of the newly organized Chicago & Alton Railroad, and Robert Hale, the General Superintendent of the Railroad Company, gave personal attention to the running of the train. Much of this line of the railroad had been surveyed by Mr. Blackstone some ten years prior when construction was undertaken.

Large accessions were made to the funeral party. Among them was the addition of the Springfield delegation appointed to escort the President's remains on the final leg of the journey to Springfield.

Upon arriving, the funeral cortege passed through the guarded station. Lincoln's coffin was taken from the hearse for the last time and carried to the waiting funeral train. It was passed through the narrow end door of the *United States* via the rollers and the Veteran Reserve Guard of Escort then picked it up, placing it on the catafalque. As the time for departure of the train drew near the parties took their place in the sleeping cars.

ELEGANT ACCOMMODATIONS FOR THE GUESTS

The final Funeral Train of May 2, was unprecedented on any American railroad. It consisted of eight elegant sleeping cars; four from the Michigan Central Railroad, and coming through from Indianapolis, four sleeping cars from the firm of Field & Pullman, the Directors' Car from the Michigan Central Railroad, the Philadelphia, Wilmington & Baltimore Directors' Car, used by the military escort, the funeral car *United States* and a baggage car.

Because sleeping cars were relatively new to railroad travel and suggested privilege; first-class and luxury, an entire train affording such accommodations was practically unheard of. It was well above the accommodations offered in the standard coach, and proper for the distinguished members of the funeral escort on this final night's journey. Such cars were made-up for day travel with chairs or seats of the day, and could be rearranged that the chairs turned into beds for sleeping.

Because of the overwhelming demand for rail transportation to move more than 100,000 mourners to Springfield for the funeral, there simply was not enough passenger equipment on the C & A to fill such demands. An equal concern was the lack of any lodging at Springfield, giving rise to the use of the sleeping cars as portable hotels while at Springfield.

Illinois legend incorrectly portrays that George M. Pullman, and the Pullman Palace Sleeping Car Company transported Lincoln's body in a Pullman sleeping car as a part of the final leg of the journey from Chicago to Springfield. At this time the Pullman Company did not exist. Some form of partnership under the name of Field & Pullman was providing sleeping cars. Records indicate George Pullman owned a few of his cars, and other business partners including Benjamin C. Field owned some cars, however, there was no formal Pullman corporation at this time.

Lincoln's coffin was handled exclusively inside the specially modified *United States*, a railroad car built and owned by the Federal Government. The coffin did not lay in state at any time inside the Pullman sleeping car

ILLINOIS

May 1 - 3, 1865

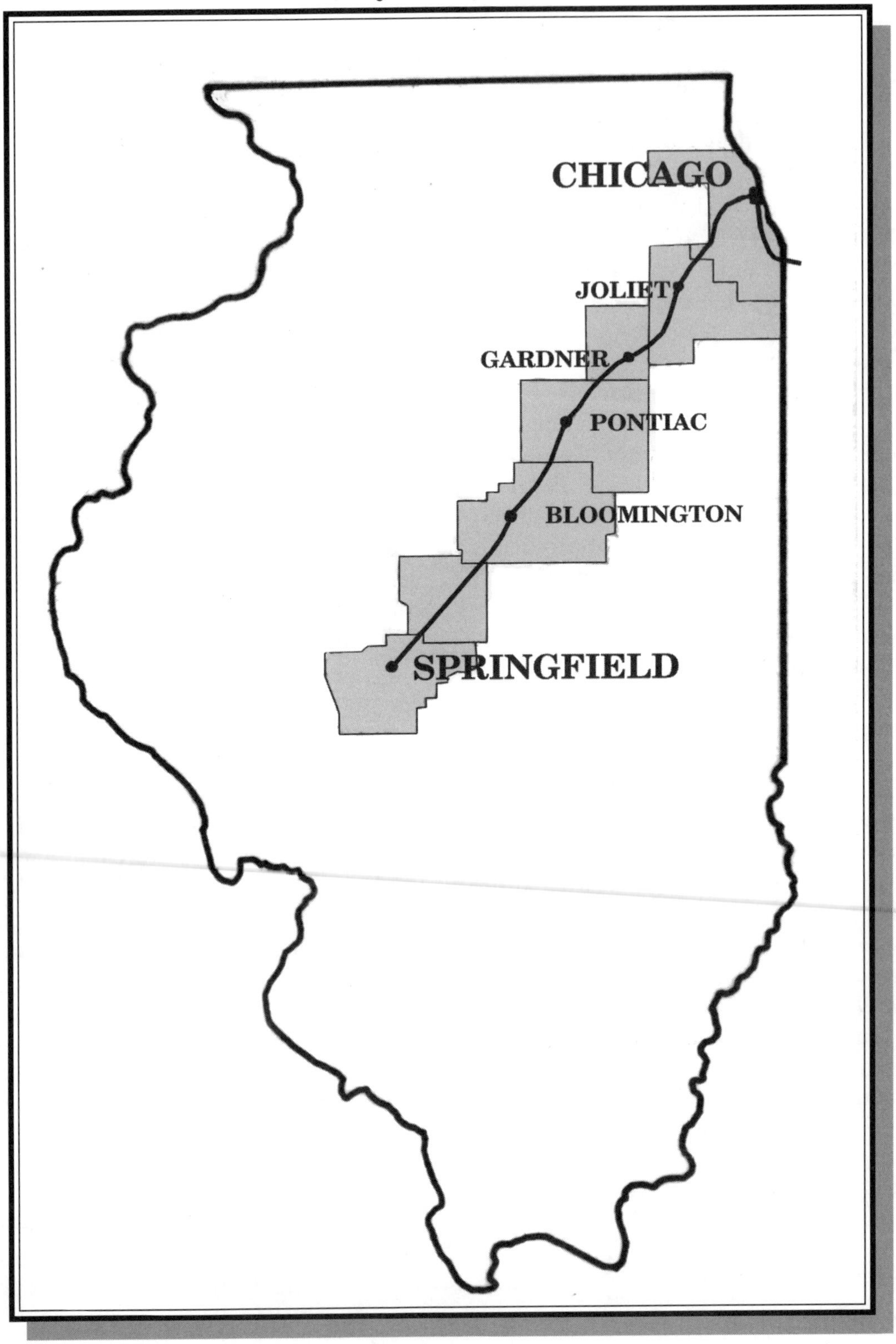

Pioneer,* or any Pullman built sleeping car.

Field & Pullman was operating a recently acquired sleeping car, which had a very similar appearance to the President's funeral car *United States*. That F & P car named *Springfield*, was at Springfield on May 4, 1865. It had 16 wheels, but was about 14 feet longer than the *United States*. It likely transported guests from Chicago in advance of the departure of the funeral train. It was being used, this date as lodging for guests to the funeral. Descriptions of the car appear in the *Wilmington Independent* on May 10, 1865.

Accounts have placed eight sleeping cars on the Funeral Train this night. Six apparently on the train when it left Chicago and two more added to the train at Joliet, Illinois. Business arrangements between the Chicago & Alton Railroad and Field & Pullman might suggest the cars were of the Field & Pullman owned cars. *The Daily Pantagraph*, at Bloomington, Illinois, reporting the trains out of Chicago states; "Mr. Blackstone, the President and Robert Hale the Superintendent of the railroad company, together with many other new accessions are on board, and Mr. Pullman, the proprietor of the sleeping cars, has amply provided a sufficient number of them for the entire party, giving his personal attention to those truly desirable accommodations."

The Funeral Train carried three sleeping cars of Webster Wagner's, New York Central Sleeping Car Company from Albany, New York, to Indianapolis, Indiana. They were replaced by four Michigan Central Sleeping cars from the Woodruff and S. C. Case firms on the Indianapolis to Chicago leg. On the Chicago to Springfield leg, the four Michigan Central sleepers remained on the train, and four Field & Pullman sleeping cars were added.

Legend has portrayed that George Pullman was nearly broke and in debt to many in Chicago, as a result of the Civil War. Because most of the Illinois Committee were Chicago business people, they allegedly held much of Pullman's debt. It is the opinion of some scholars on the topic that debt holders decided to have one of F & P sleeping cars attached to the train. In accordance with instructions for travel of the train after midnight, additional sleeping cars could be added for the accommodation of the funeral escort. This lore does not appear to be a valid portrayal of the F & P participation in the funeral, because his cars had been established for six years along this line of railroad and four F & P cars were used on the train.

Pullman lore also suggests that those holding the debt of Pullman felt that if his sleeping car was seen on the train, it would be a rolling advertisement, and would certainly attract business to the upstart sleeping car enterprise, and would save the investors from losing their money. The stories appear to be more fiction than factual. George Pullman was with his cars in Springfield, not unlike Webster Wagner, who was with his cars from Albany to Indianapolis.

Local accounts at Springfield, Illinois, on May 4, 1865, state 34-year-old George Pullman, was there with several of his cars. He invited W. R. Steele, editor of the *Wilmington Independent,* on May 4, to view, "... some four or five cars of equally handsome, but differently arranged inside." The cars apparently carried many states' officials to Springfield. Again the *Wilmington Independent* sheds some light on the mysteries on why the Pullman sleeping cars were there.

---

*According to existing newspaper accounts in surviving Pullman Records in the Newberry Library, *Pioneer* may not have been delivered and ready for test demonstrations until May 25, 1865, three weeks after the passage of Lincoln's Funeral Train. See *Daily Illinois State Register*, May 26, 1865, and *The Daily Pantagraph*, Bloomington, Illinois, May 29, 1865. One can only wonder whether if memory of the many railroad cars bringing mourners into Springfield might have confused the President's sixteen wheel funeral car *United States*, with the sixteen wheel Pullman sleeping car, *Springfield*.

George M. Pullman and Benjamin C. Field were an upstart partnership in the sleeping car business at this time. Their cars were first found on the predecessor lines of the Chicago and Alton Railroad, dating to 1859. Pullman oversaw remodeling of two of the C & A cars into his first sleepers at their Bloomington, Illinois shops, marking his entry into a growing sleeping car business.

"[cars] ... were also left to their [guests] exclusive occupancy while at Springfield, thus affording them comfortable quarters while there - an item of no small importance in the crowded state of the hotels in that city."

PREPARING FOR THE FINAL MILES

The Chicago & Alton Railroad printed and distributed a public timetable for the train along its route, in the week prior to its arrival in Illinois. The times were apparently miscalculated, and showed a 6:30 a.m., arrival in Springfield. A second corrected timetable had to be quickly produced and printed showing a corrected arrival time of 8:00 a.m., at Springfield. Copies of both schedules exist yet today. Careful examination shows the first schedule did not account for the many anticipated brief stops en route, which consumed an additional two and one-half hours over the published time in the first timetable.

At least four trains made up the final funeral cortege on May 2. The first sections of the funeral cortege consisted of two special ten-car trains departing Chicago, for Springfield at 7:30 p.m., that evening. The trains carried sleeping cars from all railroads who provided such service in Chicago. The sleeping cars provided lodging for 400 passengers. Food service was also provided with meal preparation done in Chicago before departing. The trains carried many dignitaries, whose passage was beyond the capacity of the funeral train, or who did not have passes for the funeral train. Included on the trains were Kentucky Governor Thomas E. Bramlette, and staff, who had met the train at Indianapolis, Major General Palmer and forty-three suite and staff. Indiana Governor Oliver Morton and staff were also on board this train.

There were also delegations from Wisconsin, including Governor Lewis and suite, a Michigan delegation and a large Chicago delegation. The four or five Pullman cars were used as lodging in Springfield, during the funeral. It is quite probably that other unmentioned sleeping cars from other railroads were also used by several of the passengers and guests while at Springfield. The Chicago Bar Association chartered one sleeping car solely for their occupancy.

While the Chicago ceremonies were underway, a partial train, consisting of seven cars, was moved back south over the Illinois Central trestle to a connecting switch with the Galina and Chicago Union Railway at Fifteenth Street. The empty train moved west to a connection with the Chicago and Alton Railroad near Meagher Street, where it was backed onto Chicago & Alton tracks and taken north to the station on Canal near Madison Street. The baggage car and two Field & Pullman sleepers were added on the C & A tracks.

The Funeral Train left Chicago with ten cars. Two additional sleeping cars were added to the train at Joliet, 37 miles out of Chicago, bringing the number of cars up to twelve. The pilot train, led by locomotive Number 40 pulled away from the station about 9:20 p.m. to begin the final leg of the long journey. At 9:30 p.m. as sorrowful melodies were chanted by singing societies, the Funeral Train moved away from the C & A Depot on Canal Street, guided by locomotive Number 58. It was rolling over iron rails toward its final destination. James Colting was engineer of the funeral train. This was the last leg of railroad travel and the twelfth day of the journey.

"Night was forgotten by the people in their anxiety to show all possible respect for him whom they were expecting," noted General Townsend in his report.

"Bonfires and torches threw their uncertain light upon the emblems of mourning

CHICAGO, ILL.
May 2, 1865.

Hon. E. M. STANTON:
The funeral train leaves here at 9.30 this evening.

E. D. TOWNSEND,
Assistant Adjutant-General.

Chicago & Alton Railroad Company

TIME TABLE

FOR THE SPECIAL TRAIN, CONVEYING THE FUNERAL CORTEGE WITH THE REMAINS OF THE LATE

PRESIDENT

FROM

CHICAGO TO SPRINGFIELD

Tuesday, May 2, 1865

		CHICAGO	LEAVE	9:30 P.M.
1.7	1.7	FORT WAYNE JUNCTION	"	9:45 "
3.5	1.8	BRIDGEPORT	"	9:55 "
12.0	8.5	SUMMIT	"	10:25 "
17.6	5.0	JOY'S	"	10:40 "
25.5	8.0	LEMONT	"	11:10 "
32.5	7.0	LOCKPORT	"	11:33 "
37.7	5.2	JOLIET	"	11:50 "
46.4	8.7	ELWOOD	"	12:18 A.M.
48.6	2.8	HAMPTON	"	12:27 "
53.0	4.5	WILMINGTON	"	12:42 "
58.0	4.8	STEWART'S GROVE	"	12:58 "
61.4	3.5	BRACEVILLE	"	1:08 "
65.0	3.8	GARDNER	"	1:22 "
74.0	9.0	DWIGHT	"	1:52 "
82.0	8.0	ODELL	"	2:17 "
87.4	5.2	CAYUGA	"	2:35 "
92.3	5.0	PONTIAC	"	2:52 "
97.8	5.6	OCOYA	"	3:09 "
102.6	4.7	CHENOA	"	3:25 "
110.6	8.0	LEXINGTON	"	3:52 "
118.5	7.9	TOWANDA	"	4:18 "
124.0	5.7	ILL CENTRAL R. R. JUNCTION	"	4:37 "
126.0	2.0	BLOOMINGTON	"	4:43 "
133.0	6.8	SHIRLEY	"	5:07 "
136.5	3.6	FUNK'S GROVE	"	5:18 "
141.4	4.8	McLEAN	"	5:35 "
146.0	4.8	ATLANTA	"	5:50 "
150.0	4.0	LAWN DALE	"	6:08 "
156.8	6.7	LINCOLN	"	6:26 "
164.0	7.1	BROADWELL	"	6:50 "
167.6	3.7	ELKHART	"	7:02 "
173.5	5.9	WILLIAMSVILLE	"	7:22 "
178.3	4.8	SHERMAN STATION	"	7:38 "
180.0	2.1	SANGAMON	"	7:46 "
185.0	5.0	SPRINGFIELD	Arrive	8:00 "

The following instructions are to be observed for the above train:

1. All other Trains on this road must be kept thirty minutes out of the way of the time of this Train.
2. All Telegraph Stations must be kept open during the passage of this Train.

The funeral train will pass stations at a speed not exceeding five miles and hour, the engineman tolling his bell as the train passes through the station and town.

3. A guard with one red and one white light will be stationed at all road-crossings by night: and with a white flag, draped by day, or after daylight, on Wednesday morning.
4. A Pilot Engine will run upon this time, which is to be followed by the Funeral Train, ten minutes behind.
5. Pilot Engine must not pass any Telegraph Station, unless a white flag by day, or one red andone white light bu night, shall be exhibited, which will signify that the Funeral Train has passed the nearest Telegraph Station. In the absence of said signals, the Pilot Engine will stop until definite information is received in regard to the Funeral Train.
6. The Funeral Train will pass all Stations slowly, at which time the bell of the Locomotive must be tolled.

By order ofBrevt Brigadier General D. C. McCullum, 2d Div., in Charge of Military Railroad

ROBERT HALE
General Superintendent

which were destined to stand in their places for weeks to come."

The first miles of travel from Chicago to Joliet, was over the recently leased trackage of the Chicago and Joliet Railroad. Only months earlier it had become the Chicago and Alton's access into downtown Chicago. Scarcely three miles from Chicago, expressive demonstrations of mourning along the final leg of the route began again.

It appears the engineer had instruction to stop just prior to passing each station, and to proceed through the station at a slow speed, or to stop briefly at each station.

The train passed through Bridgeport, around 10:00 p.m. Crowds lined the tracks and bonfires, along with torches illuminated the track as the trains moved slowly along.

Passing Summit, Joy's, Willow Springs, and Lemont, crowds of mourners gathered at trackside to witness passage of the funeral cortege.

A brief stop was made at Lockport, at 11:33 p.m., minute guns were fired as the train approached. Hundreds of people congregated along the track holding torches. Blazing brightly in nearby fields were immense bonfires, turning night into day. Many of the houses along the railroad were draped in mourning, and some were illuminated. The train reportedly passed all the stations slowly, the bells of the locomotives being tolled. A banner across the station offered the invitation, "Come home."

Rain commenced at Joliet. This important junction town was reached at midnight. A meteor passed through the heavens just as the train halted. Newspapers reported it appeared to fall over the funeral car. The second such scene to be witnessed en route, the other being the white dove incident at Syracuse, New York.

The train stopped for a memorial service of nearly an hour while two sleeping cars were added and locomotives serviced.* It was greeted with the report of minute guns and tolling bells. There was some confusion in the crowd as the train arrived, and it is reported a couple of ladies fainted. The depot was decorated in the traditional black and white colors of mourning, with wreaths and evergreens. Several banners expressed the sentiments of the people. A most beautiful arch, constructed of immense timbers, spanned the track, draped in mourning and most tastefully adorned with flowers, evergreens, flags, surmounted with a cross composed of evergreens and surmounted by a figure of the Genius of America.

The Joliet Coronet Band played a funeral dirge as the train arrived. Many ladies and gentlemen, arranged as a splendid choir on a heavily draped platform, sang; "There Is Rest for Thee in Heaven." Newspapers report an immense crowd, estimated at 12,000 persons were assembled. The crowd barely spoke above a whisper. *The Joliet Republican* reported, "... many of the people availed themselves of the opportunity to pass through the car containing the remains." This being the third time the general public was allowed to pass through the car while the train was stopped. The depot bore an illuminated portrait of the late President, with the motto: "Champion, Defender, and Martyr of Liberty." "Reverently the Prairie State receives the ashes of her noblest son." Bonfires lighted up this interesting scene, and draped national flags were waved.

It was raining, but this did not prevent women and children from participating in these outward marks of respect.

The calendar had rolled over to May 3, as the train passed beyond Joliet. Demonstra-

* In an article by William Porter, a brakeman on the Chicago to Springfield Funeral Train, he states two locomotives (doubleheaded), were used on the funeral train coming into Springfield. The Chicago newspapers state one locomotive was used when the train departed Chicago. The train left Chicago with ten cars, near the limit for the pulling capacity of one locomotive of that era. By adding two more sleeping cars at Joliet, it may have increased the weight of the train to the point that a second locomotive was required. Various newspapers give the names of two engineers running the funeral train; Mr. James Colting out of Chicago, and south a Joliet the name of Mr. J. Jackman begins to appear. No other discovered accounts have confirmed the use of a second locomotive.

tions of reverent respect and symbols of mourning were constant as the train was truly now in the "Land of Lincoln."

At the towns of Elwood and Hampton the people who gathered along the tracks had kindled immense bonfires to illuminate the passing train.

The Wilmington Depot, 53 miles out of Chicago, had been draped in emblems of mourning with a large emblem resembling an asterisk with a motto in the center, "Martyr yet Monarch" with mourning colors radiating out. A large crowd had gathered on the platform to await the train.

As the train neared the crest of a hill, before entering the Kankakee River Valley, the engineer whistled for "brakes down" in order to retard the speed of the train. Orders had been given to stop the train just before entering all stations this night, and to pass the stations at not more than four miles per hour. The brakes did not hold and the train flew through the Wilmington Station at an estimated 20 miles per hour. It was later recounted as purely accidental and control of the train was eventually regained.

It was 1:00 a.m., and the train was now 18 minutes off the schedule. The expressions of sympathy must have been overwhelming to cause extended delays. Reports state that at 10:00 a.m., on the morning of May 2nd, at least a hundred people were drawn up in line on each side of the track, awaiting the coming of the train with torches ready for the fall of night, some fourteen hours in advance of its passing. At Wilmington, as at many other cities on the route, minute guns were fired. More than two thousand persons surrounded the station, the men standing with their heads uncovered. Many were disappointed for the speed of the train, finally learning on May 10, the cause. At the south edge of town, exiting the Kankakee River Valley, control of the train was regained.

It was described that the trackside crowds were now constant. At Stewarts Grove, Braceville, and Gardner, the crowds were more than expected. All the houses at Gardner, were draped with emblems of mourning and illuminated. At Dwight, 74 miles south of Chicago, crowds lined the tracks, bells were tolled and minute guns fired as the train arrived. The American flag was draped as a symbol of respect. It is probable the trains made a water stop here, although the record is unclear.

The people of Odell and Cayuga were at trackside in the early hours to pay their respects with salutes of minute guns and tolling of bells.

Crowds from the Pontiac area gathered at the station, apparently confused about the time of arrival. When by 9:00 p.m., it was learned the train had not left Chicago, many left, promising to return to the station nearer the 2:00 a.m. hour. Newspapers reported that large crowds were seen at the station when the train passed through just after 3:00 a.m.

Chenoa, and Lexington also saw large crowds assembled along the tracks to pay reverent respect to the remains. The train was saluted with the firing of minute guns and the playing of appropriate music by bands. Chenoa was the crossing with the Logansport, Peoria and Bloomington Railroad.

Towanda, (Normal), highest place on the railroad between Chicago and St. Louis was reached at 4:30 a.m. Daylight was breaking over the Illinois landscape at this hour, and for the last time the torches and lanterns were extinguished. A large arch had been constructed over the tracks according to some reports.

Bloomington, 59 miles from Springfield and an important center for the Chicago & Alton Railroad, was also the town of extensive business affairs of Abraham Lincoln. On May 1, the local newspaper *The Daily Pantagraph* announced the train would arrive at, "about three o'clock on the morning of Wednesday, May 3d." The paper went on to say that it expected the citizens would be at the depot to welcome the funeral cortege. An arch was planned, apparently by railroad workers in nearby shops. Local citizens planned a torchlight ceremony as an earnest expression of sympathy to honor the dead. It was also announced the engines must take on wood and water and a stop of at least ten minutes was expected. The following day the newspaper noted a schedule change to the effect the train would not arrive until 4:43 a.m.

At 3:00 a.m., on May 3, the bells of Bloomington were tolled to awaken all and call them to the depot in plenty of time to greet the trains, due almost an hour and a half past the announced arrival time. The C & A track skirts the northwest side of town. Large crowds, estimated at over 8,000 had gathered in anticipation of the funeral cortege. The train reached Bloomington, at 5:00 a.m. *The Daily Pantagraph*, noted, "The train did not arrive according to the time laid down on the programme, and it was not only after daylight, but after sunrise before it passed the city. It stopped but a few minutes, and there was little satisfaction in gazing briefly at the funeral train...." The torchlight ceremony was cancelled because it was daylight. Other memorials are not reported.

A large arch was erected over the tracks, near the railroad shops at the end of Catharine Street. It bore the inscription, "Go to thy rest." Bloomington was where Lincoln had uttered the "Lost Speech"—lost because he held the audience so spellbound no one thought to report what he said. The locomotive's tenders were replenished with wood and water. Well behind schedule, the train quickly resumed.

According to a journal kept by a member of the Veteran Reserve Guard of Escort, an unidentified lady mourner, was struck and killed by the pilot train. Surviving records provide no detail. It is a possible reason the train arrived late.

The next day, *The Daily Pantagraph*, not happy with the showing of citizens at the station took aim at its readers. "It is greatly to be regretted that our citizens had not made more signs of mourning. The only conspicuous object was the beautiful silk flag of Engine Company No. 2 draped in mourning. After having seen such striking manifestations all along the route, those who accompanied the train, must have been surprised that the town which almost claimed Lincoln as a citizen, should not have made more demonstrations of sorrow." They expected a rebuke by the telegraphic reporters to occur, but it did not.

During the night the rain stopped and the sky cleared. Near Funk's Grove, passed at about 5:30 a.m., farm houses along the line exhibited badges and drapery of sorrow. Portraits of Abraham Lincoln were prominent in every direction. The village acknowledged the train with the tolling of bells and crowds along the margins of the railroad. A choir of ladies sang several mournful songs, contributing to the effects. Trackside torches and bonfires, which had extended nearly a thousand miles during the dark night en route, had been extinguished for the last time.

Thousands of people were assembled in Atlanta at the waking hour of 6:00 a.m., as the sun lighted the Illinois Prairie. Minute guns were fired, and there was music of the fife and muffled drum. Among the reported trackside mottoes was, "Mournfully and tenderly bear him to his grave."

The town of Lincoln was entered at 7:00 a.m. in the bright Illinois daylight. An extensive stop was made here. This town was named after Abraham Lincoln, who had been the attorney for the founders. Its population was a respectable two thousand inhabitants, most at trackside. The depot was handsomely draped in emblems of mourning, having been sincerely prepared by the local residents. The ladies, dressed in white and black, sang a requiem as the train passed under a handsomely constructed arch, on each side of which was a picture of the deceased President, with the motto, "With malice to none, with charity for all." The National and State flags were prominently displayed, and a profusion of evergreens, with black and white drapings, made up the artistic and appropriate arrangements. A memorial service was conducted while at the station.

The last 28 miles to Springfield were covered in two hours, at an average speed of just over 14 miles an hour. At Broadwell, men stood with uncovered heads, and ladies waved

SPRINGFIELD, ILLINOIS

May 3, 1865

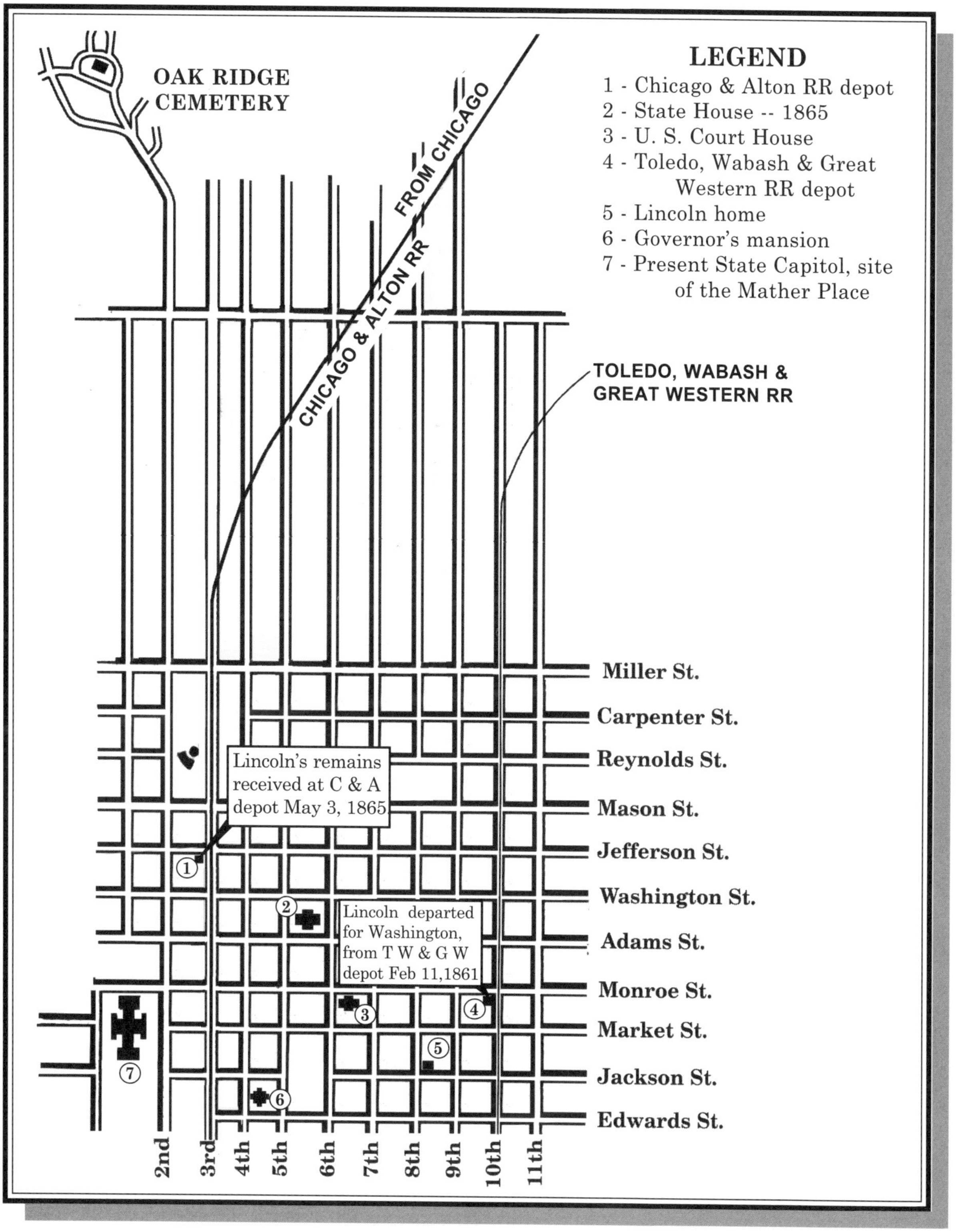

OAK RIDGE CEMETERY

FROM CHICAGO

CHICAGO & ALTON RR

TOLEDO, WABASH & GREAT WESTERN RR

LEGEND

1 - Chicago & Alton RR depot
2 - State House -- 1865
3 - U. S. Court House
4 - Toledo, Wabash & Great Western RR depot
5 - Lincoln home
6 - Governor's mansion
7 - Present State Capitol, site of the Mather Place

Lincoln's remains received at C & A depot May 3, 1865

Lincoln departed for Washington, from T W & G W depot Feb 11,1861

Miller St.
Carpenter St.
Reynolds St.
Mason St.
Jefferson St.
Washington St.
Adams St.
Monroe St.
Market St.
Jackson St.
Edwards St.

2nd 3rd 4th 5th 6th 7th 8th 9th 10th 11th

little flags, which were handsomely draped.

Elkhart honored the train where yet another arch spanned the tracks, ornamented with evergreens and national flags, all draped in mourning bearing the motto: "Ours the Cross: thine the Crown."

Now just eighteen miles from Springfield, the people of Williamsville, had constructed an arch over the tracks. The funeral train passed under it. Newspaper reporters noted it had both large and small flags, mourning drapery and evergreens. Of the latter was formed a cross intertwined with black, bearing the motto: "He has fulfilled his mission."

At Sherman Station, twelve miles from Springfield, the last reported archway over the tracks proclaimed a fitting summation of Lincoln's career: "He has fulfilled his mission." All the houses were draped, and there were many flags and portraits displayed by the crowds gathered along the margins of the tracks paying their tribute of sorrow. Beyond Sherman Station, some eight miles from Springfield, witnesses reported many people assembled on the roads, some on horseback and some in carriages, but the larger part on foot. The number increased as the train proceeded, until reaching Springfield where a sea of humanity met the train.

One of the *Chicago Tribune* reporters assigned to the 7:00 p.m., advance trains reported: "Our train arrived at Springfield about seven o'clock, but from early daybreak until that hour, the various stations on the lower end of the route were crowded with farmers, their wives and children, standing in silent order and eagerly inquiring for the funeral cortege train. Neat funeral arches were erected at most of the stations, and the depot buildings were appropriately decorated. All of the cross roads and by-paths were filled with teams decorated in mourning, and at every home were men and women standing in the doorways or beside the track waving white flags draped in crepe. Often at places where no houses were visible for miles, solitary

TRAVEL LOG

May 2-3, 1865 185 miles

Via The Chicago and Alton Railroad

Station		Time	Station	Time
Chicago	DEPART	9:30 p.m.	Ocoya	
Ft. Wayne Junction			Chenoa	
Bridgeport			Lexington	4:05 a.m.
Summit			Towanda	4:30 a.m.
Joy's			Illinois Central RR Jct.	
Lemont			Bloomington	5:00 a.m.
Lockport		11:33 p.m.	Shirley	
Joliet		Midnight	Funk's Grove	5:30 a.m.
Elwood			McLean	
Hampton			Atlanta	6:00 a.m.
Wilmington		1:00 a.m.	Lawn Dale	
Stewart's Grove			Lincoln	7:00 a.m.
Braceville			Broadwell	
Gardner			Elkhart	
Dwight		2:00 a.m.	Williamsville	
Odell			Sherman Station	
Cayuga			Sangamon	
Pontiac			Springfield	9:00 a.m.

persons standing either waving a flag or bowed down with uncovered heads, paying their silent tribute of respect."

SPRINGFIELD IS REACHED

Trains had brought thousands of people to Springfield, in advance of the funeral train. It was estimated more than 100,000 were on-hand for the arrival of the train. Many more were expected to arrive for the final viewing and funeral services.

As the sun rose on May 3rd, thousands had gathered around the Jefferson Street Station of the Chicago and Alton Railroad. Every roof top was standing with people anxious for a view of the trains. When the grounds near the station were full, people wound their way up the tracks, out to the first crossing north of the city.

The first of the four train funeral cortege to arrive were the two special trains carrying officials and part of the Chicago Committee of One Hundred Citizens and some reporters. They reached the station at 7:00 a.m. The reporter for the *Chicago Evening Journal* noted, "At every station on the route citizens were present awaiting the passage of the funeral cortege. At the time the trains reached Springfield, they were crowded with delegations from different parts of Illinois. Soon after our arrival, a large train arrived from St. Louis." This was likely the St. Louis delegation, consisting of the Old Guard and Halleck Guards, members of the city government, of the Merchants' Exchange, Governor Fletcher and Staff, and General Granville Dodge, who commands the Department of Missouri, and his Staff, together with a number of private citizens, estimated between five and six hundred persons.

The original Funeral Train schedule called for an 8:00 a.m., arrival in the city, but due to the circumstances along the line it was nearly one hour off the published schedule. A few minutes before nine the pilot train made its appearance. As it neared the depot, the feelings of the crowd became intense, and an almost breathless silence pervaded.

The Funeral Train's arrival was an-

Chicago & Alton Railroad Locomotive Number 58, at Springfield, Illinois, May 4, 1865. It pulled the funeral train the last 185 miles on May 2 and 3. -- *Allen County (Ohio) Historical Society collection*

nounced by the firing of a cannon. The funeral cortege came around that last curve, passing through the final mile of trackside crowds who had witnessed the train over the 1,600 miles. It slowly chugged the last few blocks toward the station - through dense crowds of expectant people, composed not only of the citizens of Springfield and Sangamon County, but people from all over the United States. In the immediate minutes the twelve car train slowed as the brakemen applied the brakes to bring the train to a halt. The train slowly pulled along the depot. The national funeral procession was nearly over. With brakemen cranking the car brakes down it halted at the station for the last time.

Robert Hale, General Superintendent of the Chicago and Alton Railroad, sent the following telegraph upon arrival of the train in Springfield. "The funeral train has had a fine run, and arrived on time, all right. No accident of any kind occurred. The train was very heavy. Thank God that it has been well and safely done, and to the entire satisfaction of all concerned."

Vast crowds surrounded the train. The Committee of Reception formed on Jefferson Street. The Veteran Reserve Guard of Escort departed from the train and proceeded to remove Mr. Lincoln's remains to a hearse provided by the City of St. Louis, Missouri.

W. R. Steele, Editor of the *Wilmington Independent*, wrote as the coffin was removed from the train: "Again Mr. Lincoln passes over the Springfield platform-not as when he left it, in the vigor of his mature manhood, strong in his purpose, saving the nation, and reverently asking the prayers of God of our fathers might sustain him, but cold and silent in the embrace of death-'marred by hands of traitors;' borne all unconscious of the wail that ascended to heaven by tearful friends to the scenes of his early struggles and his early triumphs."

The *Associated Press* reported, "The train stops. The pall-bearers, those old men, friends of his, lang syne, approach. The stillness among all the people is painful; but when the coffin is taken from the car, that stillness is broken, broken by sobs, and these are more painful than the stillness. The coffin is borne to the hearse; the hearse moves slowly, almost tenderly, away, followed by the mourners, and the pall bearers walk by the side. The cortege, more solemn than any that had gone before, reaches the Statehouse, where he was wont to speak face to face with his neighbors where at this hour those neighbors press to behold his face locked in death."

Into the hearse, the Veteran Reserve Guard of Escort laid the coffin. Lincoln would lie in state in the Statehouse's Hall of Representatives, in the same room in which he gave his famous "House Divided" speech. Mr. Lincoln's face had become further discolored, and Thomas Lynch, an undertaker, using rouge chalk and amber restored the face to near normal color after they reached the Statehouse. Shortly after 10:00 a.m., the doors were opened to the long line of mourners. Additionally, hundreds of people gathered around Mr. Lincoln's home.

The route of the procession from the train was direct to the Statehouse. The procession proceeded east on Jefferson Street to Fifth, then south on Fifth to Monroe, then east to Sixth, then north to the Statehouse, entering through the east gate and passing into the Hall of Representatives by the North entrance and up a winding staircase into the Representatives' Hall, in a situation not unlike that in New York City.

The train had come more than 1,600 miles and along the route, millions of people;

SPRINGFIELD, ILL.,
May 3, 1865.

Hon. E. M. STANTON,
Secretary of War:

The funeral train arrived here without accident at 8.40 this morning. The burial is appointed at 12 m. to-morrow, Thursday.

E. D. TOWNSEND,
Assistant Adjutant-General.

rich and poor, young and old, child and adult, without distinction of color or religion, crowded along the margins of the tracks, filled the highways, streets and depot grounds by day and night, in the rain and raw winds of spring to witness the train. They expressed, in every way possible, their sorrow and reverence. They demonstrated their deep sense of public loss and appreciation for the virtues of this fallen leader. Many stood with heads bowed in silent prayer, others knelt, many wept. Lines of people for hundreds of miles held torches so that Lincoln's journey along the railroad would not be in the darkness. Hymns and appropriate music were sung, salutes fired, floral immortelles presented, bells tolled as a nation expressed the intensity of their love and veneration for Lincoln's memory along the railroad tracks.

The closing accounts of the *Associated Press* reporter in Springfield summed up the journey. "All classes, without distinction of politics or creeds, spontaneously united in posthumous honors; all hearts seemed to beat as one at the bereavement, and now that the funeral processions are ended, our mournful duty of escorting the mortal remains of Abraham Lincoln is performed. ... Weeping friends with subdued and stricken hearts have taken their adieu; they turn their faces homeward ever to remember the impressive and affective scene which they have witnessed...."

PREPARATIONS AT SPRINGFIELD

When it was learned that the remains would be interred at Springfield, several efforts were immediately undertaken. While it is generally accepted the burial would take place in Springfield, it was not Mary Lincoln's first choice. Her first choice was Chicago. It was late in the evening of April 19th, when a route to Springfield was confirmed, granting burial there.

April 20th saw the appointment of Springfield committees for reception of the remains, and commencement of those other duties necessary for carrying out the last tribute of love and respect for the beloved Lincoln.

Major General Joseph Hooker was appointed Chief Marshal, assisted by Brigadier General John Cook, Brigadier General James Oakes, Brigadier General B. J. Sweet, Brigadier General I. N. Haynie, Colonel C. M. Provost and the Honorable J. A. McClernand.

The committee to meet the remains and have charge of the body while at the Statehouse included Colonel George H. Harlow, Colonel John M. Snyder, Colonel Edward P. Niles, Colonel A. J. Babcock, W. D. Crowell, W. J. Conkling and Adam Johnson.

A committee was formed for the purpose of selecting a suitable site for the resting place of Abraham Lincoln. This was contrary to the expressed wishes of Mrs. Lincoln. She had been adamant. The remains of Abraham Lincoln should be placed in the Oak Ridge Cemetery. This committee went forward with the purchase of the Mather Place, near downtown Springfield. Today it is the site of the Illinois Statehouse.

Arrangements were immediately made to build a vault for placement of the coffin until a permanent monument could be built.

On the 25th, a dispatch was sent to various newspapers giving notice the Mather Place had been purchased for $50,000. While all of these public preparation were underway, C. M. Smith, brother-in-law of Mr. Lincoln wrote, on behalf of Mrs. Lincoln, directing her desires that, "the receiving vault at Oak Ridge Cemetery to be prepared for the reception of the remains, and that they should finally be interred in that last resting place for the dead...." The City Council responded at its meeting of April 24, "... offering to donate 28 acres, most beautifully located, and comprising the most eligible grounds in the cemetery, if it should be desired to inter the body there."

Captain Robert Lincoln later sent a very clearly worded telegraph confirming his mother's wishes. History has portrayed that even after the Lincoln family wishes were made explicitly clear, some in the City of Springfield felt otherwise inclined to pursue a separate agenda for the burial of Lincoln.

Jered Irwin offered to pay for the vault, and immediately contracted with stonecutters and masons to lay-up the temporary vault on the Mather Place.

Again, Mrs. Lincoln's explicit wishes were made clear in the telegraph by Robert on May 1st, just before he left Washington for the journey to Springfield. "Mrs. Lincoln wishes to say in addition ... that if her wishes and directions in regard to her husband's remains are not complied with she will remove them to Chicago next June." The *Chicago Tribune* described it as "the urgent and preemptory request...." There was no choice. The public receiving tomb at the Oak Ridge Cemetery was prepared and the nearly completed Mather Place vault was nearly abandoned though work there was still ongoing as late as 10:00 a.m. on May 4th.

The citizens of Springfield were otherwise busy making and hanging appropriate emblems of mourning on the places of government, the retail merchant establishments, private residences and virtually every place. There were thirteen days between the time the news of the Springfield burial had been received and the arrival of the funeral trains. Thousands of yards of both black and white mourning fabrics had to be bought, most of it brought in from out of the area to satisfy the need. Several newspapers reported 150 workers were employed, working around the clock to appropriately drape the Statehouse in emblems of mourning. The former Lincoln residence at the corner of Eighth and Jackson Streets, at this point the Tilton residence, was also given full attention in light of coming events.

Extensive preparations were also under way for the thousands of mourners expected to arrive for the burial. The two depots had been hung with emblems of mourning, the immediate area was similarly prepared.

The Statehouse was decorated with taste and skill. The outside of the dome was deep black, and, together with the cornice and pillars on which it rests, was elaborately festooned with white and black fabric. Similar drapery fell from the eves and columns. The north and south entrances were corrugated with evergreens. All the windows were partially curtained with black and white trimmings. From the crown of the dome was a staff, on which the national flag was at half-mast with black streamers. The entrance to the Capitol and the rotunda was heavily draped.

The Hall of Representatives decorations corresponded with the room, which was a semicircular colonnade of eleven columns, supporting a half dome. At the apex of the dome was a rising sun, radiant to the circumference.

On the floor a dais was constructed, ascended by three steps. On the dais a hexagon canopy, supported on columns, the shaft covered with black velvet; the capitals wrought in white velvet, with silver bands, filled the canopy, tent-shaped, rising seven feet in the centre, covered with heavy black broadcloth in radiating slack folds, surmounted at the apex and at each angle with black plumes having white centres. A draped eagle was perched on the middle of each crown mould.

The lining of the canopy was white crepe in radiating folds over blue, thickly set with stars of silver, terminating at the cornice inside a band of black velvet with silver fillets. The effect of the canopy, its supports and the drapery was very imposing, the whole being unique and elegant, combining lightness with massiveness in harmony. Twelve brilliant jets of gas burning in ground glass globes sprang from the columns, lighted the interior and reflected an opaline atmosphere.

The catafalque was covered with black velvet, trimmed with silver and satin, and adorned with thirty-six burnished silver stars, twelve at the head and twelve on each side. The floor of the dais was covered with evergreens and white flowers. The steps of the dais were covered with broadcloth drapery, banded with silver lace.

The columns of the room were hung with black crepe, and the capitals festooned and entwined with the same. The cornice was appropriately draped, and, in large antique letters on a background, were the words of

President Lincoln at Independence Hall, Philadelphia, Feb. 22, 1861: - "Sooner than surrender these principles, I would be assassinated on the spot."

In front of the gallery were black panels having silver bands and centers of crossed olive branches; above the gallery looped curtains of black crepe extended around the semicircle; below the gallery white crepe curtains overhung with black crepe festoons. Each column was ornamented with a beautiful wreath of evergreens and white flowers, the gift of Mrs. Gehlman, of Springfield. On the top of the gallery, extending the entire length, was a festoon of evergreens.

Removal of the speaker's chair left a depression resembling a large panel. This was filled with flag work. At the extreme height, in the upper portion of this was placed a blue semicircular field, sixteen feet across, studded with thirty-six stars, and from which radiated the thirteen stripes on the American flag in delicate crepe. At the circumference of the blue field, increasing, breaking on the dais below and the pilasters on either side; the whole crowned with blue and black crepe, and so disposed as to correspond with the blue field, the stars, and radiated panels of the ceiling; the central red stripe fell opposite the opening in the curtains at the head of the catafalque. On the cornice, each side of the flag work, were placed two mottoes, corresponding with that on the semicircular freese, forming together these words: "Washington the Father and Lincoln the Saviour." A life-sized portrait of Washington, the frame draped in blue crepe, stood at the head of the dais. In two corners living evergreen trees and flowers were arranged. The interior decorations were perfected under the direction of the Chairman of the committee, Mr. G. F. Wright.

The catafalque was designed by Col. Schwarts. The exterior decorations and those of all other public buildings, were entirely under the superintendence of E. E. Myers, architect at Springfield.

The city outdid itself in appropriately decorating with the emblems of mourning. The newspapers reported the principal decorations of the city were confined to the buildings on the four sides of the Capitol Square. Almost every home and building had some emblem of mourning displayed, whether it was a scant piece of black cloth on the door of one of the shacks of the poor, or expansive emblems on the building of a leading merchant.

Coggeshall, using other press accounts states. "At the First National Bank a wreath of evergreen and a portrait of the deceased President surmounted the motto: *'He left us upheld by our prayers, He returns embalmed in our tears.'* "

"Over Wolf & Bergmann's was a portrait, and the motto: *'An honest man now lies at rest, As ever God with his image blest; Few hearts like his with virtue warmed, Few heads with knowledge so informed.'* "

"Hammerslough Brothers displayed a portrait of Mr. Lincoln, with the motto: *'Millions bless thy name.'* The store of J. H. Holfer & Co. was decorated with drapery and a bust of Lincoln trimmed with evergreens. John McGriery's store was decorated with drapery and flags, and the motto: *'Revere his Memory.'* The headquarters of the Illinois Paymaster's Department were appropriately draped, and displayed the flag at half mast. L. Steiners & Co.'s store had the following motto: *'Weep, sweet country weep, let every section mourn; the North has lost its champion, the South its truest friend. Let every patriot halt at our country's altar, and drop a passing tear for departed worth.'* "

"The Courthouse and the rooms of the State Agricultural Society were very beautifully draped. Little's store had the motto: *'He still lives in the hearts of his countrymen.'* "

"G. W. Chatterton's store displayed the most elegant and tasteful decoration in the city. The building was profusely draped, and had on its front a monument against a black background, inscribed: *'LINCOLN.' 'With malice towards none, with charity for all.'* In the large window, which was heavily set in black, was an eagle holding in his beak a beautiful wreath of evergreens and immortelles, the whole surmounting a bust of the departed President, at the base of which was the motto: *'Ours in life-the nation's in death.'* Robinson & Banman's store had the motto: *'Our nation mourns.' Smith* & Bros. store displayed a bust wreathed in evergreens, with the motto: *'How we loved him."* J. H. Adams' store had a bust in the window, with the motto: *'A sigh the absent claim, the dead a tear;'* also, a portrait with the motto: *'Our martyred chief.'* The Odd Fellows' Hall displayed a portrait beautifully trimmed with evergreens. Other places of business and many of the private residences in the city were beautifully draped, among them the Executive Mansion, and the residences of ex-Governor Matteson and Colonel Baker of the *State Journal.*

"The law office which Mr. Lincoln had occupied in a block of three-story brick buildings, was draped in mourning, and at the door hung a portrait of the deceased."

THE PUBLIC IS ADMITTED

Immediately after the body had been placed upon the catafalque, the waiting people were admitted to the Statehouse. Thousands upon thousands of sorrowing visitors made their way to Springfield. Newspapers estimated 150,000 came to Springfield.

The Statehouse doors were thrown open at 10:00 a.m. Mourners were obliged to ascend a winding staircase into the Representatives' Hall, and return by the same route. The passage was often jammed, but the people were patient, and rarely did confusion interrupt the stream of mourners, which continued in almost unbroken line until 10:00 a.m. May 4th.

It was estimated that at least seventy-five thousand persons visited the remains. Reporters noted all the mourners were impressed with awe by the emblems of mourning, and by the solemn reminders of the grave which met their gaze. They moved through the Hall in silence. They approached at the left hand of the corpse, passed around the head, and out on the opposite side.

All night they passed by with eyes searching through tears for resemblances and recognition of the features they knew so well. Pickpockets and common thieves also came, and worked the crowds, including members of the funeral cortege. United States Senator Henry S. Lane, of Indiana, was relieved of $90 as he awaited a train to take him home. A man from St. Louis was robbed of a watch and cash estimated at $900.

Reporters wrote on the morning of May 4: "Last night and this morning have fully doubled the immense crowd in attendance, and every street and square in Springfield ebbs and surges with a living tide of humanity. All night long has the ceaseless stream been pouring through the corridors of the Statehouse, all bent on the one sad errand of taking their farewell look at the features of the dead statesman Illinois has given to history."

Robert Lincoln arrived on the Great Western Railroad during the evening hours of May 3rd. He stayed in the home of the Honorable John P. Stuart.

MOURNERS JOURNEY TO SPRINGFIELD

The City of Springfield was overwhelmed with mourners who came to express their sorrow, witness the final ceremonies and burial. On May 1, the throngs of mourners began to arrive. Dispatches indicated incoming trains were thronged with visitors and the town was already overflowing. The Chicago and Alton Railroad offered round trips for one and one-fifth fares on special schedules from Chicago, St. Louis and intermediate stations. The Toledo, Wabash and Great Western Railroad offered similar fare schedules for originating trains as far away as Fort Wayne, Indiana. The railroad managers had no idea of the demand. They borrowed all the extra equipment that could be gotten from neighboring railroads, and when that wasn't enough to satisfy the demands for transportation, they pressed box cars into service. The *Chicago Times* reported, "Both roads centering here have made every exertion for the public accommodation; but their full resources, taxed to the utmost, are inadequate to supply the demand."

All Chicago, St. Louis and Indianapolis railroads were providing equipment and originating special trains whose passengers were destined for Springfield.

In the very early hours of May 3, thousands were walking the streets, unable to find any accommodation.

On May 3rd the day and night of public visitation, with no space available for the crowds, the railroads brought special trains, depositing mourners long enough to pass through the visitors line at the Statehouse, then they returned to the train and departed. At midnight a train came in on the Great Western Railroad, and the whole body of passengers filed at once down to the Capitol, and passed through, paying their last respects. Trains were continually arriving, bringing thousands more. Most had no lodging and slept on the streets or walked around town.

Sleeping cars were provided for many as mobile lodging. Every other space in the town was occupied.

MR. LINCOLN'S HOME

In a rather lengthy article of the scene at Springfield, the *Chicago Tribune* spent a few paragraphs to describe the Lincoln home, an item of interest to may of the visitors that day.

"The old residence of Mr. Lincoln was the center of mournful interest throughout the entire day. With the appearance of the house which has now become historic, all are familiar. Plain, unpretending and substantial, it is the type of Mr. Lincoln's character. The shrubbery in front of the house, principally rose bushes, many of them planted by Mr. Lincoln's own hand, are in full leaf, and a beautiful rose vine clambers up one of the door posts, and trails over the cornice. Lilies are sprinkled here and there, and closely shaven trim grass plats ran down to the neat picket fence surrounding the wall. The columns of the piazza at the rear of the house are also twined with vines and creepers, and the apple trees between the house and the barns, showered the ground with pink and white pedals, the blossoms filled the air with fragrance."

"The house, which is now occupied by Lucien Tilton, Esq., was very heavily draped in mourning. The windows were curtained with black and white, the corner posts wreathed with evergreens, the cornice hidden by festoons of black and white looped up at intervals, and space between the cornice of the door and the central window filled with the American Flag gracefully trimmed."

"There is little of the furniture in the house which belonged to Mr. Lincoln. In the front parlor is a whatnot and a small marble topped table on which was lying a beautiful cross of white camellias. In the back parlor, which he was accustomed to use as his study, is his bookcase. This was his favorite room, and here he toiled and wrote, unconsciously preparing himself for the great mission he was to fulfill. Idle pen! closed book! departed the writer! The mission is fulfilled. Dropped the curtain! out the lights! for the drama is over, but great thoughts and the great deeds have pervaded it are immortal. A heavy oaken bedstead and a chamber set conclude the relics."

MAY 4, 1865
A LONG JOURNEY'S END

When the train left Washington D. C., on April 21st, the plan was to arrive in Springfield on May 3. The *Wilmington Independent* reported on April 26th, plans to have Lincoln's remains lay in state through the morning of May 6, when the burial would take place. Those plans were changed enroute. It appears a modification of the plans was made April 27, to have the burial on May 4, instead, following arrival of the train in Springfield. This change most likely was due to the advancing state of deterioration of the remains.

Thursday, May 4, the day of Mr. Lincoln's Springfield funeral was a scorcher, described as an atmosphere almost intolerably hot and stifling, with little or no air stirring. The day dawned bright with a deep blue sky. Crowds which filled the streets of Springfield were greatly augmented by each train which arrived on the two railways. According to the advertised arrangements, heavy guns were fired, solemn dirges were played, and bells were tolled. All places of business were closed. The weather was propitious. At 8:00 a.m. a vast assemblage of people had collected about the State House grounds, and, while the funeral preparations were being completed, a choir of 250 singers, grouped on the Capitol steps, sang, with great sweetness and impressiveness, a hymn called "Peace, Peace, Troubled Soul." The singers were under the direction of Mr. Messner, of Springfield, assisted by Mr. Palmer, of St. Louis.

Many of the soldiers having a part in the honor guard and processional to the cemetery were held out of town because of the crowds. Many stayed at Camp Butler, east of Springfield, coming in on special trains of the Great Western Railroad that morning, and marched west over the streets of Springfield, to the Capitol. Master Sergeant Alfred Noble wrote in his diary of that morning: "On arriving in the city we stacked arms on the north side of capitol square. Soon after we marched through the building and saw the body of the late President."

At 10:00 a.m., the doors to the State House were closed, and Mr. Lincoln's body was prepared for burial by the Frank Sands, Undertaker and Dr. Charles B. Brown, Embalmer. At the appointed hour Veteran Reserve Guard of Escort entered the State House to remove the coffin from public reception for the last time. It was hoisted to their shoulders and smartly carried down the winding staircase to the elegant hearse.

While the eight Veteran Reserve Guard of Escort were carrying the coffin out on their shoulders, the choir sang, after a prelude by the band, Pleyl's beautiful hymn:

"Children of the Heavenly King, As ye journey sweetly sing; Sing our Saviour's worthy praise, Glorious in His; works and ways."

The military were drawn up on Washington Street, north of the Capitol, and when the coffin was placed in the hearse they marched east along the street, allowing it to come in the rear. The procession was then formed in the order which had been announced. The pallbearers were: Hon. Jesse K. Dubois, Hon. S. T. Logan, Hon. G. P. Kcerner, James L. Lamb, Esq., Hon. S. H. Treat, Col. John Williams, Erastus Wright, Esq., Hon. J. N. Brown, Jacob Bunn, Esq., C. W. Matheny, Esq., Elijah Iles, Esq., Hon. J. T. Stuart.

At 11:30 a.m., the cortege began to move, a band playing at the moment of its departure, "Lincoln's Funeral March."

The funeral procession was led by Major General Joseph Hooker and followed a zigzag route from the State House, past Mr. Lincoln's home, past the Governor's Mansion, and onto the country road leading to Oak Ridge Cemetery. The hearse was fol-

OBSEQUIES OF PRESIDENT LINCOLN

FUNERAL PROCESSION.

The Committtee on Ord r of Procession, have adopted the following order of Funeral Procession:

ORDER OF FUNERAL PROCESSION OF **ABRAHAM LINCOLN,**

Late President of the United States.

Under the immediate direction of Major General Joseph Hooker, Marshal in Chief.

Brig. Gen. John Cook and Staff.

Brevet Brig. Gen. James Oakes and Staff.

MILITARY.

FUNERAL ESCORT.

FIRST DIVISION.

Col. O. M. Prevost, 16th Regiment V. R. C., Marthal.

Aids—Lieut. Thomas B. Beach, A. A. A. General, Major Horace Holt, 1st Massachusetts Heavy Art., Capt. J. C. Reunison, 15th N.Y. Cavalry, Capt. E. O. Raymond, 124th Ill. Inftry., Capt. Eddy, 95th Ill. Inftry., Lieut. H. N. Schlick, 1st New York Dragoons.

To consist of Cavalry, Artillery and Infantry.

SECOND DIVISION.

Major F. Bridgeman, Pay Department U. S. A., Marshal.

Aids—Major R. W. McClaughry, Major W. W. White.

Officers and Enlisted Men of the Army and Navy, not otherwise assigned, in the order stated.

Officers in Uniform and Side Arms.

Major General John A. McClernand, Grand Marshal.

Aids—Lieut. Col. A. Schwartz, Capt. Henry Jayne, Capt. R. Rudolph, Capt. Benj. Ferguson, Thos. Owen, Hon. Charles Keys, J. L. Million, Wm. M. Springer, E. E. Myers A. N. J. Crook, Ed. L. Merritt and N. Higgins.

THIRD DIVISION.

Col. Dudley Wickersham, 1st Army Corps, Marshal.

Aids—Joshua Rogers, Isaac A. Hawley, W. F. Kimber, J. B. Perkins and Charles Canfield.

Marshals of Sections—Col. William S. Barnum, Capt. A. J. Allen, Col. S. N. Hitt, C. L. Conkling Robert P. Officer, Capt. T. G. Barnes, D. W. Smith.

Officiating Clergymen.

Surgeons and Physicians of the Deceased.

Guard of Honor.

PALL	HEARSE.	PALL
BEARERS.		BEARERS.

Horse of the late President, led by two grooms.

Mourners.

Family of the Deceased.

FOURTH DIVISION.

Col. Speed Butler, Marshal.

Aids—Major Robert Allen, Capt. L. Rosette and Capt. Albert Williams.

Marshals of Sections—William E. Bennett, Hany W. Ives, Philip C Latham, William V. Roll, K. H. Richardson, J. E. Williams and J. D. Crabb.

Civil authorities of the United States according to their relative dignities.

Foreign Ministers.

Civil authorities of the States and Territories, and of the District of Columbia, in the order stated, and according to their dignity in said order.

FIFTH DIVISION.

Hon. George L. Huntington, Marshal.

Aids—Dr. S. Babcock, George Shepherd, Charles Ridgley, George Latham, Moses B. Condell.

Municipal authorities of the city of Springfield and other cities.

SIXTH DIVISION.

Hon. William H. Herndon, Marshal.

Aids—P. P. Enos, C. S. Zane, T. W. Dresser, M. D.; John T. Jones, William G. Cochran, James Raybourne, Charles Vincent, Edward Beach, John Peters, C. W. Rearden, R. C. Huskey.

Marshals of Sections—Thomas Lyon, B. T. Hill, George Birge, Henry Yeakel, Jacob Halfen, —— Sweet, Dewitt C. Hartwell, Hamilton Hovey, Frederick B. Smith.

Members of the Christian, Sanitary, and other kindred Commissions.

Delegations from Bodies Politic, Universities and Colleges.

Clergy.

Members of the Legal Profession.

Members of the Medical Profession.

Representatives of the Press.

SEVENTH DIVISION.

Hon. Harman G. Reynolds, Marshal.

Aids—George R. Teasdale, John A. Hughes, James Smith, P. Fitzpatrick, Henry Shuck, Thomas O'Conner.

Marshals of Sections—Capt. Charles Fisher, Frank W. Tracy, M. Connor, Frederick Smith, M. Armstiong, Richard Young.

Free Masons.

Odd Fellows and other Fraternities.

Firemen.

EIGHTH DIVISION.

Hon. John W. Smith, Marshal.

Aids—Capt. Isaac Keys, S. H. Jones, Hon. John W. Priest, O. H. Abel, Henry N. Aiden, Wm. P. Crafton, G. A. Kimber, John W. Poorman, Henry Ridgely, J. H. Crow, John W. Davis, Presco Wright, N. V. Hunt, George Dalbey, Alfred A. North, John S. Bradford, Samuel P. Townsend.

Citizens at large.

Colored Persons.

FORMATION AND MOVEMENT.

MILITARY.

First Division will form on the north side of Washington street, and fronting the Capitol Square.

Second Division on Washington street, right resting on the First Division.

Third Division on Washington street, right resting on the Second Division.

Fourth Division on North Fourth street, right resting on Washington street.

Fifth Division on North Fifth street, right resting on Washington street.

Sixth Division on North Sixth street, right resting on Washington street.

Seventh Division on North Seventh street, right resting on Washington street.

Eighth Division on North Eighth street, right resting on Washington street.

Divisions from Fourth to Eighth, inclusive, will form in the order stated, faced to the south.

Bands accompanying orders, societies, fraternities, delegations, &c., &c., will be permitted to accompany their respective bodies, &c, to the point designated as their position in the funeral column. After the formation they will be assigned such places as the Committee on Music may direct.

The procession will move from Washington to Eighth street; thence south to Monroe street; thence west to Fourth street; thence directly to Oak Ridge Cemetery.

Orders, societies, fraternities, delegations, &c., are requested to appear in the order prescribed above, and to walk eight abreast, and sections in close order. Marshals will strictly enforce this direction.

No carriages or vehicles will be allowed in the procession except the funeral car and carriages containing the family of the deceased.

The Marshal in Chief, Grand Marshals, Marshals of Divisions, and their Aids, Marshals of Sections, and the Guard of Honor, will be mounted—all others will move on foot.

On the first and third days of May thirteen guns will be fired at dawn, and afterwards at intervals of thirty minutes, between the rising and setting sun, a single gun, and at the close of the day a national salute of thirty-six guns.

On the fourth day of May, twenty-one guns at dawn, and afterwards single guns at intervals of ten minutes, until the procession moves; firing then will cease until the close of the day, when national salute of thirty-six guns will be fired.

Marshals will be designated by the following sashes and scarfs:

Grand Marshal—Red, White and Blue Sash.

Aids to the Grand Marshal—Red, White and Blue Scarf.

Marshals—Red Scarf.

Aids—Blue Scarf.

Marshals of Sections—White Scarf, the same to be draped with a black rosette on the right shoulder, and tied with crape on the left side.

The procession will move on Thursday, the 4th inst., at 10 o'clock a. m., precisely.

The streets through which the procession will pass must be kept clear from sidewalk to sidewalk.

JOHN. COOK,
Brig. Gen. Comd'g Dist. of Ill.
JAMES OAKES,
Brevet Brig. Gen. U. S. A.
JOHN A. McCLERNAND,
Grand Marshal.

lowed immediately by Old Bob wearing a mourning blanket. Mr. Lincoln's only two blood relatives in attendance that day were his son, Robert, and his cousin, John Hanks. Mrs. Lincoln was still in mourning in the White House.

The procession was the largest spectacle the Midwest had ever seen. On the route to the cemetery the bands played the "Dead March in Saul," with solemn and mournful effect. The route led by the former house of Mr. Lincoln, on the corner of Eighth and Jefferson streets, then west to Fourth, and on Fourth out to Oak Ridge Cemetery, which was about three miles north of the city at that time.

Soldiers reported the marching was at slow time, company front, reversed arms.

The march was long and tedious and the heat of the sun oppressive and blistering. Several people were overcome with the heat including several soldiers, ladies, the Mayor of Springfield, and members of the delegations.

"Only a small portion of the people who had assembled to witness the ceremonies took position in the procession, but hastened by shorter routes through its line to the cemetery, which very appropriately takes its name from two high ridges, running east and west, covered principally with large oak trees. Between these is a valley about seventy-five feet in depth, winding with pleasing irregularity, and watered by a little brook of clear water. The gate of the cemetery is at the head of this valley, and for several rods it descends quite rapidly, though near the tomb it is nearly level. The tomb stands on the south side in a little cove in the bank, where it is quite steep, so that the roof of it is but a few feet in length. It is built of Joliet limestone, the architecture of the main arch being rustic. The upper range of the arch projecting a few inches from the main wall, is of rubbed stone, and rests on Doric pilasters. The whole is about twelve feet high, and ten wide. The brick walls inside

Woodcut illustration depicting the placement of Lincoln's coffin inside the reception vault at Oak Ridge Cemetery on May 4, 1865, ending the longest funeral procession ever conducted in the United States up to that time. Note the crowds on the hillside and the funeral hearse provided by the City of St. Louis, Missouri. The day was sunny and hot as the coffin was borne to the tomb, but later broke into a thunderstorm. Lincoln was officially buried in 1901, when his monument was completed. During the interim period there were two attempts made to steal the coffin from the reception vault, both were foiled.

were covered with evergreen; and in the centre stood a foundation bearing a marble slab, on which the coffin was deposited. The remains of "Little Willie" were deposited in the same tomb.

"The scene was most solemn, and, beyond the power of language to express, impressive, when in the presence of nearly all the citizens of the city which had so long been the home of Mr. Lincoln, and of a vast throng assembled from all the States of the Northwest, the imposing procession entered the cemetery under an evergreen arch, and filed toward the tomb to the music of dirges performed by many powerful bands."

Performing for the last time the melancholy service for which they had been detailed at Washington, the Veteran Reserve Guard of Escort stood around the hearse and in the immediate presence of the Guard of Honor, the President's oldest son, Robert Lincoln, and other relatives, and family friends, bore the coffin into the tomb.* Hymns were sung by a 130 voice male chorus from St. Louis, composed of members from the Social Singing Society, the Concordia Singing Choir, the Rhemish Frohsinn, North St. Louis Lieder Kranz, St. Louis Soengerbund and the Philharmonic Society. The religious exercises were then opened with prayer.

The funeral oration was given by Bishop Matthew Simpson. He gave an extremely eloquent address. When Simpson was finished, Dr. Phineas Densmore Gurley read the benediction. As he spoke the clouds gathered and darkened. A clap of thunder broke and large heavy drops of rain spat upon the crowds. They watched as the gates of iron and the heavy wooden doors of the tomb were closed and locked. It was over.

General Edward Townsend detailed a company of hand picked men to act as a guard at the tomb of Mr. Lincoln.

THE MASSES DEPART

Many delegations left Springfield soon after the services were over. Master Sergeant Alfred Noble writes, "About 3 o'clock p.m. we started on the return to the City. Waited here an hour and left for Camp Butler by another special train arriving in camp about 5 o'clock."

General Joe Hooker was extended a formal invitation to repose at Chicago, and left on one of the special trains returning there on May 4th.

Sometime over the next few hours, likely the morning of May 5, the *United States*, P W & B Officers Car, and military escort left for Washington, D. C. They arrived on May 7th.

The Ohio, Indiana and Kentucky delegations departed on the Great Western that evening for Lafayette, Indiana. Arriving there the next morning, all partook of a fine dinner at the Lepier House, hosted by "the Indianians." There were a number of speeches during the dinner and they, "gave the Copperheads a most unmerciful skinning." The parties departed for Indianapolis and separated around 5:00 p.m.

On May 5th, the newspapers reported the immense throngs were nearly gone. While trains were returning to a regular schedule, many people were coming into town to visit the different points of interest connected with Lincoln and his life. Thousands passed his former residence, the State House, Hall of Representatives where the catafalque was retained, and the tomb of Lincoln. The newspapers noted the colored people, "have already canonized him, and well they may for he has been to then the father and the savior."

It was on May 5th when Robert Lincoln and Judge David Davis returned to Oak Ridge Cemetery and selected the permanent resting spot for the late Abraham Lincoln. The site was described as, "a most beautiful one and elicits very general approbation."

*Willie's coffin was also placed inside the tomb.

The Veterans Reserve Guard of Escort Accompanying Lincoln's Body to Springfield.

VRC Veteran Reserve Corps

John P. Barry, Co. A, 24th VRC
(formerly 118th Pennsylvania Volunteer Inf.)

Luther E. Bulock, Co. E 9th VRC
(formerly 97th New York Volunteer Infantry.)

Patrick Callaghan, Co. H 9th VRC
(formerly 69th New York Volunteer Infantry.)

Frank Carey, Co. E, 12th VRC
(formerly 51st Ohio Infantry)

Samuel Carpenter, Co. K, 7th VRC
(formerly 35th Missouri Infantry)

Augustus E. Carr, Co. D, 12th VRC
(formerly 140th New York Volunteer Infantry.)

James Collins, Co. D, 12th VRC
(formerly 12th Mass. Volunteer Infantry.)

Addison Cornwell, Co. I, 7th VRC
(formerly 134th N.Y. Volunteer Infantry.)

William F. Daly, Co. A, 10th VRC
(Third Battalion Riflemen, Company C, Mass)

William W. Durgin, Co. F, 10th VRC
(formerly 1st & 9th Maine Volunteer Infantry.)

Joseph H. Durkee, Co. E, 7th VRC, 1st Lt.
(formerly 146th New York Volunteer Infantry.)

John R. Edwards, Co. E, 7th VRC
(formerly 21st Wisconsin Volunteer Infantry.)

Lloyd D. Forehand, Co. I, 18th VRC
(formerly 5th New Hampshire Volunteer Infantry.)

George E. Goodrich, Co. A, 12th VRC
(formerly 124th Ohio Volunteer Infantry.)

John Hanna, Co. B, 14th VRC
(formerly 40th New York Vol Infantry.; 2nd U.S. Cav.)

Edward Hoppy, Co. C, 12th VRC, 2nd. Lt.
(formerly 44th & 9th U.S. Infantry; 2nd U.S. Artillery)

John Karr, Co. D., 14th VRC
(formerly 1st Michigan Volunteer Infantry.)

Rufus W. Lewis, Co. E, 18th VRC
(formerly 15th Connecticut Volunteer Infantry.)

A. Judson Marshall, Co. K, 9th VRC
(formerly 94th New York Volunteer Infantry.)

James M. McCamly, Co. A, 9th VRC, Capt.
(formerly 70th New York Volunteer Infantry.)

Edward Murphy, Co. B, 10th VRC, 2nd. Lt.
(formerly 148th Pennsylvania Volunteers)

Jacob F. Nelson, Co. A, 9th VRC
(formerly 150th Pennsylvania Volunteer Infantry.)

William H. Noble, Co. G, 12th VRC
(formerly 21st Wisconsin Volunteer Infantry.)

James M. Pardun, Co. K, 24th VRC
(formerly 93rd Indiana Volunteer Infantry.)

Irvin M. Sedgwick, Co. H., 18th VRC
(formerly 8th Mass. & 93rd New York Volunteer Infantry.)

Frank T. Smith, Co. C, 10th VRC
(formerly 5th Wisconsin Volunteer Infantry.)

John P. Smith, Co. I, 14th VRC
(formerly 119th Illinois Volunteer Infantry.)

Chester Swinehart, Co. D, 7th VRC, 1st Sgt.
(formerly 14th Ohio Volunteer Infantry.)

William H. Wiseman, Co. E, 24th VRC
(formerly 139th Pennsylvania Volunteer Infantry)

CITIES HOSTING OFFICIAL CEREMONIES EN-ROUTE

CITY	STATUS	DATE	MEMORIAL SITE
Baltimore, Maryland	Major City	April 21, 1865	Exchange Place
Harrisburg, Pennsylvania	State Capital	April 21 - 22, 1865	State House
Philadelphia, Pennsylvania	Major City	April 22 - 23, 1865	Independence Hall
New York, New York	Major City	April 24 - 25, 1865	City Hall
Albany, New York	State Capital	April 25 - 26, 1865	State House
Buffalo, New York	Major City	April 27, 1865	St. James Hall
Cleveland, Ohio	Major City	April 28, 1865	Reception Building
Columbus, Ohio	State Capital	April 29, 1865	State House
Indianapolis, Indiana	State Capital	April 30, 1865	State House
Chicago, Illinois	Major City	May 1 - 2, 1865	County Court House
Springfield, Illinois	State Capital	May 3 - 4, 1865	State House

STATE AND TERRITORIAL GOVERNORS WHO RODE THE TRAIN

Governor. Richard J. Oglesby*	Illinois
Governor Oliver P. Morton*	Indiana
Governor John Brough*	Ohio
Governor William Stone*	Iowa
Governor Thomas E. Bramlette*	Kentucky
Governor Thomas Fletcher*	Missouri
Governor James T. Lewis*	Wisconsin
Governor A. I. Boreman	West Virginia
Governor Henry H. Crapo	Michigan
Governor A. W. Bradford	Maryland
Governor Stephen Miller*	Minnesota
Governor Andrew P. Curtin	Pennsylvania
Governor Ruben H. Fenton	New York
Governor Joel T. Parker*	New Jersey
Governor A. C. Gibbs	Washington Territory
Governor William Wallace*	Idaho Territory
Governor Newton Edmonds	Dakota Territory
ex-President Millard Filmore	New York

*Noted as on the Funeral Train, or on one of the escort trains upon its arrival in Springfield, Illinois.

RAILROADS OPERATED OVER

April 21, 1865 96 miles
Baltimore & Ohio Railroad
Street railways at Baltimore
Northern Central Railway [1]
Cumberland Valley Railroad [1]

April 22, 1865 106 miles
Pennsylvania Railroad
Philadelphia, Wilmington & Baltimore Railroad [1]
Junction Railroad [1]
Street railways at Philadelphia
Philadelphia & Reading Railroad [2]

April 24, 1865 86 miles
Philadelphia & Trenton Railroad [1]
Camden & Amboy Railroad [1]
New Jersey Railroad & Transportation Co. [1]

April 25, 1865 141 miles
Hudson River Railroad [3]
Rensselear & Saratoga Railroad [4]

April 25 - 26, 1865 298 miles
New York Central Railroad

April 27 - 28, 1865 183 miles
Buffalo & Erie Railroad [3]
Cleveland & Erie Railroad [3]
Cleveland & Pittsburgh Railroad [1]

April 29, 1865 135 miles
Cleveland, Columbus and Cincinnati Railway [3]

April 29 - 30, 1865 188 miles
Columbus & Indianapolis Central Railroad [1]

May 1, 1865 210 miles
Indianapolis & LaFayette Railroad [3]
Louisville, New Albany & Chicago Railroad [5]
Michigan Central Railroad [3] and via trackage rights over the Illinois Central Railroad into Chicago

May 2 - 3, 1865 184 miles
Galena & Chicago Union Railroad
Chicago & Alton Railroad [6]

Miles Traveled: 1,627 miles

FOOTNOTES

[1] Became a part of the Pennsylvania Railroad
[2] Later became the Reading Railroad
[3] Became a part of the New York Central Railroad
[4] Became a part of the Delaware & Hudson Railroad
[5] Later became the Monon Railroad
[6] Later became a part of the Gulf, Mobile & Ohio Railroad

CARS PROVIDED TO THE FUNERAL TRAIN

DATE and TRAIN SIZE	RAILROAD and EQUIPMENT MIX
April 21, 1865	
Baltimore & Ohio Railroad Train size: 9 cars	Baltimore & 0hio Railroad Equipment Baggage car, ,six coaches
Northern Central Railway Train size: 9 cars	Pennsylvania Railroad Equipment Baggage car, six coaches
April 22, 1865 Train size: 9 cars	Pennsylvania Railroad Equipment Baggage car, six coaches
April 24, 1865 Train size: 9 cars	Camden & Amboy Railroad Equipment Baggage car, six coaches
April 25 Train size: 9 cars	Hudson River Railroad Equipment Baggage car, six coaches
April 25 - 26 Train size: 10 cars	New York Central Railroad Equipment Baggage Car, two coaches, five sleeping cars
April 27 - 28 Train size: 10 cars	Mixed Roads Equipment from Buffalo & State Line Rail road, Cleveland & Erie Railroad, New York Central Railroad Baggage Car, two coaches, five sleeping cars
April 29 Train size: 9 cars	Mixed Roads Equipment from Buffalo & State Line Rail road, Cleveland & Erie Railroad, New York Central Railroad, Cleveland, Columbus and Cincinnati Railway Baggage Car, three coaches, three sleeping cars
April 29 - 30 Train size: 9 cars	Mixed Roads Equipment from Buffalo & State Line Rail road, Cleveland & Erie Railroad, New York Central Railroad, Cleveland, Columbus and Cincinnati Railway Baggage Car, three coaches, three sleeping cars
May 1 Train size: 10 cars Train size: 11 cars out of Michigan City -- one coach added	Michigan Central Railroad Equipment Baggage Car, two coaches, four sleeping cars, Directors' car
May 2 - 3 Train size: 10 cars out of Chicago 12 cars out of Joliet -- two sleeping cars added	Chicago & Alton Railroad Baggage Car, seven sleeping cars, Directors' car

IDENTIFIED LOCOMOTIVES AND FERRY BOATS USED ON THE LINCOLN FUNERAL TRAIN

	Pilot Loco	Crew Names	Train Loco	Crew Names
APRIL 21, 1865				
Washington - Baltimore	B&O 239	Engr. Wm. Galloway F'man. James Brown	B&O 238	Engr. Thomas Beckitt F'man. C. A. Miller
Baltimore - Harrisburg	?	Engr. ---- F'man. ----	?	Engr. ---- F'man. ----
APRIL 22, 1865				
Harrisburg - Philadelphia	PRR 286	Engr. John McNeal F'man. ----	PRR 331	Engr. John E. Miller F'man. Chas. W. Hambright
APRIL 24, 1865				
Philadelphia - Jersey City (New York)				
Philadelphia & Trenton RR	C&A 72	Engr. ---- F'man. ----	C&A 24	Engr. ---- F'man. ----
Camden & Amboy RR	C&A 72	Engr. ---- F'man. ----	C&A 24	Engr. ---- F'man. ----
New Jersey RR	*H. R. Remsen*	Engr. ---- F'man. ----	40	Engr. ---- F'man. ----
APRIL 25, 1865				
NEW YORK - E. ALBANY	*Constitution*	Engr. Wm. Raymond F'man. ----	*Union*	Engr. Wm. Buchana F'man. ----
East Albany - Albany via Troy (R & S RR)	--	--	?	Engr. ---- F'man. ----
APRIL 26-27, 1865				
Albany - Utica	*C. Vibbard*	Engr. Harvey Henry F'man. ----	*Edward H. Jones*	Engr. Peter Arthur F'man. ----
Utica - Syracuse	4	Engr. T. Harrett F'man. Thomas Decker	*Major Priest*	Engr. J. Vrooman F'man. ----
Syracuse - Rochester	202	Engr. R. Simmons F'man. ----	248	Engr. John H. Brown F'man. ----
Rochester - Buffalo	79	Engr. ---- F'man. ----	*Dean Richmond*	Engr. Leonard Ham F'man. ----
APRIL 27-28, 1865				
Buffalo - Erie	?	Engr. ---- F'man. ----	?	Engr. ---- F'man. ----
Erie - Cleveland	*Idaho*	Engr. J. McGuire F'man. Frank Keehan	*William Case*	Engr. John Benjamin F'man. George Martin
At Cleveland (C & P)	--	--	*Dispatch* (40)	Engr. Bill Simmons F'man. ----

	Pilot Loco	Crew Names	Train Loco	Crew Names
APRIL 28-29, 1865 Cleveland - Columbus	*Louisville*	Engr. E. VanCamp F'man. C. VanCamp	*Nashville*	Engr. Geo. West F'man. Peter Hugo
APRIL 29-30, 1865 Columbus - Richmond	?	Engr. ---- F'man. ----	?	Engr.James Gormley F'man. ----
Richmond - Indianapolis	?	Engr. ---- F'man. ----	?	Engr. ---- F'man. ----
MAY 1, 1865 Indianapolis - Lafayette	*Boon*	Engr. Thomas Culien F'man. ----	*Stockwell*	Engr. Charles Lamb F'man. ----
Lafayette - Michigan City	*Rocket*	Engr. Mr. Rhodes F'man. ----	*Persian*	Engr. Mr. A. Rupert F'man. ----
Michigan City - Chicago	*Frank Valkenberg*	Engr. ---- F'man. ----	*Ranger*	Engr. Edward Wilcox F'man. ----
MAY 2 - 3, 1865 Chicago - Springfield	40	Engr. Henry Russell F'man. ----	58	Engr James Colting F'man. Tom Freeman
			?	Engr. J. Jackman F'man. ----

FERRY BOATS

	Boat Name	Captain
APRIL 24, 1865 Jersey City, New Jersey	*Jersey City*	Captain ----
APRIL 25, 1865 Albany, New York	*New York*	Captain Seth Green

DISPOSITION OF THE FUNERAL CAR *United States*

The *United States* was put up for sale while the funeral train was enroute to Springfield, Illinois. It was purchased by the Union Pacific Railroad, during 1866. In 1874, the car was sold to the narrow gauge Colorado Central Railroad where it was stripped and converted into a simple coach. In November, 1879, the U.P. took over the Colorado Central, and the car was taken back and put into storage and used for special displays. In 1904 it was sold to Franklyn Snow, a Peoria, Illinois, historian. He sold it in 1905, to Thomas Lowry, a Minneapolis, Minnesota, real estate developer. The car passed to the ownership of the Columbia Heights Land Company, of which Lowry was a part owner. It was put on display in a shed at a Columbia Heights, Minnesota park. On March 18, 1911, a brush fire ran out of control, consuming several blocks of grass, along with the shed, the *United States* and some near-by structures. The land company permitted souvenir seekers to carry away any relics before the charred remains were dismantled.

Hotels and Places Enroute Accommodating the Funeral Escort

City	Hotel
Baltimore, Maryland	Eutaw House - Lunch only
Harrisburg, Pennsylvania	Jones House and Buchler House
Philadelphia, Pennsylvania	Continental Hotel
New York, New York	Metropolitan Hotel
Albany, New York	Delavan House
Buffalo, New York	Bloomers Railroad Dining Salon - Breakfast Mansion House - Lodging
Cleveland, Ohio	Weddell House
Columbus, Ohio	Neil House and Governor's Mansion
Indianapolis, Indiana	Bates House*
Chicago, Illinois	Tremont House and Briggs House
Springfield, Illinois	Chenery House and S. Nicholas Hotel

* Bates House served as lodging for the Kentucky delegation. It has not been determined whether it was used by the other escort on the funeral train. The hotel stood at the corner of Illinois and Washington Streets in Indianapolis, on the route from Union Station to the Statehouse. It was from this facility that Lincoln spoke in 1861, during his journey to Washington, D.C.

BIBLIOGRAPHIC RESOURCES

OBSEQUIES OF ABRAHAM LINCOLN IN THE CITY OF NEW YORK, David T. Valentine, © 1866

THE FAREWELL TO LINCOLN, Victor Searcher, © 1965

ANECDOTES OF THE CIVIL WAR, Major General Edward D. Townsend, © 1883

LINCOLN MEMORIAL. The Journeys of Abraham Lincoln:, William T. Coggeshall, © 1865

PALACE CAR PRINCE, A Biography of George Mortimer Pullman, Liston Edgington Leyendecker, © 1992

THE AMERICAN RAILROAD PASSENGER CAR, John H. White Jr., © 1978

CENTENNIAL HISTORY OF THE PENNSYLVANIA RAILROAD, George Burgess and Miles Kennedy © 1949

TWENTY DAYS, Dorothy Meserve Kunhardt and Phillip B. Kunhardt Jr., © 1965, 1993

ABRAHAM LINCOLN, The Pioneer Boy and how he Became President, William M. Thayer

LINCOLN & THE RAILROADS, A Biographical Study, John W. Starr, Jr.

CHILDREN OF A NEW ABRAHAM, Thomas E. Williams, © 1996

JERSEY'S STORY, Margaret O'Connell, © 1958 Lyons and Carnahan

CIVIC ENGAGEMENT IN AMERICAN DEMOCRACY, The Brookings Institution and Russell Sage Foundation © 1999

ABRAHAM LINCOLN,HIS GREAT FUNERAL CORTEGE AND DESCRIPTION OF THE NATIONAL MONUMENT, John Carroll Power, 1872, 1876

THE OHIO RAILROAD GUIDE, ILLUSTRATED, Ohio State Joural Company, 1854

THE HUDSON RIVER AND THE HUDSON RIVER RAILROAD—1851 Published by Bradbury and Guild

ILLUSTRATED HISTORICAL ATLAS OF INDIANA - 1876, Baskin, Forster & Co., 1876

THE NORTHERN RAILROADS IN THE CIVIL WAR 1861-1865, Thomas Weber © 1952

THE LINCOLN TRAIN IS COMING, Wayne and Mary Cat Wesolowski © 1995

THE GREAT IRON TRAIL, Robert West Howard © 1962

Diary of Sgt. Alfred Noble, Company C 24th Michigan, Bentley Historical Library, University of Michigan, Ann Arbor, Michigan

Compilation of the Official Records of the Union and Confederate Armies

NEWSPAPERS

Illinois

Daily State Register	Springfield
Chicago Tribune	Chicago
Chicago Times	Chicago
Chicago Journal	Chicago
Wilmington Independent	Wilmington
Joliet Signal	Joliet
Joliet Republican	Joliet
Free Trader & Observer	Pontiac
Pontiac Daily Leader	Pontiac
The Daily Pantagraph	Bloomington

Ohio

Daily Journal	Dayton
Ohio State Journal	Columbus
The Blade	Toledo
Greenville Democrat	Greenville
The Piqua Journal	Piqua
Piqua Daily Call	Piqua
Troy Times	Troy
Citizen & Gazette	Urbana
Cleveland Plain Dealer	Cleveland
Cleveland Daily Leader	Cleveland
Cleveland Morning Leader	Cleveland
Cincinnati Gazette	Cincinnati

New Jersey

Daily State Gazette	Trenton
Newark Daily Advertiser	Newark

New York

Courier	Palmyra
Weekly Herald	Utica
Morning Herald	Utica
The Syracuse Herald	Syracuse
Syracuse Daily Standard	Syracuse
Syracuse Daily Journal	Syracuse
The Post-Standard	Syracuse
Buffalo Morning Express	Buffalo
Commercial Advertiser	Buffalo
The Highland Democrat	Peekskill
The Putnam County News and Recorder	Cold Springs
Poughkeepsie Daily Eagle	Poughkeepsie
Schenectady Star & Times	Schenectady
New York Tribune	New York City
New York Times	New York City
Albany Journal	Albany
Argus and Atlas	Albany
Troy Daily Times	Troy
Troy Daily Press	Troy

Indiana

The Cambridge City Tribune	Cambridge City
Indiana True Republican	Indianapolis
Daily Sentinel	Indianapolis
Indianapolis Daily Journal	Indianapolis
The Palladium	Richmond
The Weekly Telegraph	Richmond

Pennsylvania

Lancaster Intelligencer Journal	Lancaster
Lancaster Daily Intelligencer	Lancaster
Gazette	Philadelphia
Philadelphia Inquirer	Philadelphia
Patriot and Sun	Harrisburg
Erie Observer	Erie
Erie Daily Dispatch	Erie

Maryland

Baltimore Sun	Baltimore

PERIODICALS and LITERATURE

Civil War Times Illustrated, March/April 1995

Railroad Magazine, December 1962

Model Railroader, February 1995

The Mutual Magazine
February 1923
March 1923
February 1941

Baltimore and Ohio Magazine
February 1928
April, 1928
June, 1928

Illustrated Sunday Magazine
July 10, 1910

Historical Happenings, Lawrenceville Historical Society (Pennsylvania), June 1997

The Biography of Major John Mead Gould Part 3 (1865 - 1867), Maine Historical Society

Poem: *"When Lilacs Last in the Dooryard Bloom'd"* by: Walt Whitman

Diaries of Rubens Peale (1784-1865), April 1865. 1 volume, 21.5 x 34 cm. Rubens Peale diaries, 1855-1865. Smithsonian Institution

Indianapolis City Directory for 1865, Hawes & Co. Publishers.

www.centralpa.org/FEBRUARY%202001/centralstories.html

Index

D

E

H

I

M

Q

R

S

T

U

V